Japanese Aesthetics and Culture

A READER

Edited by
Nancy G. Hume

1995

STATE UNIVERSITY OF NEW YORK PRESS

Albany

Grateful acknowledgement is given to the following for permission to reproduce previously published material:

J. Thomas Rimer. "Japanese Literature; Four Polarities." Originally published as "Japanese Literature on Film" in the series *Japanese Society through Film.* Reprinted with permission of the Japan Society. • Donald Keene. "Japanese Aesthetics." In his *The Pleasures of Japanese Literature.* 1988. © Columbia University Press, New York. Reprinted with permission of the publisher. • Wm. Theodore de Bary, ed., "The Vocabulary of Japanese Aesthetics, I, II, III." In *Sources of Japanese Tradition.* 1958. © Columbia University Press, New York. Reprinted with permission of the publisher. • Graham Parkes. "Ways of Japanese Thinking." In *From African to Zen.* 1993. © Rowman and Littlefield Publishers, Maryland. Reprinted with permission of the publisher. • Donald Keene. "Feminine Sensibility." In *Appreciations of Japanese Culture.* 1971. © Kodansha International Ltd. Reprinted with permission. All rights reserved. • Makoto Ueda. "Impersonality in Poetry: Bashō on the Art of Haiku." and "Imitation, *Yūgen,* and Sublimity: Zeami and the Art of the Nō Drama." In his *Literary and Art Theories in Japan.* © 1967 by Makoto Ueda. Reprinted with permission from Michigan Classics in Japanese Studies 6 (Ann Arbor: Center for Japanese Studies, University of Michigan, 1991). • Kenneth Yasuda. "An Approach to Haiku" and "Basic Principles." In his *Japanese Haiku: Its Essential Nature, History, and Possibilities in English.* 1960. Charles E. Tuttle Co., Inc. of Tokyo, Japan. Reprinted with permission of the publisher. • Donald Shively. "The Social Environment of Tokugawa Japan." In *Studies in Kabuki,* ed. Brandon et al. 1978. © University of Hawaii Press, Honolulu. Reprinted with permission of the publisher. • Haga Kōshirō. "The *Wabi* Aesthetic through the Ages." In *Tea in Japan: Essays on the History of Chanoyu.* ed. Paul Varley and Kamakura Isao. 1989. © University of Hawaii Press, Honolulu. Reprinted with permission of the publisher. • Roger Ames. "*Bushidō:* Mode or Ethic?" *Traditions* 10, 1980 (vol. III, no. 2). Reprinted with permission of the author. • H. Paul Varley. "Culture in the Present Age." In his *Japanese Culture.* 1984. © University of Hawaii Press, Honolulu. Reprinted with permission of the publisher.

Published by State University of New York Press, Albany

Production by Cathleen Collins
Marketing by Bernadette LaManna

Library of Congress Cataloging-in-Publication Data

Japanese aesthetics and culture: a reader / edited by Nancy G. Hume.
p. cm. — (SUNY series in Asian studies development)
Includes bibliographical references and index.
ISBN 0–7914–2399–9. — ISBN 0–7914–2400–6
I. Aesthetics, Japanese. 2. Arts, Japanese—Philosophy.
1. Hume, Nancy G., 1942– . II. Series.
BH221.J3J37 1995
111'.85'0952—dc20 94–12715
CIP

10 9 8 7 6 5 4 3 2

CONTENTS

PREFACE

In the foreword to Shuichi Kato's *A History of Japanese Literature: The First Thousand Years,* R. P. Dore reminds us that in this day of numerous translations of Japanese literature in English, it is hard to remember the "sense of wonder and discovery" with which English-speaking audiences first encountered Japanese literature. For the student new to Japanese literature that "sense of wonder and discovery" still exists. When the opportunity arose to teach an honors course in Japanese literature, my need to understand more about Japanese culture and the aesthetic principles that ruled its art and literature became more urgent.

A number of major works of Japanese literature have been translated into English and are now widely available. Donald Keene's *Anthology of Japanese Literature: From the Earliest Era to the Mid-Nineteenth Century* and his *Modern Japanese Literature* remain two of the best and most comprehensive introductory texts. However, because they have not been revised since their publication in 1956, they do not include the important work translated and published since then. This problem has been remedied somewhat by the recent publication of Howard Hibbett's *Contemporary Japanese Literature: An Anthology of Fiction, Film, and Other Writing since 1945*, numerous collections of short stories and poetry, and good translations of contemporary novels.

Many critical works discussing this literature are also available in translation, but they are not always easily accessible. Although most public and academic libraries have a wide selection of books focusing on Japanese business and economics, and newspapers and magazines are full of articles on these subjects, Japanese literature has not been at the forefront of discussion in the literary or scholarly journals.

The need for more information on Japanese literature and culture was brought home during the summers of 1991 and 1992 when I attended the Asian Studies Development Program sponsored by the East-West Center and the University of Hawaii. Professors from two- and four-year colleges and universities from across the country gathered to learn more about Asia, particularly China and Japan. We were teachers who were not Asianists but who were interested in preparing ourselves to teach Asian literature, culture, politics, history, or economics when we returned to our campuses. But how could we prepare ourselves to read about, to understand, and to teach a culture so fundamentally different from our own? The idea of a collection of essays that would introduce us to the basic aesthetic, cultural, and literary principles of Japanese literature and that would provide a vocabulary to mediate between the Western reader and the Japanese text was very appealing. Hence this book.

This collection of essays is *about* Japanese aesthetics, literature, and culture. It is the book I needed when I began my study of Japanese literature, and this need helped form the basic principles by which I selected the essays to be included. First and foremost, I wanted essays that are standard in the critical canon and have literary merit in their own right. They must be able to explain the basic principles of Japanese aesthetics to the Western, non-speaker of Japanese, and they must be readable and enjoyable. Most of the essays are by Western scholars because, as Thomas Rimer points out, "few commentaries of this sort were written down by Japanese creative artists."

Secondly, I selected essays of a general nature: Rimer's "Four Polarities," Keene's "Japanese Aesthetics," de Bary's "The Vocabulary of Japanese Aesthetics," Parkes' "Ways of Japanese Thinking," and Varley's "Culture in the Present Age." Thirdly, because we often study and teach literature from a genre approach, I included essays that focus on fiction, poetry, and drama: Keene's "Feminine Sensibility," Ueda's "Impersonality in Poetry," and "Imitation, *Yūgen,* and Sublimity," Yasuda's "Basic Principles," and Shively's "The Social Environment of Tokugawa Kabuki." Finally, essays that deal with cultural phenomena directly related to the literature led to Ames' "*Bushidō:* Mode or Ethic" and Kōshirō's "The *Wabi* Aesthetic through the Ages."

The intention is that these essays will spark the reader's interest for more, and to that end I have provided an extensive annotated bibliography which includes primary materials, critical studies, general histories, anthologies, encyclopedias, and sources for audio-visual materials and films. Also included is a brief outline of historical periods, notes on language and pronunciation, and a glossary of the most common terms found in discussions of Japanese aesthetics.

In editing this collection, I have remained true to the texts as they appeared in the original, particularly in the case of spelling which varies considerably from author to author. The use of diacritical marks and italics also varies (e.g., *nō,* Noh, Nō) and I have used or omitted them as they appeared in the original. The names are, for the most part, given in the traditional Japanese order, family name followed by given name, but again I have deferred to the author's use in individual essays.

Many people encouraged me to undertake this project and helped see it to completion; to them I owe my gratitude: the administration and the Board of Trustees at Essex Community College and especially Dean Andrew Snope; my colleagues at Essex Community College, including W. P. Ellis, Ralph Stephens, Peter Adams, and Gardner Pond; my honors students in Japanese literature; J. Thomas Rimer; and William Eastman, Cathleen Collins, and the production staff at SUNY Press. My husband, Jim, cheerfully offered his editing, proofreading, and computer expertise, but most of all I am grateful for his love and encouragement. I am especially indebted to my friends and colleagues who participated in the Asian Studies Development Programs in 1991 and 1992 and particularly Elizabeth Buck and Roger Ames whose vision, energy, and enthusiasm have made Asian studies an important fixture in our scholarly lives. Without them this book would not have been developed.

INTRODUCTION

In the few short decades since World War II, Japan has become an economic super power, extending its domain throughout the world so that now few developed countries can ignore Japan's role in the international marketplace. But it is one thing to know about a country's business practices and its economic influence and another to understand its culture. If we are to truly understand Japan, we must know about its business practices, but we must also know its history, its people, and its arts; only then can we truly come to understand the heart and soul of this unique and fascinating culture. The study of Japanese culture offers a window to see business just as surely as the other way around.

Japan is an island nation, separated from Asia on the east by the Sea of Japan and from the Americas, on the west, by the Pacific Ocean. Unlike many other island nations, Japan did not suffer military invasions from other countries, so for almost fifteen centuries Japan has been, with the exception of the influence from China, virtually isolated from its neighbors. As a result of this isolation, Japan developed a strong sense of cultural identity based on a homogeneous people who spoke a common language and shared strong political, social, religious, and artistic traditions.

Despite this relative isolation, Japan did have sporadic periods of cultural contact with China and the West and was influenced by their ideas and technology. As Paul Varley points out in his *Japanese Culture,* "within the context of a history of abundant cultural borrowing from China in premodern times and the West in the modern age, [the Japanese] have nevertheless retained a hard core of native social, ethical, and cultural values by means of which they have almost invariably molded and adapted foreign borrowings to suit their own tastes and purposes."

Japan's long and varied literary history, from the publication of the *Kojiki* (Record of Ancient Matters) in A.D. 712, to the more recent translation and publication of the works of Mishima Yukio and other contemporary writers in the 1970s, is at last becoming accessible to the West. It is the intention of this collection of essays on Japanese aesthetics and culture to facilitate, for the Western reader, an understanding of the aesthetic, cultural, and artistic legacy which shaped and informed Japan's literary history.

A part of this legacy is the shared aesthetic and cultural values mentioned earlier; it is these values which stand at the center of the following collection of essays. While some artistic forms and aesthetic values may be shared by Japan and the West (e.g., the masked drama of the classical Greek theater and the Nō drama), it is the continuity of aesthetic and cultural values intrinsic to Japanese literature and internalized by so many great Japanese writers, which set it apart from Western tradition. This collection of seminal essays, brought together for the first time in one place, translates Japanese aesthetic and cultural values for the Western reader, and in so doing presents the essential background contexts necessary for the Western reader of Japanese literature to develop a more thorough, appreciative understanding of that literature.

But the essays in this collection go a step beyond the literature to examine related elements of Japanese culture. A discussion of the tea ceremony, an interpretation of some assumptions about *bushidō*, and several discussions of contemporary film all show that the tradition of Japanese aesthetic principles is not limited to the literature alone, but covers a wider spectrum.

Selection of the essays was made on the basis of their position in the critical canon, their intrinsic literary merit, their accessibility and readability, and their emphasis on cultural phenomena directly related to the literature. It is a collection of scholarly writings by Western writers *about* Japanese aesthetics, not a collection of essays by Japanese writers setting forth the principles of their art. These essays are not intended to break new ground or present new theory about Japanese aesthetics, but to provide an opportunity for readers to acquaint themselves with the fundamental, defining principles of Japanese aesthetics, culture, and literature. The book can supplement traditional approaches to Japanese literature and Japanese studies. For those readers already acquainted with Japanese literature and aesthetics, the essays represent painstaking scholarship from which they might deepen their previous encounters.

The selection process for a book like this is a difficult one, and the choices here are deliberate and focused. There are not, for instance, essays on art (though Yasuda's essay on haiku does make some interesting connections between haiku and painting), music, or landscape gardening. They are omitted not because they are not essential for the understanding of Japanese aesthetics and culture nor because they have not developed their own aesthetic principles, but because the focus of this collection is literature and the literary traditions. The consideration of these arts must be left to another collection.

While each of the essays in this anthology stands on its own merit and is not necessarily related to any other essay, there are reasons for the order in which they appear in the collection. The essays are arranged in three general categories: the first four essays provide a general discussion of aesthetics, the second five more specific discussions of the genres of fiction, poetry, and drama, and the final three deal with related cultural phenomena.

Thomas Rimer's very readable essay opens the collection because it provides, in a nutshell, an introduction to both the literature and the aesthetic traditions from which it springs. His "four sets of tensions or polarities (Interior/Exterior, Poetry/Prose, Aristocratic/Popular, Fiction/Fact) . . . provide Japanese literature with its unique qualities . . . [and help] make Japanese literature particularly rich and evocative." His discussion of "Language as Form" introduces the reader to considerations of language and the *monogatari* (tale), *nikki* (diary), and Nō, Bunraku, and Kabuki (drama), literary forms which will be dealt with more specifically in later essays and are representative of the literary tradition in Japan.

The next two essays provide an *entrée* to the traditions and vocabulary of Japanese aesthetics. In his essay, "Japanese Aesthetics," noted scholar Donald Keene introduces the philosophy of the fourteenth century Shinto priest Kenkō (Urabe no Kaneyoshi). Using Kenkō's *Tsurezuregusa* (Essays in Idleness) as a focus, Keene identifies four central principles ("suggestion," "irregularity," "simplicity," and "perishability") which he feels have shaped Japanese tastes and defined the Japanese sense of beauty. Keene develops these four principles with examples from Japanese literature and occasional comparisons to Western aesthetic principles to provide an illuminating explanation of aesthetic concerns.

Closely linked to Keene's essay are excerpts from *Sources of Japanese Tradition,* edited by Wm. Theodore de Bary. The selections chosen from this classic work define a number of important aesthetic principles (*mono no aware, miyabi, yūgen, sabi),* discuss the relationship between these principles and major literary works, and also provide basic vocabulary necessary for understanding later essays. Concluding this introductory section is Graham Parkes' "Ways of Japanese Thinking." Although his essay uses, as a backdrop, the experience of Mishima Yukio's suicide (*seppuku*) and thus has a more modern focus, Parkes provides the reader with a useful introduction to "ways of Japanese thinking" while at the same time introducing similarities and differences between Western and Japanese aesthetic traditions. Parkes also discusses, as major sources of Japanese thinking, Shinto, Buddhism, and Confucianism. Through his presentation of *Bushidō,* Japanese food, modern film, and the tea ceremony, he provides important background information.

While the first group of essays introduced the reader to general principles and important works of fiction, poetry, and drama, the second group allows for a more in-depth study of these literary forms and a closer examination of individual literary works. Donald Keene's "Feminine Sensibility" uses examples from poetry, fiction, and autobiography-diary to demonstrate that the women writers of the Heian period had a significant influence on the literature produced during this era, as well as much of the literature which was to follow. The fact that they wrote in the vernacular Japanese, rather than the Chinese of the male court poets, helped to preserve the Japanese language in spite of the fact that Chinese was the official court language. Since women were not supposed to learn Chinese, "the literature of the supreme period of Japanese civilization was left by default to the women, who were at liberty both to write in Japanese and to express themselves in the genre of fiction." Keene's analysis of Murasaki Shikibu's *The Tale of Genji,* makes it clear that this "feminine sensibility" had a significant effect on the aesthetic principles and literature of Japan, particularly in the forms of the novel and diary.

The haiku poem (17 syllables, 3 lines of 5, 7, 5, syllables respectively) is perhaps the most familiar form of Japanese literature to Western readers. Two excerpts from Kenneth Yasuda's *The Japanese Haiku: Its Essential Nature, History, and Possibilities in English,* provide the reader with a solid foundation for understanding this intriguing poetic form. Yasuda makes important connections between Japanese and Western aesthetic principles as they apply to poetry and offers additional insights into the relationship between haiku and painting. Students reading haiku for the first time often dismiss it as overly simplistic and may be heard to say, "Even I could write this kind of poetry." Yasuda makes it clear, through his discussion of the concepts of the "aesthetic attitude," the "aesthetic experience," and the "haiku moment" that these "little" poems represent a complex and intricate poetic form.

Another essay on haiku by Makoto Ueda focuses on the great haiku master Matsuo Bashō. Even though, as Ueda points out, Bashō "never wrote a theory of poetry himself," his role as a master poet and teacher has had a lasting effect on the Western understanding of haiku. Ueda introduces us to Bashō's theories of the poetic spirit, *sabi, shiori,* reverberation, reflection, and lightness. These theories make it clear that this most Japanese of poetic forms is not just three lines of simplistic verse but is a form grounded in an aesthetic tradition still alive and flourishing in modern Japan.

The reader can move from poetry to theater with an important essay by Makoto Ueda on the art of the Nō drama. Although the theory of *yūgen* is explained in "The Vocabulary of Japanese Aesthetics," Ueda provides another dimension to this complex aesthetic principle by articulating the principle of "imitation" as it applies to the Nō actors' performance. Finally, his analysis of the types of Nō singing and of Zeami's nine categories of theatrical effects help make this fascinating theater more readily understandable to the Western reader.

The second essay on theater, "The Social Environment of Tokugawa Kabuki" by Donald Shively, takes a different approach by providing the reader with a glimpse of the complex social environment of the Tokugawa period (1600–1867) in which kabuki originated and thrived. Beginning with a brief history of the origins of kabuki around 1603, Shively develops the relationship of kabuki to prostitution and the prostitute quarters, the growth of theaters, elements of the theater season, the life of actors in the theater, and the presentation of actors in the *ukiyo-e* paintings and woodblock prints of the period. This essay provides not only important information about kabuki, but also allows the reader to gain a more in-depth understanding of the social environment of the Tokugawa period of Japanese history.

Of the last three essays in the collection, the first two bring the reader to an awareness of cultural elements that had an effect on the literature of Japan while the last essay shows the relationship of earlier themes to modern Japan. Haga Kōshirō's "The *Wabi* Aesthetic through the Ages," interprets for the Western reader the aesthetic principle of *wabi*, which "together with the concept of *yūgen* (mystery and depth) as an ideal of the *nō* drama and the notion of *sabi* (lonely beauty) in *haiku* poetics . . . is one of the most characteristic expressions of Japanese aesthetic principles." By connecting the idea of *wabi* to *chanoyu* (the tea ceremony) Kōshirō introduces the reader to a cultural phenomenon very important to the aesthetic traditions of Japan. As he refers to the works of Kenkō and Zeami, the principles of *yūgen* and *sabi*, and the ink painting of the Muromachi period (1336–1573), the reader once again is reminded of the interconnectedness of the Japanese aesthetic principles discussed in this collection.

A quite different, but equally important, cultural phenomenon is discussed by Roger Ames in his "*Bushidō*: Mode or Ethic?" Although both Parkes and Ames use the death of the writer Mishima Yukio as a backdrop for their discussions, it is Ames' insights into the "mode" and "ethic" of this often misunderstood concept that help make it clear to the Western reader. Using Yamamoto Tsunetomo's *Hagakure* (The Book of the Samurai) as a guide,

Ames shows how "the resolution to die" is "the center of the *bushi* mentality," as he addresses the question of "the effect of this resolve on human action and human freedom." The essay also shows the importance of *bushidō* in the Tokugawa period and its "support [of] a variety of causes and moralities, from extreme political factions to the militarism of imperial Japan, from the *kamikaze* pilots to the exploits of the Red Army." Ames argues that while *bushidō* "may appear to be negative and nihilistic, there is support, however, to suggest . . . that the dividends for this discipline do include a very real degree of personal freedom and fulfillment." To understand *bushidō* is to understand a very significant aspect of Japanese culture.

The final essay in this collection, Paul Varley's "Culture in the Present Age," brings us to post–World War II Japan. While most of the essays in this collection focus on earlier periods of Japanese history, Varley's discussions of the literary work of such post war writers as Dazai Osamu, Kawabata Yasunari, and Mishima Yukio, as well as the literary movements of that age, provide insight into the changes taking place in Japanese culture. In a particularly interesting segment of this essay, Varley sees Japanese film as "one of the most important media for the transmission of Japanese culture to the West." Discussions of modern theater, architecture, and the rise of the new religions complete the picture of culture in postwar Japan. This essay complements Parkes' essay, which also discusses literature and film.

All of the essays in this collection stand as influential, scholarly texts in their own right, and each sheds light on an important aspect of the aesthetic, literary, and cultural traditions of Japan. Readers who immerse themselves in the literature and in the aesthetic and literary traditions are preparing themselves to better understand the complexity and subtlety of Japan. As Thomas Rimer writes, "With exposure comes curiosity. The essays [in this collection] provide not only evocative accounts of the social and intellectual conditions under which Japanese artistic works have been created, but they attempt as well to explicate in English, and in a useful and unpretentious fashion, such basic concepts as *yūgen, sabi, wabi* and a variety of others. The result is a virtual handbook of cultural values and provides a continuing repair for all those who seek greater understanding."

HISTORICAL PERIODS

Although there are several earlier anthropological/historical periods, this list begins with the Nara period as it is the beginning of the historical framework covered by the essays in this collection. There are some variances in the exact years and titles of these periods; those listed are the ones most commonly identified.

Nara Period 710–794

Capital moved from Asuka to northern Nara region. Buddhism becomes court religion. Three important literary works, *Kojiki* (712), *Nihon shoki* (720), and *Manyoshū* (777) published.

Heian Period 794–1185

Capital moved to Heian. Beginning of domination of Fujiwara family at court. Founding of Tendai and Shingon schools of Buddhism. Publication of *Kokinshū* (905) and *Tale of Genji* (1010). Period of great cultural and artistic flowering.

Kamakura Period 1185–1333

Destruction of Taira by Minamoto ushers in medieval period of wars and disruption. Beginning of warrior and shogun rule. Rinzai and Sōtō schools of Zen introduced from China. Publication of *Tales of the Heike* (1225).

Muromachi Period 1333–1568

Disruption and warfare continue. Beginning of fourteen generations of Ashikaga shoguns. 1467–77: period of wars; Japan breaks up into many small domains ruled by *daimyō*. 1543: Portuguese arrive; introduction of firearms. Spread of Zen culture. Nō theater and tea ceremony develop.

Momoyama Period 1568–1600

End of Ashikaga shogunate by Oda Nobunaga. 1582: Nobunaga assassinated and Toyotomi Hideyoshi unifies Japan. 1587: proscription of Catholic missionary activity.

Tokugawa (Edo) Period 1600–1868

1603: Tokugawa Ieyasu establishes fourteen generations of Tokugawa shoguns. 1609: prohibition of Catholicism. 1635: ban on Japanese travel abroad; Japan essentially closed to foreign visitors. 1853: arrival of Perry.

Genroku Era 1688–1704

General flowering of the arts including Kabuki and the puppet theater as well as art in form of prints from *ukiyo* (floating world). Renewed interest in poetry and narrative fiction.

Meiji Period 1868–1912

1868: shogunate overthrown by samurai alliance; Emperor Mutsuhito restored to throne and capital moved to Edo (renamed Tokyo). 1896: importation of movies begins fascination with Western culture. 1904: Russo-Japanese War.

Taishō Period 1912–1926

1912: Taishō emperor succeeds. Two-party civilian government until 1932. Start of radio broadcasting. Many writers visit West, influenced by Western literary movements.

Shōwa Period 1926–

Ascension of Shōwa emperor Hirohito. 1941: Japan attacks Pearl Harbor; 1945: atomic bombs on Hiroshima and Nagasaki end war. 1945–52: Allied occupation of Japan. Postwar literary movements abound. Rise of Japanese film. Start of televised broadcasting.

NOTES ON LANGUAGE, PRONUNCIATION, AND NAMES

The first writing system in Japan occurred when *kanji* (Chinese characters) were introduced from China. The Japanese went on to develop their own syllabary (a set of written signs or characters of a language representing syllables) called *kana* which are phonetic symbols and represent pronunciation, of which there are two types.

Hiragana	*Hiragana* was developed by modifying the shape of *kanji*. It was used primarily for personal communication and poetry because it was flowing and looked pretty. It was the primary medium for court women. In modern Japanese writing there are forty-six simple *hiragana* symbols and twenty-five variations.
Katakana	*Katakana* was developed by taking part of the *kanji* and substituting it for the whole. It first emerged in the writing of Buddhist priests. In modern Japanese writing it is used primarily for Western words which have become part of the Japanese language and to make words stand out as we would use italics.
Kanji	*Kanji* are still used to write large numbers of Chinese words that have been borrowed.
Romanization	This is the form in which most foreigners read Japanese. It is simply the writing out in roman (Latin) script the Japanese language.

Pronunciation

The pronunciation of the romanized Japanese is quite simple. There are five basic vowels pronounced as follows:

a father
i *ē* as in t*ea*
u as in b*oo*t
e *eh* as in f*ea*ther
o as in b*oa*t

Long vowels are indicated by the use of a macron as in Man'yōshū. Consonants are pronounced as in English (the *g* is always hard) and there are no silent letters.

Japanese Names

In most cases Japanese names are given with the surname first and the personal name second (just the opposite of English). However, Japanese often refer to famous writers by their personal names, which we do not do in English. It is not uncommon to see names listed in both orders, thus Yasunari Kawabata or Kawabata Yasunari. For the researcher, this often means having to look in bibliographies under both names.

Chapter 1

Japanese Literature: Four Polarities

J. THOMAS RIMER

In this very interesting essay, J. Thomas Rimer introduces the reader to specific tensions within Japanese literature. While these tensions (Interior\Exterior, Poetry/Prose, Aristocratic/Popular, Fiction/Fact) are not necesarily unique to Japanese literature, they do provide useful categories for understanding that literature while also providing an overview of major literary works. His discussions of language and literary forms also present the reader with information that will be useful in understanding other essays in the collection.

I

"If you want to understand Japanese business practices," a distinguished Australian expert told a group of Midwestern business executives a few years ago, "skip all those fashionable books about how their corporations work. Read some haiku, some modern Japanese novels, *The Tale of Genji.* You have to learn who your colleagues are who live across the Pacific."

I was very struck with these comments, because I too have always felt that literature can provide us with the opportunity for a unique glimpse into the life, indeed into the soul, of another nation. Good literature, which can cast light into the interior world of the civilization in which and for which it was created, can give those of us who live in another culture a special point of access. Some of the terrain that defines this inner world will, in the case of Japan, be fairly familiar, as we and the Japanese, particularly in the modern period, share many assumptions in common. Some of what we will find in this tradition will be startling and strange. All of it will be useful, in the best sense of the word.

How often, in our ordinary lives, do we find ourselves somehow inarticulate, unable to express in any authentic degree the realities of the ebb and flow of our own emotions, our deepest convictions? How much harder still is it to convey those feelings across cultures? Literature provides a specially privileged means to effect that exchange. The works of fiction, drama and poetry that make up the Japanese tradition, whether taken from the classic canon, the best achievements of the modern period, or from the fascinating experiments of the avant-garde, have the capacity to combine pleasure with understanding.

II. Four Polarities

Japanese literature, like Japanese culture itself, has a long history. For most of us in the English-speaking world, Shakespeare forms the basis for our understanding of what literature can accomplish, setting the measure against which both later and earlier writing is judged. He was a Renaissance writer; fewer readers go back to Chaucer, whose *Canterbury Tales* dates from about 1400. My own exposure in high school to a modernized version of the earliest important text in the Anglo-Saxon tradition, *Beowulf*, left me bewildered by this glimpse into a mental world so entirely different, utterly foreign. That ancient chronicle was written in the eighth century and often strikes modern readers as rather crude and clumsy. From the vantage point of our own literary history then, it seems remarkable that the tradition of Japanese literature had already produced by that time the first, and some would say greatest, anthology of Japanese poetry, *The Anthology of Ten Thousand Leaves (Man'yōshū)*, still read and enjoyed today.

Most Western readers begin their exposure to Japanese literature by reading works from the modern period, usually novels. Yet the first successful Japanese experiments in writing fiction in such Western modes took place in the 1880s. The experiment to Westernize the traditional forms of Japanese literature is thus only a century old. Behind this hundred years of constant sometimes restless innovation, lie a thousand years of literary achievement, in which ideas and ideals of literature became firmly rooted in the minds and spirits of many, many generations of writers and readers alike. One way to understand modern Japanese literature is to grasp something of the traditions out of which it comes. Many of these older and unspoken assumptions guide, at least implicitly, the composition of contemporary drama, prose and poetry.

During the thousand years or more that make up this long parade of precedent, various important changes and developments occurred. New attitudes and fresh possibilities began to emerge as traditional Japanese culture and society changed. Indeed, literature can often serve as a kind of repository for the history of the culture in which it was created, as layer after layer of response to changing historical and social circumstances usually leave their marks on these works of the creative imagination. In Japan, the tradition was always changing. One way to understand its nature, and the power of its example, is to observe the record of how those changes occurred.

There are four sets of tensions or polarities, it seems to me, that together provide Japanese literature with its unique qualities. They are important in the traditional literature, and they remain visible today. Sometimes the movement within one set of those polarities occurred very slowly. Sometimes the shifts came rapidly. Doubtless, these four sets of contrasting attitudes can be found in various other literary traditions around the world. Nevertheless, the convergence, the interlocking of these four sets of polarities helps make Japanese literature particularly rich and evocative.

1. Interior/Exterior

Here, prose fiction provides a particularly rich example. In some works of literature, the thrust is towards the interior, psychological and spiritual world of the characters portrayed. Others move outward to stress a chronicle of the passage of external events with which the characters are involved. In the Western novel, many readers would agree that until the middle of the nineteenth century, outward events more often than not took pride of place over interior responses. The exciting plot lines that make such classic nineteenth-century novels as *Les Misérables* of Victor Hugo, *Great Expectations* of Charles Dickens, or *The Moonstone* of Wilkie Collins so vivid as reading experiences provide their energy, their very pulse. The fascinating characters that people such books often interest us primarily because of what they do, and what is done to them. The same is true of popular fiction, and television, even today. With the coming to the fore a hundred years or so ago of such writers as Flaubert in France, Turgenev in Russia, and Henry James in the United States, these polarities began to shift toward the interior psychology of the characters: who they were and what they thought about themselves began to take precedence over any actions they did or did not carry out. This shift from exterior to interior has been, in broad outline, a fairly recent development in the Western traditions of prose fiction.

On the other hand, the Japanese tradition, remarkably enough, appears to have begun the other way around. Early works that purport to tell a story, such as the *Tosa Diary (Tosa Nikki)* of 935 A.D., or the tenth century *Tales of Ise (Ise Monogatari)*, nevertheless gave pride of place to the interior feelings and responses of their respective narrators or characters. Here, for example, is a brief section from the *Tosa Diary*, which tells the story of a woman who accompanies the party of the Governor of Tosa (the traditional name for modern Kochi Prefecture), on the island of Shikoku, when she returns to Kyoto, the capital:

> As this was being said, we rowed until we came to a place called Ishizu, which had lovely pine groves, The shoreline stretched out in the distance, and we continued along it to the coast of Sumiyoshi. Someone made a poem.
>
> Now that I see them,
> I have come to understand myself,
> Ages-old the pines
> And green upon the Sumi Inlet,
> But I before them white with years[1]

Here is a brief section from *Tales of Ise*, which relates an emotional response to a love affair:

> Once a very young man and a young girl fell in love, but since both were afraid of their parents, they concealed their relationship and finally broke it off altogether. Some years later the man sent the girl this poem—perhaps because one of them wanted to revive the old affair.
>
> There is, I suppose, no one
> Who would still remember,
> Now that years have passed
> And each has gone
> His own way[2]

Such combinations of narrated event and interior response give these works a remarkably modern effect. However exotic the settings, the emotions felt make these ancient texts approachable even now.

Nowhere is this pleasure more evident than in reading the greatest of all the Japanese classic narratives, Murasaki Shikibu's *The Tale of Genji (Genji Monogatari)*, written in the eleventh century, a work often compared in the sophistication of its interiority to the French writer Marcel Proust's *Remembrance of Things Past.* In both, the ability of these two authors to conjure up the kinds of interior monologues by which the various characters respond to the vicissitudes of their lives has long been recognized as literary art of the highest sort. Remarkably enough, Lady Murasaki created her chronicle of life in the Heian court some nine hundred years before Proust set out to capture turn-of-the-century Paris. In both, the sweep of the narrative and the emotional trajectories revealed in the ebb and flow of the thoughts expressed by the characters portrayed make a powerful effect on the reader.

Here, by way of example, is a passage from *Genji* in which Prince Genji, the protagonist, finds a vulnerability within himself to the passage of time. The translation is by Arthur Waley.

> As he had promised to appear at a much earlier hour, Princess Nyogo had by now quite given up expecting him, and, much put out about this untimely visit, she bade her people send the porter to the western gate. The man made his appearance a moment later, looking wretchedly pinched and cold as he hastened through the snow with the key in his hand. Unfortunately the lock would not work, and when he went back to look for help no other manservant could anywhere be found. "It's very rusty," said the old porter dolefully, fumbling all the while with the lock that grated with an unpleasant sound but would not turn. "There's nothing else wrong with it, but it's terribly rusty. No one uses that gate now."
>
> The words, ordinary enough in themselves, filled Genji with an unaccountable depression. How swiftly the locks rust, the hinges grow stiff on the doors that close behind us! "I am more than thirty, " he thought; and it seemed to him impossible to go doing things just as though they would last, as though people would remember . . . . "And yet, " he said to himself, "I know that even at this moment the sight of something very beautiful, were it only some common flower or tree, might in an instant make life again seem full of meaning and reality. "[3]

With such a formidable model, subsequent Japanese narrative continued to privilege interior feeling over external events. As Japan entered the modern world, and social and political concerns came to occupy many writers, the polarity began to shift swiftly toward that of an exterior chronicle. Yet even so, in many of the great classics of the twentieth century, from Kawabata Yasunari's 1947 *Snow Country (Yukiguni)* and Tanizaki Junichirō's 1948 *The Makioka Sisters (Sasameyuki)* to Shiga Naoya's 1937 *A Dark Night's Passing (Anya Koro)* and Mishima Yukio's 1956 *The Temple of the Golden Pavilion (Kinkakuji)*, the emphasis continues to remain on the sometimes restless interior feelings of the central characters. The strength of this inward thrust of narrative over the centuries remains one crucial constant in the Japanese tradition.

2. Poetry/Prose

Why did this emphasis on interiority develop as it did? A major reason surely lies in the centrality of poetry in the Japanese literary tradition. Most of us have been exposed to 17-syllable haiku verse, but these represent relatively new blossoms on the very old and venerable tree of Japanese poetry. The earliest and most treasured examples of early response to life that such poetry captures reveals an intimacy that appears to modern readers as highly personal. Again, the Western tradition sends us back to the poetry of Shakespeare, which often involves grand rhetoric, the expression of powerful personalities, and the clash of wills. Early Japanese poetry, on the other hand, while sometimes created in the social environment of the court for public purposes, was, rhetorically speaking, most often couched in terms of a personal and lyrical response to nature. The way in which this situation came about goes far to explain the development of the persistent strain of lyricism in all of Japanese literature. The movement back and forth between the polarities of poetry and prose created a kind of reciprocal influence on both. Japanese poetry began to take on certain narrative functions, while prose began to develop certain lyrical qualities. The development of this central poetic tradition tells much about certain assumptions prevalent in Japanese culture as well.

In a very general way, it can be said that Japanese literature, at least in its written form, became possible because of the Chinese model. In the fourth and fifth centuries A.D., for example, Japan might have been defined in our contemporary parlance as a "Third World country." That, certainly, is how the occasional Chinese visitors of the period looked on Japan, finding the inhabitants somewhat mysterious and, of course, illiterate. From that period onwards, increased exposure to China, either directly or through the Korean peninsula, brought Japan a new religion, Buddhism, and an ability to compose written texts for the first time, using the medium of Chinese characters. As those of us who study Japanese today are all too well aware, the ultimate linguistic marriage between these two quite dissimilar languages was a very awkward one. This amalgamation required various stages. By the seventh and eighth centuries, however, many of those in court society had actually learned to express themselves with eloquence in two languages. The first was classical Chinese, which was used, predominantly by men, for a variety of public and ceremonial functions in somewhat the same manner in which medieval European monks used Latin. The second involved written composition in native Japanese, for which a written syllabary has now been developed, a kind of phonetic alphabet in which the spoken Japanese could be transcribed. Learning Chinese was difficult and time-consuming, but native phonetics were easily mastered, a phenomenon that opened up the possibilities of literary expression to men and women alike. There developed as well a sense that the world of abstract ideas might best be expressed in Chinese, but the realm of authentic feeling required the use of Japanese.

The oldest document with any literary material included is the *Record of Ancient Matters (Kojiki)* dated 712. The collection is a compilation of ancient legends and historical facts, often dealing with the consolidation of the imperial dynasty. Among the shards and pieces of myth and history comes the beginning of Japanese poetry. The first "poem" in the language, in fact, was put in the mouth of a godlike hero from Shintō mythology, Susano-o:

> When this great deity first built the palace of Suga, clouds rose from there. So he sang a song.
>
> > The song:
> > Eightfold fence of Izumo where eight clouds rise,
> > I make an eightfold fence to surround my wife,
> > That eightfold fence![4]

This is hardly a profound poetic utterance by any standards, and in fact this little verse is scarcely intelligible out of context. Yet the poem and its prose introduction provide a first rude sample of the dialectical relationship that was to drive the development of both prose and poetry down to this century and beyond.

The god's poem was composed of 31 syllables which can be broken down into a pattern of 5-7-5-7-7. This brief form came to be referred to as a *waka* (Japanese poetry) or *tanka* (short poem). Both terms were doubtless coined in order to distinguish the form from Chinese poetry, which was widely read and appreciated in the Japanese court. Chinese poetry could be composed in long forms. Therefore, the *waka* form was defined as being both Japanese and brief.

This is not to say that longer poetry was never written in early Japan. The most successful experiments were included in *The Anthology of Ten Thousand Leaves.* Some of the longer poems by such great early poets as Kakinomoto no Hitomaro (fl.680–700) and Ōtomo Yakamochi (718–785) are of great beauty and power.

On the whole, however, such early forms were not retained. By the time of the compilation of the next great anthology of traditional Japanese poetry, the *Collection of Poems Ancient and Modern (Kokinshū)* around 905, the short *waka* form had come to predominate. Some of the reasons for this were surely linguistic. The regular metrics and easy availability of rhyme in Japanese, for example, provided few opportunities for any sustained interest in the kinds of rhetorical devices available in, say, English or Chinese. Then, too, an intriguing sort of democracy of poetic possibilities was developing. Members of the court, men and women alike, were expected to possess the capacity to compose poetry as a social skill. A relatively simple form, such as the waka, was thus extremely suitable.

The importance of poetry of this sort is crucial. Prose can provide the context in which these brief lyrical statements can be fully understood. Even in that simple poem by Susano-o, prose sentences introduce the 31-syllable utterance and so prepare the reader to understand what follows. In the *Collection of Poems Ancient and Modern,* a sense of context is constantly provided, either by ordering poems into a sequence within a general subject (spring, love, cherry blossoms, and the like) or by providing prose "frames" that give necessary information. Take, for example, the following:

On gazing at the moon in China

I gaze across the
endless plains of sky can
that moon be the one
that comes from the rim of Mount
Mikasa in Kasuga

> This story is told of this poem: Long ago, Abe no Nakamaro was sent by the Mikado to China to study. For many years he was unable to return, but, when at last he was to accompany an imperial envoy back, the Chinese held a farewell banquet at a place by the sea called Mei. It is said that this poem was composed when night fell and the moon rose bewitchingly.[5]

Try reading the poem by itself. The meaning is not altogether clear. The prose and the poetry must be read and understood together. The poem "justifies" the background provided through the prose explanation.

In more popular traditional Japanese literature, medieval tales for example, prose became the ascendant of these two contrasting elements, while in more highly refined forms, poetry retained its pride of place. In virtually all forms, an emotional climax called forth the resources of poetry. Poetry provided the vehicle for the expression of the greatest truths of human condition. Those truths, in turn, were those that could be given lyrical utterance: introspective, personal, spontaneous reactions to the world of nature and of the interior self.

This principle can be seen in a striking fashion in the medieval Noh drama, that early and highly sophisticated form of Japanese theater that was to form the model for all subsequent forms of dramatic expression. The form is highly poetic and provides a unique synthesis of mime, chanting, music, dancing, acting, and other related arts in order to create what has been called in this century a "total theatre." At the heart of many of those plays lies a famous *waka* poem, often one already known to the audience from a previous familiar source. The events of the play and the characters who meet or reenact them are woven around this poem like layers of an onion. As the drama begins, a secondary character, often a traveling priest or monk, is, like the audience, at the outer layer. Then, one layer after another is stripped away until, at the moment of highest tension, the actual poem is recited. The complete Noh play thus provides not Shakespeare's clash of incident and personality but rather a crucial context that can justify the implicit emotional power of the poem. Such a structure of discovery, when the reader or spectator begins on the outside and works his or her way towards the central concern of the writer is a powerful one that, in various forms, continues in many great works of modern literature. Natsume Sōseki's great 1914 novel *Kokoro*, for example, begins with a student who comes to know an older man he refers to as *sensei*, the Japanese word for "teacher." The *sensei* becomes the young man's mentor. The student—and the reader—eventually penetrate various layers to the core of the older man's life, and in the end, that core, in the form of a long suicide note, becomes known. That note, like the classical poem in the Noh, reveals the depth of the inner truth.

In the case of a writer like Yasunari Kawabata, too, his lyric juxtapositions of exterior vision and interior sentiment produce similar effects. Some Japanese critics have suggested, for example, that the novel *Snow Country* is in fact constructed like a Noh play in prose, in which the reader is led closer and closer to elusive personality of the geisha Komako. Then, too, the construction of his 1954 *Sound of the Mountain (Yama no Oto)* resembles that of a haiku journal.

This close relationship between poetry and prose is no where more fully realized than in the travel diaries of the great haiku poet Matsuo Bashō (1644–94), considered by many Japanese to represent the highest accomplishment of traditional Japanese literature. In particular, his posthumously published diary *The Narrow Road to the Deep North (Oku no Hosomichi)* is read by most high school students in Japan, and the poet's tracks through the remote regions of northern Japan are still followed by many contemporary Japanese as a literary pilgrimage. Bashō developed the haiku form (17 syllables in a 5-7-5 sequence) from a popular pastime into a vehicle able to express an astounding variety of emotions, ranging from wry humor to powerful statements on the human condition. Bashō's masterful prose is so finely wrought that in many passages it approaches the language of poetry itself. Such refined nuance is particularly difficult to translate. Yet even in English, the beautiful reciprocity of supple prose and elegant poetry is apparent:

> At last I reached my native village in the beginning of September, but I could not find a single trace of the herbs my mother used to grow in the front of her room. The herbs must have been completely bitten away by the frost. Nothing remained the same in my native village. Even the faces of my brothers had changed, with wrinkles and white hair, and we simply rejoiced to see each other alive. My eldest brother took out a small amulet bag, and said to me as he opened it, "See your mother's frosty hairs. You are like Urashima, whose hair turned white upon his opening a miracle box." After remaining in tears for a few moments, I wrote:
>
> Should I hold them in my hand
> They will disappear
> In the warmth of my tears,
> Icy strings of frost.[6]

The prose beginning explains the poem; the poem justifies the prose. The marriage is complete, unique.

This movement in and out of lyric insights forms the pattern of movement in much Japanese prose. Modern readers, for example, regard the hilarious stories of Ihara Saikaku (1642–1693) on the foibles of city life in the Tokugawa period as "novels." Yet these tales involve many of the same literary devices and techniques developed in the world of haiku. The great theatrical masterpieces of the same period, such as the drama of Chikamatsu Monzaemon (1653–1724) move powerfully from prose to poetry in their climactic scenes. In the 1720 *The Love Suicides at Amijima (Shinju Ten no Amijima)*, the early scenes are full of the slang and banter of ordinary Osaka city life. Through his narrator and his poetic language, however, Chikamatsu is able to lift the level of his vision to one of tragic grandeur.

A particularly striking example of this modulation between poetry and prose can be observed in Kawabata's novel *Snow Country*, where narrative scenes alternate with moments of poetic insight that can propel the psychological and spiritual aspects of the story along. Here is one example. Toward the end of the story, Shimamura, who has lingered in the mountains with Komako, the geisha, has a sudden vision of her:

> He leaned against the brazier, provided against the coming of the snowy season, and thought how unlikely it was that he would come again once he had left. The innkeeper had lent him an old Kyoto teakettle, skillfully inlaid in silver with flowers and birds, and from it came the sound of wind in the pines. He could make out two pine breezes, as a matter of fact, a near one and a far one. Just beyond the far breeze he heard faintly the tinkling of a bell. He put his ear to the kettle and listened. Far away, where the bell tinkled on, he suddenly saw Komako's feet, tripping in time with the bell. He drew back. It was time to leave.[7]

An image, not an idea, precipitates the action. Poetry, supported by prose, can reveal its own kind of truth. That truth often prevails. Even in the most Westernized fiction, where prose is firmly in the ascendant, there are moments when introspection and lyric insights take command, leading the reader to the author's highest level of vision. Novels like Abe Kōbō's 1964 *The Face of Another (Tanin no Kao)*, an existentialist fable on modern identity, or Ōe Kenzaburō's 1967 *The Silent Cry (Man'en Gannen no Futtoboru)* with its revolutionary politics, reveal mingled in their complex plots moments of introspection and wonder that make such novels, for Western readers, narratives that reveal poetic, even mystic, resonances.

3. Aristocratic/Popular

A third polarity or duality so important to the Japanese literary tradition occurs between aristocratic and popular attitudes and traditions. In one way, the history of Japanese culture, very broadly defined, reveals increasingly popular encroachments in all forms of expression on an early set of aristocratic ideals. In the Heian period, virtually all cultural manifestations, from Buddhism to art, architecture and poetry, were centered in the court aristocracy. With the destruction of the court's hegemony during and after the disastrous civil wars at the end of the Heian period, those values began to spread through ever-greater segments of society. The functioning of the relationship between these aristocratic and popular traditions is certainly, from an American point of view, highly unusual and significant.

One great literary work in which this process can be observed is the colorful and moving *The Tale of the Heike (Heike Monogatari),* composed during the medieval period when the military clans were on the rise after the court's power was eclipsed in those first wars between two powerful families, the Minamoto and the Taira (the term "Heike," incidentally, is the pronunciation in Japanese of the two characters "Taira family"). This lengthy chronicle, as complex in its way as T*he Tale of Genji,* comes as close to an epic as any work in Japanese literature, since it began as a text to be recited and gradually developed many variations. The version usually read now is taken from that performed by a celebrated itinerant performer named Kakiuchi in 1371. What a prodigious feat to have remembered a text of this length and complexity!

The Tale of the Heike makes absorbing, often thrilling reading. Many of the stories recounted there formed the basics for many later works of all varieties, particularly for dramas in the Noh and Kabuki repertories. Indeed, Yoshitsune (1159–89), the young Minamoto general glorified in various incidents in the *Heike,* became, soon after his death, the grand romantic hero of medieval Japan, as the incidents in the *Heike* made clear. These incidents were adapted again and again in later periods.

Some of the stories recorded in the *Heike* show quite clearly the way in which values moved from court to commoner, city to country. Members of the Taira clan, which served the court in the capital itself, represent in a sense the villains of the story, because of their political plottings. There are many incidents recounted of attempts to overthrow their despotic power. Nevertheless, they are unequivocally admired by their rural enemies, the Minamoto clan, for the beauty of their courtly ways. That such aristocratic values found spontaneous and universal acceptance seems culturally remarkable. I can think of few other instances in other cultures where those involved in fighting their battles have admired their enemies so much. In one famous scene, the rustic warrior Kumagai, who has taken the young prince Atsumori captive, finds the boy's flute and muses to himself:

> He must have been one of the people I heard making music inside the stronghold just before dawn. There are tens of thousands of riders in our eastern armies, but I am sure none of them has brought a flute to the battlefield. These court nobles are refined men![8]

Forced to kill the boy, Kumagai, horrified by the war, gives up his prestigious military rank and becomes a Buddhist monk.

Modern observers of Japanese culture often remark on its holistic nature, on the power of the shared, often implicit cultural values that can transcend class and educational level. These same characteristics can be seen in the *Heike*, as I have pointed out. There are at least two factors that make these shared assumptions possible, and they constitute as well the reasons why the *Heike*, even in translation, can provide such a gripping experience for readers today. The first is an attitude that the past is better than the present. In the *Heike*, there is a sustained element of an elegiac, nostalgic vision of the past, the great past of the Heian court, when life was fuller, better than the present. The "golden age" had passed. Just as the Romans often looked back to the great period of the Greeks, so the medieval and later Japanese looked back to the Heian period as a great moment in their civilization, one that might never come again.

The second element that bound the culture together was a widespread sense, which followed the spread of a more popular Buddhism in medieval Japan, that the world was basically a place of sorrow, a temporary illusion to be replaced by the ultimate reality of a Nirvana. In the earliest period of Japanese history, the attitudes of the traditional "Way of the Gods" making up the Shintō religion put greatest emphasis on the vitality and purity of one's own present life. Death represented pollution and decay. Now, six centuries or so later, these values were reversed. In this attitude of pessimism lurked a strange sort of equality. None, high or low, could escape the baleful conditions of life on this earth. After all, even the power of the court itself had been virtually destroyed in the disastrous 1186 civil wars. Nothing was certain. It was no wonder that all classes of Japanese society seemed united in their respect for what had been, in objective fact, an extremely selective and aristocratic past. This pessimism in turn allowed for a more realistic assessment of life, socially as well as spiritually, than had been possible in the Heian period, which, in court circles at least, showed a tendency to self-glorification.

That respect continued on through vast social changes. In the Tokugawa period (1600–1868), the culture of the townsmen became a predominant force. Life now began to center on the pleasures and opportunities of this life. Social classes were legislated. Although the merchants were put at the bottom of the ladder by the ruling Shogunate, they nevertheless began to amass the kind of wealth, and the leisure that went with it, that made the growth of the arts possible. Japanese literature during the period also tended to develop along class lines, particularly in the theatre, where puppet Bunraku plays and the Kabuki theatre became the sorts of entertainment aimed at, and paid for, by the merchant classes. Yet even there, the heros and heroines of those dramas were often drawn from austere Noh dramas, many of those based on incidents in *The Tale of Genji* or *The Tale of the Heike.* The leisure time of these merchant audiences was sometimes spent incorporating the aristocratic arts into their busy and far more plebeian lives. To do so was, at least in part, to elevate their social status, to incorporate values from the past into the present.

In fiction as well, classical references remained an important starting point. Those who read, for example, Saikaku's 1686 *The Life of an Amorous Woman (Kōshoku Ichidai Onna)* in the delightful yet scholarly translation of Ivan Morris will find that many of the copious notes accompanying the text explain the often aristocratic cultural baggage Saikaku considered appropriate for his readers to carry around with them. The same was true for haiku poetry, which became so important to the period. Bashō paid consistent homage to his sources from the early, high traditions.

The past, then, aristocratic and in some ways austere, and the artistic and cultural lessons to be learned from it, continued to form and shape the expectations of writers and readers alike. It may thus come as no surprise that Kawabata, in accepting the Nobel Prize for literature in 1968, could stress the influence on him as a modern man of the Japanese classics, indicating that he had read the Heian classics as a child and that *The Tale of Genji* has been a profound influence on his own writing. The other great novelist of this interwar period, Tanizaki Jun'ichirō (1886–1965), spent several years rendering the *Genji* into modern Japanese and paid his own homage at least twice, once in his novel, *The Makioka Sisters (Sasameyuki)*, written largely during the war as an evocation of the peaceful time that existed a generation before, and once in his erotic and disquieting set of variations on a theme in his cunningly created 1959 short story "The Bridge of Dreams" (Yume no Ukihashi).

The movement between these polarities of aristocratic and popular cultural attitudes has, in one sense, provided a means toward a refinement in popular sensibilities. This shift has been accomplished by the aid of the classics which made it possible for the older sensibilities to inform and render more sophisticated those of a new generation. When, for example, the gauche and shy Kazuko, the heroine of Dazai Ōsamu's 1947 nihilistic novel *The Setting Sun (Shayō)*, is forced to go to work as a kind of occasional day laborer towards the end of the war, she is given kind treatment by a lieutenant in an incident that eerily resembles the encounter between a similarly shy and introspective woman with a gentle courtier in the famous Heian diary, the *Sarashina Nikki* (called in its English translation *As I Crossed a Bridge of Dreams*). Eerie indeed, until Dazai openly mentions the diary itself a few pages later. In every civilization, art is as often made of older art as much as it is of life. Given the nature of the Japanese heritage, it is no wonder that such introspective and understated themes and values have tended to prevail in so many works of serious literature in all periods.

4. Fiction/Fact

Truth may be stranger than fiction, as the expression goes. In the Japanese tradition, at any rate, real facts have often been privileged over works created entirely out of the imagination. From early on in the tradition, for example, what we now call narrative fiction was frowned upon in certain circles as useless, even dangerous lies. Part of the reason for such a prejudice may have to do with certain attitudes prevalent in the Chinese literary tradition that influenced Japanese literature so profoundly in its formative stages. For the Chinese of the classical period, poetry and the essay represented the art of the gentleman; stories and tales were worthy only of the marketplace. There were many reasons for such attitudes in China, some of them involving the distance between the classical and spoken languages, some due to certain Confucian pieties. Suffice to say that when the Japanese unwittingly absorbed some of these prejudices, they did so without a full understanding of the Chinese background. Indeed, had they absorbed those attitudes more fully, there might well have been no *Tale of Genji* for us to read.

Fiction, however, had its powerful defenders. One of the best places to see these tensions at work is in the text of *Genji* itself. It is clear from the conversations among the various characters in the novel that many in the Heian court read fictional narratives with great enthusiasm. A number of titles of stories and tales are mentioned in these discussions; now lost, they were obviously once staples. In a long and celebrated discussion over the merits of fiction, Prince Genji himself defends the art of the imagination. The conversation he holds with his ward Tamakatsura is far too long to reproduce here, but the following extract is telling:

> He smiled and went on: "But I have a theory of my own about what this art of the novel is, and how it came into being. To begin with, it does not simply consist in the author's telling a story about the adventures of some other person. On the contrary, it happens because the storyteller's own experience of men and things, whether for good or ill—not only what he had passed through himself, but even events which he has only witnessed or been told of—has moved him to an emotion so passionate that he can no longer keep it shut up in his heart. Again and again something in his own life or in that around him will seem to the writer so important that he cannot bear to let it pass into oblivion. There must never come a time, he feels, when men do not know about it."
>
> (Murasaki, *The Tale of Genji*, p. 501)

So Genji defends art over nature. Some later writers in the Buddhist tradition attempted to defend fictional narrative as a kind of "accommodation" (*hōben*), in which the story was created as a kind of sweetener to make the moral lesson of the writer easier for the reader to swallow. This line of argument is not unfamiliar in the English tradition. After all, Chaucer made use of the same principles in *The Canterbury Tales.*

Nevertheless, this ongoing tension between the polarities of fiction and fact often provided writers with the inclination to use factual characters and incidents as a basis for their stories, perhaps as an unconscious means of grounding, validating their own art. The further development of these assumptions is particularly important in the Tokugawa period. Stories and plays began to be wedded ever more firmly to a basis in fact. There were, it seems to me, two sorts or varieties of "facts" that those writers chose for this self-validating process.

The first of them involved the use of actual contemporary incidents as a basis for works of the creative imagination. To take a particularly obvious example, Chikamatsu, in writing his plays on domestic themes, took his often sensational plots and characters from what we might now define as "local news events," sometimes vying with rival playwrights in order to dramatize the sensational material as quickly as possible. Like rival accounts of the Watergate revelations rushed to press, Tokugawa playwrights transformed scandals into dramatic form with the utmost speed possible, artificially re-arranging events in order to excite and titillate their audiences. However over-wrought the resulting dramas, the audiences knew that the outline of the story itself, based on the facts, was accurate.

In a play like *The Love Suicides at Amijima,* for example, Chikamatsu actually conducted interviews in order to obtain certain details correctly. The story possesses another level of significance for readers in our time however, who may find themselves more involved in the symbolic and mythical qualities inherent in the story.

This grounding in actual fact, however, should not suggest that Chikamatsu and his contemporaries were writing what we might call in modern terms realistic drama. Rather, the realistic elements allowed the writer to use his own imagination in order to develop the story's psychological and religious elements that the headlines, as it were, left out. Chikamatsu's question to himself is not *what* happened—that was a given—but *how* and *why* it happened. Every aspect of his literary and dramatic skill was marshalled in order to create the kind of drama that, as he once put it, "lies in the slender margin between the real and the unreal."[9]

In a similar fashion, the comic tales of Saikaku, as I mentioned earlier, grew from a close observation of the details of everyday life, combined with a sense of the foibles of his own contemporaries from many walks of life. Saikaku, as a comic artist, adopts, like Chikamatsu, the art of the "slender margin," but his distancing techniques stress the amusing and ironic, producing a smile rather than a tear. Without a firm base in the observed details of ordinary life, however, there would be little means to create distance.

The second sort of "facts" in which writers tended to ground their art is at once more subtle and complex, the "facts" of history itself. As I mentioned previously, the use of historical figures in imaginary situations goes back at least as far as *The Tale of the Heike.* By the Tokugawa period, the practice had become firmly entrenched. However fanciful the treatment given to historical characters represented on the stage, for example, that they once actually existed gave their utterances and postures credibility to audiences. In fact, in Chikamatsu's times, his historical dramas, in which he chose protagonists from Japanese and Chinese history, were far more popular than his domestic dramas of contemporary life. His play, *The Battles of Coxinga (Kokusenya Kassen)*, written in 1715, was one of the most popular dramas written in the history of Japanese theatre. Donald Keene, who has translated the text, quotes scholarly estimates that over 240,000 persons, a high percentage of the population of the city of Osaka, witnessed the play.

On some occasions, history was used to mask contemporary concerns, particularly in areas of political sensitivity where potential Shogunate censorship was involved. The most famous of all traditional dramas, *The Treasury of Loyal Retainers (Kanadehon Chūshingura),* provides a prime example of this process. Written in 1748, almost half a century after the sensational political scandal that threatened to bring down the whole regime, the three playwrights who composed this lengthy drama in eleven acts moved the action backwards by four centuries. The sensational actions portrayed on stage were thus given a double sanction, the first from a relative fidelity to the occurrences that took place at the time of the original 1703 vendetta, the second from the authority of the historical trappings, which turned incident into myth.

There exist many kinds of history, including literary history. The existence of old texts became in itself a principle for artistic validation, and a rerendering of these older materials provided access to still another sort of "truth." The effectiveness of this principle can easily be seen in the travel diaries of the haiku poet Matsuo Bashō, mentioned earlier. Bashō travelled in the footsteps of the great poets and writers he most respected and loved.

Perhaps the greatest work written in the literary/historical vein is the collection *Tales of the Moonlight and Rain (Ugetsu Monogatari)*, published in 1776, the work of that consummate storyteller Ueda Akinari. Each of the nine stories in the collection deals with some aspect of the supernatural. Written in an elegant style, the work shows another aspect of Akinari's brilliant and fanciful imagination. The tales have continued to resonate ever since. Lafcadio Hearn, the American writer resident in Japan towards the end of the nineteenth century, loved the stories and adapted some of them in his own work. The great film director Kenji Mizoguchi used elements from several of them in his 1953 homage to Akinari entitled *Ugetsu.*

Akinari, however, is always careful, perhaps puzzlingly so to the modern reader, to document his sources. He is able to indulge in composing these works of peculiar poetic fancy, he seems to be saying, because his renditions are actually retelling "facts," old Japanese and Chinese tales. In retelling them, he remains faithful to their "truth" just as Chikamatsu was faithful to the outlines of the life of an historical figure like Coxinga or the other heroes he chose for his dramas. Like Chikamatsu, Akinari's own stories often make use of their antecedents as only the slightest of pretexts, depending fully on the workings of his own imagination. Still, that anchor in history, literal or literary, remained a vital principle.

With the opening of Japan, and the beginnings of a new society, the felt need to relate the realm of the imagination to the truth of contemporary or historical events continued to be important. The great modern novelist Shimazaki Tōson (1878–1943), for example, composed his lengthy masterpiece *Before the Dawn* (*Yoakemae*, 1929–35) on the basis of his close study of the lives of his father and his friends in order to document the enormous changes that had come to Japan during the end of the Tokugawa period and the opening of the country. Mori Ōgai (1862–1922), another giant of the period, wrote several novels on Meiji life, such as his *Wild Geese (Gan)*, then went on to compose toward the end of his life a number of remarkable evocations of actual personalities in earlier periods of Japanese history, using the distance between the lives of his characters and his own in order to establish his own "thin line between the real and the unreal." Akutagawa Ryūnosuke (1892–1927) a brilliant teller of Poe-like stories often took for his sources medieval tales, including the well-known "Rashō Gate" ("Rashōmon"), which along with his "In a Grove" ("Yabu no naka") formed the basis for the famous 1950 film by Kurosawa Akira.

In the postwar period, prominent writers such as Mishima Yukio used both contemporary events, such as the burning of a treasured Kyoto temple by a crazed acolyte in his 1956 *The Temple of the Golden Pavilion (Kinkakuji)* or political scandal in *After the Banquet* (*Utage no Ato*, 1960). He also incorporated historical figures and events into his work, ranging from the family of the Marquis de Sade of eighteenth-century France in his 1965 play *Madame de Sade (Sado Kōshaku Fujin)* to the Japanese political figures of the 1880s in his celebrated play *Rokumeikan* (1957). The word, incidentally, is the name of a building, sometimes translated as "Deer Horn Hall," built to give parties for foreign dignitaries during the period. (The play is as yet untranslated.) Mishima uses such facts, but merely to ground his evocations of his own highly personal and idiosyncratic vision.

In one contemporary masterpiece, Ōe Kenzaburō's 1967 *The Silent Cry*, the author illustrates the psychic power that the validation of history can provide for the lives of his characters. Takashi, the younger brother, brilliant, peculiar, and a revolutionary himself, continually attempts to measure himself and his success against the life of his own grandfather, who had evidently led an uprising in the same rural village just before the beginning of the Meiji period. Takashi's own self-understanding, and self-forgiveness, is always measured, sometimes tragically, against this precedent, and it becomes his burden, his quest to seek out the precise nature of those historical facts. A work like Ibuse Masuji's 1966 *Black Rain (Kuroi Ame)* deals with one of the most heart-rending facts of our century, the atomic bombing of Hiroshima, yet in his novel too, introspection renders the facts sufficiently palatable to permit the creation of a work of art.

For Western readers, this reciprocity of fiction and fact can be quite helpful in providing an important sense of authenticity, if you will, for what we read ourselves. The grounding of literary works in the specifics of society and history can provide us in turn with a necessary and useful background for entering the unusual worlds that are the property of the best Japanese writers.

III. Japanese Literature: Language as Form

So intensely you had been waiting for lemon,
In the sad, white, light deathbed
you took that one lemon from my hand
and bit it sharply with your bright teeth.
A fragrance rose the color of topaz.
Those heavenly drops of juice
flashed you back to sanity.
Your eyes, blue and transparent, slightly smiled.
You grasped my hand, how vigorous you were.
There was a storm in your throat
but just at the end
Chieko found Chieko again,
all life's love into one moment fallen.
And then once
as once you did on a mountaintop, you let out a great sigh
and with it your engine stopped.
By the cherry blossoms in front of your photograph
today, too, I will put a cool fresh lemon.

(Sato and Watson, *From the Country of Eight Islands: An Anthology of Japanese Poetry*, p. 469)

So wrote one of the great modern poets of Japan, Takamura Kōtarō (1883–1956). This poem, entitled "Lemon Elegy," describes the death of his beloved wife in 1938. In Hiroaki Sato's eloquent translation, the poem is as moving in its new English dress as in the original. Emotions such as these are familiar to us from our own lives and our own traditions of self-expression. In this century, Japan, her writers included, has become an enthusiastic participant in world culture. Takamura, himself the son of a sculptor, went to study art in New York and Paris, fell under the spell of Rodin, and returned to Japan in 1909 to lead the avant-garde movement in the visual arts.

For some, the blending of cultures was difficult to achieve. Natsume Sōseki, perhaps the finest writer of the modern period, whose novels range from the amusing 1906 *Botchan* to powerful critiques on a modernizing Japan, such as his 1910 *And Then (Sorekara)* to the bleak and penetrating *Kokoro*, mentioned above, lived in London from 1900 to 1903, where he learned, as he later wrote, of the pain of being a Japanese in an alien world. Other writers of the period, such as Shimazaki Tōson, felt the same difficulties and a similar pain of separation from the past.

In the postwar period, Japanese and Western cultures began to draw even closer together. By now, such writers as Mishima and Abe Kōbō have earned a wide and loyal readership around the world. The growing ascendancy of popular culture has placed the contemporary Japanese arts, including literature, in the center of what is becoming an international marketplace.

This phenomenon is new, however. If Japanese culture and literature have been part of our consciousness for a few decades, the preceding thousand years of culture require for us, as for many young Japanese who have grown up in the new world of popular culture, a certain amount of transposition. Both in language and literary form, the differences are greater.

Take, for example, the case of the literary language employed at various periods in Japan's long history. Until the example of Western literature became known in Japan, a kind of literary language was used which, although quite beautiful and effective on its own terms, was not intended to be responsive to ordinary speech. In fact, ordinary spoken Japanese was seldom written down as such. This situation, of course, prevails in every literary tradition. You need only pick up a copy of a supposedly "realistic" novel by Henry James, say *The Portrait of a Lady*, and read out loud a page or so of the conversations to realize that the author actually employs a highly stylized syntax and vocabulary. Still, their words are quite recognizable in terms of our contemporary speech patterns.

Modern Japanese fiction is now as close to the rhythms and patterns of the spoken language as is the literary language of our own tradition. The older literary language, however, with its high rhetorical devices, is now particularly hard to comprehend when spoken, since there is not sufficient time for the listener to reflect on its complex overtones of meaning. I was rather startled several years ago at a performance in Tokyo of an eighteenth-century Kabuki play to notice that a high proportion of the audience wore rented transistor headsets. A delegation from Hawaii? "No," I was told by an usher, "these are regular patrons listening not in English or French but in modern Japanese, so they can follow the plot."

Works written in still earlier periods cause greater problems. My first introduction to Japanese classical literature, in the late 1950s, came in the form of an elegant Arthur Waley translation of Lady Murasaki's *The Tale of Genji*, given to me by an elderly Japanese couple who had themselves lived in London and wanted to share with me their enthusiasm for that masterpiece. Greatly touched, I told them how much more they must have enjoyed reading it in the original. "Oh certainly not!" they replied, "We can't read a word of it! Mr. Waley has always been our guide." Anyone who has some knowledge of modern Japanese knows, looking at the bewildering original, exactly what they meant.

I mention the difficulties of the classical language as a reminder that, when we read in translation, we are perforce making do with an adaptation. Reading modern Japanese literature in English may, on the whole, require no more of a transposition, a danger, than reading French or Russian literature in English. Nuances are inevitably lost, values occasionally shifted, but the same sense of the original, with a good translator, can be conveyed. Reading works from the classical tradition in translation smooths them out and so risks making them, in a sense, falsely familiar. The transpositions required remove, inevitably, something rich and strange from our experience.

Transformations figure as well in matters of literary form. Although, as I indicated before, modern Japanese literature tends to employ genres used and appreciated around the world, some of the older classics are composed in forms that make them excitingly different from those in use in our Western tradition. Take, for example, *The Tale of Genji*. I have avoided using the word "novel" to describe it, because the associations we have with our English term are at some variance with the term employed in the title *monogatari*, "telling of something." Actually, the word "tale," employed by the translators, is perhaps a better, if far from perfect, English equivalent. True enough, certain features of the differences themselves are also revealing. Indeed, a criticism made of the Waley version is that, in making his translation he used a model implicit in his mind of the modern Western psychological novel, thereby perhaps heightening certain passages to an unrealistic degree.

Another traditional Japanese literary form that puzzles and intrigues modern readers is the literary diary, or *nikki.* Some of the most evocative works written in the Heian period and later are composed in this form. The *Tosa Diary* and *As I Crossed a Bridge of Dreams* were mentioned earlier, and there are a half-dozen others of equal accomplishment available now in English. Perhaps most famous of all is *An Account of My Hut (Hōjōki)* by Kamo no Chōmei (1153–1216), which has long come to constitute a fundamental statement on Buddhist aesthetics. It is read in every school today, and most Japanese will recognize, if nothing else, some of its beautiful opening phrases:

> The flow of the river is ceaseless and its water is never the same. The bubbles that float in the pools, now vanishing, now forming, are not of long duration . . . which will be first to go, the master or his dwelling? One might just as well ask this of the dew on the morning glory. The dew may fall and the flower remain—remain, only to be withered by the morning sun. The flower may fade before the dew evaporates, but though it does not evaporate, it waits not the evening. (Keene, *An Anthology of Japanese Literature, from the Earliest Era to the Mid-nineteenth Century*, pp. 197–98)

Most of these literary diaries are cast as first-person narratives, and the modern reader therefore may usually assume one of two things. On one hand, it may appear that they are "true," that is, that the events described in them actually occurred, and that the diary serves as a kind of report. On the other hand, the reader may decide that the texts are fiction, like a novel written in the first person. Actually, neither response accurately portrays the quality of the originals, which usually shift between fact and fantasy, art and life. Such forms open up new modes of expression if we, as readers, do not flatten them out by imposing too firmly our own preconceptions.

In the theatre too, we tend, however inadvertently, to impose implicitly our modern standards on a bewildering variety of dramatic forms. In our own Western tradition, we use the word "drama" or "play" to define, at least loosely, works ranging from *King Lear* to *Death of a Salesman.*

In a sense we can do this, since the development of our tradition has been more or less continuous. By extension, it is easy enough to refer to works for the stage written by Abe Kōbō or Minoru Betsuyaku, another contemporary Japanese playwright whose works have been translated, as "plays," because in their dramaturgy they partake of the basic assumptions of Western traditions that took root in Japan since the plays of Ibsen and Chekhov were first imported and performed at the beginning of this century. Yet to describe works of the traditional repertory of Noh, Bunraku, and Kabuki as "plays" or "dramas," however, is to impose Western categories on very different traditions. All three, indeed, might best be compared very loosely to Western opera librettos, since mime, dance, and music are, in various ways, as important to the total spectacle as the text itself. Reading a Chikamatsu puppet play in translation may give us something of the same experience we might have in reading a Western play text. In translation, however, it is all too easy to forget that, in actual performance, one male chanter, using a slim musical accompaniment, must perform all parts, imitating the voices of the characters, and then provide linking narration as well. The remarkable puppets follow his lead, not the other way around. Reading the text is an experience rather far removed from the effect intended for the original.

As more and more translations of Japanese literature become available, the possibilities to increase our sense of these older traditions allows for expanding creative possibilities on our own side. Earlier in this century, writers as diverse as William Butler Yeats, Bertolt Brecht, and Paul Claudel composed new kinds of dramas based on their understanding of the medieval Noh theatre, learned from translation. Indeed, in the case of Claudel, he was directly influenced by seeing Noh plays staged in Japan between 1921 and 1926, during the period he served as the French Ambassador to Japan. By now, virtually every American elementary and junior high school student has a chance to try composing haiku. The forms of Japanese literature, however they may vary from our own ideas of genre, can open up new horizons.

Notes

1. Ki no Tsurayuki, *Tosa Diary (Tosa Nikki)*, translated and introduced by Earl Miner in *Japanese Poetic Diaries* (Berkeley: University of California Press, 1969), p. 83. Reprinted with permission.

2. *Tales of Ise: Lyrical Episodes from Tenth-Century Japan (Ise Monogatari)*, translated by Helen Craig McCullough and published by the Stanford University Press, 1968, p. 129. Reprinted with permission.

3. From *The Tale of Genji (Genji Monogatari)* by Lady Murasaki, translated by Arthur Waley and published by Unwin Hyman Ltd., and Houghton Mifflin Company in 1935, p. 390. Reprinted with permission.

4. Excerpts from *From the Country of Eight Islands: An Anthology of Japanese Poetry*, translated and edited by Hiroaki Sato and Burton Watson. Copyright 1981 by Hiroaki Sato and Burton Watson. Reprinted by permission of Doubleday, a Division of Bantam, Doubleday, Dell Published Group, Inc.

5. Laurel Rasplica Rodd, translator, *Kokinshū: A Collection of Poems Ancient and Modern.* Copyright 1984 by Princeton University Press. Selection, p. 164, reprinted with permission of Princeton University Press.

6. *The Narrow Road to the Deep North and Other Travel Sketches (Oku no no Hosomichi)* by Bashō, translated by Nobuyuki Yuasa (London: Penguin Classics, 1966), p. 55. Copyright Nobuyuki Yuasa, 1966. Reprinted by permission of Penguin Books Ltd.

7. Yasunari Kawabata, *Snow Country (Yukiguni)*, translated by Edward G. Seidensticker (New York: Alfred A Knopf, 1955. Reprinted with permission.

8. *The Tale of the Heike (Heike Monogatari)*, translated by Helen Craig McCullough (Stanford University Press, 1988), p. 317. Reprinted with permission.

9. Cited by Hozumi Ikan, "Chikamatsu on the Art of the Puppet Stage," in Donald Keene, ed., *An Anthology of Japanese Literature, from the Earliest Era to the Mid-nineteenth Century* (New York: Grove Press, 1955), p. 389. Reprinted with permission.

Chapter 2

Japanese Aesthetics

DONALD KEENE

Using the Shintō priest Kenkō's Tsurezuregusa *(Essays in Idleness) as a focus, Donald Keene introduces the reader to his notion of "the pleasures of Japanese literature." His discussion of "suggestion," "irregularity," "simplicity," and "perishability," echoed in many other essays in this volume, provides essential background for the student of Japanese aesthetics and literature. Even though contemporary Japanese culture may resemble that of the West, the principles put forward by Keene will persuade the reader that the "Japanese aesthetic past is not dead."*

It would be difficult to describe adequately in the course of a few pages the full range of Japanese aesthetics or even to suggest the main features of Japanese taste as it has evolved over the centuries. It probably would be even more difficult to discuss any aspect of Japanese culture without alluding to the Japanese sense of beauty, perhaps the central element in all of Japanese culture. I will attempt to describe some of the characteristics of Japanese taste in terms of one book *Tsurezuregusa* (Essays in Idleness), a collection of short essays by the priest Kenkō, written mainly between 1330 and 1333. This work does not explain the whole of Japanese aesthetics, obviously not the developments of the last six hundred years, but I believe that it contains much that illuminates Japanese preferences today, despite the long interval of time since it was written and despite the immense changes that Japanese civilization has undergone, especially during the past century. The author is generally known by his name as a Buddhist priest, Kenkō. His name when he was born in 1283 was Urabe no Kaneyoshi, and he came from a family of hereditary Shintō priests. It is somewhat surprising that a man of a Shintō background should have become a Buddhist, but the two religions of Japan, though antithetical in many respects, were both accepted by the Japanese; in general, the Japanese in the past (and the present) have turned to Shintō for help in this life, and to Buddhism for salvation in the world to come.

Kenkō, though his rank as a Shintō priest was modest, seems to have won a secure place in court circles thanks to his skill at composing poetry. This alone should suggest how highly poetic skill was valued by the court, which in most respects was acutely conscious of rank and ancestry. For courtiers, an ability to compose poetry was an indispensable accomplishment, and Kenkō may have been welcomed to the palace less as a poet than as a tutor in poetry to those who lacked outstanding poetic talent.

Kenkō took Buddhist orders in 1324 at the age of 41, after the death of the Emperor Go-Uda, whom he had served. Many reasons have been adduced for his decision to "leave the world," but nothing in his writings suggests that it was an act of despair. Buddhist thought figures prominently in *Essays in Idleness,* and it can hardly be doubted that Kenkō was sincere when he urged readers to "flee from the Burning House" of this world and find refuge in religion. But he did not in the least resemble the typical Buddhist monks of the medieval period, who either lived in monasteries or else were hermits. Kenkō lived in the city and was as familiar with worldly gossip as with Buddhist doctrine. Certain Buddhist beliefs, notably the impermanence of all things, run through his work, but even though he insisted that the possessions that people accumulate in this world do not last, he did not condemn them as hateful dross, as a more orthodox Buddhist priest might have. Obviously, he did not reject the world. Ultimately this world was not enough, but Kenkō seems always to be saying that while we are here we should try to enrich our lives with beauty.

Essays in Idleness consists of 243 sections. They are not systematically presented; it was in the nature of a work in the *zuihitsu* tradition of "following the brush," to allow one's writing brush to skip from one topic to another in whichever direction it was led by free association. Kenkō did not enunciate a consistent philosophy—it is easy to find contradictions among the various sections, and some are so trivial in content that we may wonder why he included them. But a concern with beauty is never far from his thoughts, and this aspect of the work, much more than its Buddhist message, has influenced Japanese taste. *Essays in Idleness* was unknown to the reading public during Kenkō's lifetime, but it came into prominence at the beginning of the seventeenth century, and since then has been one of the best known of the Japanese classics. Kenkō's tastes at once reflected those of Japanese of much earlier times, and greatly contributed to the formation of the aesthetic preferences of Japanese for centuries to come.

A typical section of *Essays in Idleness* will illustrate Kenkō's manner. It is section 81.

> A screen or sliding door decorated with a painting or inscription in clumsy brushwork gives an impression less of its own ugliness than of the bad taste of the owner. It is all too apt to happen that a man's possessions betray his inferiority. I am not suggesting that a man should own nothing but masterpieces. I refer to the practice of deliberately decorating in a tasteless and ugly manner 'to keep the house from showing its age,' or adding all manner of useless things in order to create an impression of novelty, though only producing an effect of fussiness. Possessions should look old, not overly elaborate; they need not cost much, but their quality should be good.[1]

Some years ago, when writing an essay on Japanese tastes, I chose four characteristics that seemed to me of special importance: suggestion, irregularity, simplicity, and perishability. These still seem to me to be a valid way to approach the Japanese sense of beauty, though I am fully aware that they do not cover everything. Generalizations are always risky. If, for example, one says of the Nō drama that it is a crystallization of Japanese preferences for understatement, muted expression, and symbolic gesture, how is one to explain why the Japanese have also loved Kabuki, which is characterized by larger-than-life poses, fierce declamation, brilliant stage effects, and so on? The clean lines of the Katsura Palace are today recognized everywhere as representative of the essence of Japanese architecture, but it was a European who first described the beauty of the palace in writings published in the 1930s, and Japanese over the centuries have usually praised instead the garishly decorated mausoleum of the shoguns at Nikkō, built about the same time.

Again, I feel quite sure that no people are more sensitive to beauty than the Japanese, but one Japanese critic, Sakaguchi Ango, wrote in 1942, "A more convenient life is more important to the Japanese than the beauty of tradition or of the authentic Japanese appearance. Nobody would be discomforted if all the temples in Kyoto and Buddhist statues in Nara were completely destroyed, but we would certainly be inconvenienced if the streetcars stopped running." Sakaguchi was being cynical, but there is more than a grain of truth in what he wrote, and it took some courage to publish such ideas in 1942, at a time when the Japanese were otherwise asserting the spiritual superiority of their culture. With these cautions in mind, I would like to discuss the four aspects of Japanese taste I noted above, referring particularly to Kenkō's opinions in *Essays in Idleness.*

Suggestion

The most eloquent expression of Kenkō's advocacy of suggestion as an aesthetic principle is found in section 137.

> Are we to look at cherry blossoms only in full bloom, the moon only when it is cloudless? To long for the moon while looking on the rain, to lower the blinds and be unaware of the passing of the spring—these are even more deeply moving. Branches about to blossom or gardens strewn with faded flowers are worthier of our admiration. . . . People commonly regret that the cherry blossoms scatter or that the moon sinks in the sky, and this is natural; but only an exceptionally insensitive man would say, "This branch and that branch have lost their blossoms. There is nothing worth seeing now."
>
> In all things, it is the beginnings and ends that are interesting. Does the love between men and women refer only to the moments when they are in each other's arms? The man who grieves over a love affair broken off before it was fulfilled, who bewails empty vows, who spends long autumn nights alone, who lets his thoughts wander to distant skies, who yearns for the past in a dilapidated house—such a man truly knows what love means.
>
> The moon that appears close to dawn after we have long waited for it moves us more profoundly than the full moon shining cloudless over a thousand leagues. And how incomparably lovely is the moon, almost greenish in its light, when seen through the tops of the cedars deep in the mountains, or when it hides for a moment behind clustering clouds during a sudden shower! The sparkle on hickory or white-oak leaves seemingly wet with moonlight strikes one to the heart. . . .
>
> And are we to look at the moon and the cherry blossoms with our eyes alone? How much more evocative and pleasing it is to

> think about the spring without stirring from the house, to dream of the moonlight though we remain in our room!

Kenkō presents his views so compellingly that we may assent without noticing that they contradict commonly held Western views on the same subjects. The Western ideal of the climactic moment—when Laocoön and his sons are caught in the terrible embrace of the serpent, when the soprano hits high C, or when the rose is in full bloom—grants little importance to the beginnings and ends. The Japanese have also been aware of the appeal of climactic moments: they celebrate the full moon far more often than the crescent, and the radio breathlessly informs listeners when the cherry blossoms will be in full bloom, not when they are likely to scatter. But although the Japanese share with other peoples a fondness for flowers in full bloom, their love of the barely opened buds and of fallen blossoms is distinctive. The Japanese seem to have been aware that the full moon (or the full flowering of a tree), however lovely, blocks the play of the imagination. The full moon or the cherry blossoms at their peak do not suggest the crescent or the buds (or the waning moon and the strewn flowers), but the crescent and the buds do suggest full flowering. Beginnings that suggest what is to come, or ends that suggest what has been, allow the imagination room to expand beyond the literal facts to the limits of the capacities of the reader of a poem, the spectator at a Nō play, or the connoisseur of a monochrome painting.

Kenkō did not create the preference for beginnings and ends that he describes, but he was probably the first to state it as a principle. We find a similar phenomenon in earlier collections of Japanese poetry, though no one ever explained the reason. The innumerable love poems preserved in anthologies of Japanese poetry almost never express the joy of meeting the beloved; instead, they convey the poet's yearning for a meeting, or else his—or more commonly, her—sorrow at the realization that an affair is over and there will not be another meeting.

In Japanese painting, especially of the period when Kenkō was writing, the use of suggestion is carried to great lengths, a few brush strokes serving to suggest ranges of mountains, or a single stroke a stalk of bamboo. A desire to suggest rather than to state in full was surely behind the preference for ink paintings. No people has a surer sense of color than the Japanese, and there are many splendid Japanese works of art in brilliant colors; but in the medieval period especially, many painters renounced color in favor of monochromes. I have never seen any reason stated for this preference, but I wonder whether it was not dictated also by an awareness of the power of suggestion. A mountain painted in green can never be any other color but green, but a mountain whose outlines are given with a few strokes of black ink can be any color. To add even the most delicate colors to a monochrome would be as disconcerting as adding color to Greek marbles, or in as bad taste as the rubies and emeralds with which the sultans decorated their Chinese porcelains.

Irregularity

A second notable characteristic of Japanese taste is irregularity and once again I turn to Kenkō for an illustrative passage. In section 82 he says, "In everything, no matter what it may be, uniformity is undesirable. Leaving something incomplete makes it interesting, and gives one the feeling that there is room for growth. Someone once told me, 'Even when building the imperial palace, they always leave one place unfinished.'" Kenkō gave an example of what he meant: "People often say that a set of books looks ugly if all volumes are in the same format, but I was impressed to hear the Abbot Kōyū say, 'It is typical of the unintelligent man to insist on assembling complete sets of everything. Imperfect sets are better.'" I doubt that many librarians would agree with the Abbot Kōyū, but anyone who has ever faced a complete set of the Harvard Classics or any similar series knows how uninviting it is.

The Japanese have been partial not only to incompleteness but to another variety of irregularity, asymmetry. This is one respect in which they differ conspicuously from the Chinese and other peoples of Asia. In ancient (and modern) Iranian art there is often a tree in the center of the picture or pattern with beasts on either side. If a line is drawn vertically through the tree, what is on the right side is likely to be a mirror image of what is on the left. One finds symmetry also in Chinese art and architecture, though it is not quite so rigid. The typical plan of a Chinese monastery has the same buildings on one side of a central axis as on the other. But in Japan, even when the original plan called for symmetry along Chinese lines, it did not take long for the buildings to cluster, seemingly of their own volition, on one side or the other.

In literary style, parallelism in poetry and prose is a staple feature of Chinese expression. Japanese writing that is not specifically under Chinese influence avoids parallelism, and the standard verse forms are irregular numbers of lines—five for the *tanka*, three for the *haiku*. This is in marked contrast to the quatrains that are typical poetic forms not only in China but throughout most of the world.

We find the same tendency in calligraphy, too. The Japanese, ever since they acquired skill in writing Chinese characters, have excelled in "grass writing," the cursive script, but there are few outstanding examples of the more formal style of calligraphy, which the Japanese happily leave to the Chinese. Japanese children are taught in calligraphy lessons never to bisect a horizontal stroke with a vertical one: the vertical stroke should always cross the horizontal one at some point not equidistant from both ends. A symmetrical character is considered to be "dead." The writing most admired by the Japanese tends to be lopsided or at any rate highly individual, and copybook perfection is admired only with condescension.

Irregularity is also a feature of Japanese ceramics, especially those varieties that are most admired by the Japanese themselves. The Bizen or Shigaraki wares that are the delight of connoisseurs are almost never regular in shape. Some of the finest examples are lopsided or bumpy, and the glaze may have been applied in such a way as to leave bald patches here and there. A roughness caused by tiny stones in the clay is also much admired. These would be serious faults if the potter had intended to make a bowl or jar in a symmetrical shape with an even glaze and failed, but that was clearly not his aim. The Japanese have produced flawless examples of porcelain, and these too are admired, but are not much loved. Their perfection, especially their regularity, seems to repel the hands of the person who drinks tea from them, and flowers arranged in porcelain vases seem to be challenged rather than enhanced.

Irregularity is present too in flower arrangements (notably those based on "heaven, earth, and man") and in gardens. The gardens at Versailles, with their geometrical precision, would hardly have struck the Japanese of the past as a place for relaxation. The celebrated Japanese gardens insist on irregularity as determinedly as the classical European gardens insisted on symmetry. One European authority on gardens, D. P. Clifford, expressed in *A History of Garden Design* (1963) his distaste for the famous sand and stone garden of the Ryōan-ji, in these terms:

> It is the logical conclusion of the refinement of the senses, the precipitous world of the abstract painter, a world in which the stains on the cover of a book can absorb one more utterly than the ceiling of the Sistine Chapel; it is the narrow knife edge of art, overthrowing and discarding all that man has ever been and achieved in favour of some mystic contemplative ecstasy, a sort of suspended explosion of the mind, the dissolution of identity. You really cannot go much

further than this unless you sit on a cushion like Oscar Wilde and contemplate the symmetry of an orange.

The symmetry of an orange was hardly likely to absorb the attention of the architects of this exceedingly asymmetrical garden, and far from being artless "stains on the cover of a book," the Ryōan-ji garden is the product of a philosophical system—that of Zen Buddhism—as serious as the one that inspired the ceiling of the Sistine Chapel. And, it might be argued, even a European might derive great pleasure from daily contemplation of the fifteen stones of the Ryōan-ji garden, without "overthrowing and discarding all that man has ever been and achieved." The Sistine Chapel is magnificent, but it asks our admiration rather than our participation; the stones of the Ryōan-ji, irregular in shape and position, allow us to participate in the creation of the garden, and thus may move us even more. But that may be because in our age, Western artistic expression is closer to that of the Ryōan-ji than to that of Michelangelo.

Simplicity

Kenkō has much to say about the third characteristic of Japanese aesthetics that I would like to discuss, simplicity. I will quote a few of his views, from section 10 of *Essays in Idleness:*

> A house, I know, is but a temporary abode, but how delightful it is to find one that has harmonious proportions and a pleasant atmosphere. One feels somehow that even moonlight, when it shines into the quiet domicile of a person of taste, is more affecting than elsewhere. A house, though it may not be in the current fashion or elaborately decorated, will appeal to us by its unassuming beauty—a grove of trees with an indefinably ancient look; a garden where plants, growing of their own accord, have a special charm; a verandah and an open-work wooden fence of interesting construction; and a few personal effects left lying about, giving the place an air of having been lived in. A house which multitudes of workmen have polished with every care, where strange and rare Chinese and Japanese furnishings are displayed, and even the bushes and trees of the garden have been trained unnaturally, is ugly to look at and most depressing. How could anyone live for long in such a place?

Kenkō expresses himself so well that we are likely to agree, perhaps a little too easily; houses which multitudes of workmen have polished with every care have generally been considered very desirable, as we know from old photographs showing the profusion of treasures with which the drawing rooms of the rich used to be adorned. Gardens where even the bushes and trees have been trained unnaturally still attract visitors to the great houses of Europe. Kenkō asks rhetorically "how could anyone live for long in such a place?" but generations of Europeans and even some Americans seem to have had no trouble.

Perhaps Kenkō would answer this with another passage from *Essays in Idleness:* "It is excellent for a man to be simple in his tastes, to avoid extravagance, to own no possessions, to entertain no craving for worldly success. It has been true since ancient days that wise men are rarely rich" (section 18). Kenkō's professed dislike for possessions may stem from Buddhist convictions. Elsewhere in his book he states it even more strongly:

> The intelligent man, when he dies, leaves no possessions. If he has collected worthless objects, it is embarrassing to have them discovered. If the objects are of good quality, they will depress his heirs at the thought of how attached he must have been to them. It is all the more deplorable if the possessions are ornate and numerous. If a man leaves possessions, there are sure to be people who will quarrel disgracefully over them, crying, "I'm getting that one!" If you wish something to go to someone after you are dead, you should give it to him while you are still alive. Some things are probably indispensable to daily life, but as for the rest, it is best not to own anything at all. (section 140)

Obviously, however, people have to live in houses of some sort, and Kenkō, for all his insistence on simplicity, was certainly not urging people to live in hovels. Here is how he described the kind of house he liked: "A house should be built with the summer in mind. In winter it is possible to live anywhere, but a badly made house is unbearable when it gets hot. . . . People agree that a house which has plenty of spare room is attractive to look at and may be put to many uses" (section 55).

Kenkō's prescription has been followed by many Japanese, as anyone who has spent a winter in a Kyoto house knows. When the Japanese settled Hokkaidō in the late nineteenth century they still went on building with the summer in mind, and quietly froze in the winter. But leaving aside the matter of temperature, Kenkō's insistence on having plenty of spare room has typified Japanese houses at their most artistic. It is easy too for us to accept the principle that it is better to have too little rather than too much furniture; we have been trained to believe that "less is more," but this was not true of people at the beginning of this century.

It is by no means inexpensive to build a Japanese house of the kind Kenkō favored. Simplicity is probably more expensive than ornateness, a luxury concealing luxury. Walls decorated with gilt cupids can be repainted or re-gilded from time to time, and the wood need not be absolutely first-rate; but the unpainted wood of the *tokonoma* cannot be so easily disguised. The Japanese preference for unpainted wood is today much admired abroad and even imitated, but it was not so in the past. When the distinguished British diplomat and author Harold Nicolson visited Kyoto early in this century he remarked that it looked like a town in the Wild West because the exteriors of the buildings were not painted; and more recently, during the Occupation, it is said that Americans painted the woodwork to brighten the houses they occupied.

Simplicity as an aesthetic principle is, of course, not confined to houses and their furnishings. Perhaps the most extreme example of the Japanese love for unobtrusive elegance is the tea ceremony. The ideal sought by the great teamaster Sen no Rikyū (1522–1591) was *sabi,* related to the word *sabi*, for "rust," or *sabireru*, "to become desolate." This may seem like a curious aesthetic ideal, but it was perhaps a reaction to parvenu extravagance in an age when military men obtained sudden power and wealth. Rikyū's *sabi* was not the enforced simplicity of the man who could not afford better, but a refusal of easily obtainable luxury, a preference for a rusty-looking kettle to one of gleaming newness. The tea ceremony is sometimes attacked today as a perversion of the ideal of simplicity. The prized utensils are by no means ordinary wares but may cost fortunes. But the spending of a great deal of money in order to achieve an appearance of bare simplicity is quite in keeping with Japanese tradition.

The Portuguese missionary João Rodrigues (1561–1633) described with admiration a tea ceremony he had attended, but he could not restrain his astonishment over the lengths to which the Japanese carried their passion for unobtrusive luxury:

> Because they greatly value and enjoy this kind of gathering to drink tea, they spend large sums of money in building such a house, rough though it may be, and in purchasing the things needed for drinking

> the kind of tea which is offered in these meetings. Thus there are utensils, albeit of earthenware, which come to be worth ten, twenty or thirty thousand *cruzados* or even more—a thing which will appear as madness and barbarity to other nations that know of it.[2]

Madness perhaps, but surely not barbarity! The avoidance of a display of conspicuous wealth, regardless of how much the objects actually cost, is typical of the Japanese insistence on simplicity. But surely it would be far more barbarous to calculate the value of objects solely in the terms of typical European collectors of exotic bric-a-brac: how many workmen have gone blind to make them?

One more example of the Japanese preference for simplicity is found in Japanese food, and not only the variety served in connection with a tea ceremony. Japanese food lacks the intensity of flavor found in the cuisines of other countries of Asia. Spices are seldom used, garlic almost never. Just as the faint perfume of the plum blossom is preferred to the heavy odor of the lily, the barely perceptible differences in flavor between different varieties of raw fish are prized and paid for extravagantly. The taste of natural ingredients, not tampered with by sauces, is the ideal of Japanese cuisine; and the fineness of a man's palate is often tested by his ability to distinguish between virtually tasteless dishes of the same species. The early European visitors to Japan, though they praised almost everything else, had nothing good to say about Japanese food. Bernardo de Avila Girón wrote, "I will not praise Japanese food for it is not good, albeit it is pleasing to the eye, but instead I will describe the clean and peculiar way in which it is served." His judgment was repeated by foreign visitors for the next three hundred years. The current popularity of Japanese food may be another sign of the general trend I have already mentioned towards a congruence of contemporary American and traditional Japanese tastes.

Perishability

The last of the four qualities of Japanese aesthetic preference that I have chosen to describe is the most unusual, perishability. In the West, permanence rather than perishability has been desired, and this has led men to build monuments of deathless marble. The realization that even such monuments crumble—proof of the inexorability of the ravages of time—has led men since the age of the Greeks to reflect on the uncertainty of the world.

Lafcadio Hearn (1850–1904), a widely-read popularizer of Japanese landscapes and customs, wrote in *Kokoro* (1896):

> Generally speaking, we construct for endurance, the Japanese for impermanency. Few things for common use are made in Japan with a view to durability. The straw sandals worn out and replaced at each stage of a journey; the robe consisting of a few simple widths loosely stitched together for wearing, and unstitched again for washing; the fresh chopsticks served to each new guest at a hotel; the light *shōji* frames serving at once for windows and walls, and repapered twice a year; the mattings renewed every autumn,—all these are but random examples of countless small things in daily life that illustrate the national contentment with impermanency.

Hearn's comments were astute, but it might be even more accurate to say that the Japanese have not only been content with impermanency, but have eagerly sought it. Once more, a passage from Kenkō helps to illuminate this traditional preference:

> Somebody once remarked that thin silk was not satisfactory as a scroll wrapping because it was so easily torn. Ton'a replied, "It is only after the silk wrapper has frayed at top and bottom, and the mother-of-pearl has fallen from the roller that a scroll looks beautiful." This opinion demonstrated the excellent taste of the man. (section 82)

Signs of wear and tear such as the fraying of a silk wrapper or the loss of mother-of-pearl inlay from the roller would probably dismay most other people, and it is likely that the owner would send for a restorer, but in Japan an object of such perfection, such gleaming newness that it might have been made yesterday has seemed less desirable than a work that has passed through many hands and shows it. Such an object acquires the mysterious quality that, according to Robert Graves in a lecture I once heard, is called *barak* by the Arabs. Even a typewriter one has banged at for thirty years acquires *barak* because one has grown to know and perhaps even to love its little eccentricities; how much more true this is of a work of art, whose flaws are sometimes as attractive as its intrinsic beauty. A pottery bowl that has been cracked and mended, not invisibly but with gold, as if to call attention to the cracks, is human, suggesting the long chain of people who have held it in their hands—

more human than a bowl that looks as if it might have been made very recently. The common Western craving for objects in mint condition, that look as if they were painted or sculpted the day before, tends to deprive antiques of their history; the Japanese prize the evidence that a work of art has been held in many hands.

Western traditions seem to go back to the Greeks, who constantly bewailed the uncertainty of fate and insisted that no man should be called happy until he was dead, lest cruel Nemesis catch up with him. The Japanese were perhaps the first to discover the special pleasure of impermanence, and Kenkō especially believed that impermanence was a necessary element in beauty. He wrote early in *Essays in Idleness,* "If man were never to fade away like the dews of Adashino, never to vanish like the smoke over Toribeyama, but lingered on forever in this world, how things would lose their power to move us! The most precious thing in life is its uncertainty." The frailty of human existence, a common theme in the literature of the world, has probably not been recognized elsewhere than in Japan as a necessary condition of beauty. This may explain the fondness for building temples of wood, even though stronger materials were available: the very signs of aging that made Harold Nicolson recall the wooden buildings of frontier towns give greater aesthetic pleasure to the Japanese than age-repellent walls of brick or stone.

The special love the Japanese have for cherry blossoms is surely also connected with the appreciation of perishability. Cherry blossoms are lovely, it is true, but not so lovely as to eclipse totally the beauty of peach blossoms or plum blossoms. But the Japanese plant cherry trees wherever they can, even in parts of the country whose climate is not suitable for these rather delicate trees. Several years ago I visited Hirosaki in the north of Japan, a town known for its huge apple orchards. When I went to buy postcards I discovered not one that showed apple blossoms, but many devoted to cherry blossoms, which, though lovely, are hardly unique to Hirosaki. Perhaps the greatest attraction of the cherry blossoms is not their intrinsic beauty but their perishability: plum blossoms remain on the boughs for a month or so, and other fruit trees have blossoms for at least a week, but cherry blossoms normally fall after a brief three days of flowering, a fact that countless poets have had occasion to lament. Ornamental cherry trees do not produce edible fruit and they attract caterpillars and other disagreeable insects, so many that it is wise to carry an umbrella when passing under them in the late summer; but the Japanese happily plant these trees wherever they can, for their three days of glory.

Japanese when traveling abroad are sometimes startled by the indifference of people in the West to the passage of time in nature. The tea master

Rikyū is said to have scattered a few leaves over a garden path that had recently been swept, in order to give it a natural look and to emphasize the sense of process; and the great novelist Natsume Sōseki, when traveling in Europe at the beginning of this century, was struck by the insensitivity of Europeans to the beauty of the changes effected by nature. He wrote,

> When I was in England, I was once laughed at because I invited someone for snow-viewing. At another time I described how deeply the feelings of Japanese are affected by the moon, and my listeners were only puzzled. . . I was invited to Scotland to stay at a palatial house. One day, when the master and I took a walk in the garden, I noted that the paths between the rows of trees were all thickly covered with moss. I offered a compliment, saying that these paths had magnificently acquired a look of age. Whereupon my host replied that he soon intended to get a gardener to scrape all this moss away.[3]

Natsume Sōseki was a novelist, that is, a man who invented stories as his career, so we need not take his anecdote as literal truth. But it is unquestionable that Sōseki responded more to snow-viewing, the moon, and gardens with mossy paths than to herbaceous borders or avenues of carefully trimmed evergreens. He was heir to tastes that had evolved in Japan over many centuries, partly under the influence of Kenkō's writings. Sōseki had also read a great deal of English literature and possessed a remarkable store of knowledge concerning such varied authors as Shakespeare, Laurence Sterne, and George Meredith, but apparently at the most fundamental level, the level of his appreciation of beauty, concepts other than those he found in Western books still dominated.

The Western visitor to Japan today who expects to find exquisite beauty wherever he looks is likely to be disappointed and even shocked by his first encounters with contemporary culture. He will notice Kentucky Fried Chicken establishments and other fast-food shops, the ugliness of commercial signs, the blank looks on the faces of people hurrying to places of business that more clearly resemble contemporary models in the West than anything traditional. But the past survives in aesthetic preferences that often find surprising outlets for expression—a box of sushi, a display of lacquered zori, branches of artificial maple leaves along a commercial street. And the man who prides himself on his elegantly tailored Western clothes will be delighted to sit in Japanese style, destroying the creases, at a restaurant where traditional food is served with traditional elegance. The Japanese aesthetic past is not dead. It accounts for the magnificent profusion of objects of art that are produced each year, and its principles, the ones I have escribed, are not forgotten even in an age of incessant change.

Notes

1. *Essays in Idleness: The Tsurezuregusa of Kenkō*, trans. Donald Keene (New York: Columbia University Press, 1967), p. 70. All subsequent quotations from this work are from this edition.

2. Quoted in Michael Cooper, *They Came to Japan* (Berkeley: University of California Press, 1965), p. 265.

3. Translated by Matsui Sakako, in *Natsume Sōseki as a Critic of English Literature* (Tokyo: Center for East Asian Cultural Studies, 1975), p. 34.

Chapter 3

The Vocabulary of Japanese Aesthetics, I, II, III

WM. THEODORE DE BARY, ED.

First published in 1958, Sources of Japanese Tradition, *from which the following three excerpts are taken, introduces the reader to both the literature and aesthetic principles which shape the Japanese tradition. "Vocabulary of Japanese Aesthetics I," introduces the terms* aware, mono no aware, *and* miyabi *as they are reflected in the* Manyōshū, *the eighth-century collection of poetry and in* The Tale of Genji, *Murasaki Shikabu's classic novel of Heian Japan. "Vocabulary of Japanese Aesthetics II" shifts to medieval Japan and a discussion of the Nō theater and the principles of* yūgen *and* sabi, *with excerpts from the great Nō playwright Seami's treatise on the Nō theater. "Vocabulary of Japanese Aesthetics III" focuses on the Tokugawa period's interest in* ukiyo *(floating world) as it relates to the theater, woodblock prints, and literature. Chikamatsu's comments on the puppet theater and* joruri *conclude the essay. This collection of important aesthetic principles serves as a background for several of the essays to follow, especially Ueda's "Imitation,* Yūgen, *and Sublimity: Zeami and the Art of the Nō Drama."*

The Vocabulary of Japanese Aesthetics I

It is surprising how often we find the same few terms used to express the preferences or ideals of Japanese creative artists throughout the ages, so often indeed that we can identify them as a special "vocabulary of Japanese aesthetics." Such terms varied in meaning with the times and with the individual critics, as was only to be expected of words employed for well over a thousand years in some cases. Nevertheless, some knowledge of this vocabulary may serve as a key to Japanese canons of taste in literature and the other arts.

The most famous of these words, and one which has had whole volumes of serious research devoted to it, is *aware.* In old texts we find it first used as an exclamation of surprise or delight, man's natural reaction to what an early Western critic of Japanese literature called the "ahness" of things, but gradually it came to be used adjectivally, usually to mean "pleasant" or "interesting." One scholar who analyzed the uses of *aware* in the *Manyōshū,* the great eighth-century collection of poetry, discovered that an *aware* emotion was most often evoked in the poets by hearing the melancholy calls of birds and beasts. An inscription from the year 763 contains the word *aware* used to describe the writer's emotions on seeing the spring rain. Gradually, therefore, *aware* came to be tinged with sadness. By the time of *The Tale of Genji* only the lower classes (or the upper classes in moments of great stress) used the word *aware* as a simple exclamation: elsewhere it expressed a gentle sorrow, adding not so much a meaning as a color or a perfume to a sentence. It bespoke the sensitive poet's awareness of a sight or a sound, of its beauty and its perishability. It was probably inevitable that with the steady heightening of the sensitivity of poets to the world around them the tone of sadness deepened.

The famous eighteenth-century critic of Japanese literature Motoori Norinaga (1730–1801) once characterized the whole of *The Tale of Genji* as a novel of *mono no aware,* a phrase which has sometimes been translated as "the sadness of things." Motoori, however, seems to have meant by it something closer to a "sensitivity to things"—sensitivity to the fall of a flower or to an unwept tear.

Some of the early works of criticism use the word *aware* so often as to make it almost the exclusive criterion of merit. In a work written about the year 1200, for example, there occurs this discussion of *The Tale of Genji.*

> "Someone asked, 'Which chapter is the best and creates the most profound impression?'
>
> "'No chapter is superior to *Kiritsubo.* From the opening words, "At the Court of an Emperor (he lived it matters not when)" to the final description of Genji's initiation to manhood, the whole chapter is filled with a moving *(aware)* pathos which colors the language, the circumstances portrayed, and everything else. In *The Broom-Tree* the discussion on a rainy night of the categories of women

contains many praiseworthy things. The chapter *Yugao* is permeated with a moving (*aware*) sadness. *The Festival of Red Leaves* and *The Flower-Feast* are unforgettable chapters, each possessed of its own charm (*en*) and interest. *Aoi* is an extremely moving *(aware)* and absorbing chapter. The chapter *Kashiwagi* contains the scene of the departure for Ise, which is at once charming *(en)* and magnificent. The scene when, after the death of the Emperor, Fujitsubo takes vows as a nun is moving *(aware). Exile at Suma* is a moving (*aware*) and powerful chapter. The descriptions of Genji leaving the capital for Suma and of his life in distant exile are extremely moving *(aware).*' "[1]

As this excerpt shows, the word *aware* was used to describe almost every chapter considered to be of unusual beauty, and in each case the meaning, though vague, was associated with deep emotions, and not a mere exclamation as in early times. But *aware* had not yet darkened to its modern meaning of "wretched," which represents perhaps the final evolution in its long history.

In the same excerpt one other word appears several times—*en,* which may be translated as "charming." Its use as a term of praise indicates that not only the melancholy but the colorful surface of the *Genji* was appreciated. Indeed, if we look at the superb horizontal scroll illustrating the *Genji,* which is roughly contemporary with this piece of criticism, we are struck far more by its exquisite charm than by the sadness of the scenes (although, of course, the two conceptions are not mutually exclusive). *En* evokes the visual beauty in which much of the literature of the time was clothed.

Another term of aesthetic criticism of a cheerful nature was *okashi,* a word we find in many Heian works, in particular the celebrated *Pillow Book.* It seems originally to have meant something which brought a smile to the face, either of delight or amusement. It was not applied to the serious or sad things of life except ironically and thus, as one Japanese critic has pointed out, in its making light of the tragic was just the opposite of the attitude of *aware* which sought to impart to the otherwise meaningless cries of a bird or the fall of a flower a profound and moving meaning.

Both *aware* and *okashi*—the former best represented by Murasaki Shikibu, who saw the *aware* nature of a leaf caught in the wind, the latter by Sei Shōnagon, whose witty essays are dotted with the word *okashi*—are standards which are typical of an aristocratic society of great refinement. That aristocrats of the Heian period were aware of the special nature of their society is attested by one other word of their aesthetic vocabulary—*miyabi,* literally "courtliness" but in general "refinement." The court was a small island of refinement and sophistication in a country otherwise marked by ignorance and uncourtliness; it is therefore not surprising that people at court tended to think with horror of the world outside the capital. By "courtliness" was meant not only the appropriate decorum for lords and ladies at the palace, but also the Japanese reflection of the culture which had originally come from China. One can imagine in our own day a somewhat similar situation existing somewhere in Africa, where the Oxford-educated prince of a still largely uncivilized tribe listens to records of the music of Debussy or tries his hand at composing avant-garde verse.

Miyabi was perhaps the most inclusive term for describing the aesthetics of the Heian period. It was applied in particular to the quiet pleasures which, supposedly at least, could only be savored by the aristocrat whose tastes had been educated to them—a spray of plum blossoms, the elusive perfume of a rare wood, the delicate blending of colors in a robe. In lovemaking too, the "refined" tastes of the court revealed themselves. A man might first be attracted to a woman by catching a glimpse of her sleeve, carelessly but elegantly draped from a carriage window, or by seeing a note in her calligraphy, or by hearing her play a lute one night in the dark. Later, the lovers would exchange letters and poems, often attached to a spray of the flower suitable for the season. Such love affairs are most perfectly portrayed in *The Tale of Genji,* and even if somewhat idealized in that novel, suggest to what lengths a feeling for "refinement" could govern the lives of those at court. Perhaps nowhere is insistence upon the refinement of taste more clearly revealed than in the passage known as the Gradations of Beauty,[2] in which Prince Genji and his sophisticated companions discuss the relative virtues of the women they have known. In love, no less than in art, the same aristocratic hierarchy of values, the same subtlety of discrimination prevailed as in social relations. Indeed, it was in just such a society as this that so much importance was attached, even in religious matters and contrary to the equalitarian trend of Mahāyāna Buddhism, to the ascending hierarchy or gradations of religious consciousness.

The influence of *miyabi* was not wholly beneficial, it must be admitted. In refining and polishing down the cruder emotions such as may be found in the *Manyōshū,* it severely limited the range of Japanese poetry and art. *Miyabi* led poets to shun the crude, the rustic, and the unseemly, but in so doing it tended to remove or dilute real feeling. In reading today much of the later Japanese poetry we cannot help wishing at times that the poet would venture forth from the oft-sung themes of the moon, the cries of birds, and the fall of cherry blossoms, and treat instead harsher and more compelling subjects.

Miyabi was in a sense a negation of the simpler virtues, the plain sincerity (*makoto*) which *Manyōshū* poets had possessed and which poets many centuries later were to rediscover. "Refinement" gave to the courtiers a justification for their own way of living and at the same time a contempt for the non-courtly similar to the attitude which has given the English words "peasant-like," "boorish," and "countrified" their uncomplimentary meanings. But in a curious way this specifically aristocratic standard was transmitted to the military classes when the latter rose to power, and later to the common people and even the peasantry, so that today much of what it represented is part of the common heritage of all Japanese. The hackneyed imagery of Heian poetry—the falling of the cherry blossoms, the reddening of the autumn leaves, and the rest—has become very much a part of even the least aesthetic of Japanese. Steel mills dismiss their employees for the day to enable them to admire the cherry blossoms (and to drink sake under them), and the hardest-headed businessman will not begrudge an afternoon off that is spent at Takao when the maples are their most brilliantly colored. Even the shoeshine boy in front of the railway station may in summer talk of the flickering beauty of the fireflies. Nothing in the West can compare with the role which aesthetics has played in Japanese life and history since the Heian period. If *aware* and *okashi* are no longer used in the present-day vocabulary of aesthetic criticism, the *miyabi* spirit of refined sensibility is very much in evidence.

Murasaki Shikibu

On the Art of the Novel

(From *The Tale of Genji*)

The Tale of Genji has been read and commentated on ever since it was first written, almost a thousand years ago, and many theories have been advanced as to what the author Murasaki Shikibu was attempting to express in her novel. In this excerpt from *The Tale of Genji* we find what is perhaps the best answer to this question. It seems likely that Murasaki was here, in one of the earliest and most famous examples of Japanese criticism, stating her own views on the function of the novel.

From Arthur Waley (tr.), *A Wreath of Cloud*, pp. 253–57

One day Genji, going the round with a number of romances which he had promised to lend, came to Tamakatsura's room and found her, as usual, hardly able to lift her eyes from the book in front of her. "Really, you are incurable," he said, laughing. "I sometimes think that young ladies exist for no other purpose than to provide purveyors of the absurd and improbable with a market for their wares. I am sure that the book you are now so intent upon is full of the wildest nonsense. Yet knowing this all the time, you are completely captivated by its extravagances and follow them with the utmost excitement: why, here you are on this hot day, so hard at work that, though I am sure you have not the least idea of it, your hair is in the most extraordinary tangle. . . . But there; I know quite well that these old tales are indispensable during such weather as this. How else could you all manage to get through the day? Now for a confession. I too have lately been studying these books and have, I must tell you, been amazed by the delight which they have given me. There is, it seems, an art of so fitting each part of the narrative into the next that, though all is mere invention, the reader is persuaded that such things might easily have happened and is as deeply moved as though they were actually going on around him. We may know with one part of our minds that every incident has been invented for the express purpose of impressing us; but (if the plot is constructed with the requisite skill) we may all the while in another part of our minds be burning with indignation at the wrongs endured by some wholly imaginary princess. Or again we may be persuaded by a writer's eloquence into accepting the crudest absurdities, our judgment being as it were dazzled by sheer splendor of language.

"I have lately sometimes stopped and listened to one of our young people reading out loud to her companions and have been amazed at the advances which this art of fiction is now making. How do you suppose that our new writers come by this talent? It used to be thought that the authors of successful romances were merely particularly untruthful people whose imaginations had been stimulated by constantly inventing plausible lies. But that is clearly unfair. . . ." "Perhaps," she said, "only people who are themselves much occupied in practicing deception have the habit of thus dipping below the surface. I can assure you that for my part, when I read a story, I always accept it as an account of something that has really and actually happened."

So saying she pushed away from her the book which she had been copying. Genji continued: "So you see as a matter of fact I think far better of this art than I have led you to suppose. Even its practical value is immense. Without it what should we know of how people lived in the past, from the Age of the Gods down to the present day? For history-books such as the *Chronicles of Japan* show us only one small corner of life; whereas these diaries and romances which I see piled around you contain, I am sure, the most minute information about all sorts of people's private affairs. . . ." He smiled, and went on: "But I have a theory of my own about what this art of the novel is, and how it came into being. To begin with, it does not simply consist in the author's telling a story about the adventures of some other person. On the contrary, it happens because the storyteller's own experience of men and things, whether for good or ill—not only what he has passed through himself, but even events which he has only witnessed or been told of—has moved him to an emotion so passionate the he can no longer keep it shut up in his heart. Again and again something in his own life or in that around him will seem to the writer so important that he cannot bear to let it pass into oblivion. There must never come a time, he feels, when men do not know about it. That is my view of how this art arose.

"Clearly then, it is no part of the storyteller's craft to describe only what is good or beautiful. Sometimes, of course, virtue will be his theme, and he may then make such play with as he will. But he is just as likely to have been struck by numerous examples of vice and folly in the world around him, and about them he has exactly the same feelings as about the pre-eminently good deeds which he encounters: they are more important and must be garnered in. Thus anything whatsoever may become the subject of a novel, provided only that it happens in this mundane life and not in some fairyland beyond our human ken.

"The outward forms of this art will not of course be everywhere the same. At the court in China and in other foreign lands both the genius of the writers and their actual methods of composition are necessarily very different from ours; and even here in Japan the art of storytelling has in course of time undergone great changes. There will, too, always be a distinction between the lighter and the more serious forms of fiction. . . . Well, I have said enough to show that when at the beginning of our conversation I spoke of romances as though they were mere frivolous fabrications, I was only teasing you. Some people have taken exception on moral grounds to an art in which the perfect and imperfect are set side by side. But even in the discourses which Buddha in his bounty allowed to be recorded, certain passages contain what the learned call *Upāya* or 'Adapted Truth'[3]—a fact that has led some superficial persons to doubt whether a doctrine so inconsistent with itself could possibly command our credence. Even in the scriptures of the Greater Vehicle there are, I confess, many such instances. We may indeed go so far as to say that there is an actual mixture of Truth and Error. But the purpose of these holy writings, namely the compassing of our Salvation, remains always the same. So too, I think it may be said that the art of fiction must not lose our allegiance because, in the pursuit of the main purpose to which I have alluded above, it sets virtue by the side of vice, or mingles wisdom with folly. Viewed in this light the novel is seen to be not, as is usually supposed, a mixture of useful truth with idle invention, but something which at every stage and in every part has a definite and serious purpose."

The Vocabulary of Japanese Aesthetics II

The collapse of the Heian society is all too apparent in the terrible wars that mark the close of the period, in the growth of new religious sects (some of which preached that the world had entered its last, degenerate days), and in the successive disasters which befell the once lovely capital. During much of the period from 1100 to 1600 there was bitter warfare, marked usually by the triumphs of the lower rank of warlord over the higher, a tendency which culminated in the victory of Hideyoshi, a man of extremely humble birth. The wars brought so much destruction and death that it must have seemed at times the whole country would become one huge graveyard. It is small wonder that ghosts so frequently figure in the literature, and that the prevailing tone is one of intense tragedy. *The Tale of the Heike,* written at the beginning of this long period of warfare, opens with the words: "In the sound of the bell of the Gion Temple echoes the impermanence of all things. The pale hue of the flowers of the teak-tree show the truth that they who prosper must fall. The proud ones do not last long, but vanish like a spring night's dream. And the mighty ones too will perish in the end, like dust before the wind."

It might be expected that parallel changes in aesthetic principles would at once have developed and that the new masters of Japan would have imposed new standards of taste. We find, however, that although changes did occur, they were soon softened by the influence of *miyabi* and the son of an upstart warlord was likely to compose verses on the sadness of the falling cherry blossoms. The third of the Kamakura shoguns prided himself on being an accomplished poet of the traditional school and exchanged *aware*-laden verses with members of the court.

The new aesthetic standards in literature and art which eventually emerged did not represent any sharp break with the past, but were instead an intensifying and a darkening of the Heian ideals. Fujiwara no Shunzei (1114–1204) declared, "We should seek to express emotions which our predecessors have not already described, but in so doing retain the language which they used." In other words, he did not advocate a rejection of the means of earlier poets, but rather the use of the old means in the search for new ends. It was the ends involved which characterize the period from the end of the twelfth century to the seventeenth century.

The aesthetic ideals which pervaded the poetry, drama, painting, gardens, tea ceremony, and most other artistic activities during this period were summarized largely in the concept of *yūgen. Yūgen* was a word used to describe the profound, remote, and mysterious, those things which cannot easily be grasped or expressed in words. Its closest equivalent in Western terms is probably "symbolism," not the obvious symbolism of a flag standing for a country or a bird in a cage for a captive spirit, but what Poe called "a suggestive indefiniteness of vague and therefore of spiritual effect." To intimate things rather than state them plainly was what Japanese of the medieval period no less than nineteenth-century Europeans were trying to do.

The connection between the ideal of *yūgen* and that of *aware* is obvious, but there was a difference. The Heian poet felt *aware* when he saw wrinkles reflected in the mirror and realized that time was passing by and the years of his youth vanished. But this realization was in a sense the end of the emotion: it did not extend to the dark and mysterious regions of *yūgen.* On the other hand, when a Nō actor slowly raises his hand in a play, it corresponds not only to the text which he is performing, but must also suggest something behind the mere representation, something eternal—in T. S. Eliot's words, a "moment in and out of time." The gesture of the actor is beautiful in itself, as a piece of music is beautiful, but at the same time it is the gateway to something else, the hand that points to a region as profound and remote as the viewer's powers of reception will permit. It is a symbol, not of any one thing, but of an eternal region, of an eternal silence. Again, in T. S. Eliot's words,

> . . . Words, after speech, reach
> Into the silence. Only by the form, the pattern,
> Can words or music reach
> The stillness, as a Chinese jar still
> Moves perpetually in its stillness.[4]

To suggest the stillness there must be form or pattern. If that form or pattern is beautiful, it is enough for many people, and they do not feel a need for any deeper meaning. Others might even doubt whether such a thing as silence beyond the form really exists, and whether one can seriously consider anything like *yūgen* which defies definition or description.

Such doubts are not peculiar to our time. A work written in the year 1430 contains these words: "*Yūgen* may be comprehended by the mind, but it cannot be expressed in words. Its quality may be suggested by the sight of a thin cloud veiling the moon or by autumn mist swathing the scarlet leaves on a mountainside. If one is asked where in these sights lies the *yūgen,* one cannot say, and it is not surprising that a man who does not understand this truth is likely to prefer the sight of a perfectly clear, cloudless sky. It is quite impossible to explain wherein lies the interest or the remarkable nature of *yūgen.*"[5]

It may be impossible to explain *yūgen,* but we can intuitively sense it. "It is just as when we look at the sky of an autumn dusk. It has no sound or color, and yet, though we do not understand why, we somehow find ourselves moved to tears."[6] *Yūgen* is the quality of the highest realm of art, an absolute domain to which all forms point. It tends to be expressed in bare and simple terms, as if to keep the mind from dwelling too long on the beauty of the form presented, and thereby to allow it to leap to that realm. There is *yūgen* in the simple perfection of the Chinese jar which "moves perpetually in its stillness," but not in the Dresden figurine. There is *yūgen* in the sound of the Nō flute, which stirs us imprecisely but with an almost painful urgency to an awareness of the existence of something beyond the form, but not in the ravishing melodies of the sextet from *Lucia.* There is *yūgen* in the sight of a tea-master dipping water into a kettle with simple movements that have about them the lines of eternity.

Although *yūgen* may be discovered in many forms of Japanese medieval art, the Nō theatre was the medium which carried it to the highest degree. It was in fact the effect at which the masters of the Nō, and particularly the great Seami (1363–1443), consciously aimed. From what little we know of the Nō before Seami's day it seems clear that it was essentially a representational theatre, with the attempt being made in a manner not very different from that employed in the West to portray on the stage the actions of dramatic personages. Seami, however, chose to make of the Nō a symbolic theatre, in which the most important actions were not represented but suggested. The central character in many of his plays is a ghost, someone from a world beyond our own which can only be symbolized. Often this ghost returns in his former appearance in the second part of the play, and during the interval between the first and second parts harsh music and inarticulate cries from the musicians suggest the distance of the world of the dead and the pain of being born. The climax of the play is the final dance which symbolizes and resolves the character's anguish.

Seami wrote that spectators of the Nō sometimes found the moments of "no action" the most enjoyable, when it was not any gesture of the actor which suggested the eternity beyond gestures, but only the unconsciously revealed spiritual strength of the actor. However, *yūgen* was more normally achieved through the means of beautiful forms, and in deciding what was beautiful Seami was guided by the Heian principle of *miyabi.* He says, for instance, that "the *yūgen* of discourse lies in a grace of language and a complete mastery of the speech of the nobility and the gentry so that even the most casual utterance will be graceful." This is another instance of how it was attempted to achieve *yūgen* by using Heian aesthetic means and not by denying them. But what had stopped at the level of being "charming" or "touching" in the Heian period became in the medieval period the profoundly moving *yūgen.* It is tempting to speculate that in an age of painful changes and destruction like the Japanese medieval period, the need for eternal incorruptible values might well give rise to such an aesthetic ideal as *yūgen.*

Towards the end of the medieval period another aesthetic ideal, that of *sabi,* joined *yūgen. Sabi* was a very old word, found as far back as the *Manyōshū* where it has the meaning of "to be desolate." It later acquired the meaning of "to grow old" and it is related to the word "to grow rusty." In *The Tale of the Heike* we find it used in the sentence, "It was a place *old* with moss-covered boulders, and he thought it would be pleasant to live there." It seems likely that already by this time (the thirteenth century) *sabi* suggested not only "old" but the taking of pleasure in that which was old, faded, or lonely. To achieve the end of *yūgen,* art had sometimes been stripped of its color and glitter lest these externals distract; a bowl of highly polished silver reflects more than it suggests, but one of oxidized silver has the mysterious beauty of stillness, as Seami realized when he used for stillness the simile of snow piling in a silver bowl. Or one may prize such a bowl for the tarnished quality itself, for its oldness, for its imperfection, and this is the point where we feel *sabi.*

If the Nō is the highest expression of *yūgen, sabi* is most profoundly felt in the tea ceremony, and to attend one even today is to get a glimpse of *sabi* at its purest. The tea hut is extremely bare and almost devoid of color. If a flower is arranged in a vase, it is usually a single, small blossom of some quiet hue or white. The tea utensils are not of exquisite porcelain but of coarse pottery, often a dull brown or black and imperfectly formed. The kettle may be a little rusty. Yet from these objects we receive an impression not of gloominess or shabbiness but one of quiet harmony and peace, and watching the ceremony we may experience an intimation of *yūgen.*

The love of imperfection as a measure of perfection in pottery and other forms of art and nature is very old with the Japanese. We find a beautiful statement of it in the *Essays in Idleness (Tsuredzure-gusa)* Yoshida Kenkō (1283–1350) when he asks:

> Are we only to look at flowers in full bloom, at the moon when it is clear? Nay, to look out on the rain and long for the moon, to draw the blinds and not to be aware of the passing of the spring—these arouse even deeper feelings. There is much to be seen in young boughs about to flower, in gardens strewn with withered blossom. . . . They must be perverse indeed who will say, "This branch, that bough is withered, now there is nought to see."[7]

The love for the fallen flower, for the moon obscured by the rain, for the withered bough is part of *sabi.* Unlike *yūgen* (to which, however, it is not opposed) *sabi* does not necessarily find in these things symbols of remoter eternities. They are themselves and capable in themselves of giving deep pleasure. *Sabi* also differs from the gentle melancholy of *aware:* here one does not lament for the fallen flower, one loves it. This quality is superbly captured in the *haiku* of Bashō (1644–94) who, although he lived after the end of the medieval period, was heir to its aesthetic traditions. Many of his *haiku* give expression to a love for old and faded things.

Kiku no ka ya	Scent of chrysanthemums—
Nara ni wa furuki	And in Nara all the many
Hotoketachi	Ancient Buddhas.

In this *haiku,* which unfortunately depends a great deal for its effect on an exquisite choice of words that cannot be approximated in translation, there is suggested the correspondence between impressions of *sabi* received through different senses. The scent of chrysanthemums, astringent and somewhat musty, blends into the visual impression of the statues in the old capital of Nara—dark, with flaking gold leaf and faded colors. The *sabi* quality found alike in the chrysanthemums and the ancient statues may be contrasted with the Heian love for the fragrance of plum blossoms, recalling the memories of past springs, and for richly colored images, or with the common Western preferences for the heavy perfume of the rose and the polish of white marble statues.

In *sabi* art is valued as a refuge, a haven of tranquility, as is not surprising when we read the early history of the tea ceremony, born amidst the terrible warfare of the medieval period. Even when the warfare ceased in the seventeenth century the need for spiritual peace continued to be met largely by the *sabi* aspects of beauty.

Yūgen can probably only be understood by a person of developed aesthetic perceptions who is spiritually capable of seeing beyond symbols to the eternal things adumbrated, but *sabi* has become very much a part of Japanese life. The Japanese, like every other people, love bright colors, but they are unusual in that they also love the old, the faded, and the underdecorated. This is not always understood by foreigners. During the days of the American occupation, for example, Americans who requisitioned Japanese houses often painted the woodwork to "brighten" the subdued harmonies of the buildings, much to the dismay of the Japanese owners. More recently, when the Golden Pavilion was rebuilt in Kyoto, its dazzlingly gilded walls reflected in the temple pond brought delight to many tourists, but the people of Kyoto said, "Wait ten years, wait till it acquires some *sabi*." This love for the old and unobtrusive may be the best defense the Japanese have against the harsher aspects of mechanization which are otherwise all too apparent today.

Seami

On Attaining the Stage of Yūgen

Yūgen is a term which it is difficult either to define or to translate. It primarily means "mystery," and however loosely used in criticism generally retains something of the sense of a mysterious power or ability. The term was employed as a standard of criticism long before Seami, but it was only with him that it attained its full meaning as the unifying aesthetic principle underlying all parts of the Nō. In this section of a longer essay he gives some of the ways of attaining *yūgen*. It should be noted, however, that he concludes by insisting that it is not enough for an actor to learn about *yūgen* from others—he must attain it through his own efforts.

[From Nosé, *Seami Jūrokubushū Hyōshaku* 1, 358-66]

Yūgen is considered to be the mark of supreme attainment in all of the arts and accomplishments. In the art of the Nō in particular the manifestation of *yūgen* is of the first importance. In general, a display of *yūgen* in the Nō is apparent to the eye, and it is the one thing which audiences most admire, but actors who possess *yūgen* are few and far between. This is because they do not in fact know the true meaning of *yūgen*. There are thus none who reach that stage.

In what sort of place, then, is the stage of *yūgen* actually to be found? Let us begin by examining the various classes of people on the basis of the appearance that they make in society. May we not say of the courtiers, whose behavior is distinguished and whose appearance far surpasses that of other men, that theirs is the stage of *yūgen?* From this we may see that the essence of *yūgen* lies in a true state of beauty and gentleness. Tranquility and elegance make for *yūgen* in personal appearance. In the same way, the *yūgen* of discourse lies in a grace of language and a complete mastery of the speech of the nobility and gentry, so that even the most casual utterance will be graceful. With respect to a musical performance, it may be said to possess *yūgen* when the melody flows beautifully and sounds smooth and sensitive. In the dance there will be *yūgen* when the discipline has been thoroughly mastered and the audience is delighted by the beauty of the performer's movements and by his serene appearance. In acting, there will be *yūgen* when the performance of the Three Roles is beautiful. If the characterization calls for a display of anger or for the representation of a devil, the actions may be somewhat forceful, but as long as the actor never loses sight of the beauty of the effect and bears in mind always the correct balance between his mental and physical actions and between the movements of his body and feet,[8] his appearance will be so beautiful that it may be called "the *yūgen* of a devil."

All these aspects of *yūgen* must be kept in mind and made a part of the actor's body, so that whatever part he may be playing *yūgen* will never be absent. Whether the character he portrays be of high or low birth, man or woman, priest, peasant, rustic, beggar, or outcast, he should think of each of them as crowned with a wreath of flowers. Although their positions in society differ, the fact that they can all appreciate the beauty of flowers makes flowers of all of them.[9] Their particular flower is shown by their outward appearance. An actor, by the use of his intelligence, makes his presentation seem beautiful. It is through the use of intelligence that the above principles are thoroughly grasped; that poetry is learned so as to impart *yūgen* to his discourse; that the most elegant costuming is studied so as to impart *yūgen* to his bearing: though the characterization varies according to the different parts, the actor should realize that the ability to appear beautiful is the seed of *yūgen.* It is all to apt to happen that an actor, believing that once he has mastered the characterization of the various parts he has attained the highest stage of excellence, forgets his appearances and therefore is unable to enter the realm of *yūgen.* Unless an actor enters the realm of *yūgen* he will not attain the highest achievements. If he fails to attain the highest achievements, he will not become a celebrated master. That is why there are so few masters. The actor must consider *yūgen* as the most important aspect of his art and study to perfect his understanding of it.

The "highest achievement" of which I have spoken refers to beauty of form and manners. The most careful attention must therefore be given to the appearance presented. Accordingly, when we thoroughly examine the principles of *yūgen* we see that when the form is beautiful, whether in dancing, singing, or in any type of characterization, it may properly be called the "highest achievement." When the form is poor, the performance will be inferior. The actor should realize that *yūgen* is attained when all of the different forms of visual or aural expression are beautiful. It is when the actor himself has worked out these principles and made himself their master that he may be said to have entered the realm of *yūgen*. If he fails to work out these principles for himself, he will not master them, and however much he may aspire to attain *yūgen*, he will never in all his life do so.

On the One Mind Linking All Powers

> The influence of Zen Buddhism is particularly apparent in the following section. The "mindlessness" which transcends mind, the moments of "no-action" which excite greater interest than those of action, the mind which controls all the powers—all these are familiar ideas of Zen, and show to how great an extent Seami's aesthetic principles relied on the Zen teachings.
>
> From Nosé, *Seami Jūrokubushū Hyōshaku, I,* 375–79

Sometimes spectators of the Nō say, "The moments of 'no-action' are the most enjoyable." This is an art which the actor keeps secret. Dancing and singing, movements and the different types of miming are all acts performed by the body. Moments of "no-action" occur in between. When we examine why such moments without actions are enjoyable, we find that it is due to the underlying spiritual strength of the actor which unremittingly holds the attention. He does not relax the tension when the dancing or singing come to an end or at intervals between the dialogue and the different types of miming, but maintains an unwavering inner strength. This feeling of inner strength will faintly reveal itself and bring enjoyment. However, it is undesirable for the actor to permit this inner strength to become obvious to the audience. If it is obvious, it becomes an act, and is no longer "no-action." The actions before and after an interval of "no-action" must be linked by entering the state of mindlessness in which one conceals even from oneself one's intent. This, then, is the faculty of moving audiences, by linking all the artistic powers with one mind.

Life and death, past and present—
Marionettes on a toy stage.
When the strings are broken,
Behold the broken pieces.[10]

This is a metaphor describing human life as it transmigrates between life and death. Marionettes on a stage appear to move in various ways, but in fact it is not they who really move—they are manipulated by strings. When these strings are broken, the marionettes fall and are dashed to pieces. In the art of the Nō too, the different sorts of miming are artificial things. What holds the parts together is the mind. This mind must not be disclosed to the audience. If it is seen, it is just as if a marionette's strings were visible. The mind must be made the strings which hold together all the powers of the arts. If this is done the actor's talent will endure. This resolution must not be confined to the times when the actor is appearing on the stage. Day or night, wherever he may be, whatever he may be doing, he should not forget this resolution, but should make it his constant guide, uniting all his powers. If he unremittingly works at this his talent will steadily grow. This article is the most secret of the secret teachings.[11]

The Nine Stages of the Nō in Order

The *Nine Stages* is a summary and systematization of the aesthetic principles found in his various other writings. It appears to be a late work, and of all his works of aesthetic criticism is the most difficult to understand, partially because of the unexplained technical terms and partially because of its Zen form of expression. As the leading authority on the work, Nosé Asaji wrote, "In order to understand this work properly one must have had considerable experience with Zen practices and have discovered how to decipher the Zen riddles *(kōan)*. One must also have studied Seami's aesthetic criticism thoroughly. Unless this work is approached with the wisdom gained from both aspects of it, it will not be possible to give any definitive explanation of the text." Nevertheless, thanks mainly to Nosé's work, we can now understand much of what Seami was seeking to express in his deliberately elusive manner.

The influence of Zen teachings is apparent throughout this work. Most of the sentences or phrases used to characterize the different stages of the Nō are taken from poems written by Japanese Zen monks; the use of such symbols itself is a typical Zen device. But the general structure, synthetic character, and much of the terminology of this essay are reminiscent of Tendai and Shingon doctrine.

From Nosé, *Seami Jūrokubushū Hyōshaku, I,* 547–83

THE HIGHER THREE STAGES

1. The flower of the miraculous

"At midnight in Silla the sun is bright."[12]

The miraculous transcends the power of speech and is where the workings of the mind are defeated. And does "the sun at midnight" lie within the realm of speech? Thus, in the art of the Nō, before the *yūgen* of a master-actor all praise fails, admiration transcends the comprehension of the mind, and all attempts at classification and grading are made impossible. The art which excites such a reaction on the part of the audience may be called the flower of the miraculous.

2. The flower of supreme profundity

"Snow covers the thousand mountains—why does one lonely peak remain unwhitened?"

A man of old once said, "Mount Fuji is so high that the snow never melts." A Chinese disagreed, saying, "Mount Fuji is so deep. . . ."[13] What is extremely high is deep. Height has limits but depth is not to be measured. Thus the profound mystery of a landscape in which a solitary peak stands unwhitened amidst a thousand snow-covered mountains may represent the art of supreme profundity.

3. The flower of stillness

"Snow piled in a silver bowl."

When snow is piled in a silver bowl the purity of its white light appears lambent indeed. May this not represent the flower of stillness?

THE MIDDLE THREE STAGES

1. The flower of truth

"The sun sinks in the bright mist, the myriad mountains are crimson."

A distant view of hills and mountains bathed in the light of the sun in a cloudless sky represents the flower of truth. It is superior to the art of versatility and exactness, and is already a first step towards the acquisition of the flowers of the art.

2. The art of versatility and exactness

"To tell everything—of the nature of clouds on the mountains, of moonlight on the sea."

To describe completely the nature of clouds on the mountains and of moonlight on the sea, of the whole expanse of green mountains that fills the eyes, this is indeed desirable in acquiring the art of versatility and exactness. Here is the dividing point from which one may go upward or downward.

3. The art of untutored beauty

"The Way of ways is not the usual way."[14]

One may learn the Way of ways by traveling along the usual way. This means that the display of beauty should begin at the stage of the beginner. Thus the art of untutored beauty is considered the introduction to the mastery of the nine stages.

THE LOWER THREE STAGES

1. The art of strength and delicacy

"The metal hammer flashes as it moves, the glint of the precious sword is cold."

The movement of the metal hammer represents the art of strong action. The cold glint of the precious sword suggests the unadorned style of singing and dancing. It will stand up to detailed observation.

2. The art of strength and crudity

"Three days after its birth the tiger is disposed to devour an ox."

That the tiger cub only three days after its birth has such audacity shows its strength; but to devour an ox is crude.

3. The art of crudity and inexactness

"The squirrel's five talents."

Confucius said,[15] "The squirrel can do five things. He can climb a tree, swim in the water, dig a hole, jump, and run: all of these are within its capacities but it does none well." When art lacks delicacy it becomes crude and inexact.

In the attainment of art through the nine stages, the actor begins with the middle group, follows with the upper group, and finally learns the lower three. When the beginner first enters the art of the Nō, he practices the various elements of dancing and singing. This represents the stage of untutored beauty. As the result of persistent training, his untutored style will develop into greater artistry, constantly improving until, before he is aware of it, it reaches the stage of versatility and exactness. At this stage if the actor's training is comprehensive and he expands his art in versatility and magnitude until he attains full competence, he will be at the stage of the flower of truth. The above are the stages from the learning of the Two Disciplines to the mastery of the Three Roles.

Next the actor progresses to the stage of calm and the flower that arouses admiration. It is the point where it becomes apparent whether or not he has realized the flower of the art. From this height the actor can examine with insight the preceding stages. He occupies a place of high achievement in the art of calm and the realization of the flower. This stage is thus called the flower of stillness.

Rising still higher, the actor achieves the ultimate degree of *yūgen* in his performance, and reveals a degree of artistry which is of that middle ground where being and nonbeing meet.[16] This is the flower of supreme profundity.

Above this stage, words fail before the revelation of the absolute miracle of the actor's interpretation. This is the flower of the miraculous. It is the end of the road to the higher mysteries of the art.

It should be noted that the origin of all these stages of the art may be found in the art of versatility and exactness. It is the foundation of the art of the Nō, for it is the point where are displayed the breadth and detail of performance which are the seeds of the flowers of the highest forms of the art. The stage of versatility and exactness is also the dividing line where is determined the actor's future. If he succeeds here in obtaining the flower of the art he will rise to the flower of truth; otherwise he will sink to the lower three stages.

The lower three stages are the turbulent waters of the Nō. They are easily understood and it is no special problem to learn them. It may happen, however, that an actor who has gone from the middle three stages to the upper three stages, having mastered the art of calmness and the flower of the miraculous, will purposely descend and indulge in the lower three stages.[17] Then the special qualities of these stages will be blended with his art. However, many of the excellent actors of the past who had mounted to the upper three stages of the art refused to descend to the lower three. They were like the elephant of the story, who refused to follow in the tracks of a rabbit. There has been only one instance of an actor who mastered all the stages—the middle, then the upper, and then the lower: this was the art of my late father.[18] Many of the heads of theatres have been trained only up to the art of versatility and exactness and, without having risen to the flower of truth, have descended to the lower three stages, thus failing in the end to achieve success. Nowadays there are even actors who begin their training with the lower three stages and perform with such a background. This is not the proper order. It is therefore no wonder that many actors fail even to enter the nine stages.

There are three ways of entering the lower three stages. In the case of a great master who has entered the art by way of the middle stages, ascended to the upper stages of the art, and then descended to the lower stages, it is quite possible to give a superb performance even within the lower stages. Actors who have dropped to the lower stages from the level of versatility and exactness will be capable only of parts which call for strength with delicacy or crudity. Those actors who have wilfully entered the art from the lower three stages have neither art nor fame and cannot be said even to be within the nine stages. Although they have taken the lower three stages as their goal, they fail even in this, to say nothing of reaching the middle three stages.

The Book of the Way of the Highest Flower (Shikadō-sho)

In this piece Seami, one of the great masters of the Nō drama, sets forth the criteria for consummate mastery in the performance of this art. "Flower" here signifies "beauty" or "perfection," a meaning which derives from the use of the Lotus as a symbol of supreme truth or perfection in Buddhism, especially as represented in the *Lotus (Hokke)* and *Flower Wreath (Kegon) Sūtras.*

Seami was chiefly instrumental in defining and shaping the Nō drama, and his views reflect the synthetic character of the art form which he and his father, Kan'ami, helped to develop. In it elements from earlier dance-drama forms, especially temple and folk dances, were combined to produce an art of the greatest refinement and sophistication. Much of the subtlety and striking simplicity of the Nō manifest the influence of Zen Buddhism, then dominant at the Ashikaga court in Kyoto. But the extreme stylization, precision, and gorgeous costuming of the Nō also reveal the deep and lasting influence of Esoteric Buddhism on Japanese art, though this is today less generally appreciated. The elaborate symbolism, conventionalized movements, and stylized gestures of the Nō relate it closely to the mandala, that typical expression of the esoteric teaching in the field of painting, which, like the Nō, is so inaccessible to those who are ignorant of the conventions which have surrounded these arts from the beginning. To them Esoteric Buddhism has contributed, not so much the conventions themselves, as the essential concern for proper form in the representation of sacred mysteries and the performance of symbolic acts. Through the exercise of all men's faculties, not just the intellectual, Esoteric Buddhism made the widest use of all the riches of the natural world to enhance the efficacy of its secret formulas and thus achieve the unity of matter and spirit in the perfection of Buddhahood. To accomplish this was a great art, requiring perfect mastery. Seami's conception of mastery in the Nō, his insistence on prolonged training in orthodox disciplines and in imitation of one's teacher, as well as his neat numerical formulations and philosophical categories all attest to the formative influence of this earlier tradition. Seami served his apprenticeship in Nara, the stronghold of Buddhist catholicism which left its seal on the fundamentals of his art. Only later, in the Ashikaga court at Kyoto did he find in Zen the final quickening insight which brought these dramatic elements into sharp focus and raised his mature art to the threshold of perfect ease and freedom.

From Nosé, *Seami Jūrokubushū Hyōshaku*, I, 435–80

1. THE TWO MEDIUMS AND THE THREE ROLES

Although there are many different items of training in the art of the Nō, the initial preparation should be confined to the Two Mediums and the Three Roles. By the Two Mediums is meant dancing and singing; the Three Roles refer to the types of people represented. First of all, singing and dancing must be thoroughly studied and practiced under the guidance of a master. While the actor is still a boy, from his tenth to his fifteenth years, he should not study the Three Roles; he should merely perform the singing and dancing of these roles while remaining in a boy's attire. He should not wear a mask. His miming should be nominal, and his appearance in keeping with his age. It is similar to the way in which the dancing-boys perform the Ryō-ō, the Nassori, and other court dances in outline only, wearing Nō masks, and retaining their youthful appearance. This training as a boy is the root of the flower which will maintain its beauty in all an actor's later performances.

When an actor has been initiated into manhood[19] and has come of age, he wears a mask and changes his appearance according to the role he assumes. There are many types of impersonation, but the beginner may attain to the highest flower of true art through the Three Roles only. The old man, the woman, the warrior—these are the three. These roles must be thoroughly studied and practiced, and then combined with the various types of singing and dancing which have already been learned. No other training exists in the art of the Nō.

The other forms of miming all derive from the Two Mediums and the Three Roles, and one should wait for ability in them to develop naturally. The noble perfection of the dances of the gods derives from the mastery of the role of the old man; beauty and elegance in the singing and gestures derive from the role of the woman; and vigor in the movements of the body and the feet derives from the role of the warrior. The actor will naturally express in his performance his own conception of the role. If his talents are inadequate and natural mastery does not develop, he may still be considered an actor of the highest flower if he is thoroughly trained in the Two Mediums and the Three Roles. That is why they are known as the measure, essence, and basis of the art of the Nō.

When we examine contemporary methods of training in the Nō, we find that the initial steps are not made on the main road of the Two Mediums and the Three Roles, but instead all kinds of unorthodox fashions of miming are practiced. This results in a lack of mastery, a feebleness of performance and general inferiority—there are thus no actors today who are worthy of the name of "masters."

Having entered the art in a way other than the Two Mediums and the Three Roles, to indulge in fripperies of style constitutes a denatured and peripheral training.

(Author's note: It should be borne in mind that the beauty of an actor's boyhood appearance is preserved in the Three Roles, and the mastery derived from the three roles can impart vividness to every performance.)

2. THE LACK OF MASTERY

In the art of the Nō a lack of mastery is to be deplored. This matter deserves careful consideration. It seems likely that natural gifts make one a master. May it not be also that natural gifts are developed through an accumulation of experience in this art? Take the case of singing and dancing. As long as in actor is trying to imitate his teacher, he is still without mastery. Even once he has perfected his imitation, until he makes the performance his own it will be lacking in vigor and inadequate: he will still be an actor without mastery. The master-actor is one who has trained himself thoroughly in imitation of his teacher, and having absorbed his art and made it his own, part of his own body and mind, thus achieves effortless proficiency. His performance is then imbued with life. An actor may be said to be a master when, by means of his artistic powers, he quickly perfects the skills he has won through study and practice, and thus becomes one with the art itself. I must insist on the importance of recognizing the demarcation between mastery and lack of mastery. Mencius said, "To do is not difficult; to do well is difficult."[20]

3. THE MASTER-ACTOR

In the art of the Nō it sometimes happens that a master-actor who has scaled the topmost heights of the profession and who is aware of his degree of attainment will perform in an unusual manner, which is then copied by beginners. The perfect freedom exercised by the accomplished veteran should not be imitated thoughtlessly. What, I wonder, do beginners think that they are doing when they copy him?

The art of the accomplished veteran lies in the spiritual strength of his interpretations. It may occasionally lead him to demonstrations of the skill which he has attained after having spent the years from youth to old age in intensive training in all aspects of the Nō, and after having gathered to himself all the good techniques and rejected the bad ones. He may then at his stage of perfection mix a little of the bad techniques, which he has hated and rejected during his years of training, with the good ones. Why, it may be wondered, should a master indulge in faulty techniques? The answer is that it is a method of demonstrating his virtuosity. The master-actor by definition has only good techniques. Thus, if, as it may happen, his excellences lose their unusualness and become somewhat stale to the audience, he may occasionally introduce faulty techniques which will be acclaimed for their novelty in a master's performance. In this way, faulty techniques may actually seem good ones to the audience. This is a case where the talents of the master seem to transform faults into merits. It thereby creates an interesting effect.

If beginners in the art, finding such techniques an interesting method of winning applause, believe that they should copy them, their imitations will represent the admixture of essentially faulty techniques with their own immature style; it will be "adding fuel to the flames" of their mediocrity. Imagining that maturity in art is a matter of techniques, they may not realize that it comes from the attainment of mastery. This fact requires careful attention.

The actions which the master performs with full awareness that they are wrong are imitated by the young actors in the delusion that they are right. They thus differ as much as black and white. How can the beginner hope to attain the level of the master-actor without having accumulated experience? When a beginner imitates the mannerisms of the master actor, he is imitating faults, which make him all the worse an actor, do they not? Mencius said, "To do what you do to seek for what you desire is like climbing a tree to seek for fish."[21] He adds, by way of comment, "If you climb a tree to seek for fish, it is merely stupid, and does you no harm. But to do what you do to seek for what you desire assuredly does you harm." The fact that faults of technique in the hands of the veteran master-actor may actually become merits shows that artistic achievements may be obtained by a master-actor, but this does not lie within the competence of an unskilled performer. Thus, if with the limited powers at his disposal, he seeks to emulate the inimitable feats of the master-actor, there is certain to be harm done. It is like "doing what you do to seek for what you desire." As long as the beginner confines his imitations to consummate performances of the correct techniques, however inadequate he may be there is not likely to be much harm done. It is like "climbing a tree to seek for fish." I repeat: the beginner must not imitate the eccentricities and mannerisms of the master-actor's performance. To do so invites mishaps.

Beginners should remain close to their master, ask his advice on their problems, and find out everything they can about their art. Even when they witness examples of the kind of unusual performance I have described they should direct their efforts towards the mastery of the Two Mediums and the Three Roles. The *Lotus Sūtra* states, "Be wary of those who consider enlightenment yet to come as enlightenment attained, and mystic insight yet to be achieved as mystic insight won." Bear this in mind.

4. THE SKIN, FLESH, AND BONES

The art of the Nō has its skin, flesh, and bones, but the three are never found together. In calligraphy as well they say that the three have never been found together except in Kūkai's writing. The skin, flesh, and bones of the Nō may thus be identified: the display in this art of the special powers which have enabled one to become a master-actor naturally, by virtue of inborn abilities, may be designated the bones; the display of the perfect powers which have come from study and experience of dancing and singing may be called flesh; and an appearance which exhibits these qualities at their highest pitch, with perfect gentleness and beauty, may be termed the skin. If these three aspects are equated with the senses, seeing may be called the skin, hearing the flesh, and feeling the bones. Moreover, the three aspects may be found in singing alone or dancing alone. (In singing the voice is the skin, the style the flesh, and the breathing the bones; in dancing, the appearance is the skin, the movements the flesh, and the expression the bones.) These distinctions should be noted carefully.

When I look over the contemporary Nō performers, not only do I fail to find anyone who possesses these three aspects of the art, but there is not a single person who even realizes that such things exist. I myself learned of them through the secret teachings of my late father. The contemporary performers whom I have seen limit themselves to a feeble representation of just the skin, and even that is not the real skin. Again, the fact that they imitate only the skin proves that they are actors without mastery.

Even if an actor happens to possess all three qualities, there is another point to be borne in mind: he may have natural gifts (the bones), consummate attainments in dancing and singing (the flesh), and personal beauty (the skin), but it may be that he merely *possesses* the three. He still cannot be said to be an actor with full control of them. To say of an actor that he has attained full control of the three qualities means that he has developed to their limits all of his inborn talents, and being already in the highest rank, reaches to effortless and ineffable performance. His performances on the stage will offer pure enjoyment, and the audience will lose itself in the wonder of his art. Only on careful reflection after the performance will the audience appreciate its flawlessness; this is the feeling aroused by accomplishment in the art of the bones. The audience will then also be aware of the actor's inexhaustible wealth of skill: this is the feeling aroused by accomplishment in the art of the flesh. And it will realize that, in whatever way it might be considered, the performance was of perfect beauty: this is the feeling aroused by accomplishment in the art of the skin. In view of the effect that he has produced on the audience, the actor may then be known as a master in full control of the skin, flesh, and bones.

5. ESSENCE AND PERFORMANCE[22]

We must distinguish in the art of Nō between essence and performance. If the essence is a flower, the performance is its fragrance. Or they may be compared to the moon and the light which it sheds. When the essence has been thoroughly understood, the performance develops of itself.

Among those who witness Nō plays, the connoisseurs see with their minds, while the untutored see with their eyes. What the mind sees is the essence; what the eyes see is the performance. That is why beginners, seeing only the performance, imitate it. They imitate without knowing the principles behind the performance. There are, however, reasons why the performance should not be imitated. Those who understand the Nō see it with their mind and therefore imitate its essence. When the essence is well imitated, the performance follows of itself. The untutored, believing that the performance is the thing to follow, imitate it; they show themselves unaware of the fact that the performance when imitated becomes an essence as well.[23] Since, however, it is not the true essence, both the essence and the performance are doomed eventually to perish, and the style which they are imitating will cease to exist. It will then be Nō without direction and without purpose.

When we speak of the essence and the performance, they are two. Without the essence, however, there cannot be any performance. There is no such thing as performance by itself, and it thus does not deserve to be imitated. If, however, it is considered to exist and is copied, does it not become a false essence? The connoisseur realizes that the performance lies in the essence and not apart from it and that there is no reason to imitate it. Such a person understands the Nō.

Since there is no reason to imitate the performance, it must not be imitated. It should be realized that to imitate the essence is in fact to imitate the performance. I repeat: he who bears in mind the fact that to imitate the performance is to create a false essence may be termed an actor who has distinguished between essence and performance. It has been said, "What one should desire to imitate is skillfulness; what one should not imitate is skillfulness."[24] To imitate is performance, to have achieved resemblance is essence.

These items of training in the Nō, some simple and some profound, were not very much considered in the past. A very few of the actors of the old style were able by their innate talents to attain the heights of the art. In those days, the criticism made by the courtiers consisted entirely of praise for the excellences which they observed; they did not criticize the faults. At present, however, their powers of observation have greatly developed, and they have come to criticize the most trifling faults. Thus, unless performances are as polished jade or chosen flowers, they will not meet with the approval of the patrons on high. That is why there are few masters of this art. The Nō is steadily declining as an art, and if training in it is neglected, it may well perish. With this in mind I have recorded in outline my convictions about the Nō. The rest of the instruction will depend on the degree of talent of the inquirer, and must be privately transmitted in person.

Oei 27 [1420] Sixth Month [*signed*] SEAMI

The Vocabulary of Japanese Aesthetics III

The student of Tokugawa Japan is everywhere faced with seeming contradictions. He finds first of all a military dictatorship which ruled the country for more than two hundred and fifty years virtually without warfare, and which sacrificed the chance of an overseas empire in favor of peace. He finds also a society which subscribed to strict Confucian principles but which distinguished itself especially by its devotion to sensual pleasures. And when he considers the aesthetic vocabulary of the period he discovers no less curious contradictions.

Part of the difficulty in attempting to establish the typical words used by Tokugawa writers in making aesthetic judgments stems from the fact that there was no uniformity. That is, we have no reason to suppose that the touchstone of taste in 1650 remained such in 1850, or that the ideals which guided a chronicler of the glories of the gay quarters were the same as for a poet living in a tranquil hermitage. Nevertheless, certain words and ideas can be mentioned as having possessed especial significance during much of the period.

The most brilliant part of the Tokugawa period was undoubtedly the Genroku era (1688–1703), which lent its name to much of the culture of the late seventeenth and early eighteenth centuries. One term which first came into prominence about this time was *ukiyo,* a word which in another meaning was much older. In Heian literature the word was used to mean "sorrowful world," and was a typical Buddhist description of the world of dust and grief. However, about 1680 the same sounds acquired a new meaning, by making a pun between *uki* meaning "sorrowful" and *uki* meaning "floating." The new term, the "floating world," was quickly taken up, probably because it gave so vivid a picture of the unstable volatile society which had succeeded the medieval world of sorrow and gloom. One typical expression of the "floating world" may be found in the numerous Genroku paintings of waves—the most changeable and exciting of natural forms. The word *ukiyo* itself came to be applied to many products of Genroku culture, including the *ukiyo-e,* the woodblock prints which were the most famous if not the best works of Tokugawa art. *Ukiyo* was used especially of the licensed quarters—the brothels and other places of amusement which were the center of urban society at the time. The Genroku literary figure par excellence, the hero of the novel *The Man Who Spent His Life at Love-making* (1683), was named Ukiyonosuke, and his complete familiarity with the denizens and arts of the "floating world" made him the envy and the object of emulation of many lesser men. This book (an outstanding example of *ukiyo-zōshi,* or demi-monde fiction) was written by Ihara Saikaku (1642–93), the leading Genroku novelist, who portrayed in a fascinating manner the two great interests of the "floating world"—sex and money. He who gained a full mastery of these two disciplines was entitled to be known as a *tsūjin,* or expert. Saikaku himself was a great *tsūjin* and could boast of many and varied experiences in the *ukiyo.* His description of the ideal woman of Genroku times proves, among other things, how careful a study he made of his chosen field:

> When I asked what type of woman he was hoping to get, the old man took from a scroll-case of paulownia wood a picture of a beautiful woman, saying that he would like to hold in his arms a living replica made from this model. When I examined it I saw that the woman in the picture was from fifteen to eighteen years of age. Her face, which had an up-to-date look, was roundish and of the color of pale cherry blossoms. Her features were flawless: the eyes, by his wish, were not narrow; the thick brows did not grow too close together; the nose was straight; the mouth was small with regular, white teeth; and the long ears, which had delicate rims, stood away from the head so that one could see through to the roots. Her hair at the forehead grew naturally and with no trace of artificiality. The back hair fell over her downless slender neck. Her fingers were pliant and long with thin nails. Her feet could not have had the breadth of eight copper coins; the big toes curled upwards and the soles were translucently delicate. Her body was above average in size.

> The hips were firm and not fleshy, the buttocks full. Elegant in movement and in dress, her bearing possessed both dignity and gentleness. She excelled in the arts required of women, and was ignorant of nothing. There was not a single mole on her entire body.[25]

Saikaku's ideal woman differed greatly from the one described in *The Tale of Genji.* The Heian beauty was distinguished primarily by her accomplishments and her tastes, and her genealogy was never overlooked. She was, of course, ravishingly beautiful too, but no Heian writer would have entered into the precision of details to which Saikaku treats us. It was obviously more important for him that his ideal woman's toes curl up than that she write with exquisite brush strokes. And, since Saikaku does not even mention what moral qualities she should possess to complement her physical charms, there is no reason to suppose that he sought any in this paragon of women.

In the plays of Chikamatsu (1653–1725), however, we find depicted quite a different type of woman—which serves to show how far from uniform the aesthetic ideals of the Tokugawa period were. Chikamatsu's heroines were usually either figures from Japanese history or else women from the same *ukiyo* milieu that Saikaku so lovingly treated. But unlike Saikaku's heroines, who surrendered themselves entirely to their passions, Chikamatsu's were also influenced by *giri,* a concept of great importance in Tokugawa Japan. *Giri* had both Buddhist and Confucian antecedents, developing equally from the awareness of the law of causality and the concern for moral justice. The word may be translated as "duty" or "moral obligation," but its implications extended far beyond the usual sphere of the English words. To control the passions *(ninjō)* one had to exercise *giri;* when the passions were too strong to be controlled there was likely to be tragedy, as Chikamatsu demonstrated.

The *ukiyo* world of the passions and the stern dictates of *giri* remained dominant themes in Tokugawa literature. Well into the nineteenth century we find books with such titles as *The Ukiyo Bath-house* or *The Ukiyo Barbershop,* as well as numerous works with the avowed intention of "encouraging virtue and chastising vice" (*kanzen chōaku*). The *ukiyo* books usually consisted of gay (and even pornographic) material; the other type of literature which enjoyed great popularity was the didactic romance, in which the author attempted painlessly to inculcate moral teachings. The outstanding work in the latter category was Bakin's monumental *Hakken-den* ("Biographies of Eight Heroes"), written between 1814 and 1841. Each of Bakin's eight heroes represents one of the Confucian cardinal virtues, a device similar to that employed by Spenser in *The Faerie Queene.* In the course of the thousands of pages of the *Hakken-den,* the various heroes are often sorely tempted and tried, but their Buddhist conviction that good brings only good while evil leads only to evil enables them to surmount all difficulties. In its time the *Hakken-den* enjoyed immense popularity because of its combination of exciting incidents with sage admonitions. And, even though most modern readers prefer Saikaku's *ukiyo* to Bakin's *giri,* the *Hakken-den,* both by its magnitude and its summary of ways of thought developed during the preceding two hundred years, may be considered to represent the grand culmination of the Tokugawa culture and aesthetic ideals.

Chikimatsu Monzaemon

On Realism in Art
(From the preface to *Naniwa Miyage,* by Hozumi Ikan)
(From Keene, *The Battles of Coxinga,* pp. 93–96)

This is what Chikamatsu told me when I visited him many years ago. *"Jōruri* differs from other forms of fiction in that, since it is primarily concerned with puppets, the words should all be living things in which action is the most important feature. Because *jōruri* is performed in theatres that operate in close competition with those of the *kabuki,* which is the art of living actors, the author must impart to lifeless wooden puppets a variety of emotions, and attempt in this way to capture the interest of the audience. It is thus generally very difficult to write a work of great distinction.

"Once, when I was young and reading a story about the court, I came across a passage which told how, on the occasion of a festival, the snow had fallen heavily and piled up. An order was then given to a guard to clear away the snow from an orange tree. When this happened, the pine tree next to it, apparently resentful that its boughs were bent with snow, recoiled its branches. This was a stroke of the pen which gave life to the inanimate tree. It did so because the spectacle of the pine tree, resentful that the snow has been cleared from the orange tree, recoiling its branches itself and shaking off the snow which bends it down, is one which creates the feeling of a living, moving thing. Is that not so?

"From this model I learned how to put life into my *jōruri.* Thus, even descriptive passages like the *michiyuki,* to say nothing of the narrative phrases and dialogue, must be charged with feeling or they will be greeted with scant applause. This is the same thing as is called evocative power in poets. For example, if a poet should fail to bring emotion to his praise of even the superb scenery of Matsushima or Miyajima in his poem, it would be like looking at the carelessly drawn picture of a beautiful woman. For this reason, it should be borne in mind that feeling is the basis of writing. . . .

"The old *jōruri* was just like our modern street story-telling and was without either flower or fruit. From the time that I began to write *jōriru*. . . I have used care in my writing, which was not true of the old *jōruri*. As a result, the medium was raised one level. For example, inasmuch as the nobility, the samurai, and the lower classes all have different social stations, it is essential that they be distinguished in their representation from their appearance down to their speech. Similarly, even within the same samurai class, there are both daimyō and retainers, as well as others of lower rank, each rank possessed of distinct qualities; such differences must be established. This is because it is essential that they be well pictured in the emotions of the reader.

"In writing *jōruri*, one attempts first to describe facts as they really are, but in so doing one writes things which are not true, in the interest of art. To be precise, many things are said by the female characters which real women could not utter. Such things fall under the heading of art; it is because they say what could not come from a real woman's lips that their true emotions are disclosed. If in such cases the author were to model his character on the ways of a real woman and conceal her feelings, such realism, far from being admired, would permit no pleasure in the work. Thus, if one examines a play without paying attention to the question of art, one will probably criticize it on the grounds that it contains many unpleasant words which are not suitable for women. But such things should be considered as art. In addition, there are numerous instances in the portrayal of a villain as excessively cowardly, or of a clown as being funny, which are outside the truth and which must be regarded as art. The spectator must bear this consideration in mind.

"There are some who, thinking that pathos is essential to a *jōruri*, make frequent use of such expressions as 'it was touching' in their writing, or who when chanting do so in voices thick with tears, in the manner of the *Bunyabushi*.[26] This is foreign to my style. I take pathos to be entirely a matter of restraint.[27] Since it is moving when all parts of the art are controlled by restraint, the stronger and firmer the melody and words are, the sadder will be the impression created. For this reason, when one says of something which is sad that it is sad, one loses the implications, and in the end, even the impression of sadness is slight. It is essential that one not say of a thing that 'it is sad,' but that it be sad of itself. For example, when one praises a place renowned for its scenery such as Matsushima by saying, 'Ah, what a fine view!'

one has said in one phrase all that one can about the sight, but without effect. If one wishes to praise the view, and one says numerous things indirectly about its appearance, the quality of the view may be known of itself without one's having to say, 'It is a fine view.' This is true of everything of its kind."

Someone said, "People nowadays will not accept plays unless they are realistic and well reasoned out. There are many things in the old stories which people will not now tolerate. It is thus that such people as *kabuki* actors are considered skillful to the degree that their acting resembles reality. The first consideration is to have the chief retainer in the play resemble a real chief retainer, and to have the daimyō look like a real daimyō. People will not stand for the childish nonsense they did in the past."

Chikamatsu answered, "Your view seems like a plausible one, but it is a theory which does not take into account the real methods of art. Art is something which lies in the slender margin between the real and the unreal. Of course it seems desirable, in view of the current taste for realism, to have the chief retainer in the play copy the gestures and speech of a real retainer, but in that case should a real chief retainer of a daimyō put rouge and powder on his face like an actor? Or, would it prove entertaining if an actor, on the grounds that real chief retainers do not make up their faces, were to appear on the stage and perform, with his beard growing wild and his head shaven? This is what I mean by the slender margin between the real and the unreal. It is unreal, and yet it is not unreal; it is real, and yet it is not real. Entertainment lies between the two.

"In this connection, there is the story of a certain court lady who had a lover. The two loved each other very passionately, but the lady lived far deep in the women's palace, and the man could not visit her quarters. She could see him therefore only very rarely, from between the cracks of her screen of state at the court. She longed for him so desperately that she had a wooden image carved of the man. Its appearance was not like that of any ordinary doll, but did not differ in any particle from the man. It goes without saying that the color of his complexion was perfectly rendered; even the pores of his skin were delineated. The openings in his ears and nostrils were fashioned, and there was no discrepancy even in the number of teeth in the mouth. Since it was made with the man posing beside it, the only difference between the man and this doll was the presence in one, and the absence in the other, of a soul. However, when the lady drew the doll close to her and looked at it, the exactness of the reproduction of the living man chilled her, and she felt unpleasant and rather frightened. Court lady that she was, her love was also chilled, and as she found it distressing to have the doll by her side, she soon threw it away.

"In view of this we can see that if one makes an exact copy of a living being even if it happened to be Yang Kuei-fei,[28] one will become disgusted with it. Thus, if when one paints an image or carves it of wood there are, in the name of artistic license, some stylized parts in a work otherwise resembling the real form; this is, after all, what people love in art. The same is true of literary composition. While bearing resemblance to the original, it should have stylization; this makes it art, and is what delights men's minds. Theatrical dialogue written with this in mind is apt to be worthwhile."

Notes

1. *Mumyō sōshi*, pp. 17–18.
2. *Shina no sadame*—literally, "the determination of rank or value."
3. Sutras presenting divergent doctrines were said to represent different formulations of the same teaching, adjusted by the Buddha to his hearers' level of comprehension.
4. Burnt Norton, in *Four Quartets*, p. 7.
5. *Shōtetsu Monogatari* in *Zoku gunsho ruijū*, book 16, p. 929.
6. *Mumyō Hisho* in *Gunsho ruijū*, book 13, p. 366.
7. Sansom, "Tsuredzure-gusa," p. 85.
8. Seami elsewhere discusses the relation between what the actor expresses with his body and what he knows but does not overtly express. At first an actor who has studied with a master does not know any more than what he has learned and what he expresses, but as he himself acquires mastery there are things which he comes to understand beyond what he has been taught and which he suggests rather than expresses.

The relation between the movements of the body and feet refers to a principle of Seami's that if the body and feet move in the same manner the effect will be crude. Thus, in an agitated passage if the feet are stamping wildly, the movements of the body should be gentle. Otherwise a disorderly effect will be produced which will mar the enjoyment of the spectators.

9. That is, their love of beauty makes them beautiful, however humble their station may be.
10. Buddhist verse by an unknown Zen master. The last two lines may mean, "When life comes to an end the illusions of this world also break into pieces."
11. The tradition of secret teachings transmitted from teacher to student is here indicated.

12. From a Chinese Zen work also paraphrased in Japan by Musō Kokushi. The reason for mentioning Silla (Korea) here is uncertain, but since Korea is to the east of China it may signify that the sun is already rising there while it is still night in China—a typical device in Taoism and Zen to show that nothing is impossible but only appears so due to the limitations in time and place of the individual.

13. Both the "man of old" and the Chinese are as yet unidentified. The meaning is apparently that height can be measured, but depth cannot.

14. Paraphrased from the opening of the *Tao Te Ching*, but the meaning given by Seami to the phrase is not the one currently accepted.

15. Said by Hsün-tzu and not Confucius.

16. Expression used in Tendai philosophy of a region "which is not being and not nonbeing, and is being and nonbeing."

17. Suggested by the Mahāyāna doctrine of the bodhisattva who voluntarily leaves the highest rank to go down to save those at the bottom.

18. Kan'ami (1333–84), the first great master of the Nō.

19. The *gembuku* ceremony took place when a boy reached the age of fifteen. His personal name was changed and he wore for the first time the hat and clothes of an adult.

20. This statement is not by Mencius; it is not even in normal Chinese.

21. Legge, *The Chinese Classics, Mencius* IA:7. The passage concerns the use of improper means to achieve an end, aspiring to greatness without first qualifying for it through personal cultivation.

22. By essence is here meant the inner understanding of the Nō, the true accomplishment of the actor; the performance is the actual manifestation on the stage of his qualities.

23. That is, sets up within the actor a basic misconception of the art.

24. One should supply the words "of essence" and "of performance" to complete the meaning of each part of this curious statement.

25. *Kōshoku ichidai onna*, I, in *Saikaku zenshū*, I, 320.

26. The style of Okamoto Bunya, noted for its sentimentality.

27. The word here translated as "restraint" is *giri*, which normally means "propriety" or "duty." If one acts in accordance with propriety one will not gush over into uncontrolled emotion but will be restrained.

28. The most celebrated of Chinese beauties, concubine of the Emperor Hsüan-tsung (r. 712–55).

Chapter 4

Ways of Japanese Thinking

GRAHAM PARKES

*Using the life and ritual suicide (*seppuku*) of the contemporary Japanese novelist, Mishima Yukio, as a backdrop, this insightful essay by Graham Parkes clarifies for the Western sensibilities the multiple elements of the Japanese tradition. With an emphasis on philosophical thought (both Western and Japanese), Parkes discusses the traditions of food and the eating of meals,* bushidō *(The Way of the Warrior), calligraphy,* chanoyu, *Nō theater, and Japanese film. All these elements of Japanese culture combine to provide the reader with new ways of understanding the Japanese aesthetic tradition.*

In February of 1936, twenty-one junior officers in the Imperial Army of Japan led an uprising calculated to overthrow the government and restore supreme command of the armed forces to the emperor. They managed to assassinate three government ministers and occupy a small area of Tokyo near the imperial palace. Emperor Hirohito, however, demanded that the uprising be quashed. Overwhelmed by the imperial forces, two of the officers committed *seppuku* (ritual suicide by disembowelment) and the rest were executed.

In 1960, Mishima Yukio, who was becoming one of the best known writers in Japan, wrote a short story entitled "Patriotism," which was based on the abortive rebellion of 1936.[1] The hero of the story is a young officer in the Imperial Guard, from whom his comrades have kept the dangerous conspiracy a secret since he is newly married and they want to obviate the risk of his young bride's being prematurely widowed. After the rebellion is launched, the officer is ordered to participate in the attack on the rebel forces; but rather than take up arms against his comrades he resolves to commit *seppuku.* His wife expresses her desire to join him in death, and the officer agrees.

The husband and wife bathe, and then make love, the eroticism of the scene heightened by the prospect of imminent death. Mishima is one of the great prose stylists in modern Japanese, and the story builds to a climax that is overwhelmingly powerful even in English translation. The officer's self-disembowelment is described in loving and excruciating detail, as he plunges the sharp sword into the left side of his abdomen and pulls it across to the right. It is almost a relief when the wife follows her husband in death by stabbing herself in the neck with a dagger.

Five years after writing "Patriotism" Mishima made a film of the story, entitled *The Rite of Love and Death,* in which he himself played the role of the young officer who commits *seppuku.* Five years later, in 1970, at the head of a small band of comrades in a paramilitary organization he had founded, Mishima gained entry to the headquarters of the Army Self-Defense Force in Tokyo and captured its commander. From a balcony on the second floor he proceeded to harangue the troops whom he had ordered assembled outside, encouraging them to abolish the democratic form of government that had been established after the Second World War and to restore to Japan its true identity by reestablishing the emperor system.

Greeted by howls of derision, Mishima went back into the room where his comrades were holding the commander hostage, knelt down facing the balcony, and committed *seppuku.* His right-hand man, a university student by the name of Morita, followed his previous orders to behead him so as not to prolong the agony. (The beheading by a "second" was a part of the ancient ritual.) Morita then disembowelled himself, and was beheaded in turn by a third member of the group. Mishima had been the most admired writer of his generation, and the Japanese public was profoundly shocked by his death—in part because this was the first incident of *seppuku* in Japan since just after World War II.[2] A number of critics have remarked that with Mishima's death a special epoch of Japanese literature came to an end.

While there have been some forms of ritual suicide in the Western tradition, there is something profoundly alien to the Western sensibility about the particular form of *seppuku.* We can, many of us, imagine killing ourselves; but the idea of plunging a sword into one's abdomen and having the strength of will to keep the blade in (the musculature of the lower body naturally tries to eject it) as one pulls it across to the other side, slicing through a variety of vital organs and entrails, is surely incomprehensible to the large majority of

Westerners. Mishima was a gifted writer of extraordinary intelligence, and his voracious intellectual appetite encompassed a wide range of European literature and philosophy as well as classical East Asian learning. Being a great admirer of the German philosopher Friedrich Nietzsche, he was surely familiar with the chapter in *Thus Spoke Zarathustra* called "On Free Death," and his suicide can certainly be seen as a consummate response to Zarathustra's dictum, "Die at the right time!" On the other hand, the method of his self-annihilation is quite alien to Western sensibilities, and he chose *seppuku* precisely because it is so quintessentially Japanese.

Insofar as philosophy is "the uncommonly stubborn attempt to think clearly," it is hard for us to be "philosophical" about Mishima's suicide. But if we try to think clearly about this man who saw his life and death as embodying traditional Japanese ideas, we stand to learn some things about the way the Japanese have traditionally thought about life—and death. As in the case of China, however, we cannot expect philosophical thinking to look the same as it does in the Western tradition. Insofar as philosophy seeks "to discover how things, in the most general sense, hang together, in the most general sense," Japanese philosophy tends to concentrate on concrete things and relations *within* the world rather than on abstractions beyond it. In this it is again like Chinese philosophy, in part because the development of Japanese thought was greatly influenced by Confucianism, Taoism, Chinese Buddhism, and Neo-Confucianism.

Indeed, the Japanese tradition is above all *multiple*, being composed of many heterogeneous elements; and Japan is one of the most fascinating of modern cultures because of the ways its enduring indigenous tradition has continually incorporated a wide range of foreign influences. A feature of this tradition that makes it quite different from its Western counterparts is that philosophy did not develop as a separate discipline in isolation from life, but was rather embodied in particular forms of practice. (It is significant that the Japanese word for philosophy, *tetsugaku,* was coined only a little over a hundred years ago, to refer to the European systems of thought that began to be studied when Japan was opened up to the West.)

This is not to say that there are no texts in the Japanese tradition that contain thinking of the kind we call philosophical in the West. There are many such works, but relatively few of them have been translated into English, and many of these make very difficult reading. For one thing the content is often inherently complex, being an amalgam of native ideas with ideas from India, China, or—in the modern period—Europe. For another, the

Japanese language possesses far more inherent ambiguity and indeterminacy than do Indo-European languages, which makes a faithful translation quite taxing for the reader accustomed to Western philosophy.

Because Japanese philosophy is so closely allied to a variety of practices, one of the best ways to approach it is to read Japanese literature in translation, to look at Japanese art and architecture, see Japanese films, study Japanese martial arts, go to Japanese theater, visit Japanese restaurants, and so on. The last part of this suggestion is not as frivolous as it may sound. In fact it is worth developing a little, so that we may appreciate how reflection upon a practice can bring to light a philosophy behind it—and also how an approach informed by inappropriate presumptions can blind us to what is really going on.

The first thing to notice about a Japanese meal is that how it *looks* is as important as how it tastes: the best Japanese cuisine is almost as much a feast for the eyes as it is a treat for the palate. Even in the most modest eating establishment, far from the metropolis, care is taken as a matter of course concerning the aesthetic appearance of the meal. And insofar as it provides satisfaction for the senses of sight and touch as well as taste, one usually eats less than usual before feeling satisfied. (The particular sense of satisfaction experienced after a good Japanese dinner is rarely accompanied by a feeling of overfulness—perhaps in part because savoring of the visual and tactile pleasures inclines one to eat more slowly.) Another thing to notice is that most of the meal is served at one time, rather than course by course as in the West. The advantage of this "nonlinear" way of eating is a remarkably wide range of tastes, as one gradually works one's way through the various combinations of flavors afforded by a large number of small dishes laid out at the same time.

One of these dishes is usually miso soup served in a lacquer bowl.[3] Now if the diners, following the injunction so beloved of Western mothers to "Drink your soup before it gets cold," finish the soup first, before going on to the other dishes, he will have lost the opportunity to appreciate what Japanese cuisine is really about. But if they consume the soup Japanese-style, slowly and intermittently, they are able not only to savor the progression of different tastes as it cools but also to orchestrate the combinations of these changing tastes with the flavors of the other dishes. The meal can then be appreciated as a multilayered process rather than a single linear event—an appreciation that is impossible if the meal is approached from the perspective of Western preconceptions of ingestion.

But let us return from the sustenance of life to its curtailment in suicide. The death Mishima chose to end his life with and that life itself are emblematically Japanese. (On being criticized for affecting a Western lifestyle—a home furnished in European rococo and a wardrobe of Italian suits, Levi's, and T-shirts—Mishima responded that those were just the outer trappings. His real life, as a writer working late at night in his study, was Japanese through and through.) It is possible to extract from that life some salient features that serve to articulate a kind of intellectual framework with which to approach some of the ways of thinking that are the topic of this chapter. In short, Mishima chose his *death,* through destroying the *body,* in a *ritual* action that consummated his life as an *aesthetic* whole.

To choose one's death as Mishima did is to consummate one's life in a way that is impossible if one just lets things take their course and dies from natural causes. This kind of suicide affirms an understanding of death as inseparable from life rather than as an event that simply comes after it. When Socrates describes the true philosopher as "practicing dying," or the Christian advocates "dying to the world" in order to be reborn, it is on the basis of an understanding of death as a separation of the soul from the body which grants access to a world beyond. But when the Japanese Zen thinkers speak of the "great death," they refer to death experienced *within* life that leads to a rebirth in *this* world; and thus insofar as they distinguish something like a soul from the body, the major focus tends to be on the latter. Modern Japanese thinkers like to remark that whereas in the West philosophies of life have predominated, Eastern thought has tended to produce philosophies of life-*and*-death such as Buddhism and Taoism. In broad terms this is true, with some of the more recent "existential" philosophies in the West providing the exception that strengthens the general rule.[4]

The tendency of the Platonic-Christian tradition to privilege the soul over the body is manifest in the fact that it was not until Schopenhauer and Nietzsche in the nineteenth century—and then, later, Merleau-Ponty—that European thinkers began to develop extensive philosophies of the body. In East-Asian thought, by contrast, the body has consistently been a focus of philosophical reflection, whether by virtue of the emphasis on ritual performance in the teachings of Confucius, the development of breathing and concentration techniques or physical skills in Taoism, or the practice of meditation in sitting, walking, and other physical activity in Zen Buddhism.[5]

Even though the ancient Greeks attached great importance to the training of the body, Plato's association of the head with intellect and rational thought distracted the attention of the subsequent philosophical tradition from the body as a whole. Thinking came to be understood as an "internal" process, the outward somatic manifestations of which are relatively unimportant. Descartes' denial of the body as in any way essential to our true nature as "thinking beings" exaggerated this trend. The idea of mental interiority was, however, quite foreign to the thinkers of the classical Chinese tradition. For Confucius, the major task was to cultivate oneself as a human being in society by engaging in the ritual practices handed down from the ancestors: Tradition was in this way literally *embodied*. By disciplining the movements and postures of the body through ritual practice, one could refine the faculties and capacities of the whole human being. This attitude was maintained in the Taoist tradition that developed after Confucius—and thus was incorporated into Chinese Buddhism as well as the Japanese forms of Buddhism that were descended from it. This is why the ideas of Zen have traditionally embodied themselves in such activities as archery, swordplay, tea ceremony, Noh drama, painting, and calligraphy.

Chinese thought is predicated upon an aesthetic rather than a rational notion of order, and the same is true in general of the Japanese tradition. Aesthetics did not develop as a separate field of Western philosophy until the eighteenth century, and philosophies of art have traditionally been regarded as peripheral in comparison with metaphysics, epistemology, and ethics. In East Asian thought there has been no such marginalization of the aesthetic viewpoint: The texts of classical Taoist philosophy are some of the finest poetry ever written; the eighth-century Japanese thinker Kūkai was a Buddhist priest and an accomplished painter and calligrapher; the Zen thinker Dōgen (born 1200 C.E.) wrote exquisite poetry as well as poetic works of philosophy; the eighteenth-century Zen master Hakuin was a renowned poet, painter, and calligrapher as well as a thinker of the first rank.

But let us begin our approach by stepping back for some historical perspective. Because in Japan—more so than in most cultures—the past persists alongside (beneath or behind) the present, our understanding of Japanese ways of thinking will be all the more enhanced if we can get a sense of some of the factors that have historically conditioned them.[6]

The Major Sources: Shinto, Confucianism, Buddhism

The drama of Mishima's "Patriotism" is played out against the backdrop of a devotion to Shinto. Holding pride of place in the young lieutenant's home is a tablet from the Great Shrine at Ise, the religion's most sacred site, and a photograph of the emperor, the high priest of Shinto—before which the lieutenant and his wife solemnly bow every morning. The code of honor and ethics followed by the hero of "Patriotism"—and the philosophy that Mishima himself came to espouse—was that of *bushidō,* "the way of the samurai." This philosophy is precisely a synthesis of elements of Shinto with ideas from the Confucian tradition and Buddhism.

Up until the last part of the nineteenth century, when Japan was opened to the West after several hundred years of self-imposed isolation, Japanese thinking had been fed by the three streams of Shinto, Buddhism, and Confucianism. Let us begin with Shinto, which was the indigenous religion of Japan prior to the influx of any influence from outside, and which still informs many aspects of life in Japan today. (There are thousands of well attended Shinto shrines in Japan, and most marriage ceremonies are still performed by Shinto priests.)

Shinto—the Japanese word means literally "way of the divine spirits"—is an animistic nature religion, according to which the entire cosmos is "ensouled" and animated by spirits, and which is in many respects similar to the religion of ancient Greece. Its two major components are a *cult of nature,* in which the sun, mountains, trees, waterfalls, rocks, and certain kinds of animals are worshipped as divine, and an *ancestor cult* in which reverence is paid to the spirits of the ancestors—again often as divinities. Another important idea in Shinto is that the Japanese nation is one large, extended family, with the emperor—as high priest and "father"—at the head. This notion began to be literalized in the so-called "nativist" philosophies of the eighteenth and nineteenth centuries, which held that the Japanese imperial family was directly descended from the gods of the primeval period. The idea of the Japanese nation as a family whose forefathers were of divine origin tends to give rise to a belief in the inherent superiority of the Japanese to all other races—a belief that formed the basis of the ultranationalist movements of the 1930s.

A salient feature of Shinto illustrates a contrast between the Japanese and the Western understandings of age and the reality of the past. The Great Shrine at Ise is dedicated to the ancestor of the imperial family, the sun goddess Amaterasu. This most ancient shrine in the country is also the newest: In order to avoid the impurity that comes with the decay of aging, the Ise shrine is destroyed and built anew every twenty years. Whereas in the West the age of a building depends on how old the materials of which it is made are, in Japan it is the *form* that counts. Not form in the Platonic sense of some antecedent pattern beyond the world of change, but form as concretely embodied in a finite, impermanent building. The ephemeral nature of existence, of which the Japanese appear to possess an especially keen awareness, is enacted in the perpetual destruction and reconstruction of the most sacred structure of the national religion.

The Japanese propensity for the intelligent and thorough appropriation of foreign influences is nowhere more apparent than in the massive borrowings from Chinese culture that took place in the sixth century and continued, on and off, over the next thousand years. The Japanese had developed no writing system of their own, and so the first and most basic thing to be "imported" was the ideographic system of written Chinese. Along with it came the philosophies embodied in that writing: namely, Confucianism, Buddhism, and Taoism.

The first two of these had originated around a thousand years prior to their arrival in Japan. Buddhism, which arose in India in the sixth century B.C.E., was transmitted in the first century of the Christian Era to China, where its development was influenced by the indigenous philosophy of Taoism during the five hundred years before it spread to Japan. A primary feature of Buddhist thinking is expressed in what it calls the "three characteristics of existence"—which turned out to harmonize especially well with the Japanese worldview. Most forms of Buddhism view existence being characterized by *duhkha,* frustration or unsatisfactoriness, *anitya,* impermanence, and *anatmam,* which refers to the idea that nothing possesses an intrinsic "selfness." In the Buddhist view, it is the failure or refusal to acknowledge that existence is transitory through and through that gives rise to frustration. If existence is a continual process of "arising and passing away," then the idea that there are enduring, self-identical things—including human egos or selves—may be shown to be an illusion, a fabrication designed to mask the radically ephemeral nature of existence.

Buddhist thought is particularly opposed to the substantialist view that there are *independently* existing things, claiming that everything is "itself" only in relation to a set of conditions that make it what it is. And again, the same is true for the "non-thing" that is the human self: It, too, is what it is only in relation to other things. The idea that things do not possess any inherent "self-nature" was already current in some schools of Chinese thought, as was the idea of the world as constant process or flux. Thus when Buddhism spread from India to China, certain forms of it especially resonated with the indigenous philosophies of Confucianism and Taoism.[7]

With respect to the influence of Confucian thought on Japanese thinking, the important ideas concern the ethical teachings: the "virtues" of sincerity, humaneness, rightness, and filial piety. Equally important are the ideas underlying these virtues: an understanding of the self as a matrix of familial and social relationships rather than as something substantial, and an emphasis on ritual activity as a means toward a harmonious "ritual community."

Out of the interactions between Buddhism and Confucianism and Taoism there arose in the Tang dynasty in China (seventh and eighth centuries) an eminently practical form of Buddhism known as "*Chan*"—the Chinese rendering of the Sanskrit *dhyana*, meaning "meditation." Chan Buddhism renounced the reciting of holy scriptures (sutras) and the discussion of metaphysical theories in favor of the practice of meditation. However, the goal of this practice, enlightenment, was understood not as the attainment of some transcendent realm beyond the world of everyday affairs, but rather as the realization of a more authentic way of being *within* the realm of day-to-day life.

The basic premise of Chan Buddhism (as of its transformation into Zen in Japan) is that our normal, pre-enlightenment experience is conditioned by layers of conceptualization that prevent us from experiencing the world *the ways* it is. (The plural marks a difference from the common Western conception of *the way* the world is.) This conceptualization is something we all grow up into quite naturally as we are acculturated into a particular social context through the acquisition of language. To use a visual metaphor for experience generally, it is as if the linguistic categories we acquire as we grow up place various kinds of filters over our eyes that color and distort our experience of the world.

The practice of Zen effects a return to the preconceptual level of the individual's being and to the most basic context of the person, which is understood as *mu*, or nothingness. The radical nature of this return is brought into relief when we recall that in China and Japan the person is normally understood as a function of social relationships. In stark contrast to the modern Western notion of the individual (especially as developed in the liberal democratic tradition), in East-Asian thought it is the group—whether the nation or the family—that is ontologically primary, and the individual a derivative aberration. Thus when one enters a Zen monastery—giving up one's former possessions, clothing, social standing, head of hair, and even one's name—all ties to one's former existence are severed and the context of one's personal identity is completely abandoned. In spite of the new and highly disciplined order prevailing within the monastery, the point of the Zen regime is to show the novice that the ultimate context for his being is precisely *nothing*.[8]

Dōgen, the founder of the Soto school of Zen, refers to this process of self-transformation in which one's ordinary identity falls away as "the molting of body-mind." This molting allows one to experience and act from the "field of emptiness"—another Zen expression for the context of nothingness—without preconceptions, which in turn allows one's experience and actions to be totally spontaneous and appropriate to the current situation. (People sometimes fail to realize that, according to Zen, if the situation happens to call for conceptualization, the appropriate response is to conceptualize.)

The founder of the other major school of Zen, the ninth-century Chinese master Rinzai, expresses a similar conception of the person by talking about "the true human of no rank." We have seen that the Japanese understanding of the self is above all relational, and especially in terms of social standing; the Rinzai Zen idea of "no rank" suggests that all human relations (to things as well as persons) are possible only in the deeper context of nothingness. Hakuin, a Japanese Zen master who flourished in the early eighteenth century and is responsible for a revitalization of the Rinzai school, was fond of talking about the "great death" rather than the return to nothingness. In order to see into the depths of one's true nature it is necessary, according to Hakuin's quite existential understanding of Zen, to undergo the "great death": One must "be prepared to let go one's hold when hanging from a sheer precipice" if one is to be able to "die and return again to life."[9] This talk of the "great death" brings us now to a consideration of the philosophy and practice of *bushidō*, the major tenet of which is summed up in the dictum, "The way of the samurai is death."

The Way of the Sword

The pretext on which Mishima paid his apparently cordial visit, on the day of his suicide, to the commander of the Army Self-Defense Force was that of showing him a beautiful ceremonial sword. From ancient times in Japan the sword has been regarded with an almost religious awe, and famous swordsmiths, who regard their art as being primarily spiritual rather than material, pass down the secrets of their special craft from master to pupil over the generations. Zen ideas and practice began to influence swordsmanship (the use as well as the making of the sword) around the beginning of the fourteenth century, and they played an increasingly important role in the development of the way of the sword over the succeeding centuries of civil strife in the country.[10]

Because Buddhism, with its emphasis on cultivating compassion for all sentient beings, has a reputation of being one of the world's more peaceable religions, it may be thought strange that Zen should have such a close connection with swordsmanship. But from the Zen perspective everything depends on the character and integrity of the one wielding the sword: If one's will is directed toward annihilating evil and against agents that stand in the way of justice and harmony, then the sword—even though it kills—becomes what Zen calls a "sword of life" rather than of death.

The *bushi*, or samurai warrior, carried two swords: a long one for combat, and a short one to kill himself with—if that should be necessary. The most important thing for a samurai was his honor as a loyal servant of his master, and if he were humiliated by defeat or about to be taken prisoner, he would have no hesitation in turning the short sword upon himself. This attitude is a manifestation of a more general readiness to die—and especially to die for one's lord—that is the distinguishing mark of the Japanese samurai. Let us consider the role of this idea that "the way of the samurai is death" in the teaching and discipline of swordsmanship.[11]

The most important principle of samurai swordsmanship is the injunction to enter combat, when combat is unavoidable, *absolutely prepared to die*—with no concern whatsoever for saving one's skin. This somewhat paradoxical idea is more comprehensible if one considers the combination of Confucian and Zen Buddhist elements in *bushidō*. In speaking of the difficulty of attaining the ideal of true "humaneness," Confucius emphasized that the requisite ritual activity must not only be technically precise but must also be informed by the performer's heart or spirit. Similarly, *bushidō* stresses the discipline of the whole person, the training of the psychological and spiritual aspects of the warrior as well as the physical. The idea is that once one has undergone the requisite self-discipline and trained the body to its utmost limits, the appropriate activity will flow effortlessly.

To understand this idea (which is also quite Taoist) it may help to consider an example from the field of competitive sports in the West. Even given an innate talent for tennis, for instance, the training necessary to acquire the psychological coordination that it takes to win a championship game is long and demanding. But once one has undergone such training, which may involve considerable analytical reflection upon various swings and strokes (not to mention a good deal of boredom and frustration), the appropriate frame of mind in which to play a championship match would appear to be one of relative "emptiness." As in Zen, the idea is to free oneself of preconceptions and expectations. If one starts to think about how to respond to a particular serve, one is certain to fluff the return. And even amateur players learn early on that emotional upset or nervousness about losing a crucial point virtually guarantees that one will lose it.[12]

What is called for—and the corresponding point can surely be made about most competitive sports—is an attitude that is open, yet free from all extraneous influences, a relaxed but intense concentration on the event of the opponent's striking the ball. Then the return happens as if "by itself"—without one's having to think "Now the opponent is in that part of the court moving in this direction, so I need to place the ball over there" and then issue commands to the musculature to move in such and such a way so as to put one's body in the right position to execute a forehand volley at the appropriate angle.

In the Zen Buddhist tradition one enters into the spirit of a physical discipline by cultivating the condition of *mushin,* or "no-mind," which again connotes an openness untrammeled by ego-centered prejudices or preconceptions. (The Sino-Japanese word *shin* means "heart," and thus carries broader and less strictly intellectual connotations than the English "mind.") The term also suggests the respect accorded to what one might call the deep "wisdom of the body." As mentioned earlier, the Japanese tradition in general, and Zen in particular, tends not to employ as strict a dichotomy between mind and body as Western thought does—as evidenced by the common use in Zen texts of Dōgen's compound term "body-mind."

On the question of where to direct the mind or focus one's body awareness, the master of the sword is likely to tell the student at first to keep the mind in the lower part of the abdomen, just below the navel. (This area is regarded by the Chinese and the Japanese as the center of the body's vital activity. The Japanese call it the *hara,* which is why the alternative reading of *seppuku* is *hara-kiri,* "cutting the abdomen.") The more advanced student is instructed to expand that focus throughout the entire body. In the words of Takuan, addressed to the sword master Yagyū Munenori: "If you don't put the mind anywhere, it will go to all the parts of the body and extend throughout its entirety."[13] In this way one's awareness will extend through to the sword as well, which thus virtually becomes part of the body—just as the racket becomes an extension of the arm in the case of the championship tennis player.

The parallel with tennis goes only so far, however, because the stakes in swordsmanship are infinitely higher. An instant of emotional upset or a moment's reflective thought on the court at Wimbledon can mean the loss of a valuable prize, it is true. But the Japanese sword is such a fiendishly sharp instrument that a corresponding lapse in a sword fight means the loss of a hand, a limb, or one's head. And losing one's head in that context is a literal and irrevocable loss.

If we recall now that the samurai is encouraged to enter combat absolutely prepared to die and with no thought of preserving himself, we can see that the openness or emptiness of "no-mind" coincides in an interesting way with the nothingness of death. We can also appreciate the further paradox that the Zen emphasis on *natural* action, when it re-emerges as a consequence of intense physical and mental discipline in something like the spontaneous activity of the consummate swordsman, coincides now with a way of being that is quite *unnatural.* This is not meant to suggest that it is artificial, but rather that the way to realize one's full humanity lies in going against what is naturally given so that one may sublimate, as it were, one's human nature.

In animals the instinct for self-preservation is fundamental and pervasive, and it is naturally strong in humans, too. However, the almost superhuman achievement of the Zen swordsman, which manifests in activity that appears equal to the most finely honed instinctual responses in the animal world, goes hand in hand with a remarkable suspension of the instinct for self-preservation. Many of the stories told about the best known Zen masters of the sword suggest that they have acquired extraordinary powers (some of the better samurai films convey a sense of this). At this level of achievement it is as if the life-force is negated in such a way that one becomes totally—and almost supernaturally—alive.

Let us now go on to consider some other, less violent arts of the hand that have been inspired by the ideas of Zen.

Arts of the Hand

Although Mishima was a writer, he lived in an era during which writing was less an art of the hand than it was before the advent of printing (a Chinese invention). Formerly in Japan, as in China, writing well meant not only authoring fine poems and essays, but also producing manuscripts that were themselves works of art. Because of the special nature of the Chinese ideographic writing system, the fine poem will look as beautiful as it sounds—and indeed the way it looks is an important part of the poetry. For someone writing after the invention of printing, the act of writing is bound to seem a less immediate type of action than it was in the days when readers would have before them the actual traces of the author's moving hand.

We shall see later how this perceived lack of connection with the world drove Mishima to take up more dynamic arts of the hand and body than writing, like kendō (a kind of fencing with swords of bamboo, but more in the style of sabers than foils). In so doing he was following an East-Asian tradition—grounded in the teachings of Confucius, among others—with respect to which the Western dichotomy between theory and practice, or reflection and action, fails to hold. Japanese history is full of figures whose achievements undercut such dichotomies: emperors who were exquisitely cultured individuals, Zen masters who were consummate swordsmen, and warriors who were exemplary men of letters. Over the centuries in which Japan was torn by civil wars, there grew up a tradition of samurai who were at the same time literati, men of refined culture who wielded the pen (or, rather, the brush) with as much skill as the sword.

Closely related to the art of calligraphy *(shōdō:* literally, "the way of writing") is *sumi-e,* monochrome painting with brush and ink. The most striking thing about both Chinese and Japanese brush painting at first sight is the large amount of "empty space." Until fairly recently it was traditional in most Western painting to have the canvas completely covered with paint, for the space outlined by the picture frame to be filled. By contrast, in many masterpieces of Japanese brush painting as little as 15 to 25 percent of the surface of the scroll has ink on it. In view of the influence of Taoism and Zen on this art form, the relative emptiness of the canvas can be understood as an evocation of the nothingness that forms the context of all particular things.

The technique of monochrome painting has much in common with that of swordsmanship: The training under a master is long and rigorous, and the goal is to let the brush move itself. The appropriate condition for painting is one of "no-mind," and one's awareness is dispersed throughout the whole body—and even beyond the brush to the blank paper. In the case of painting a persimmon, a branch, or a bird, the idea is to have contemplated the subject long enough so that one has actually become one with it; then the subject literally paints itself. (Something like this can happen in the case of stillife or landscape painting in the West, too, insofar as the artist contemplates the subject with sufficient concentration to achieve a kind of union with it.)

While it is a delight to watch the exquisite movements of a master calligrapher or *sumi-e* artist letting the ink flow on to the paper, it is the product rather than the process that is regarded as the work. But in several other art forms inspired by Zen the moving body of the artist is itself part of the work of art.

One of the most quintessential expressions of Japanese culture is the tea ceremony (*chadō,* "the way of tea," or *chanoyu,* literally, "hot water for tea").[14] Tea was originally brought to Japan from China some time during the sixth or seventh century, and the practice of drinking tea appears to have established itself first of all in the Buddhist seminaries and schools. The green tea that is still the staple in Japan is a vitalizing beverage that helps keep one alert during meditation—and in life in general. After relations with China were broken off at the end of the ninth century, the custom went into decline, and was not revived again until the twelfth century, thanks to the Zen master Eisai.

At first tea gatherings were rather grand social affairs that took place in elaborate Chinese-style tea pavilions and often involved tea-tasting competitions. In the course of the Middle Ages the ceremonies gradually became simpler and at the same time more strictly governed by rules of ritual. This happened in part through the adoption of the tea ceremony by the samurai class, whose rules of conduct were being formulated at the time, and also under the influence of the simple rules of life-style of the Soto school of Zen, whose founder was Dōgen. There is also a strong Confucian element in the tea ceremony, as we shall see.

While the primary requisite for the tea ceremony consists of simplicity and an avoidance of ostentation, the specifications for the utensils, the room, and the surroundings are remarkably strict, on the principle, not entirely foreign to Western thinking, that it is only within a context of the most rigid discipline that the utmost freedom for creativity can be exercised. On the surface, the ceremony is simple; a small number of guests gather in an anteroom. They proceed through a modest but carefully laid out and well tended garden to a simple thatched hut built of wood and plaster. Before entering the hut, which usually consists of one rather small room, each guest washes his or her hands in a stone water basin—a symbolic cleansing from the dust of the everyday world. They enter across a stone threshold and through a low entranceway with a simple sliding door covered with white rice paper.

The room is small, some ten feet square, and suffused by a subdued light coming through the translucent sliding screens that make up much of the walls. The only form of ornament is an alcove built into one of the walls: a vase with a simple arrangement of flowers in it, or else a hanging scroll inscribed with Chinese characters or a monochrome painting. In the middle of the floor of tatami (rectangular mats made of tightly woven rice straw) is a hearth in which charcoal is burned to heat the iron kettle for water.

The host enters through a sliding door in one of the other walls, greets the guests and passes round a dish of small cakes while preparing the tea. In a precisely determined sequence of ritual movements, the host uses a special ladle to rinse the tea bowl with hot water, puts two spoonfuls of powdered tea into the bowl, pours a ladleful of hot water into the tea bowl, and stirs the tea with a whisk made of split bamboo. Originally the guests would share one bowl, wiping the rim with a piece of rice paper before passing it on; a variation of the ceremony uses one bowl for each guest. As the guests slowly sip the tea, they may compliment the host on its taste and color, admire the tea bowls and utensils, and converse for a while before taking their leave. That is all; and yet when it goes well, those present have the impression of contacting the deepest levels of human being, and of experiencing from the narrow confines of that simple hut a far wider world.

All features of the room, of the ornaments, and the utensils for brewing and serving the tea are precisely specified as to their optimal size, shape, color, and so on. The specifications change, however, according to the time of day the ceremony is performed as well as the season of the year. Certain kinds and colors of flowers, for example, are recommended for certain times of day but not for others. The ritual gestures of the hands with which the host makes and serves the tea are too complex to be described: They have to be seen to be appreciated. As in the practice of the Zen sword, the techniques are learned over a long period of instruction under a master of the discipline, until they can be performed quite naturally. To watch an accomplished tea person simply lay the ladle on top of the kettle, for instance, is to witness an action quite awe inspiring in its elegance and economy.

The Zen ideas that inform the ceremony ensure that all the participants are *there* with full attention to the present activity. At the same time, aware of the age of the ceremony itself and of many of the utensils being used to perform it (the form of the activities being centuries old, and the utensils fashioned long before the participants were born), they feel the flow of the past rise up through the present moment. A beautiful account of this phenomenon is to be found in the well-known short novel by Kawabata Yasunari, *A Thousand Cranes*.[15] The tea ceremony serves as a background to the entire narrative, and two or three bowls play a role in the story that is—strangely—almost human, insofar as they are three to four hundred years old and so have passed through the hands of generations of tea connoisseurs.

More recently the bowls in question have been owned by the young protagonists' parents and their respective lovers, and after the deaths of the parents the bowls evoke the presence of the deceased with an almost supernatural power, at the same time prompting premonitions of the deaths of the survivors in turn. The young man and woman, Kikuji and Fumiko, are looking at a bowl that was a favorite of Kikuji's deceased father, when Fumiko remarks how like the father the bowl is. And so reminiscent of its previous owner is a bowl inherited from her late mother that the bowls together look like "two beautiful ghosts." And yet since the bowls are completely "sound and healthy," "life seemed to stretch taut over them in a way that was almost sensual."

In the tea ceremony the bowl is handled with such care and reverence that—while of course it will not last for ever—it is likely to survive beyond the death of any particular owner or user. (Should the bowl be broken, it is often repaired using gold.) The awareness that this bowl will continue to exist long after I have passed on, even though a part of my being may somehow survive with it—to the extent that it has been closely associated with me during my lifetime—helps me to focus on the series of unique moments in which I drink from it. The realizations that there are a finite number of such moments yet to come and that every sip is potentially the last, serve to intensify the experience of the present moment.

An important dimension of the ceremony is illuminated if we recall the Confucian conception of the place of ritual activity in human life, where such practice is understood to be integral to cultivating and refining one's essential humanity. For a ceremony to be genuine in the Confucian sense, not only must the technique be faultless and effortless, but the performer must perform the actions with "heart and soul." (Lack of heart is as obvious to a connoisseur as a perfunctory handshake is to a sensitive individual, or a coldly mechanical rendition of a piano sonata to a true music lover.) In the case of tea, consummate technique must be accompanied by a sense that the participants are fully engaged in the human interaction. As the host serves the tea, or the guest bows to the host, the activity expresses an awareness that here are two human beings who have come together under the heavens and on a particular piece of the earth, and in the context of a particular configuration of the elements of fire and water, wood and metal, in order to partake of a unique and vivifying beverage.

Just as in Zen the awareness that accompanies sitting meditation (*zazen*) is to be extended throughout one's waking life, so the atmosphere of the tea ceremony optimally comes to pervade the practitioner's entire being, so that every meal and all other waking activities may become occasions for experiencing the ultimate context of nothingness that is the womb of all human possibilities. The greatest contrast would be the kind of "eating on the run" encouraged by the institution of the drive-through fast food outlet. The consumption while driving of a bland styrofoam-enclosed mass is something that—even if it helps sustain life—barely enters the consumer's consciousness (perhaps just as well) let alone vivifies the experience of life itself.

Even as present-day Japan succumbs to the institution of fast food, there remains a custom that faintly recalls the Zen attitude underlying the way of tea. In the otherwise prosaic situation of drinking beer, for example, whether in a public place or a private home, one may find one's companion proffering the bottle, neck first. The appropriate response is to lift one's glass a little off the table so that the other person can fill it. The roles are usually reversed on the second round. Rather than dismiss this custom as a minor bit of useless ritual, one might see it as analogous to the tea ceremony in its function of bringing to awareness the uniqueness of the human situation in which the participants find themselves.

Noh Drama: Poetry, Music, Dance

Several critics maintain that the plays Mishima wrote based on the traditional Noh drama are among his finest accomplishments. Noh (the word means literally "accomplishment," and was used early on to refer to the special abilities of actors, singers, and dancers) is another Zen-influenced art form in which the human body is part of the work.[16] It was developed during the fourteenth century from a mixture of art forms such as the sacred dances of Shinto, court dances concerning warriors, and other forms of recitation and proto-opera. The traditional founder, Kan'ami had a son, Zeami, who became a protégé of the shogun of Japan at the time, an enlightened ruler who was a great patron of the arts and a devotee of Zen. This high regard for Zen was shared by Zeami, and Buddhist ideas influenced both the many classic plays he authored and his treatises laying out the basic principles of the art.

Noh is a highly refined art form that combines poetry, drama, music, song, and dance in a way that is somewhat reminiscent of ancient Greek tragedy. The plays are generally based on simple, ancient, and archetypal themes deriving from some of the most familiar poems, stories, and legends in the Japanese canon. (This is just as well, since the highly poetic dialogue is delivered in such an idiosyncratic combination of song and chant that it is more or less incomprehensible even to native Japanese speakers, many of whom attend the plays equipped with the written texts.) There is generally very little in the way of plot in these plays; they aim rather at the development of a particular mood or emotion or attitude basic to human psychology.

A primary aim of the drama, according to Zeami, is the production of the mood of *yūgen,* a Zen term that connotes "what lies beneath the surface," the subtle as opposed to the obvious. The original meaning of the word is "obscure and dark," but it came to refer to a special kind of beauty that is only partly revealed, that is elusive yet full of meaning and tinged with a wistful sadness. It also has connotations of the graceful elegance of the refined aristocrat. The talk of something "beneath the surface" is not meant to suggest the dichotomy between appearance and reality familiar in Western metaphysics, but comes rather from the Zen idea that layers of conceptualization obscure our experience, and that certain art forms may enable us to "see through" those layers.

There is no attempt in Noh at realism. The back of the stage consists of simple wood paneling on which is painted a stylized pine tree, and a chorus and several musicians sit on the stage in full view of the audience. The "orchestra" comprises a flute and two hand drums, with sometimes a third stick drum in addition. The rhythms of the percussion are based on an extremely long and often irregular beat, which has the effect after a while of profoundly altering the audience's sense of time. (Zen adepts might claim that the rhythms help one to break through the conceptual overlay; psychologists, that they modify the brainwaves in such a way as to activate the deep unconscious.) On occasion, in some of the dances, the music can become remarkably Dionysian in its frenzied crescendos, evoking no doubt the music of the Shinto festivals of which Mishima was so enamored. The singing of the chorus sometimes comments on the action and sometimes substitutes for the singing of the principal actor when he is too involved in the dance to be able to sing. But the most striking feature of the Noh is the way the acting techniques combine with the specially designed costumes and masks.

With the movements and gestures of Noh drama we are again on familiar ground—a ground prepared by our discussion of the role of ritual activity in refining the human being. The gestures are highly stylized and for the most part extremely subtle and restrained—only occasionally building up into climaxes of wild dance—and they are perfected only after years of the most intense physical training on the part of the actor. The costumes, which generally cover the entire body, are themselves works of art, and when worn by an accomplished actor they become kinetic sculptures of breathtaking beauty. Some of the costumes have an uncanny way of making the wearer appear to be defying the laws of gravity. It sometimes looks, for instance, as if it is physically impossible for a human being to stand that way without falling over; this phenomenon conduces to the often desired effect of a more-than-human presence.

The Noh mask is carved from wood, usually cypress, and then covered with layer upon layer of paint. The making of these masks is another Japanese art that has been handed down from master to apprentice over the centuries, and some of the older ones are today regarded as "national treasures." There are many different types of mask, and one of their primary functions is to enable the principal actor (all Noh actors and musicians are men) to play a wide range of parts: young girl, old man, angry demon, and so on. Sometimes a different mask is used for the second part of the play, since the text often requires a warrior or a woman to turn into a ghost, a demon, an animal, or even a god.

Unlike the masks that were used in Greek tragedy, the Noh mask is slightly smaller than the face, and this has the effect of delocalizing the sound of the actor's voice in such a way that it seems to come, strangely, from "around" the figure rather than from it. The masks are designed to have a neutral, intermediate expression, so that very slight movements of the actor's head, in combination with the appropriate bodily gestures, are able to produce the illusion of a remarkable variety of facial expressions. The synergism of all these features gives the masked figure of the actor a strangely nonhuman or even superhuman appearance—again in a way similar to the overall effect of the masked actors of Greek tragedy.

During the half-hour before he goes on stage, the Noh actor sits alone and in silence in what is called the "mirror room" and contemplates the mask he is about to put on. During the last five minutes, he looks into the eyes of the mask, at the center of which is nothing, in order to "see" the character about to be acted. This period of meditation allows him to empty himself so that he will be able to act out of the context of no-mind, or nothingness, thus letting the archetypal figure he is to portray "play through" him. Correspondingly, the more the audience is able to let its preconceptions concerning what it is seeing fall away, the more profound the experience that will ensue. The effects of the music and the somewhat hypnotic chanting of the poetry of the text can thus combine to short-circuit everyday consciousness and elicit a profound response from the deeper layers of the self.[17]

Because Zen is not a set of dogmas but rather a practice that transforms one's relationships to the world, it is not surprising that the ideas behind it should continue to inform Japanese thought and culture even after the radical break effected by modernization, which began a little more than a century ago. In the last part of this chapter we shall consider some later transformations of Japanese thinking through the correspondingly modern medium of cinema.

Projections in a Western Medium: The Art of Film

In 1853 several warships of the U.S. Navy commanded by Commodore Matthew Perry sailed into Edo Bay, carrying a request (amounting to a demand) that Japan open her ports to foreign trading ships. The island had been closed to foreign influence for almost three hundred years. A number of people in the government were quick to gauge the situation. They realized that the only way for Japan to avoid the fate of colonization that had befallen all her neighbors in Asia was to modernize quickly enough to develop technology to defend the country against foreign aggression. In 1868 the feudal system that had held sway for several centuries was abolished, and some measure of political power was restored to the imperial house of Meiji (hence the name *Meiji Restoration*). Western technology and culture were imported with amazing rapidity and thoroughness: Promising Japanese political leaders and scholars in all areas of the arts and sciences were sent by the hundreds to the major countries of Europe, as well as to the United States. Their assignment was to learn the ways of the West so that they could return home and supervise the appropriation of Western ideas in fields ranging from philosophy to physics.

Toward the end of the nineteenth century, not only were French positivism and British utilitarianism being received with special enthusiasm, but also—in the interests of a thorough historical understanding of Western thought—ancient Greek and Roman thought. But it was German philosophy that found the most fertile ground for transplantation—from Leibniz and Kant, through German Idealism, to the more recent philosophies of Schopenhauer and Nietzsche.[18] To this day, philosophers in Japan are more likely to be fluent in German than in English or French; and if one wants to study Buddhist philosophy there, for example, one has to go to a department of religious studies, since most philosophy departments are concerned only with continental European thought and Anglo-American (analytic) philosophy.

The fact that relatively few contemporary philosophers in Japan are interested in Japanese philosophy is a symptom of just how massive and comprehensive the importation of Western ideas after the Meiji Restoration was. While the appropriation of Western philosophical ideas has greatly enriched Japanese culture, it was undertaken with such zeal as to almost preclude a continuing engagement with the indigenous tradition of Japanese thought. It is true that Shinto still functions on the everyday level as a vessel for whatever thoughts and feelings the average Japanese may have concerning "the meaning of life," the nature of death and the beyond, and so on. However, it seems that the majority of the contemporary population has been cut off from the traditional ideas and practices of Buddhism and Confucianism—and the arts and disciplines that sprang from them—which sustained the development of so many centuries of Japanese culture. The "Kyoto School" philosopher Nishitani Keiji argues in a book on nihilism written in 1949 that this severance from the tradition on the intellectual and existential levels has introduced into modern Japanese life a deep-seated nihilism that is all the more powerful for remaining mostly unconscious.[19]

There is really no equivalent in the West to the shock caused by modernization in Japan. A country with a two-thousand-year-old tradition cuts itself off from the rest of the world for a period of a dozen generations, and then is suddenly forced into the wholesale adoption of a totally alien set of values—a process that necessitates in large part a radical break with indigenous traditions. The situation was exacerbated because the importation of Western ideas was carried out uncritically, so it passed unnoticed that many of the systems of thought that were brought in were themselves beginning to collapse. The import of Nietzsche's proclamation of "the death of God" was lost on the avid Japanese appropriators of turn-of-the-century European culture. Nobody realized that the ideals that had sustained the enormous expansion of the Western powers were themselves crumbling from within, that the virus of nihilism was present in the ideational stock that was so indiscriminately transplanted to Japanese soil.

This is not to deny that much of the past persists alongside the manifestations of modernity in Japan. But while the integration of modern Western ideas with the quite different ways of thinking that formerly sustained the development of the indigenous culture has been enormously fruitful—as evidenced by Japan's current economic domination of the world—it has also engendered a certain tension between an outer fullness and an inner void. Nietzsche remarked on the efficacy of hard and prolonged work as a way of covering over the abyss of nihilism, and it is hard to resist the impression that the frenetic industriousness of contemporary Japanese life serves to conceal a yawning emptiness at the core of it. The question of what "Japaneseness" consists in has been something of a national obsession since even before the Meiji period, and one suspects that the periodic outbreaks of aggressive nationalism that have occurred during this century may also stem from an inadequate response to the issue of nihilism. If all other sources of meaning for one's life appear to have dried up, then at the very least the meaning of it all is that one is Japanese.[20]

This line of thinking is going to take us back full circle to Mishima, but on the way let us consider another engagement with the problem of nihilism that dates from shortly after the publication of Nishitani's book on the topic. The art of film, which provides another example of the way Japan has appropriated from the West in order to produce work of the first rank, will afford us a final approach to Japanese thought by way of a peculiarly modern medium.

While Kurosawa's *Rashomon* (1950) is probably the Japanese film that is best known in the West, his *Ikiru* (1952) is in many ways more profound.[21] The title is the plain form of the verb "to live" and may best be translated as "living." In any case, the topic of the film is living, or how to live, in the face of death—and with this we return to a major theme in our discussion of *bushidō*.

The film begins with a close-up of an X-ray of the protagonist's stomach, which (the narrator's voice-over tells us) shows symptoms of cancer. The protagonist's exterior is presented in the next shot, where we see him—his name is Watanabe and he is the chief of the Citizens' Section in City Hall—sitting at his desk. Shortly thereafter the narrator informs us that the main character "is not very interesting yet. He's just passing the time. . . . It would be difficult to say that he is really alive." As Watanabe looks through a pile of papers, stamping them as he goes—the epitome of the automaton like bureaucrat—the narrator remarks, "This is pretty bad. He is like a corpse, and in fact he has been dead for the past twenty-five years."

In the context of the strict work ethic of postwar Japan, the film's opening scenes are a stinging indictment of the stultifying nature of office work in the public sector—but also, by extension, of all the kinds of work with which modern Japanese narcotize their existence. And because a much larger part of one's identity in Japan comes from one's occupation than is the case in most other countries, Kurosawa's criticism cuts deeply into the question of what it means to be a human being in modern Japanese society. On the other hand, one could argue that at least one feature of *bushidō* persists in contemporary Japanese life: the sense of honor and duty to one's superiors. It is common, for example, for politicians or heads of companies in Japan to resign at the first public sign of impropriety on their part, in order to save face and leave the image of the party or company untainted. (This response seems incomprehensible to chief executive officers in this country, where the immediate reaction is always to announce one's intentions to fight to the bitter end while one searches for someone else to lay the blame on.)

Watanabe goes to the hospital to get the results of some tests that have been done because of a stomach problem. The doctor has diagnosed the cancer and reckons that the patient has only six months to live, but when Watanabe comes in, the doctor lies to him (as is still the custom in Japan in such cases), saying "it's just a light case of ulcers." But, as a result of a strange encounter just before going into the doctor's consulting room, Watanabe knows the truth. The realization of his imminent death serves to pull him out of his absorption in his job, with the result that he abruptly stops going in to the office—after not missing a day's work for twenty-five years!

He hopes for some solace from his son and daughter-in-law, with whom he lives, but they callously reject him before he can tell them about his devastating realization. Thus an even more fundamental context for Watanabe's identity than his job—his relationship to his family—is shattered. We learn later that after Watanabe's wife died he declined to remarry out of consideration for his son, and Watanabe himself at one point explains his total dedication to his deadening work as being "all for my son's sake." Such parental self-sacrifice (though usually on the part of the mother) is the norm in Japan, and is the counterpart of the Confucian filial piety that parents expect from their offspring. So, to a degree that may be extreme even in Japan, Watanabe has devoted himself to the raising of his son in addition to his work; and now, with his son's rejection of him, as well as his alienation from his job, everything that gave his life meaning has collapsed. The abyss of nihility yawns as it seldom does in a normal Japanese life; the nothingness of death stares him in the face in true existentialist fashion.[22]

The protagonist's response to his confrontation with death is quite consonant with Western existentialist thinking as well as with Zen. Rather than reject or attempt to transcend the everyday routines of his life, Watanabe re-engages them, transfigured, with an unprecedentedly vital enthusiasm. He throws himself back into his job, but in a completely new way, devoting his energies to having an insalubrious swampy area drained and a neighborhood park built in its place. He thereby succeeds, in his last months, in getting something genuinely meaningful done in the context of his formerly deadening occupation. But this account of some of the major themes of the film gives no indication of the cinematic techniques with which Kurosawa elaborates these themes and lends them such power. The movie is one of the great masterpieces of mid-twentieth-century cinema—as are the works of another Japanese director during the same period, whose primary concern is with stresses within the family that are occasioned by the modernization of the country. (With this focus we move away from the major concerns of Mishima, but the Japanese sense of self is so intimately bound up with the family that the detour is justified.)

Ozu Yasujiro, who between 1927 and 1962 made around sixty-five feature films, is often referred to as the most "Japanese" of Japanese film directors.[23] If a feature of being "Japanese" is being eclectic in one's ability to appropriate foreign influences—Ozu was a keen admirer of early Hollywood movies—

then this judgment is apt. At any rate, there are few better ways to get a feel for the modernizing Japanese culture of the 1950s than to see some of Ozu's films of the period.[24]

Ozu's films almost invariably take as their subject the family, with whatever drama there is being provided by the process of the family's dissolution. Since the sense of self in Japan is always closely bound up in relationships, and especially family relationships, the breaking up of the family provides rich material for human drama. Ozu's treatment is sufficiently penetrating psychologically that in his films the family become a microcosm for the whole society and even—insofar as his characters transcend cultural boundaries—for the human world in general.

The portrayal of the family takes place mostly in the home, and no other director has been as successful as Ozu in presenting the internal architecture of the Japanese house as an embodiment of the soul and spirit of its inhabitants. Ozu is also famous for his low positioning of the camera: It is usually only three feet from the floor, which might seem odd until one realizes that this is eye-level for someone sitting in the traditional Japanese way (on one's heels or cross-legged) on a tatami-matted floor. Ozu uses silence, stillness, and the stark contrasts of black and white film in ways that evoke a mood strongly reminiscent of Zen. Over the decades he refined his filmic technique relentlessly, returning repeatedly to the same stories and themes, and using the same actors and cowriter over long periods of time, in order to strip down the essentials of his art to the bare minimum. In his mature work, pretty much the only form of transition is the cut; the camera hardly ever moves, and the length of the shots stays remarkably constant. On the one hand, this pacing gives Ozu's films a somewhat meditative tone with an occasionally hypnotic effect, and on the other it conveys a strong sense of the inevitability of fate in human affairs.

Some of Ozu's films directly invoke the spirit of Zen. *Late Spring,* for instance, contains scenes of a tea ceremony (though very much a "society" affair), a Noh play, and the famous sand and rock garden at Ryoanji temple in Kyoto. (There are also several scenes in this film where characters pour drinks for each other.) The extent to which Ozu has distilled the essence of Japanese culture of that period is remarkable. And in the course of elaborating his customary theme of the breakup of the family, he conveys a powerful sense of the dichotomy that is probably more radical in Japan than in any other modern society: that between outer appearances and one's true inner feelings.

The story of *Late Spring* is simple: A widowed university professor lives with his daughter Noriko, who in her fondness for her father is happy to take care of him. Being in her late twenties, however, she is under tremendous social pressure—both from other members of her family and from her friends—to get married, since that is simply what "one does." (Arranged marriages were still the norm in 1949, and are common to this day in Japan.[25]) Noriko is able to resist this pressure until she is tricked into believing that her father is going to remarry and will thus have someone else to take care of him. Her aunt arranges a meeting with an excellent prospective husband (who is said to resemble Gary Cooper!), and after the meeting Noriko eventually—simply for the sake of some peace, one imagines—consents to marry the man. She leaves on her honeymoon, and the father is left alone in the house.

The film conveys an extreme sense of the overwhelming power of social pressures on individual freedom in Japanese society, and is at the same time—thanks to the superb acting—a very moving film emotionally. Just as restraint is a quality highly prized in human relationships in Japan because of the harmony it imparts to social interactions (and restraint is the keynote of Ozu's technique as a director), so does it also characterize the emotional lives of the protagonists in this film. Thanks to the consummate artistry with which the actors play the father and daughter, the emotional power generated (but never directly expressed) is excruciating in its intensity. On several occasions the daughter says "yes" when every fiber of her being is screaming "no" (or vice versa), and yet that scream comes silently, through facial expression alone. The film's ending is extremely poignant because both the main characters are unhappy. The viewer is left with the impression that the daughter has condemned herself to a life of utter misery and that the father will miss her terribly—and yet they have done what "one does." But such is life in the world of Japan.

Ozu worked with the same actors over and over again from film to film, and he was able to elicit performances from them that are on occasion overwhelming in their hieratic beauty. Whether Ozu was aware of it or not, his technique in directing his actors had a great deal in common with the Zen approach to physical discipline, as well as with the technique of the Noh. He apparently had his actors and actresses repeat certain movements and gestures over and over again, ad nauseam, until every drop of spontaneous feeling had been eliminated. After that point was surpassed, he would film, and the results are often uncanny in the impression they give of controlled spontaneity. The combination of this technique and the reappearance in film after film of the same actors—often in very similar roles and even bearing the same names—further enhances the archetypal quality of the characters.[26]

Having left the world of Mishima, it will be in the spirit of Ozu to effect an abrupt cut back, in order to gather together the threads of Japanese thought we have been considering.

Mishima's Ends

At the age of thirty, having devoted the major part of his life up to then to literature, which—though itself a form of action—is hardly a very physical activity, Mishima resolved to take up bodybuilding, a discipline he engaged in for the rest of his life. This was partly an attempt (apparently successful) to overcome a tendency toward ill health, but it was also Mishima's way of counteracting the tendency of writing to "corrode reality away" before he had a chance to experience life directly. Over the ensuing fifteen years he became proficient at boxing, karate, and *kendō*. Having been born into an aristocratic family, Mishima may, in a certain sense, have been returning to his roots in these endeavors. He also saw himself as participating in a revival of the old samurai ideal of combining the ways of the martial and the literary arts. He gives a fascinating and, at times, enigmatic account of this aspect of his life in the long essay *Sun and Steel,* written in 1968.[27]

While there was surely a strong element of narcissism in Mishima's concern for the body during the last part of his life (a concern intensified, it seems, by his homosexuality), his devotion to various forms of physical regimen nevertheless situated him authentically in the Japanese tradition of arts and letters. He was obsessed from early on by the desire to die "a beautiful death," and believed this would be impossible unless the body had been developed to perfection. It is an impressive fact about Mishima's suicide that on the morning of the day he ended his life he sent to the publisher the final installment of the fourth volume of his last work, *The Sea of Fertility.*[28] There is a sense that Mishima had reached the height of his powers, that he knew it, and that he had no wish to go on to live a life of both physical and artistic decline. His suicide would thus be his ultimate aesthetic act.

Toward the end of his life, Mishima developed an interest in Japanese Neo-Confucianist philosophy, and especially in its idea of the importance of the unity of thought and action.[29] Since he had come to think that Japanese culture had degenerated lamentably since the Second World War, and his recent attempts to call attention to this decline through polemical essays had fallen on deaf ears, it was a logical consequence of his philosophy that he should take more drastic action. To this extent Mishima's suicide was in keeping with the tradition of *kanshi,* a type of *seppuku* whose purpose was remonstration with one's feudal lord or a more general reproach of the ruling powers.[30]

One can assemble a multiplicity of plausible perspectives, negative as well as positive, on Mishima's suicide—which appropriately reflects the inherent multiplicity of Japanese thought. One can see him as the consummate exemplification of the way of the samurai, in knowing the right time to die and having the courage to act accordingly. He can be reproached for vain egocentrism in his irresponsible disregard for his wife and the sacred institution of the family. One can argue that since he was beyond the peak of his powers, nothing of value was lost in his ending his life when he did, and that a great deal was gained, because all was not right in the state of Japan at the time, and his *seppuku* shocked at least some people into a realization of the crisis. We can say that he acted out of pure vanity, unable to bear the prospect of the disintegration of the body he had worked so hard to perfect. A Nietzschean could argue that he died at just the right time—or else that his obsession with the body was too literal and blinded him to the fact that old age would be incapable of destroying the magnificent body of work he had produced. Or one could say from the perspective of someone like Nishitani Keiji that his response to the problem of nihilism was too shallow: that the way in which he wanted to reassert the ancient Japanese spirit suggests that he failed to plumb the depths of the self sufficiently to reach a layer deeper than that of national identity.

Mishima came in for a great deal of criticism, both in Japan and abroad, for the right-wing views and support of the emperor system expressed in his later polemical essays and speeches. However, it is hard to take those views too seriously, in view of Mishima's quite apolitical stance during most of his career. And indeed they are peripheral to his main work—a body of literature, some of which is the finest in any modern language, and which embodies an important philosophy of existence that partakes genuinely of the best of the Japanese tradition.

Notes

1. An English translation of the story by Geoffrey W. Sargent can be found in *Yukio Mishima, Death in Midsummer and Other Stories* (New York: New Directions, 1966). When not used in citations, Japanese names will be given Japanese style, with the family name first.

2. Two biographies of Mishima are available in English: John Nathan, *Mishima: A Biography* (Boston: Little, Brown & Co., 1974), and Henry Scott Stokes, *The Life and Death of Yukio Mishima* (New York: Farrar, Straus & Giroux, 1974). An outstanding poetic celebration of Mishima's work is Marguerite Yourcenar, *Mishima: A Vision of the Void* (New York: Farrar, Straus & Giroux, 1986). Available on videotape, and well worth seeing, is Paul Schrader's film *Mishima: A Life in Four Parts.* A comprehensive list of films and videos on Japan, entitled *Audio Visual Resources,* is available on request from the New York office of the Japan Foundation.

3. The novelist Tanizaki Junichiro offers a lyrical description of the aesthetic delights of eating soup from a lacquer bowl in his essay *In Praise of Shadows,* trans. Thomas J. Harper and Edward G. Seidensticker (New Haven: Leete's Island Books, 1977). Although amusingly cranky in parts, this essay is an excellent introduction to certain aspects of Japanese aesthetic culture by one of the country's greatest novelists.

4. The most striking example would appear to be the existential conception of death elaborated by Martin Heidegger in his masterpiece *Being and Time,* which bears a remarkable similarity to the understanding of death that informs the philosophy of the Japanese samurai tradition. For some evidence that Heidegger may have been influenced by Japanese ideas concerning death, see Graham Parkes, "Heidegger and Japanese Thought: How Much Did He Know, and When Did He Know It?" in Christopher Macann, ed., *Heidegger: Critical Assessments* (London: Routledge, 1992).

5. For a good account of East Asian philosophies of the body, see Yuasa Yasuo, *The Body: Toward an Eastern Mind-Body Theory,* trans. Thomas P. Kasulis and Nagatomo Shigenori (Albany: SUNY Press, 1987).

6. An excellent cultural history of Japan is H. Paul Varley, *Japanese Culture* (Honolulu: University of Hawaii Press, 1973).

7. A helpful overview of the transmigration of Buddhist ideas from India to China and then Japan is provided by Alan Watts, *The Way of Zen* (New York: Pantheon Books, 1957). For a more detailed analysis see the monumental two-volume study by Heinrich Dumoulin entitled *Zen Buddhism: A History,* trans. James W. Heisig and Paul Knitter (New York: Macmillan, 1989).

8. An excellent treatment of the philosophy of Zen Buddhism, with a special focus on Dōgen and Hakuin, is T. P. Kasulis, *Zen Action, Zen Person* (Honolulu: University Press of Hawaii, 1971). See, on the present topic, the section entitled "*Mu* as the Context of the Zen Person" (pp. 40–42).

9. A selection of Hakuin's writings is available in English: *The Zen Master Hakuin: Selected Writings,* trans. Philip Yampolsky (New York: Columbia

University Press, 1971). The experience of the "great death" as described by Hakuin bears a striking resemblance to the revelation of "the abyss" in Nietzsche and the encounter with the nothingness disclosed by *Angst* described by Heidegger. For a comparative treatment of some of the ideas of Rinzai Zen, see Graham Parkes, "The Transformation of Emotion in Rinzai Zen and Nietzsche," *The Eastern Buddhist* 23/1 (1990): 10–25.

10. An account of the relation of Zen to swordsmanship can be found in Daisetz T. Suzuki, *Zen and Japanese Culture* (Princeton: Princeton University Press, 1959), chapters 5 and 6. A real gem of a Zen treatise relating the way of the sword to experience in general is Takuan Sōhō, *The Unfetterd Mind*, trans. William Scott Wilson (Tokyo and New York: Kodansha International, 1986); see especially the first section, "The Mysterious Record of Immovable Wisdom."

11. Excerpts from the classic text of *bushidō* have been translated into English: Yamamoto Tsunetomo, *Hagakure: The Book of the Samurai,* trans. William Scott Wilson (Tokyo and New York: Kodansha International, 1979). Also of interest are Mishima's reflections on the contemporary relevance of the text in *Yukio Mishima on Hagakure: The Samurai Ethic and Modern Japan*, trans. Kathryn Sparling (Tokyo and Rutland, Vt.: Tuttle, 1978).

12. Not surprising is the appearance of a number of books about sports with titles like "Zen and the Art of . . ." and "The Tao of . . ." The first of these is still, I think, the best: Eugen Herrigel, *Zen in the Art of Archery* (London: Routledge Kegan Paul, 1953).

13. Takuan, *The Unfetterd Mind*, pp. 30–31.

14. A concise introduction to the tea ceremony is Horst Hammitzsch, *Zen in the Art of the Tea Ceremony* (New York: St. Martin's Press, 1980). For a more detailed account, see A. L. Sadler, *Cha-no-yu: The Japanese Tea Ceremony* (London, 1933).

15. Kawabata Yasunari, *A Thousand Cranes,* trans. Edward G. Seidensticker (New York: Knopf, 1958).

16. A good introduction is Donald Keene, *Nō: The Classical Theater of Japan* (Tokyo and Palo Alto: Kodansha International, 1966). Classic translations of some of the classic plays can be found in Arthur Waley, *The Nō Plays of Japan* (London, 1921), and Ezra Pound and Ernest Fenollosa, *The Classic Noh Theater of Japan* (New York: New Directions, 1959). The latter was first published in the United States in 1917, but the 1959 edition includes an interesting essay on the Noh by William Butler Yeats.

17. A modern version, as it were, of Noh drama is *Butoh,* a quintessentially Japanese form of theater involving music and dance, but which generally uses

white-face, makeup, and body paint instead of masks. The only comprehensive treatment in English is Jean Viala, *Butoh: Shades of Darkness* (Tokyo: Shufunotomo, 1988). A fine collection of photographs can be found in Mark Holborn, et. al., *Butoh: Dance of the Dark Soul* (New York: Aperture, 1987). See also the videotape *Butoh: Body on the Edge of Crisis.*

18. The only overview of modern Japanese Philosophy in English has unfortunately long been out of print: Gino K Piovesana, S.J., *Contemporary Japanese Philosophical Thought* (New York, 1969). Some aspects of the early appropriation of Western philosophy in Japan are touched on in my essay, "The Early Reception of Nietzsche's Philosophy in Japan," in Graham Parkes, ed., *Nietzsche and Asian Thought* (Chicago: University of Chicago Press, 1991), pp. 177–99. Discussions of correspondences between Japanese philosophy and the thinking of Martin Heidegger can be found in Graham Parkes, ed., *Heidegger and Asian Thought* (Honolulu: University of Hawaii Press, 1987).

19. An excellent account of this process, in the context of an insightful discussion of the phenomenon of nihilism in general, is to be found in Keiji Nishitani, *The Self- Overcoming of Nihilism*, trans. Graham Parkes with Setsuko Aihara (Albany: SUNY Press, 1990).

20. This suggestion is based on Nishitani's discussion of the import of nihilism in the Japanese context in *The Self-Overcoming of Nihilism.*

21. *Ikiru* is available under that title both on videotape and on laser disc.

22. There is no evidence that Kurosawa was familiar with the writings of the European existential thinkers, but the film is uncannily reminiscent of the treatments of such themes as anxiety, nothingness, and death in Kierkegaard, Nietzsche, and Heidegger.

23. If this output seems considerable, one should bear in mind that the Japanese film has always been one of the most prolific in the world. It is just that most of it has been, until fairly recently, for domestic consumption only.

24. An excellent trio of films by Ozu (available on videotape) dealing with the stresses on the Japanese family structure caused by modernization is: *Late Spring* (1949), *Early Summer* (1951), and *Tokyo Story* (1953). An exquisite later film dealing with a slightly earlier period (available on laser disc as well as videotape) is *Floating Weeds* (1959; one of Ozu's few films in color). Two good sources in English on Ozu are Donald Richie, *Ozu* (Berkeley & Los Angeles: University of California Press, 1974) and David Bordwell, *Ozu and the Poetics of Cinema* (Princeton: Princeton University Press, 1988).

25. A survey a few years ago estimated that as recently as 1966 fully fifty percent of marriages in urban areas in Japan were arranged *(o-miai)*—in rural

areas the figure was 63 percent—while nowadays the figure has dropped to around 25 percent.

26. After seeing *Late Spring, Early Summer, and Tokyo Story* the viewer is bound to see Hara Setsuko as *the* (good) daughter, Ryu Chishu as *the* (benevolent) father, and so on. Ozu's apparently obsessive return to the same characters and themes in film after film has, of course, its counterparts in Western art—in Cézanne's persistent return to the Montagne St. Victoire, for example.

27. Yukio Mishima, *Sun and Steel*, trans. John Bester (Tokyo and New York: Kodansha International, 1970).

28. The novels of the tetralogy, which—while they are perhaps not his best works—contain many interesting philosophical ideas, are: *Spring Snow, Runaway Horses, The Temple of Dawn,* and *The Decay of the Angel.* His greatest novels, and the most interesting philosophically, are (in my opinion) *The Temple of the Golden Pavilion* (1956) and *The Sailor Who Fell from Grace with the Sea* (1963).

29. Japanese Neo-Confucianism arose in the sixteenth and seventeenth centuries, the major interest being in the work of the medieval Chinese philosophers Chu Hsi and Wang Yang-ming.

30. A discussion of the various types of *seppuku* can be found in Jack Seward, *Hara-Kiri: Japanese Ritual Suicide* (Tokyo and Rutland: Tuttle, 1968).

Chapter 5

Feminine Sensibility in the Heian Era

DONALD KEENE

The influence of women writers on Japanese literature has been significant, and this essay by Donald Keene discusses the cultural and literary ramifications of this influence. Using examples from poetry, autobiography-diary, and fiction, Keene demonstrates that the "feminine sensibility" of the Heian period is an important feature of Japanese culture and aesthetics.

One of the most striking features of Japanese literature is that so many masterpieces were written by women. This is not true, however, of all periods. Although women poets and novelists were prominent between the eighth and twelfth centuries, hardly a woman writer of distinction appeared between the thirteenth and nineteenth centuries, and in modern Japanese literature the role of the woman writer has been relatively modest. Obviously, the varying position of women at different epochs of Japanese history accounts in large part for the extent of their participation in literary activity. During the long medieval period, when women were badly educated and kept in a position of subservience to men, they had little opportunity to display literary talent. In contrast, the position of women at the Heian court in the tenth and eleventh centuries was perhaps the highest of any period in

* From his *Appreciations of Japanese Culture,* 1971.

Japanese history, at least until recent days. Of course, only a few thousand people enjoyed the particular kind of freedom that prevailed at the court. Elsewhere in the country the people lived under conditions of extreme duress. But these few thousand people created a body of writing that is considered today to be the finest flowering of Japanese literature, and the chief works were written by women.

In this essay I shall consider both the reasons why women played so conspicuous a part in Heian literature and the peculiar significance for Japanese literature in general of the triumph of feminine sensibility. If we examine the *Manyōshū,* the oldest anthology of Japanese poetry, compiled in the middle of the eighth century, we find poems by women even among the earliest works included. One by the Empress Kōgyoku, who died in 661, indicates how far back the tradition of women writing artistic poetry goes. Other examples are found from every period covered by the anthology. Many poems were exchanged with men, as part of a real or pretended courtship; this was to become an important function of Japanese poetry in later times. In the *Manyōshū* we find already a characteristically feminine poetry that later became the dominant tone of Japanese poetry as a whole, but the *Manyōshū* is prevailingly masculine in its tone. The most masculine of the poems are the *chōka,* or long poems, written by such men as Kakinomoto no Hitomaro and Yamanoe no Okura. Their poems are often public: that is, they describe not the poet's private emotions but the splendor of a new palace, the grief of the nation over the death of a princess or perhaps the misery of poverty or the uncertainty of life. The greater amplitude of the *chōka,* which might be in as many as fifty or a hundred lines, as contrasted with the five lines of the *tanka,* which became the classic verse form, permitted the poets to treat themes of greater intellectual complexity than was possible in the *tanka.* Women rarely wrote *chōka,* either at this time or later, and those they wrote are identical in tone with their *tanka,* taking no advantage of the greater scope. On the other hand, their *tanka* differ not only from the *chōka* written by the male poets of the *Manyōshū,* but also from their poems in the same form. To make this more concrete, let me give the example of *tanka* by Lady Kasa and her lover Ōtomo Yakamochi, two *Manyōshū* poets. Here is a poem Lady Kasa sent to Yakamochi:

In the loneliness of my heart
I feel as if I should perish
Like the pale dewdrop
Upon the grass of my garden
In the gathering shades of twilight.[1]

The images found in this poem occur in much later Japanese poetry, and all are feminine. The woman is alone, waiting in vain for her lover to come. In her grief she imagines she will fade away like the dew. The lover's negligence does not arouse her anger, nor is she torn by violent jealousy or apprehension. Instead, she yields despondently to her fate. And the time of day is twilight, not the glare of noon nor the blackness of the night, but the hour of melancholy and bittersweet pain rather than of tragedy. In contrast, here is a poem by Yakamochi, possibly addressed to Lady Kasa:

> Over the river ferry of Saho,
> Where the sanderlings cry—
> When can I come to you,
> Crossing on horseback
> The crystal-clear shallows?[2]

This obviously is an entirely masculine poem in both its tone and imagery. But even in a sadder poem by Yakamochi, suggesting an unhappy love affair, the masculinity is apparent:

> Rather than that I should thus pine for you,
> Would I had been transmuted
> Into a tree or a stone,
> Nevermore to feel the pangs of love.[3]

The disappointed lover, unlike his mistress, has no desire to fade away like the dew. Instead, he would prefer to become an object insensitive to the pangs of love.

This difference between masculine and feminine expression is obvious, and parallels may of course be found in many other literatures. What makes it of special relevance to Japanese literature is that the masculine tone of the *Manyōshū* was to yield in future centuries to a feminine sensibility even on the part of male poets. In other words, the poetry in the *Manyōshū* written by women was to set the tone for later compositions both by men and women.

It is hard to say why this should have been true, but probably it was related to the functions of poetry in Japan. Already in the time when the *Manyōshū* was compiled men at the court were composing chiefly poems in the Chinese language. The court, in the attempt to emulate the great continental civilization, had taken over bodily the framework of Chinese government and laws, imported Chinese architecture and sculpture, and adopted Chinese dress. All these importations were presently modified to suit the different Japanese temperament, but their origins were unmistakably Chinese. The Japanese court also felt the need of proving to the Chinese that their country was civilized. Earlier, the Japanese had compiled in 720 an official history of the country, the *Nihon Shoki,* written in Chinese after a Chinese model, and they probably felt the need of showing off a literature in Chinese as well. Chinese had the dignity enjoyed by Latin in medieval Europe, and writing in the vernacular was considered to be undignified if not vulgar. Promotion at court was granted to noblemen who could produce poems in Chinese, but not in Japanese. Furthermore, in keeping with Chinese views, literature came to mean poetry and learned essays, and did not include fiction or works of a frivolous nature. The members of the court, who had ample leisure for such pursuits, devoted themselves increasingly to writing poetry and essays in Chinese.

Chinese, however, was a foreign language, and the Japanese could not acquire it easily. Most of them achieved in their compositions no more than grammatical accuracy, though even this was sometimes beyond their capacities. Their poems in Chinese were rather like the Latin poems composed by schoolboys today; though they are incapable of expressing themselves freely in Latin they can get good marks by patching together phrases from Latin writers and observing the rules of metrics. Composition in Chinese not only involved using a language totally dissimilar to Japanese both in structure and sounds, but also the characteristic imagery of the language. The poets of the *Manyōshū* had used such familiar Japanese imagery as the swaying seaweeds in the ocean, the great ship one can trust in, the clarity of the mountain stream, but these are not typical of Chinese poetry. Instead, the Japanese poets writing in Chinese were forced to describe mountains in China they had never seen, compare sad or felicitous occurrences in their own lives to ancient Chinese examples, or to sing the praises of flowers or trees merely because their names fitted easily into Chinese metrics. As may easily be imagined, most of this poetry is exceedingly poor.

Women, however, were not expected to learn Chinese. For one thing, they did not serve as officials, and had no need therefore of proving their ability at Chinese. Chinese, in any case, was considered to be unladylike, rather as the study of surgery or hydraulic engineering would be in our day. The women of the court in fact sometimes learned Chinese, but it was considered to be in bad taste if they revealed this. They therefore continued to write poetry in Japanese, usually in the *tanka* form. By the ninth century the invention and widespread adoption of the Japanese syllabary, the *kana,* made it far easier to write Japanese poetry than with the Chinese characters used by the *Manyōshū* poets. The *kana* naturally came to be associated with women's writings since men were expected to write in Chinese. However, men still composed Japanese poetry when addressing themselves to women, as a part of courtship. Had it not been for this circumstance the writing of Japanese might have been discontinued altogether, or relegated to a minor place. In Korea and Viet Nam, two other countries that had fallen into the orbit of Chinese culture and adopted the Chinese writing, literature in the vernacular was almost swamped by the superior prestige of Chinese.

The first statement of the ideals of Japanese poetry was given by a man, Ki no Tsurayuki, in the preface to the collection *Kokinshū*, completed in 905. It enumerated the circumstances under which men composed poetry: "When they looked at the scattered cherry blossoms of a spring morning; when they listened on an autumn evening to the falling of the leaves; when they sighed over the snow and waves reflected with each passing year by their looking-glasses; when they were startled into thoughts on the brevity of their lives by seeing the dew on the grass or the foam on the water; or when, yesterday all proud and splendid, they have fallen from fortune into loneliness; or when, having been dearly loved, they are neglected."

These occasions are all melancholy, in the vein of Lady Kasa's poetry. The list suggests that poets were not likely to be moved to write poetry by joy or cheerful sentiments, and that powerful tragedies, such as the death of a wife or child, the destruction of one's city by a disaster, or the horrors of war were not proper themes for Japanese poetry. These limitations would not have been admitted by the *Manyōshū* poets, who wrote in exhilaration or admiration and sometimes with a sharp awareness of tragedy. Of course, the shortness of the *tanka* did not permit the poet to treat adequately an intellectual subject or, for that matter, emotions harsher than melancholy. But the list of circumstances when men are moved to poetry also indicates that a feminine sensibility had become dominant by the time of the *Kokinshū,* in the early tenth century. If we analyze this list, the items reduce themselves to regret over the passage of time, especially to the decline of beauty, in itself a feminine preoccupation.

By far the most common subjects of Japanese poetry are the cherry blossoms and the reddening maple leaves of autumn. If one were obliged to read through the twenty-one imperial anthologies between the tenth and fifteenth centuries, one would certainly end by being thoroughly bored with both cherry blossoms and maple leaves. Both were used to suggest the passing of time, being symbols for the end of spring or the end of autumn. Although the cherry blossom is now established as the national flower of Japan, it does not figure importantly in the *Manyōshū,* where the most often mentioned blossoms are the plum. Plum blossoms seem to have been displaced because of an aesthetic consideration: they linger on the boughs for weeks, unlike the cherry blossoms that fall dramatically after two or three days. The perishability of beauty never failed to excite the tears of the beholders; perishability, as we have seen, came to be a necessary condition of beauty. The innumerable poems on the cherry blossoms are therefore rarely concerned with their appearance but instead with their significance as symbols for the perishing beauty of the beholders. The ladies of the Heian court, grieving over their loneliness or over being abandoned by their lovers, turned to writing poetry for consolation, and did not hesitate to use familiar, even hackneyed imagery to suggest their emotions. They infused this poetry with an intense sense of melancholy, as in a great poem by Ono no Komachi, a ninth-century poetess:

> The flowers withered,
> Their color faded away,
> While meaninglessly
> I spent my days in the world
> And the long rains were falling.

The best poetry of the Heian period, whether written by men or women, tends to be in this vein, though of course more masculine poetry existed. Not only did men abandon the public themes of the *Manyōshū* poetry or Yakamochi's powerful statements in favor of suggestion, but sometimes they even wrote in the guise of women, describing their anguish over a faithless lover. Women, as far as I know, never wrote in the guise of men.

The first important sustained work of Japanese prose by a known author is the *Tosa Diary,* written in 936 by Ki no Tsurayuki, the compiler of the anthology *Kokinshū.* It begins, "Diaries are things written by men, I am told. Nevertheless, I am writing one to see what a women can do." The author, a man, pretends to be a woman so that he may write this diary in Japanese, instead of Chinese, as would be customary in a man. Why did Tsurayuki wish to write in Japanese? Probably he felt that the highly personal nature of the contents could not be expressed in the formal Chinese the court scholars learned. Such personal writing, in any case, belonged to the domain of women. No earlier diaries by women survive, if any were written, but the introspective nature of the *Tosa Diary,* which describes, under the surface account of a sea journey, the grief of a man whose daughter has recently died, made it imperative to use Japanese.

Nevertheless, most literary men of the Heian period avoided using the Japanese language or creating anything resembling fiction. This meant that the literature of the supreme period of Japanese civilization was left by default to the women, who were at liberty both to write in Japanese and to express themselves in the genre of fiction.

The first major literary work of the Heian period is the *Kagerō Nikki,* translated by Edward Seidensticker into English as *The Gossamer Years,* an autobiography-diary covering the period 954 to 974. There can hardly be a more intensely feminine piece of writing. It is concerned almost exclusively with the personal feelings of the author. Not one word is devoted to the social or political life of the time, though the author was the wife of the prime minister, and not one trace of objectivity may be found in the author's descriptions of her activities. So intent is she on describing her woes that she gives no thought to possible reactions to her attitudes. She writes with a candor no man could approximate. We are stunned to read such a paragraph as:

> It began to appear that the lady in the alley [her husband's mistress] had fallen from favor since the birth of her child. I had prayed, at the height of my unhappiness, that she would live to know what I was then suffering, and it seemed that my prayers were being answered. She was alone, and now her child was dead, the child that had been the cause of that unseemly racket. The lady was of frightfully bad birth—the unrecognized child of a rather odd prince, it was said. For a moment she was able to use a noble gentleman who was unaware of her shortcomings, and now she was abandoned. The pain must be even sharper than mine had been. I was satisfied.[4]

The author states at the beginning of *Kagerō Nikki* that she decided to write her diary because she felt dissatisfied with the fabrications of the old romances. She tells us that she will be honest, and indeed, such undiluted honesty, when she gloats over a rival's downfall or rejoices over the death of her baby, would be hard to encounter elsewhere in literature. Certainly it does not make us feel affectionately towards the woman, but, on the other hand, we feel no barrier whatsoever between us and this tenth-century court lady. We may not approve of her, but we understand her perfectly. Because she confines herself to describing her emotions, always with the same naked honesty, and does not describe ephemeral events or intellectual speculations, her diary, like most other products of the Heian feminine sensibility, has a modernity that astonishes us today.

Kagerō Nikki is devoted mainly to the description of a woman unhappily married to a man who betrays her for many other women. Although of high birth herself, she is not the first wife of the prime minister but the second, and has therefore little hope of drawing her husband back once his affections begin to wander. We sympathize with her when she discovers he has taken up with another woman, but gradually her feelings become obsessive, and she is in the end incapable of responding when her husband attempts to make amends. She even seems to take a perverse delight in destroying what is left of his affection and she almost pleasurably records his coldness or his infidelities. When, after her husband has neglected her for some time, he finally pays her a visit, she pours out all her resentment. She records, "It may not have been entirely gracious of me, but I behaved like a stone for the rest of the night, and he left early in the morning without a word."

The author almost always feels sorry for herself. Again and again we find such sentences as, "The loneliness the pain, the sorrow I felt as we set off down the river can surely have had few parallels." Her absorption with herself makes her indifferent to other people's suffering: "There was a dead body lying in the river bottom as we passed, but I was quite beyond being frightened by that sort of thing."[5] In the *Manyōshū* there is a repertory of poems written by men on seeing dead bodies lying by the road or on the shore, in which the poet wonders who the man was and sympathizes with his family waiting for someone destined never to return. But the author of *Kagerō Nikki* has no compassion to spare.

The manner in which I have described the author may make her sound unattractive, but this perhaps is a hypocritical male judgment. The male poet on seeing a dead body felt he must respond to it in the appropriate manner, whether or not it actually aroused his deep emotions, and he attempted therefore to imagine the sufferings of others. For the poetess, however, a dead body and falling cherry blossoms had the same meaning: they tell her of her own mortality, her own loss of beauty. If the essential meaning is the same, it is clearly more elegant to speak of cherry blossoms than of corpses; hence, the development of a strict poetic diction in the Heian period. But if the author of the *Kagerō Nikki* does not react in the approved, hypocritical manner to news of her rival's unhappiness or to the death of someone she hates, there can be no doubting the genuineness of her feelings. She is bored, she has nothing to do but brood over her misfortunes, she feels that no one can be as unfortunate as herself, but she is a woman of extraordinary sensitivity, and she captures her feelings with such precision that we, reading her diary a thousand years after it was written, and living in a civilization that has nothing to do with hers, feel she is one of us. She is as much to be pitied and despised and loved as we are.

This diary, more than the various fairy tales and adventure stories of the tenth century, is the ancestor of *The Tale of Genji* by Lady Murasaki, the supreme masterpiece of Japanese literature. The earlier stories sometimes have charm, but we cannot believe in their characters any more than we can in the characters of the Greek romances with their incessant and tedious adventures. We believe in the characters of *The Tale of Genji* as we believe in the author of *Kagerō Nikki.* That no doubt is why it has often been referred to as the oldest novel in the world. It is also a modern novel in that it is introspective. The characters are not simply good or bad, young or old, but complex people torn by doubts and uncertainties. Grief arises not because of the machinations of villains or the spite of malevolent demons but as a necessary part of the human condition.

Lady Murasaki describes in her novel a supremely accomplished man. Prince Genji is peerlessly handsome, endowed with every artistic talent, intelligent and witty, an incomparable lover; but, above all, he is sensitive. He is a hero quite dissimilar to those found in normal Western novels or even in Japanese novels written by men. Not one word is said about Genji as a statesman, though we are told he occupies high office; not one word suggests he was accomplished at arms or possessed physical strength. He is not required to avenge his father's death, protect his country, rescue distressed damsels or, for that matter, to govern his country for the benefit of the people. The novel hardly contains any action in the normal sense, though it runs to over twelve hundred pages in English translation. Yet it is always absorbing, whether read in the manner of a conventional novel, or as the creation of a world. It describes a court that could never have existed, not because it is haunted by monsters or under some magic spell, but because it is totally lacking in ugliness. The world is incredibly beautiful. The nobles of the Heian court having no need to occupy themselves with warfare or administration or economic planning, devoted themselves entirely to the cult of beauty. In most societies where men have possessed unlimited wealth and unlimited leisure they have turned naturally to depravity, like the Roman emperors, but in the world of Lady Murasaki's novel the creation of beauty in every aspect of life was the chief concern. Infinite care was given to the palaces and gardens, to costuming and furnishings; but above all, the center of the courtiers' lives was love.

Courtship was extremely elaborate. The court ladies were almost always hidden, seated behind screens from which they could see out but which rendered them invisible, even to their lovers. A young man, hearing rumors about a beautiful woman, might pay a visit. Of course he could not hope to see her or even to hear her voice, but she might condescend to exchange poems with him. He would eagerly scan her answer, judging by the calligraphy, the ink, the paper, even by the way the paper was folded (as well as by the contents of the poem) whether or not he should pursue the affair. Or perhaps he might catch a glimpse of the long, trailing sleeves of her elaborate, twelve-fold robes, and decide from the exquisite harmonies of the colors of the different layers, revealed at the opening of her sleeve, that this indeed was a woman worth courting. Even when he had made his way behind her screen and into her chamber he might never enjoy a proper look at her. Not only was she enveloped in a tent-like set of robes, but she lived in the dark, hidden from the light of day, and her lover was obliged by custom and the fear of rumors to leave before the dawn. Even after a nobleman had married a woman he often did not live with her, and his visits at night hardly differed from those of a secret lover.

The world that appears in *The Tale of Genji* is so compelling that we have no choice but to believe in it. Yet we know from other evidence that the courtiers of the day were not all flawlessly behaved. There was violence, drunkenness, cruelty, all the familiar elements of our world. The fact that we do not miss these ugly elements is a tribute to the triumph of Lady Murasaki's feminine sensibility. Genji is the lover every woman dreams of. In the course of the novel he has a great many love affairs, but he is quite the opposite of Don Juan, at least as we see him in Mozart's opera. Don Juan is summed up by Leporello's catalogue. We are told how many women he has conquered in France, Turkey, Italy, and Spain, that some are tall and some short, some blond and some dark, but nothing suggests that all these women mean anything more to Don Juan than numbers. The more women the better, and once a woman's name has been entered in Leporello's catalogue Don Juan wants to get rid of her as quickly as possible. If, like Dona Elvira, she insists on pursuing Don Juan even after he has lost interest in her, he humiliates her by having Leporello make love to her. Despite the number of Genji's affairs, however, he never forgets or abandons a woman. Moreover, he acts differently towards each, responding to her temperament. He is the great noble when he makes love to Lady Rokujō, the demon lover when with Yūgao, tender and unassertive with the timid Lady of Akashi, fatherly to Tamakazura. He needs each woman for precisely this reason: if, having found his ideal in

Murasaki, who becomes his wife, he had forsaken all other women, or had, on the other hand, merely conquered women instead of giving himself to them, his greatest artistic accomplishment, his skill at lovemaking, would have been wasted. This would have choked him artistically and it would also have deprived many women of their greatest happiness, for they were content even with the smallest part of Genji's affection. Genji never abandons a mistress merely because she had become old. Even when he makes a serious mistake and courts a woman who, when at last he sees her, proves to be comically ugly, he does not run from the scene like Don Juan, but looks after her as tenderly as if he truly loved her.

When we read this novel it never occurs to us to doubt that Genji could be so considerate, so sensitive, yet surely no such man has ever existed. His is a perfection we can believe in, an ideal that becomes a reality. This is not only a tribute to the novelistic skill of Lady Murasaki but to her femininity. No male author could have created such a character. The one thing Murasaki could not do with Genji was to allow him to grow old. The last glimpse she gives of him, as a man in his forties, is of a man handsomer than ever before.

The next chapter, which occurs about two-thirds of the way through the novel, opens with the words, "Genji was dead." I can think of no other novel in which the principal character dies at that point in the work, but Murasaki, by a stroke of genius, realized that to give full dimension to Prince Genji she must move from the world of his perfection to one more recognizably like our own. The last third of the novel deals mainly with two princes, Niou and Kaoru. Both are handsome and accomplished, but they are only fragmentations of Genji. Niou has Genji's ardor, his success with women, but he is insensitive and even at times cruel. Kaoru has Genji's sensitivity, but it is overdeveloped and renders him neurotic and incapable of action. The world, though still beautiful, is tinged by failure. It is a world where people love but misunderstand, where Niou conquers women he does not love and Kaoru is so paralyzed by his love for a woman that he cannot conquer her.

In the novels and diaries that followed *The Tale of Genji,* most of them by women, Kaoru rather than Genji is evoked. Genji, the ever-triumphant, flawless lover proved inimitable. Perhaps, as the Heian court itself lost its brilliance, it became harder for women to hope for a Genji. Instead we have many touching, sometimes heartbreaking accounts of frustrated love. The author of the *Sarashina Diary,* writing not long after the composition of *The Tale of Genji* in the early eleventh century, describes how she grew up in the provinces, far away from the capital. She heard about *The Tale of Genji,* apparently from people who recited chapters from memory, and prayed devoutly she might go to the capital where she would be able to read the whole work. In 1020, when she was twelve, her prayers were granted when her father took her to the court. She tells us that she was still ugly and immature, but she hoped that one day she would develop into a beautiful woman like Yūgao whom Genji had loved, or Ukifune, loved by Kaoru. She imagined herself especially as Ukifune, living in some lonely mountain retreat. She wrote, "Even if he came but once a year I would be content." But even that much happiness was denied her. Perhaps she never became a beauty; in any event, she was neglected. No Genji ever took pity on her and courted her. She spent her time alone, with nothing better to do than to immerse herself in *The Tale of Genji* and other old romances, finding in them a refuge from her life.

One night, at a religious ceremony, a certain gentleman addressed her. She writes, "He spoke gently and quietly. There was nothing about him to be regretted. . . . He said nothing rude or amorous like other men, but talked delicately of the sad, sweet things of the world, and many a phrase of his enticed me by its strange power into the conversation." The two talked of the beauty of the different seasons, and the man described a visit on a wintry night to the Great Shrine of Ise. He ended with, "Hereafter every dark night with gentle rain like tonight will touch my heart; I feel this has not been inferior to the snowy night at the palace of the Ise vestal." He left with these words. Not until the following year did the author of the diary have another glimpse of the man. He approached and assured her he had never forgotten the night of softly falling rain, but before they could converse people interrupted them.

She writes, "In the next year one tranquil evening I heard he had come into the princess's palace, so I crept out of my chamber with my companion. But there were many people waiting within and without the palace, and I turned back. He must have been of the same mind. He had come because it was so still a night, and he returned because it was noisy." She concludes the section, "There is nothing more to tell. His personality was excellent and he was not an ordinary man, but time passed, and neither called to the other."[6]

This is a far cry from *The Tale of Genji* where even an ugly princess can hope for a visit from the peerless Genji. But the *Sarashina Diary,* though a miniature work in a minor key, is curiously affecting.

In many other later works of the Heian period the failure of love is chronicled. The most unusual example is the story of *The Lady Who Loved Insects,* the twelfth-century account of a young woman who refuses to obey the social conventions. She deliberately allows her eyebrows to grow instead of plucking them, does not blacken her teeth in the manner expected of a court lady, and instead of admiring cherry blossoms and maple leaves, spends her time collecting disagreeable insects like caterpillars. She dislikes anything smacking of artifice, and asserts that her only interest is to "inquire into everything that exists and find out how it began." A certain captain, hearing of this curious young lady, goes to her house and peeps in on her. Intrigued, he sends in a poem, to which she can barely be persuaded to vouchsafe a reply. The captain apparently has had enough of this fantastic creature by this time, for he writes another poem, "In all the world, I fear, no man exists so delicate that to the hairtips of a caterpillar's brow he could attune his life."[7]

The comic resolution is unusual, but we are left with a pang of disappointment that the captain could not recognize the merits of this unconventional but somehow attractive girl. The failure of love becomes a conspicuous feature of the novels written by women; in those by men a happy ending is generally achieved, however unnaturally. For all its exaggeration, *The Lady Who Loved Insects* is entirely believable. The heroine with her alarmingly white teeth lives only for a moment, but she lives. In the works of fiction written by men of the time it is impossible to believe in the characters even for a moment. Such works as *Utsubo Monogatari* or *Ochikubo Monogatari*, presumably by men, are totally lacking in the introspection of the works by women authors, and tend to be crude and fantastic. The diaries by men are unrelievedly boring, consisting mainly of careful notations on meteorological phenomena and lists of ceremonies and promotions.

It is not hard to imagine why this was the case. The members of the Japanese court, despite the way they are portrayed in *The Tale of Genji,* were much occupied with official business. Love-making was undoubtedly of great importance to them, as to anyone else, but it was only a part of their lives, whereas it was everything to the court ladies. The women, as we know from their diaries, were bored and rarely left their quarters save for an occasional visit to a temple. Yet, unlike the ladies of a Turkish harem, they were well educated and their status was high. They were by no means mere playthings or the passive victims of the men's appetites. They spent their time reading, composing poetry and, above all, waiting for something to happen. They brooded over their lives, they worried about other people's feelings and motives, they imagined men who would be more considerate than the ones that actually visited them. Fiction was for them an extension of their lives, and not an excursion into fantasy, as it was for the men.

Not all the women writers were given to melancholy. The finest example of humorous writing in Japanese, perhaps the only truly witty book in the language is the *Pillow Book* by Sei Shōnagon, who wrote in the late tenth century. Sei Shōnagon served the Empress Sadako, a learned and accomplished woman who gathered around her a salon of amusing court ladies. For this small and special group of women there were more pleasant occupations than waiting for evening and the chance some man would visit them. Their privileged position enabled them to deal with men on equal terms. Sei Shōnagon especially delighted in discomfiting men with a well-placed witticism or with a display of her erudition. George Meredith in his *Essay on Comedy* put forward the proposition that only in a society where men and women met on equal footing was wit possible, though lower forms of humor always exist. Perhaps this was the one time that wit in Meredith's sense was possible in Japan. Be that as it may, the *Pillow Book* is unique in Japanese literature in its sharp observations, its brilliantly evoked vignettes of the court society, its apt generalizations on human nature. Its prevailingly cheerful tone distinguishes it from other writings by women of this period, but it shares with them a contemporary quality that comes from direct description of human experiences.

The appearance of this extraordinary group of women writers was to mold the shape of Japanese literature for centuries to come. The shadow of *The Tale of Genji*, the last third especially, lay over the novels composed for the next six hundred years. Imitations, variations, and distortions of its plot recurred in works written by men and women alike. The diary too, thanks to the Heian court ladies, developed in Japan into an important literary genre, rather than being considered as in the West a marginal form of literature. Again, whether the writer was a man or a woman, the style and manner of composition was tinged by the femininity of the Heian period. For centuries the court writers produced imitations of Heian literature, clinging to a language that had become archaic or obsolete. This kind of feminine sensibility was more likely to produce works that are still readable today than the masculine stories of a moralistic or didactic nature. The melancholy of a rainy evening, the preciousness of a beauty soon faded, the unspoken overtones of a casual remark, and all the rest of the characteristic features of the writings inspired by feminine sensibility in the Heian period, became the heritage not only of the handful of nobles at the court but of the entire Japanese people.

Notes

1. Translation from *Manyōshū*, edited by Nihon Gakujutsu Shinkōkai (Columbia University Press, 1965), p. 106.

2. Ibid., p. 134.

3. Ibid., p. 134.

4. *The Gossamer Years*, translated by Edward G. Seidensticker.

5. Ibid., p. 88.

6. Translation by Doi and Omori, in Keene, *Anthology of Japanese Literature*, p. 161.

7. Translation by Arthur Waley, in Keene, *Anthology of Japanese Literature*, p. 176.

Chapter 6

"Approach to Haiku" and "Basic Principles"

KENNETH YASUDA

Of all the types of Japanese literature, the haiku poem (17 syllables, 3 lines of 5, 7, 5 syllables respectively) is perhaps the most familiar to Western readers. Kenneth Yasuda's "Approach to Haiku" and "Basic Principles" provide a solid foundation for understanding this intriguing poetic form. Of particular interest to the Western reader is the connections Yasuda makes between haiku and painting and haiku and the aesthetic concerns of Western poetry. His description of the "aesthetic attitude," the "aesthetic experience," and the "haiku moment," with a number of poems as examples, will inform readers new to haiku as well as those already familiar with this most Japanese of literary forms. Additional information on haiku and the great haiku master, Bashō, can be found in Makoto Ueda's essay, "Impersonality in Poetry: Bashō on the Art of the Haiku," also in this collection.

An Approach to Haiku

A definition of the term haiku which will cover not only its formal characteristics but will also embody something of its breathing beauty and its allusive life is a difficulty which probably faces the definers of any art form. An additional hurdle in the case of haiku is the tendency of critics in the past to dismiss it as inconsequential for a variety of reasons which seem to have no relationship to its function and no appreciation of its accomplishments. We are not, however, so rich in beauty or tranquility or joy to be able to discard any creation so directly concerned with these qualities as is the haiku, concerning which Bashō noted: "From ancient times, those with a feeling for refinement . . . find joy in knowing the truth and insight of things."[1] For as the haiku is a major poetic form in Japan, I feel that it can become so in other countries, given some understanding of its nature and its aesthetics and its sort of power, a power which is similar in some respects to that of painting. I shall begin then by comparing haiku to painting.

Each time I look at an old painting on rich silk by a Chinese master of the T'ang Dynasty—especially one of the monochromes in Chinese ink, *mo*, by such a painter as Wang Wei or some later master of the Sung period—I am left speechless, my breath taken away in admiration. The effect of the picture, in black and white and with subtle gradations from white to black, is one of mysticism and extreme delicacy. Unlike an oil painting, this fills the space without filling it; as a sampan rises out of a silver mist on the Yangtse River, the faint outlines of distant mountains appear far beyond, and a pagoda's darker lines float between and above the misty veil over the rich valley.

A picture, whether the scene described above or a portrait painting, is easy to appreciate; even the inexperienced in matters of art can enjoy it just by looking at it. This is called intuition. Intuition is immediate, as the perception of color is immediate. In its essence it is non-judgmental, amoral, non-verbal, and uncritical, although after the intuiting moment the spectator may be filled with scorn or praise, and so on. Thus I hold with Croce, Dewey, and other thinkers on aesthetic matters that any work of art can be enjoyed through this act of immediate perception without conscious effort or reasoning.

The same holds true of poetry and, to a degree undreamt of in the West, of haiku in particular. Perhaps the inability of Western readers and critics to grasp the nature of haiku lies here. They are not yet accustomed, in spite of the efforts of the Imagists and their heirs, to a poetry that as Ford Maddox Ford said arouses "emotions solely by rendering concrete objects, sounds and aspects."[2] Perhaps as a vestige of the Victorianism they decry, an explicit interpretation is somehow felt as a necessity, not only by the reader but even by the poet. A far more complex reason, and one which serious Western critics have lately exposed as fallacious, probably lies in the attempts of poetry to justify its sort of intuitive material against the empirical successes of scientific thought; the age, unable to understand or to accept the values of poetry, assigns to it didactic, humanitarian, or propagandistic functions, a phase through which a certain Japanese group also passed.[3] As Allen Tate has said, "we are justifying poetry by 'proving' that it is something else, just as, I believe, we have justified religion with the discovery that it is science."[4] Is there almost a fear that the concrete experience, the intuition, is somehow "not enough" in the following comments of Cleanth Brooks on the general structure of Robert Penn Warren's poems, which he finds on the whole admirable?

> There is a rich and detailed examination of the particular experience with the conclusion, which may be drawn from the experience, coming as a quietly ironical statement or as modest and guarded understatement. It is as though the poet felt that only the minimum of commentary was allowable if he was not to do violence to the integrity of the experience.[5]

It would perhaps be a sly question to ask how much commentary is so minimum as not to "do violence to the integrity of the experience." And it is interesting to note that in discussing Yeats' poem "Blood and the Moon," Brooks finds that its value resides in part in the poet's refusal "to define the moralization except in terms of the specific symbols."[6]

The question as to whether "minimum commentary" is a valid part of the long poem or of certain types of subject matter is one which I do not feel is within the scope of this book. If this appears to be an ambiguous area in certain types of Western poetry, the attitude of the haiku poet is sharply defined. There can be no commentary, no conclusion; the concrete, sensuous material to be intuited must stand alone. While the latter concept is by no means strange to Western poetic thought, it may be that the clear-cut position of the haiku form may serve a useful purpose within the large body of Western poetry. Where Brooks has said that some poems demand a revision of our ideas of poetry, perhaps haiku can force a clarification of them. ("From time to time poets appear, who if they are accepted at all, demand a radical revision of the existing conception of poetry." *Modern Poetry and the Tradition*, p. vii.)

Even that most persistent of imagistic poets, William Carlos Williams, would not escape censure from Japanese critics, even though he has maintained that "all art is necessarily objective. It doesn't declaim or explain; it presents."[7] Yet the function of the explicit, prose statement in the first line of the following, beautiful poem seems primarily explanatory:[8]

so much depends
upon

a red wheel
barrow

glazed with rain
water

beside the white
chickens

Let us compare this with the following poem by Bashō, remembering that enjoyment that comes from a haiku comes intuitively and immediately, rather than through logical reasoning:

On a withered bough
A crow alone is perching;
Autumn evening now.

How clear it is that a great deal depends upon the crow, perching upon the withered bough; yet Bashō, complying with the exacting standards of haiku poetry, conveys its importance only through the concrete objects. Perhaps this is part of what he meant when he said: "The haiku that reveals seventy to eighty percent of its subject is good. Those that reveal fifty to sixty percent we never tire of."[9]

We feel instinctively that the air is clear in Bashō's haiku; the sky hangs gently above the horizon like a cobalt mirror. There, against a tranquil background of the autumn blue turning almost into deep black-purple, we can see the tall tree standing, distinct and still, above the gathering gloom of the autumn twilight, and a black crow perching alone on one of the withered branches. A loneliness is there, and a mystic power which holds us close with an acute feeling akin to melancholy sadness, tinged with acceptance. The three objects mentioned—the withered bough, a crow, autumn evening—have the same feeling and we are moved by and impressed with this common emotion existing among those three; and only through them can we feel that emotion, that sense of the essence of this autumn evening, through our intuition.

Here we want no adjective to blur our impression; the picture speaks for itself. We seek no metaphor or simile to make the picture clear, but simply let the objects do their part. If the picture is so beautiful that he who looks must admire, how superfluous and intrusive would it sound if the author were to exclaim, "Oh, how beautiful it is" and the like. If sad, we do not want him to tell us so, but we demand that he make it sad; then our understanding will supply the necessary adjectives. One advantage of this method, as Hughes has remarked, is that "there is a kind of force gained from the expression of this emotion once and once only through an appropriate image."[10] Indeed, the simple treatment of this kind, whether of a picture or of a haiku, is always the most difficult. It demands the true, mature artist, like the master Bashō.

Here is another example:

Underneath the eaves
A blooming large hydrangea
Overbrims its leaves.

Here we see the hydrangea growing with its large disks of clustered flowers by the house. "Overbrims its leaves," the poet puts it, to say aesthetically how the flowers bloom among and above the deep-green enamelled leaves. The poem has a bright light; it gives the impression of a rich oil painting drawn with the dynamic strokes of a masterful hand.

Another equally colorful picture is this haiku:

Scattered the peony!
One beside another pile,
Petals two or three.

The beauty of the splendid peony expresses itself. The richness of the flower has a magic touch to keep our attention; yet here, viewing its large petals piled one upon another rather than lying one above the other, we can feel their movement, a sense of weight exquisite enough to give the living texture of the petals, further vivified with a definite number of the petals—"two or three"—to give a concrete impression. Contrasted with the softness and barely perceptible weight, how appropriate is the dynamic cadence, "Scattered . . . !"

Color can be as important to haiku as to painting:

In the twilight gloom
Of the redwood and the pine
Some wisterias bloom.

There is a twilight touch to this scene. The lovely wisterias hang their clusters against the background of the semi-darkness of the redwood and the pine, whereby the sweet purple of the flower gains in softness and visual contrast. It reminds us of the rich coloring of some exotic painting, especially of the southern school of Wang Wei in the Sung period.

Thus haiku has something in common with painting, in the representation of the object alone, without comment, never presented to be other than what it is, but not represented completely as it is. For if the haiku poet moves us by presenting rather than describing objects, he does so by presenting the particulars in which the emotional powers of the things or scenes reside. And from these particulars comes the significance and the importance of his particular haiku. He renders in a few epithets what he experiences, so that imagination will fill those spaces with all the details in which the experiential value of the images reside. He does not give us meaning; he gives us the concrete objects which have meaning, because he has so experienced them. When we read such a poem, how true it is that the "meanest flower can give thoughts That do oft lie too deep for tears."

Basic Principles

In the foregoing section we have seen what haiku is like when compared with painting. For the more than five hundred years that Japanese poets have been composing haiku, they have found it a fit instrument for giving utterance to their experiences; it is the most compact, evocative verse-form crystallized by Japanese talents. Santei, the haiku poet with whom I lived for almost two years, has well expressed the supreme position that the form has for the Japanese literary artist; even though he attained great success as a novelist under his actual name, Masao Kume, he felt that the haiku was the greatest and most enduring flower of Japanese art:

> For me haiku was truly the gate which opened my literary career and even now I think of and yearn for the joy of appreciating and creating haiku as a haiku poet. Often I wonder why I did not spend my whole life as an artist as a pure haiku poet. . . . In regard to a unity in life, art, and mental attitude, there is no other artist for whom it is so harmonized as for the haiku poet. . . . Though Bashō and Issa are masters of the past, even now there are haiku poets like

> them. So the feeling that in a country like Japan haiku will always be the first and last art form is deeply held.[11]

Its long history, in itself, shows that it is able to satisfy certain poetic needs. Its ability to do so is, I feel, because its underlying aesthetic principles are the same as those for any art form in the East or West.

A haiku can be a thing of joy to any reader for the same reasons that a sonnet can be, although the techniques may seem so different that even as acute a reader as John Gould Fletcher, the noted Imagist poet, could occasionally be led astray in his judgment of it.* I hope therefore in the following pages to discuss the aesthetic nature of haiku, following generally the theories of Benedetto Croce, John Dewey, and others, many of whose basic positions seem to me shared by those Japanese haiku poets whose random observations have been preserved by Japanese critics. Such a discussion will have two purposes: first, to organize and unify basic aesthetic theory in regard to haiku; and second, to demonstrate that haiku, far from being an esoteric, purely Japanese form, incomprehensible to the West, shares common ground with all art in an important and significant manner.

1. Aesthetic Attitude

Let us suppose that a poet is looking at a rye field one sunny afternoon with two friends, one a farmer who owns the field and the other an entomologist. The farmer is explaining how lovely and rich his field is and how many bushels of rye it produces every year. While they are thus talking, a red dragonfly passes before them, and immediately the entomologist notices it. Perhaps he classifies it as an idle mental exercise, and may even remark on its beauty aloud to his friends. The poet, standing beside them, also sees the dragonfly and notices it light on a blade of rye, as do the other two. He is immediately interested in the dragonfly—in its color, form, and quality.

This is a happening shared by the three men. The farmer, in seeing the dragonfly, may have agreed with his friend the entomologist about its beauty,

* "The relationship of the Chinese classical poets to the Japanese *tanka* and *hokku* poets is, psychologically speaking, like the relation of full-grown and mature human figures to a group of rather small and temporarily attractive children. The *tanka* or the *hokku* poem is nothing more than a sketch." "The Orient and Contemporary Poetry" in *The Asian Legacy and American Life*, p. 159.

but it does not affect him. He is probably thinking of something else; perhaps he feels very proud of the rich rye field he owns. The value he places on his field is directly referable to the price the grain will bring him in the market place. His attitude might be called commercial.

The entomologist's attitude is scientific. As soon as he sees the red dragonfly, he ceases seeing it directly and sees it only as a part of his system of categories. If he had not recognized it, he would most likely have observed its characteristics by counting the number of its wings, legs, and so on, in reference to his entomological knowledge, and tried to arrive at some sort of conclusion. As Allen Tate has concisely put it, the scientific statement is "about a thing, a person, an experience, which relates it to something else, not for the purpose of giving us intensive knowledge of the thing, person, or experience, in itself and as a whole; but simply to give us, in varying degrees depending upon the exactness of the science under which it is viewed, the half-knowledge that limits us to the control of its extensive relations."[12]

In contrast to these two attitudes, the poet's is neither commercial nor scientific. His attention is directed not to his knowledge about the dragonfly, nor to the value of the rye field. He is interested in the object for its own sake. Furthermore, he is not aware even of how beautiful the object is or of how he is affected by it. An attitude such as this is aesthetic. I shall call it a haiku attitude.

This haiku attitude is a readiness for an experience for its own sake. The value of the experience does not lie outside the object as the value of the rye field lies outside of the object for the farmer; for the scientist, the value of the dragonfly lies in the object, but only as that object can be classified, generalized about, and related. Nor does the aesthetic value lie in the observer's emotion about the object or in the emotion aroused in him by the object, as when the scientist casually remarked on its beauty. A poet, when he is being a poet, cannot make such a statement. That is to say, he cannot interject anything of his personal or egoistic needs between himself and the experience; and it is interesting to note that Japanese critics and poets are most insistent upon the importance of this point.

As Otsuji (Seki Osuga), a noted poet and one of the greatest haiku theorists, puts it: "[We can enter the world of creation] when we are completely sincere and humble before nature, yet free and fearless; when we are never separated from nature; when we do not introduce idle fancy or fall into cogitation."[13] One aspect of the sincerity and humility he calls for is the poet's willingness to surrender cherished intellectual concepts before the reality of his experience: "It is unnecessary to believe in some ideology or personal philosophy in order to compose haiku, because, since they contain ideas, there is a danger that the poet will compose haiku through logic where pure feeling should be the motive."[14] This understanding is of course shared by Western critics such as Allen Tate, who points out that while there are poets who understand "the poetic use of their ideas," still a "conscious cultivation of ideas in poetry is always dangerous."[15]

Bashō notes that the poet must also surrender personal vanities and attitudes: "The verse of some poets tries to speak with charm but, on the contrary, is completely without it; the quality of charm is not to speak of charm. . . . Again the verse of some is over-ambitious and loses its sincerity."[16]

As for the poet's emotions, Otsuji remarks, as have many Western thinkers,* that far from aiding him toward clarity of vision, they will actually hinder him when they are of a certain sort: "When one is overwhelmed by sorrow, that sorrow cannot produce a haiku. When one is joyful and immersed in happiness, that feeling cannot produce a haiku."[17] Asō calls such emotions crude and hints at the reason why they have no place in aesthetic experience; they do not arise from the experience: "[In the aesthetic attitude] what we call feeling is not human feelings like joy, sadness, anger, etc. In Bashō's art of *haikai* these fresh, crude feelings are rather avoided. Such feelings as joy, anger, sadness or delight are subjective and are merely another form of subjectivism."[18] For, as Rainer Maria Rilke has said, "Verses are not, as people imagine, simply feelings; they are experiences."[19] The whole question of the role of emotion in experience is dealt with more fully in the succeeding pages.[20] I wish here only to point out that it can serve to separate the poet from experience.

When a person is interested and involved in the object for its own sake, then, a haiku attitude is formed. It is therefore said that a haiku attitude is a state of readiness for an experience which can be aesthetic. Without such an attitude it is impossible to have an aesthetic experience. However, the relationship between the attitude and the experience is not causative; when a person with a haiku attitude looks at an object, he does not necessarily have an aesthetic experience. Therefore I call it a state of readiness, of receptivity. As Otsuji has remarked, "the writer faces these conditions [which produce a haiku attitude] and his sympathetic activity is very strong; this alone cannot produce haiku."[21]

---

* E.g., John Dewey: "Portrayal of intoxication is a common device of the comic stage. But a man actually drunken would have to use art to conceal his condition if he is not to disgust his audience." (*Art as Experience*, p. 80.)

This readiness, moreover, must be for a disinterested form of single-minded activity. If it is not disinterested, it will be commercial, the farmer's attitude, or scientific, like his friend's. If it is not single-minded—i.e., for the sake of the experience alone—there will be only a relationship, not an experience. To clarify this point, let us remember that both the farmer and the entomologist related to the dragonfly; the act was casual, fleeting, and did not involve them in any serious manner. What is meant here by single-mindedness will be explored in the following section.

2. Aesthetic Experience

I have stated that a haiku attitude and an aesthetic experience are inseparable and coexist, but that a haiku attitude does not necessarily cause an experience to be aesthetic. Here the question arises as to the nature of the aesthetic experience which has been characterized above as being among other things, single-minded. By this is meant that during such an experience the observer has no awareness of himself as separate from what he sees or hears, from what he is experiencing. As he contemplates and experiences, becomes submerged in the object, there comes in Coleridge's phrase "a coalescence of subject and object" into one. As Otsuji has said, then "consciousness is completely unified"[22] and "the poet's nature and environment are one."[23]

John Dewey has called this state the "common pattern of experience": "The outline of the common pattern [of experience] is set by the fact that every experience is the result of interaction between a live creature and some aspect of the world in which he lives."[24] The condition exists until we reflect upon it. As Ernst Cassirer has put it, "If we consult immediate experience unmixed with reflection, the opposition of subject and object is shown to be wholly foreign to it. . . . What is grasped by consciousness here and now 'is' and is precisely in the form offered by direct experience."[25]

Otsuji has expressed almost the identical thought, indicating that the immediate experience is the aesthetic experience: "At the instant when our mental activity almost merges into an unconscious state—that is, the relationship between the subject and object is forgotten—we can experience the most aesthetic moment. This is what is implied when it is said that one goes into the heart of created things and becomes one with nature."[26]

The "form of direct experience" is the realization of what the object is, in its unity and oneness, in and for itself. It is an experiencing of what, in being itself, the object is, so that it becomes unique. It is, as Croce has maintained, an experiencing of the quality of the object.[27] The form of the color red is red—as we see it. The form of the crow, as Bashō saw it, is the crow. Experience then is always the interaction of a man and his environment.

What then are the uses of such words as *subject* and *object*—a dualism that has long plagued Western philosophy*—in dealing with aesthetic experience? They are convenient tools to distinguish aspects of a whole, to deal with its parts, and to analyze it. They are useful terms, as long as it is remembered that, in the aesthetic experience, the subject cannot exist without the object, nor the object without the subject, since they are one. Only as they are one, in a concrete and living unity, is there an aesthetic experience.† Otsuji, too, remarks on how inappropriate these dualistic terms are as applied to haiku arising out of a true aesthetic moment: "When one reaches the state where he is unattached and sings naturally, he can produce true haiku. The haiku composed under this condition transcend what we call the subjective or objective attitude."[28]

So far I have dealt with the role of the object in the aesthetic experience. To consider the role of the subject, let us begin with the question as to a particular artist's choice of a particular object out of the limitless objects available. That is to say, not all objects speak to an artist, inviting contemplation and absorption into an experience. Which one will become a part of a realization is dependent upon what Dewey has called "funded experience."

Let us take a musician, a painter, and a poet who are looking at a scene in which all three find a mountain, a brook murmuring through a flowering dale, and birds singing. As Dewey has observed, they cannot face this scene with no interests and attitudes, with no meanings and values drawn from their prior experience; he goes on to say: "Before an artist can develop his reconstruction of the scene before him . . . he observes the scene with meanings and values brought to his perception by prior experiences. . . . They cannot vanish and yet the artist continue to see an object."[29] Waggoner maintains the same position, emphasizing the reciprocity between object and subject:

---

* Alfred North Whitehead, in his enormously influential book, has suggestively described the situation: "The enormous success of the scientific abstractions, yielding on the one hand *matter* with its *simple location* in space and time, on the other hand, *mind*, perceiving, suffering, and reasoning, but not interfering, has foisted onto Philosophy the task of accepting them as the most concrete rendering of fact. (*Science and the Modern World*, p. 81.)

† These particular terms have never become as rigidly dualistic in Japan as in Occidental thinking and their oneness in experience is generally understood and accepted. Due to the historical associations around words such as *subject* and *object*, or *form* and *content*, the English words themselves seem immediately to suggest separate entities rather than distinguishable aspects of a whole. Wherever these terms occur hereafter, they are to be understood as defined in the text.

> The poet today then . . . must constantly concern himself with the immediately presented data of experience. . . . But concrete experience has meaning,—indeed, it has form, has existence—only in terms of values. . . . Even on the rudimentary level this is so: the phenomenon of attention, without which experience could not be said to exist because it would be, if anything, an indescribable blur, means exclusion as much as it means concentration. We contribute a part of the meaning. We interpret even as we see, not simply after we have seen. Awareness is a dynamic and purposeful activity.[30]

So categorical is the role of the observer's funded experience in his experience of the environment that Cassirer points out that "thus no content of experience can ever appear as something absolutely strange."[31]

The way, then, that each of our three artists synthesizes his experience is different not only because of their respective fields of art, but in Dewey's words because of "those memories, not necessarily conscious, but retentions that have been organically incorporated in the very structure of self."[32] Otsuji, in referring to "our real life" in the following passage, seems to mean what Dewey calls the "very structure of the self": "The spirit of composing haiku must be a searching which is both passive and active, to feel the dignity of unadorned nature in such a way as to reflect our real life, in all its diversities."[33] Croce, in dealing with the same concept, reveals the flexibility of the artist's funded experience and its capabilities for growth and change:

> The research of which we speak does not concern the superficial but the profound character of the man; it is not concerned with the congealed and solidified stratum [e.g., any political beliefs, any openly professed religion] but with the tide that flows beneath it. . . . Presuppositions are the philosophemes that everyone carries with him, gathering them from the times and from tradition, or forming them anew by means of his observations and rapid reflections. In poetical works, they form the condition remote from the psychological attitude, which generates poetical visions.[34]

In expanding what Croce above calls the poet's presuppositions gathered from the times, Waggoner concurs in the following manner: "All poetry exhibits to a greater or less degree—greatest of all in didactic poetry . . . and least in pure lyrics . . . —the patterns of assumption, attitude, and idea of the age and of the poet."[35]

Consequently, even were our three artists poets, they would not experience the common scene except differently, for in virtue of their different funded experiences, any aspect of the scene is potentially significant. As Bashō has said, "There is no subject whatever that is not fit for hokku."[36] What each selects out of the scene is what meaning he finds as the quality of the experience he realizes.

Why the artist contemplates this aspect of his environment rather than that is not his concern. Indeed, he is not completely free in the choice. He is solely interested in experiencing the object that does present itself, in and for itself. When he contemplates a scene, in virtue of his funded experience, any object that has meaning resonatory enough to respond to and answer the impulsion generated in him becomes his subject. He becomes so aware of it that his self is that awareness; he does not reflect on it. He is like a tuning fork placed before a vibrating one of the same frequency. When he contemplates the impassionate, living object he immediately realizes its quality just as the sound from the tuning forks will become audible. He is in a state of aesthetic resonation, a harmonized whole of all the meaningful experiences he has had, brought to bear upon the moment of aesthetic contemplation.

Every man, poet or not, as Dewey remarks, possesses a funded experience through which his insights are indeed his own: "I have tried to show . . . that the aesthetic is no intruder in experience from without, whether by way of idle luxury or transcendent reality, but that it is the clarified and intensified development of traits that belong to every normally complete experience."[37] But often we see only superficially, through the eyes of convention, prejudice, or tradition; as I have said, we can relate casually to objects instead of experiencing them. This is fatal for the poet, as a poet. His perceptions can become sharp only as his funded experience becomes easily available to him, as he strives to be sincere, to be devoted single-mindedly to the realization that is his. Only by doing so can he achieve an aesthetic experience or, as Otsuji calls it, a unity in life, arising from the poet's very being: "Before a poet can compose haiku, he must find a unity within his life which must come from the effort to discover his true self."[38]

It is in this area that questions of what sincerity, morality and truth in art are can be most satisfactorily resolved, without reference to standards that lie beyond the concern of art. Bradley has shown the comic implications of evaluating art by direct reference to other values:

> If we [determine the intrinsic value of poetry by direct reference to other human values] we shall find ourselves maintaining what we

> did not expect. If poetic value lies in the stimulation of religious feelings, *Lead Kindly Light* is no better a poem than many a tasteless version of a Psalm; if in the excitement of patriotism, why is *Scots, wha hae* superior to *We don't want to fight*? if in the mitigation of the passions, the Odes of Sappho will win but little praise; if in instruction, *Armstrong's Art of Preserving Health* should win much.[39]

Mistaken notions as to what constitutes poetic sincerity are many: an attempt to espouse good "humanitarian" principles, to re-affirm without qualification the values of religion, or a given moral or political position, or to deal with "beautiful" subject matter rather than what a reader finds gross or crude. As both perceptive Japanese and Western critics have maintained, such concepts or artistic sincerity are irrelevant. They can result in sheer sentimentality, as Cleanth Brooks declares:

> [An older view] expresses itself as a vigilance which keeps out of the poem all those extraneous and distracting elements which might seem to contradict what the poet wishes to communicate to his audience. It is the sincerity of the conscientious expositor who makes his point, even at the price of suppressions and exclusions. Poetry which embodies such a conception of sincerity, when it is unsuccessful, has as its characteristic vice, sentimentality. For sentimentality nearly always involves an over-simplification of the experience in question.

Rather, as he goes on to say, a more tenable position will deal with art in its own terms; sincerity lies in a single-minded devotion to the totality of the realization:

> The second conception of sincerity . . . reveals itself as an unwillingness to ignore the complexity of experience. The poet attempts to fuse the conflicting elements in a harmonious whole.[40]

In dealing with the experience, Asō has pointed out that Onitsura, one of the outstanding haiku poets of the seventeenth century, had pertinent observations to make to poets. For aside from the necessity of rejecting the claims coming from without the area of art, the poet must also be sincere in his own artistic practice:

> At the center of Onitsura's haiku theory is his statement about truth. Everywhere in his writing he uses the word *makoto.* This term is used in various ways and its meaning is not fixed. However, he uses this term in the sense of *sincerity.* In his writing entitled *Soliloquy,* he said, "When one composes a verse and exerts his attention only to rhetoric or phraseology, the sincerity is diminished." The fact that no artistic effort in the form or no decorative expression in the content [should be present] is Onitsura's ideal, which is the way to sincerity.[41]

And as has been previously pointed out[42] the poet can become single-mindedly devoted to his experience only as he abandons the needs of the self and submits humbly to his vision.

Here also lies the crux of the question of morality in art, which is synonymous with the poet's sincerity of devotion to his realization, not with his treatment of morally enlightening subject matter or with pious conclusions appended to his works. This is not to maintain that a valid work of art cannot have morally sound effects or should not treat of moral subject matter; but morality *per se* is not the artist's concern. Rather it is the experience, which is unique if it is truly his and which it is his function to grasp. Such an experience may be profoundly moral and religious, as indeed the Zen quality is in many of Bashō's haiku; but it was not his concern to make his poems so. His concern was to grasp the intuition. As Croce has maintained, "if art be beyond morality, the artist is neither this side of it nor that, but under its empire, in so far as he is a man who cannot withdraw himself from the duties of man, and must look upon art itself—art which is not and never will be moral—as a mission to be exercised as a priestly office."[43]

The importance of the artist's attitude toward his art is a commonly recognized concept by Japanese thinkers, who maintain further that his "life, art, and mental attitude"[44] must be unified and harmonized, so great must be his devotion to his "priestly office." Asō's comments on Bashō may be taken as representative:

> In the life of a haiku poet, his attitudes from day to day were very important. The haiku he composed each day was his "death verse"* for that day, according to Bashō. . . . [Consequently] the

* Following Japanese tradition, each poet was supposed to compose one final poem shortly before his death, which was then his "death verse."

> art of haiku should be the outbursting of attitudes he holds every day. . . . The attitude of the haiku poet is to find the way of art in the common modes of living.
> One of the outstanding characteristics of Bashō is that life and art are in perfect harmony. . . . In his work, art is the expression of the whole man, and in it, the whole man was able to emerge in the art.[45]

Otsuji expressed the same idea: "Therefore as regards the attitude necessary for composing haiku, it requires endless effort to find a unity in life and to make life an art."[46]

Unlike the Japanese, Western critics have for the most part tended to avoid such phrases as to make "One's life an art," not insisting upon the relationship between an artist's mode of life or sense of artistic morality and his works. The hesitancy is due undoubtedly to a wish to escape any identification with the school that cultivates a so-called aesthetic life, which usually degenerates into an esthete, pseudo-Bohemian display in which the arty rather than art became the standard; or with the school that adversely criticizes the art product because of the unconventionality or irregularities of the artist's life—a remnant of the Victorian attitude. Students of art have also tended to feel that the matter lay outside of their area, which is perhaps another instance of the fragmentation of learning in the West. As Allen Tate makes clear, however, there is an awareness of a connection between literary practice and the problems of morality: "I assume that a poet is a man eager to come under the bondage of limitations if he can find them. As I understand John Peale Bishop's poetry, he is that eager man. It is a moral problem, but that phase I cannot touch here."[47]

Morality lies then in the artist's sincerity as he searches for artistic truth. When Onitsura states that without truth there is no haiku, he is not referring to actual truth, but rather to what something, actual or not, is. The true in the sense of the actual is not what the artist presents. In the case of one of Bashō's poems, this point is well illuminated. He wrote the following haiku on the seashore of Kuwana:

> Fallen snows are light,
> And the lancelets appear
> No more than an inch white.[48]

The poem represents what Bashō saw on a beach where the snow had fallen lightly. This is factual, not the poetic truth that Bashō was seeking. For in composing the poem, he was too much bound by factual truth and failed to grasp a deep insight of what it was that he saw, actual or not. Of course I do not mean by this that the factual is not important, but rather that, through factual truth, the poet can realize poetic truth. Bashō, apparently feeling some dissatisfaction with the above version, perhaps along some such line of reasoning as that presented, later changed the poem to read:

In the dawn twilight
There the lancelets appear
No more than an inch white.[49]

He made the following remark about his revision, which is recorded in the Sanzōshi: "This verse was first composed beginning with the five syllables, 'Fallen snows are light.' It is a matter of great regret to me."[50] It may be said that, from the factual point of view, the revised version is false, since the happening did not occur in this way. However, it is poetic truth, of the sort that not only Japanese but Western poets try to realize. As Eliot has remarked of philosophical theories when they have entered the realm of art, the first kind of truth then becomes irrelevant: "A philosophical theory which has entered into poetry is established, for its truth or falsity in one sense ceases to matter, and its truth in another sense is proved."[51]

Suzanne Langer points out, too, that factual truth is not artistic truth, for this arises from the total poem: " 'Artistic truth' does not belong to statements in the poem or their obvious figurative meanings, but to its figures and meanings *as they are used*, its statements *as they are made* . . . in short, to the poem as 'significant form.' "[52] What she means by significant form may be illustrated in the way Bashō realized his insight based on the actual happening. When we compare the two poems above, this point becomes clear.

In the first version we find a small, actual world, flattened by the seashore on which the light snows are white; the whiteness of the snow and that of the lancelet destroy each other's life and nothing remains significant. There is only the actual scene, which is no more than a mere fragment of the poet's intuition. But in the revised verse the seashore becomes a part of the great universe aesthetically wrapped in the twilight of dawn. And the lancelet, no more than an inch white, breathes in significant form, its transparent beauty alive against the atmosphere at early dawn.

Otsuji has pointed out why it is essential for the poet constantly to apply effort and discipline in the realization of his intuition: "A sense of immedicacy does not come alive for a poet with any deep significance without such past effort."[53] That is, with such effort, every experience can become excitingly and meaningfully his own, not arrived at second-hand. Only thus, too, can his critical judgment be sharpened and enable him to recognize falseness in his work. Kyorai, a disciple of Bashō's, reports that Kyoroku, another follower, put it thus: "'I am tired of my self of yesterday.' What a good saying this is. The decreased master [Bashō] often spoke thus."[54] What Kyoroku meant, one supposes, is that he is wearied of the self who yesterday created a haiku that today he finds false.

The aim of aesthetic contemplation, then, is intuitive insight into the nature of experience, "the toal revelation" in Allen Tate's words.[55] That the revelation is knowledge is somewhat defensively maintained by Western critics. For example, Stephen Pepper: "[Aesthetic experience] is the most illuminating of activities. It gives us direct insight into the nature of the world. It shows us what is real there, it realizes events. . . . Art is thus as fully as cognitive, fully as knowing as science, so that the contextualists are fond of calling intuition of quality a realization."[56] One of the uses of that knowledge, as Croce points out, is to provide the insights which may lead to concepts or generalizations:

> If we have shown that the aesthetic form is altogether independent of the intellectual and suffices to itself without external support, we have not said that the intellectual can stand without the aesthetic. This *reciprocity* would not be true. . . . Concepts are not possible without intuitions. . . . Intuitions are: this river, this lake, this brook, this rain, this glass of water; the concept is: water, not this or that appearance and particular example of water, but water in general.[57]

Another use which both Whitehead and Dewey point out is that the artist's direct intuitions are correctives against the fallacy of "misplaced concreteness," the name Whitehead has given to the error of mistaking abstract logical constructions for the concrete fact: "Wordsworth, Shelley are representative of the intuitive refusal seriously to accept the abstract materialism of science."[58] As Dewey puts it: "The conception that objects have fixed and unalterable values is precisely the prejudice from which art emancipates us."[59]

Yet what that knowledge is that art yields through insight is still a difficult question. For example, although Waggoner states that "poetry deals with, includes, is in some sense knowledge," still he is forced to admit that what the knowledge is has not yet been "adequately defined or agreed upon."[60] The background of this question as Western critics deal with it is of course the low esteem to which all disciplines based on an intuitive approach, not publicly demonstrable—for example, art, religion, philosophy—fell, during the nineteenth century particularly, because of the stunning successes of science and of the scientific method. Reality, as painted by science for its own needs, has been mistaken for ultimate reality, which, being based on a positivistic, mechanistic naturalism, wrought havoc with traditional religious, philosophic, and aesthetic assumptions. As has been suggested,[61] recent thinkers have demonstrated that a "denial of a large part of man's experience because a smaller part seemed to demand it"[62] is unnecessary. It is, in fact, impossible. As Cleanth Brooks has put it: "The refusal to accept the scientific account in matters where the scientific method is valid and relevant is unrealistic, but there is nothing 'escapist' about a hostility to science which orders science off the premises as a trespasser when science has taken up a position where it has no business to be."[63]

Although I do not feel that it is within the scope of this book to explore this question fully, it may be interesting and perhaps enlightening to see how similar are the pronouncements of Japanese haiku scholars to those of Western critics in this area. The similarity seems to me to demonstrate that, no matter how vague or unprecise the language used, as compared to scientific language, to describe the nature of the knowledge yielded by art, there is a common core to their discussions. Moreover, the Japanese as yet unburdened by invidious comparisons between science and art, are not so defensive as the Western thinkers and speak more freely.

A common point of departure seems to lie in Waggoner's following statement: "The poet working as poet includes more of total meaning than the scientist or the practical man does, and works more intimately with the concrete wholes that make up the material of total meaning than the philosopher does. . . . [Therefore] poetry conveys more humanly relevant, which is to say more meaningful, more philosophical knowledge about life and man than science does."[64] When the haiku poet or critic speaks of the "knowledge about life and man" that haiku conveys, he almost invariably does so in terms of man's knowledge of nature, and in terms of his insights into it, leading eventually to a realization of his relationship to nature. Representative statements along this line follow. Let us first take Otsuji: "What is expressed in a haiku is a very small aspect of phenomena; yet what the poet experiences is the reality hidden behind what he expresses, which may be said to be a universal feeling arising from the union of the poet with nature."[65] Asō's description of the thinking of both Onitsura and Bashō is revealing:

> Once an abbot asked Onitsura what the essence of haiku art was, and he replied: "In front of a garden, a camellia tree blooms with white flowers." Since the truth of the universe lies even in a single flower, insight into the universe and into God can be grasped by understanding this truth. . . . Onitsura thinks that the true way of haiku art is to discover poetic refinement in the truth of natural phenomena, whether in the snow, the moon, or flowers, with a selfless attitude. [Bashō] tried his utmost to master the hidden aspects of nature and to reveal its secrets. What he tried to find was not the outward appearance of nature, but to touch its very heart.[66]

The master Bashō himself said: "In the sound of the frog leaping from the bank overgrown with wild grass, a haikai is heard. There is the seen; there is the heard. Where there is hokku as the poet has felt it, there is poetic truth."[67]

For the Japanese haiku poet, insights into nature are most usually expressed through the important element called by them the seasonal theme. Briefly described, it refers to the inclusion in a haiku of the sense of the season of the year with which the haiku deals. Otsuji, in one of his characteristically penetrating insights, declared that once the concept was accepted as absolutely essential to haiku, a most important consequence followed:

> Viewed against the popular idea that the seasonal theme is a man-made concept, the contention that it is unnecessary to haiku has some justification; however, if one comes to my idea that the seasonal theme is the natural object itself in all its naturalness—that its function is to symbolize nature—then for the first time will he come face to face with the problem of the relationship between nature and himself. Here the poet should think deeply of the problem of the self.[68]

One supposes that W.M. Urban had the same thought in mind when he said that the language of poetry, among its other concerns, always says one thing, "namely, that human life and man are unique, free, and self-determining parts of nature."[69] Although the Japanese might not agree with the characterization of man's relationship to nature as given by Urban in his three adjectives, he would unequivocally agree that haiku dealt with it, and deals with it because, as Asō says, insight into it will reveal the "truth of the universe"[70] or what Waggoner calls "the supreme or unifying value."[71]

To summarize, aesthetic contemplation is, then, a disinterested awareness of an object. The scientist also shares this awareness, but he, in scientific contemplation, has no other end than scientific knowledge of it. The artist, on the other hand, is not occupied, as is the scientist, in drawing conclusions from the object observed. Nor is he interested in making any judgments about it. He is interested in the object only for its own sake. Aesthetic contemplation is also characterized by single-mindedness, for in the state of aesthetic contemplation the subject and object are one. Only as the poet remains completely devoted to the totality of experience in contemplation does the concept of artistic sincerity have meaning. Morality for the artist also lies in his sincerity as he searches for poetic truth; the concept applies to the art work only in reference to the sincerity of the poetic intent and not to values outside the area of art. Poetic truth also arises from aesthetic sincerity, for it is a function of a realized insight, and is not to be determined only by reference to fact or actuality. During the state of realization the quality of the object is grasped. The anecdote is told of Seihō, the famous Japanese painter, that in looking at a picture of a chicken drawn by a student he clucked several times. Here awareness of the object was his whole being and he became that chicken. But had he exclaimed on the beauty of the painting, he would have been separated from the object he was observing; he would have been passing judgment upon it and would no longer have been one with it; and the experience would no longer have been aesthetic. The content of aesthetic experience is judged to be a kind of knowledge, different from the scientific, offering intuitive insight into the deepest levels of meaning.

3. Haiku Moment

Aesthetic contemplation is contemplation of an object and the object's quality which the artist, in virtue of his funded experience, can experience. When an aesthetic contemplation is completed and the quality of the object is fully realized, the artist having felt the perception as a totality, this I call an aesthetic moment. At this moment, and indeed just prior to it as we sense that it is about to come into being, "one's feeling already has reached an enlightened, Nirvana-like harmony,"[72] timeless since "the poet's nature and environment are unified," as Otsuji has said.[73] This moment is common to all art. It is characteristic of it that the completion of the reading of, let us say, a full-length novel or of the hearing of a long symphony does not end its effects. These persist, as many can testify, as did Gustave Flaubert when he said that he loved best those works which made him "dream all day long";[74] as did

John Gould Fletcher, who remarked of certain poems that they had the "extraordinary power to set up echoes in the reader's mind";[75] or as did Bashō, who said that experiencing was a "going back."[76]

What these remarks seem to refer to is what might be called the power of "resonation" of the aesthetic moment, which arises of course from the words of the work. However, the relationship between the words and the resonation is that while a temporal element is inherent in the reading of the words, the insight into what is expressed through them, as they attain their full meaning simultaneously, is immediate. In this simultaneity and immediacy, obviously impossible with a novel, a sonnet, or even a quatrain, the words, although of course they give rise to these effects, do not function directly. It is physically impossible for them to do so, where possibly a hundred thousand or so words, as in a novel, are concerned. It is, as I stated, even impossible in a sonnet or a quatrain. Yet there is a literary form in which the words themselves can occur as a simultaneous happening. When this kind of aesthetic moment does take place, I call it a *haiku moment.*

A haiku moment is a kind of aesthetic moment—a moment in which the words which created the experience and the experience itself can become one.[77] The nature of a haiku moment is anti-temporal and its quality is eternal, for in this state man and his environment are one unified whole, in which there is no sense of time. The total implication of the words in the realization of experience creates that sense of immediacy which Ezra Pound declared was essential for art: "[The image is] that which presents an intellectual and emotional complex in an instant of time. . . . It is the presentation of such a 'complex' instantaneously which give that sense of sudden liberation; that sense of freedom from time limits and space limits; that sense of sudden growth, which we experience in the presence of the greatest works of art."[78]

The truly realized haiku moment is the goal toward which every haiku poet strives. It is as difficult to create a haiku arising from it as to create a tanka or a sonnet. But if a poet overcomes its difficulties, we are charmed by its perfections. It is this that "moves Heaven and Earth—srikes devils and deities with pity—softens man and woman."[79] The haiku challenges the great poets, taxing their power and revealing vividly their individuality and differences in temperament. Rare indeed is the well-realized haiku, as Bashō repeated to his disciplines in many ways:

> He who creates three to five haiku poems during a lifetime is a haiku poet. He who attains to ten is a master.

> [A disciple said]: "Does even a master sometime nod?" The answer was: "In every poem."[80]

This seemingly quixotically high standard was shared by Ezra Pound: "It is better to present one Image in a lifetime than to produce voluminous work."[81] The haiku moment results, then, in a new insight or vision which the haiku poet must render as an organic whole. It is aesthetic truth, wherein beauty lies and sincerity, when the poet is devoted to realizing it alone. It is all that a poet can accept.

Nor are such moments and experiences confined to artists alone. For when the ordinary man confronts a work of art, or indeed experiences aesthetically any object, his process of realization is identical to that of the artist. Insofar as he experiences it, he realizes its quality, what kind of thing it is. As Croce has said, there is no difference between the artist and his audience in the kind of experience each has: "Great artists are said to reveal us to ourselves. But how could this be possible unless there be identity of nature between their imagination and ours and unless the difference be one only of quantity? It were well to change *poeta nascitur* into *homo nascitur poeta*; some men are born great poets, some small."[82] The artist, then, when he is successful, communicates an experience valuable to the spectator for the new insight afforded him. The artist, however, must be able, as the layman need not, to embody and objectify his realization in terms of his particular discipline and of his individual insight. This leads to a consideration of various aspects of form and technique.

I wish to limit this area to haiku and to show how the preceding general remarks on aesthetic experience are illustrated in this form which is the gem of Japanese poetry.

Notes

1. Bashō, *Haikai Ronshū*, (Collected Haikai Theory), ed. T. Komiya and S. Yokozawa, 3rd. ed. (Tokyo: Iwanami, 1951), p. 71 (*Kyoroku ni Okuru ben.*) The titles of original works of Bashō, in which given quotations are found, will be cited in parentheses after the bibliographical data.

2. Hughes, Glenn, *Imagism and the Imagists* (Palo Alto: Stanford University Press: 1931), p. 47.

3. Yasuda, Kenneth, *The Japanese Haiku: Its Existential Nature, History,*

and Possibilities in English (Rutland, Vermont: Charles E. Tuttle Company, 1957), pp. 35–38.

4. Allen Tate, *Reactionary Essays on Poetry and Ideas* (New York: Scribner's, 1936), p. x.

5. Brooks, Cleanth, *Modern Poetry and the Tradition* (Chapel Hill: University of North Carolina Press, 1939), p. 78.

6. Ibid., p. 182.

7. Gregory, Horace, and Marya Zaturenska, *A History of American Poetry* (New York: Harcourt and Brace, 1942), p. 207.

8. Williams, *Spring and All. I–XXVIII.* In Louise Bogan, *Achievement in American Poetry* (Chicago: Henry Regnery, 1951), p. 130.

9. Bashō, *Haikai Ronshū*, p. 103. (*Hai mon haikai Goroku*).

10. Hughes, *Imagism*, p. 5.

11. Masao Kume, *Bikushō Zuihitsu* (Bitter-Sweet Essays) (Tokyo: Bangei Shumju Shinsa, 1953), p. 258.

12. Tate, *Reactionary Essays*, p. 108.

13. Otsuji (Seki Osuga), *Otsuji Hairon-shū* (Otsuji's Collected Essays on Haiku Theory), ed. Toyo Yoshida, 5th ed. (Tokyo: Kaede Shobō, 1947), p. 18.

14. Ibid., p. 262.

15. Tate, *Reactionary Essays*, p. 17.

16. Bashō, *Haikai Ronshū*, p. 98. (*Kurozōshi*.)

17. Otsuji, *Hairon-shū*, p. 30.

18. Isoji Asō, *Haishumino no Hattatsu* (The Development of Haiki Taste), 2nd ed. (Tokyo: Tokyodō, 1941), p. 234.

19. Quoted by Herbert Read, *Form in Modern Poetry* (London: Vision Press), 1953, p. 79.

20. Yasuda, *Japanese Haiku*, pp. 49–50.

21. Otsuji, *Hairon-shū*, p. 19.

22. Ibid., p. 11.

23. Ibid., p. 47.

24. John Dewey, *Art as Experience* (New York: Mentor Balch, 1934), p. 44.

25. Ernest Cassirer, *Substance and Function and Einstein's Theory of Relativity*, trans. by W.C. and M.C. Swabey (Chicago: Open Court, 1923), p. 272.

26. Otsuji, *Hairon-shū*, p. 4.

27. Benedetto Croce, *Aesthetic as a Science of Expression and General Linguistic*, trans. Douglas Ainslie (London: Macmillan, 1922), p. 127.

28. Otsuji *Hairon-shū*, p. 31.

29. Dewey, *Art as Experience*, p. 89.

30. H.H. Waggoner, *The Heel of Elohim* (Norman, Okla.: University of Oklahoma Press, 1950), p. 13.

31. Cassirer, *Substance and Function*, p. 150

32. Dewey, *Art as Experience*, p. 89.

33. Otsuji, *Hairon-shū*, p. 13.

34. Benedetto Croce, *Ariosto, Shakespeare, and Corneille*, trans. Douglas Ainslie (London: George, Allen and Unwin, 1920), pp. 153–54.

35. Waggoner, *Heel of Elohim*, p. 73.

36. Bashō, *Haikai Ronshū*, p. 49. (*Kurozōshi.*)

37. Dewey, *Art as Experience*, p. 46.

38. Otsuji, *Hairon-shū*, p. 262.

39. A.C. Bradley, *Oxford Lectures on Poetry* (London: Macmillan, 1909), p. 6.

40. Brooks, *Modern Poetry*, p. 37.

41. Asō, *Haishume*, pp. 190–192.

42. Yasuda, *Japanese Haiku*, pp. xix–xx.

43. Benedetto Croce, *Essence of Aesthetic*, trans. Douglas Ainslie (London: Heineman, 1921), p. 16.

44. Yasuda, *Japanese Haiku*, p. 8.

45. Asō, *Haishume*, pp. 273–74.

46. Otsuji, *Hairon-shū*, p. 262.

47. Tate, *Reactionary Essays*, p. 56.

48. Bashō, *Bashō Haikushū* (Collected Haiku of Bashō), ed. Ebara Taizō, 18th ed. (Tokyo: Iwanami, 1953), p. 30.

49. Ibid., p. 30.

50. In *Bashō Kōza* (Lectures on Bashō), comp. and ed. Ebara Taizō and Katō Shūson (Tokyo: Sanshōdō, 1943), I, p. 355.

51. T.S. Eliot, *Selected Essays* (New York: Harcourt, Brace, 1932), p. 248.

52. S.K. Langer, *Philosophy in a New Key* (Cambridge, Mass: Harvard University Press, 1942), p. 261.

53. Otsuji, *Hairon-shū*, p. 262.

54. Bashō, *Haikai Ronshū*, p. 69. (*Ryōshinron.*)

55. Tate, *Reactionary Essays*, p. 88.

56. Stephen Pepper, *Aesthetic Quality* (New York: Scribner's, 1938), p. 31.

57. Croce, *Aesthetic*, p. 36.

58. Alfred North Whitehead, *Science and the Modern World* (New York: Macmillan, 1925), p. 120.

59. Dewey, *Art as Experience*, p. 95.

60. Waggoner, *Heel of Elohim*, pp. 192, 203.

61. Yasuda, *Japanese Haiku*, p. 4.
62. Waggoner, *Heel of Elohim*, p. 6.
63. Brooks, *Modern Poetry*, p. 174.
64. Waggoner, *Heel of Elohim*, p. 219.
65. Otsuji, *Hairon-shū*, p. 131.
66. Asō, *Haishume*, pp. 191, 270.
67. Bashō, *Haikai Ronshū*, p. 49. (*Shirozōshi.*)
68. Otsuji, *Hairon-shū*, p. 50.
69. W.M. Urban, *Language and Reality* (London: Macmillan, 1939), p. 495.
70. Asō, *Haishume*, p. 191.
71. Waggoner, *Heel of Elohim*, p. 219.
72. Otsuji, *Hairon-shū*, p. 4.
73. Ibid., p. 47.
74. Gustave Flaubert, *La Correspondance de Flaubert* (Paris: Conard, 1926–33), II, p. 294.
75. Fletcher, Introduction to *A Pepper Pod* in Yasuda, Kenneth, *A Pepper Pod* (New York: Alfred A. Knopf, 1947), p. viii.
76. Bashō, *Haikai Ronshū*, p. 95. (*Kurozōshi.*)
77. Yasuda, *Japanese Haiku*, p. 23ff.
78. Ezra Pound, "A Few Dont's by an Imagist," *Poetry: A Magazine of Verse,* vol. I (October–March, 1912–13), p. 200.
79. *Kokinshū*, ed. by Hachirō Onoe, 19th ed. (Tokyo: Iwanamui, 1951), p. 11.
80. Bashō, *Haikai Ronshū*, pp. 64, 84. (*Haiki Mondō Aone ga Mine.*)
81. Pound, "A Few Dont's."
82. Croce, *Aesthetic*, p. 24.

Chapter 7

Bashō on the Art of the Haiku: Impersonality in Poetry

MAKOTO UEDA

If haiku is the most well-known of Japanese literary forms, then Bashō is perhaps the most well known haiku poet. To understand the works of Bashō is to understand the aesthetic underpinnings of haiku, even though, as Ueda points out, Bashō "never wrote a theory of poetry himself." As a teacher/poet, Bashō's influence had a profound effect on haiku as an art form. Ueda's discussion of the "poetic spirit, sabi, shiori, *reverberation, reflection, and lightness" provides the reader with insight into the poetry and aesthetic spirit of this most influential figure. In this volume, see also Kenneth Yasuda's essay on haiku.*

Japanese poetics reached another high point in its history with the appearance of Matsuo Bashō (1644–94) in the seventeenth century. Bashō is chiefly known as a great writer of the Haiku, one of the world's shortest verse forms that consists of only three lines with a total of seventeen syllables. Yet his immense influence over contemporary and later poets is due in no small measure to his poetic ideas as well as to his poetic works. Besides being a talented poet, Bashō was also an excellent teacher of verse-writing who had numerous disciples all over Japan. He and his disciples followed certain poetic principles of their own and clearly distinguished themselves from other poets, so their contemporaries called them the poets of *shōmon,* or the Bashō school. As is well known, it was this school that came to form the main current of the Haiku through succeeding centuries. To examine Bashō's poetics, then, is to study the poetics of the Haiku in its most orthodox form.

Bashō, however, never wrote a theory of poetry himself. He seems to have thought that fixed rules would be too binding and too restrictive on each poet's creative imagination. There is plenty of evidence to show that he tried to encourage his disciples' individual talents instead of imposing his own rules upon them. Yet he did have a series of poetic ideas with which he could have formulated a set of rules consistent within itself, if only he had been inclined to do so. "Those disciples of mine who are so inclined," Bashō once said, "can talk with me personally, write down what they understand from me, and use it privately as the teaching of our school." Fortunately for us, many of Bashō's disciples were so inclined and left us with a considerable number of essays and miscellaneous pieces expounding the poetic ideas of Bashō and his school. Of those writings, Kyorai's and Dohō's are most valuable, since these poets were not only Bashō's leading disciples but themselves tried to be as faithful as possible to their master's teaching.[1] The writings of Shikō, Kyoroku, Rogan, and others are generally less reliable, whether because of their dogmatic tendency, lack of understanding, or plain misinformation: but within these limits they still throw light on Bashō's teaching.[2] Those pieces, together with Bashō's own essays, journals, letters, and other miscellaneous reminiscences, provide more than ample material to study his ideas on the art of the Haiku. These ideas were many and various and some were so elusive that modern scholars differ widely in their interpretations. But at all events they should include such concepts as the poetic spirit, *sabi, shiori*, slenderness, inspiration, fragrance, reverberation, reflection, plainness, and lightness, all of which appear frequently in the writings of the *shōmon* poets.

Of those ideas the poetic spirit occupies the central position: one might almost say that all the ideas are different aspects of it. "Of the Haiku there is a style that remains unchanged for thousands of years," says Kyorai. "There is also a style that prospers only for a time. There are the two poles of the late Masters's teaching, and they are really the same in essence. They are the same, because they both resort to a single source, the poetic spirit." "Of the Master's Haiku, there is a style that remains unchanged for thousands of years," Dohō reiterates. "There is also a style that changes with time. All other styles are ultimately reduced to these two, which in turn can be traced back to a single origin. That single origin is the poetic spirit." Two of Bashō's most faithful pupils are here making the point in almost the same vocabulary; Bashō must have been quite emphatic on it. According to Bashō, then, all the styles of the Haiku fall into two large categories; the one that has qualities transcending time and place, and the other that is rooted in the taste of the time. Both styles are good, the former because of its universal appeal, the latter because of its freshness in expression. Bashō, however, thinks that the two are ultimately one—the poetic spirit. All good Haiku, whatever style they may show, spring from this common source. In truth, the poetic spirit was conceived by Bashō on an even grander scale. He believed that this spirit went far beyond the realm of the Haiku, that, indeed, it pervaded all areas of creative arts. Bashō says this in his own writing:

> There is a common element permeating Saigyō's lyric poetry. Sōgi's linked verse, Sesshū's painting, and Rikyū's tea ceremony.[3] It is the poetic spirit, the spirit that leads one to follow the ways of the universe and to become a friend with things of the seasons. For a person who has the spirit, everything he sees becomes a flower, and everything he imagines turns into a moon. Those who do not see the flower are no different from barbarians, and those who do not imagine the flower are akin to beasts. Leave barbarians and beasts behind; follow the ways of the universe and return to nature.

Somewhat metaphysically Bashō has here conceived a spirit that underlies all creative activities. It is a spirit that produces all works of art, and ultimately it goes back to the creative power of the universe. The universe creates beautiful flowers, and the lovely moon, and so does the artist; they are both creative, and appreciative, of things beautiful. The creation and appreciation of beauty is essentially what distinguished civilized men from barbarians and beasts; it is the prime factor of culture. Thus Bashō's poetic spirit comes to assume a form of cultured primitivism; his concluding words are, fittingly enough, "return to nature."

Yet Bashō's primitivism was necessarily of a specific kind, as it was based on his poetic spirit. In this respect a remark by Bashō, recorded by Dohō, is revealing: "Attain a high stage of enlightenment," he said, "and return to a world of common men." The poetic spirit has two aspects; a high spiritual attainment and a life of the laity. The former, with its Buddhist overtone, would presume those serene, quiet, ascetic qualities that were the concerns of medieval Japanese artists. The latter, with its emphasis on the mundane, points toward that gay, pleasure-loving world of newly emerging Japan, often called the "floating world." The two sets of values are inevitably in conflict with one another at times, Bashō himself was well aware of the conflict: he often criticized himself for being neither a priest nor a layman. But certainly Bashō's ideal must have overcome that conflict, to reach a realm where those two sets of values are not antithetical but dialectical. Before we proceed to see whether and how this could be done, we need to examine one by one the values that make up the two aspects of the poetic spirit. The first set of values, which are to help the poet to attain a high stage of enlightenment, would include *sabi, shiori*, slenderness, inspiration, and so on. The second set of qualities, which form the world of common men, would contain such ideas as plainness and lightness. Each of those values is interesting in itself, as it reveals some phase of Bashō's poetics as well as the poetics of the Haiku.

Sabi is perhaps the best known of all these ideas pertaining to Bashō's poetics. Bashō, however, seldom used that term himself, although he often used the word *sabishi* from which it was derived. *Sabishi* primarily means solitary or lonely, referring to a man's state of mind when he is in want of company. But Bashō seems to have used that word in a more limited sense. Here is, for instance, Bashō's Haiku using the word *sabishi*:

Loneliness—.
Standing amid the blossoms,
A cypress tree.

It is spring, and cherry blossoms are in full bloom. But in the middle of them there is something that does not harmonize with the loveliness and gaiety of the scene: a green cypress tree. Because of that cypress, the scene somehow yields the atmosphere of loneliness. In this poem, then, loneliness is not referring to a man's personal emotion; it is describing an impersonal atmosphere, a mood created by a natural landscape.

Sabi, derived from *sabishi*, seems to connote this sort of objective, non-emotional loneliness. There is only one poet remaining today that Bashō reportedly said had *sabi*, and this quality of loneliness is manifest is that poem, too. In fact, that poem is strikingly close to the cypress poem just cited:

Under the blossoms
Two aged watchmen,
With their white heads together—.

This is not purely a nature poem; there are two men placed in the heart of the landscape. Yet the Haiku says nothing about the men's inner feelings. They are part of the natural scene, just as a cypress tree was in the previous poem. And again like the cypress tree, the image of the aged watchmen provides a sharp contrast to the colorful cherry blossoms, thereby creating an atmosphere of loneliness. Lovely as the blossoms are, they must eventually fall with the passing of time, as suggested by the white hair of the watchmen. Important is the fact that these old men are not grieving over the impending fall of the blossoms or over the anticipated end of their lives. They are there simply to fulfill their place in nature, together with the blossoms; they are part of impersonal nature. Such seems to be the implication of *sabi*, the lonely mood latent in this sort of natural scenery.

Bashō conceived loneliness as an impersonal atmosphere, in contrast with grief or sorrow, which is a personal emotion. The contrast cannot be over-emphasized, because loneliness thus conceived lay at the bottom of Bashō's view of life, pointing toward a way in which his plea "return to nature" can be fulfilled. For Bashō, sorrow was the word to describe life and the world at large; in his view this life was a "demoniac world of the lusts" and mankind was "drowning in a filthy ditch." Life is filled with sorrow because men, each pursuing his own desires, hurt one another. There is not escape for men from sorrow, since it is inherent in humanity. If there should be an escape, it would be only through a denial of humanity, through men's dehumanizing themselves. They can escape from sorrow only when they transform it into an impersonal atmosphere, loneliness.

This metamorphosis of sorrow into loneliness is the theme of one of Bashō's most famous poems. Bashō composed the Haiku while staying alone at a temple in the mountains:

> My sorrowful soul—.
> Make it feel lonesome,
> You, a cuckoo.

The poet, as he set out to compose the poem, was still in the world of humanity, with a personal feeling like sorrow. The cuckoo, on the other hand, seemed to have already transcended sorrow, as it was closer to the heart of nature. Thereupon the poet wished that the bird's cry might enlighten his soul and eventually lead him into the realm of impersonal loneliness, where he would no longer feel sorrow.

Bashō makes a similar point on another occasion, this time in his diary. It was a rainy morning, and Bashō, trying to kill time did some idle scribbling:

> A person in mourning makes Grief his master, and a person who drinks wine makes Pleasure his master. When Priest Saigyō sang:

"Even casual visitors
Ceased to think about
This mountain village
It would be sorrowful, indeed,
If here were no loneliness to live with."

he made Loneliness his master.

Again sorrow and loneliness are clearly distinguished. While sorrow is something hard to live with, loneliness is something enjoyable to have around; in fact, loneliness is what gives solace to a sorrowful life. Though the poem is Saigyō's, Bashō, in quoting it in his diary, must have felt exactly the same way; Saigyō had long been his model both in life and in poetry.

Such a dissolution of personal emotion into an impersonal atmosphere constitutes the core of Bashō's attitude toward life. It was the way in which Bashō tried to bear the sorrows inherent in human life. Bashō was quite determined in keeping this attitude, so much so that he at times looked cold-hearted, or even inhuman. One striking instance of this appears in one of his journals. One day on his journey he came across a little infant abandoned on the roadside and crying bitterly. His remark, addressed to the infant, was a very calm one: "Are you hated by your father, or are you neglected by your mother? No, it is not that your father hates you, nor that your mother neglects you. It is merely fate, Grieve over your adverse fate." A similar attitude prevails in all of his poems produced on grievous occasions, for example, this poem composed by Bashō at the death of his beloved disciple:

In the autumn gust
It is sorrowfully broken:
A mulberry stick.

As a self-contained entity, the poem does not much differ in mood from another Haiku by Bashō that simply describes a scene of nature:

All flowers are dead.
Sprinkling sorrows
Are the grass seeds.

Bashō's poems on death, even on the death of those dearest to him, do not show the intensity of grief that is the merit of a dirge or elegy. It was not that

Bashō was inhuman; rather, he was *un*human. He tried to overcome his grief by transforming it into something impersonal.

This attitude toward life held by Bashō was his attitude toward poetry, too, especially in his later years when he established a style distinctly his own. A poem containing a personal emotion was inferior to a poem presenting an impersonal atmosphere. Here are two contesting Haiku for which Bashō was the judge.

> The town where they pound cloth–.
> A dog is howling for his mate
> Piteously.

> A garden of taros outside-
> I listen to the gusty rain
> From inside the hut.

Bashō judged the second poem to be the winner. One of the reasons for that verdict was, as he tells us, that the scene of the rain falling on the large leaves of taros at night was "truly desolate and lonesome." Compared with it, the image of a dog barking for his mate was too human, too abundant in personal sentiments.

Indeed the finest of Bashō's poems seem to be devoid of ordinary human emotions. Here, for instance, are three of his poems universally acknowledged as among his best:

> Quietness—
> The cicada's cry
> Penetrates the rocks.

> The rough sea—
> Far over Sado Isle,[4] extends
> The Milky Way.

> Gathering the rains
> Of June, how swiftly flows
> The Mogami River![5]

These poems contain no personal emotion: no joy, sorrow, love, hatred, anger, jealousy. All there is is the atmosphere of the quiet, the vast, or the swift. It is the atmosphere of impersonal nature, and not an emotion of human life.

Sabi, is such an atmosphere. It is loneliness, not the loneliness of a man who has lost his dear one, but the loneliness of the rain falling on large taro leaves at night, or the loneliness emerging out of a cicada's cry amid the white, dry rocks, or the Milky Way extending over the rough sea, or a huge river torrentially rushing in the rainy season. Nature has not emotion, but is has life, through which it creates an atmosphere. This impersonal atmosphere, with an overtone of loneliness, is the core of *sabi.* In this respect it comes close to Rikyū's *wabi.* But *sabi* seems to differ from *wabi* in that it dissolves, rather than withdraws from, ordinary human emotions. Here *sabi* is more like Zeami's sublimity. Yet it differs from sublimity in one significant way. While sublimity transcends ordinary life and enters the world of the supernatural, *sabi* does not attempt to go into the other world. The beauty of sublimity is symbolic; that of *sabi* is not. For Zeami a cedar tree is beautiful because an eternal god is behind it. For Bashō a cypress tree is beautiful because it is a cypress tree, because it is part of impersonal nature.

While *sabi* derives its connotation of loneliness from the poet's attitude toward life, *shiori* seems to produce loneliness out of the structure of the poem. The former is related to the poet's philosophy, and the latter to his poetic technique, both bringing out a poem with the same overtone of loneliness. Etymologically, *shiori* stems from a verb *shioru,* which means "to bend" or "to be flexible." Originally, therefore, *shiori* described a poem flexible in meaning, a poem ambiguous enough to allow several different interpretations. But is so happened that there was another verb, *shioru,* written differently and declined differently but pronounced the same, which meant "to wither," "to droop," or "to wilt." This meaning seems to have found its way into the other meaning of *shiori,* too. Thus, when the poets of the Bashō school use it, *shiori* appears to refer to a poem containing several levels of meaning and yet altogether yielding the mood of loneliness, an atmosphere created by the image of a withering flower.

Let us take an example. Here is a haiku that Bashō said had the quality of *shiori*:

> The Ten Dumplings
> Have become smaller, too—
> The autumn wind.

The Ten Dumplings, so called because they were strung together in a unit of ten, were the special product of a certain mountain village in central Japan, where they were sold to travelers on the roadside. But it is now autumn, and travelers have become fewer. As the sales drop, the villagers now make their dumplings smaller and get more profit from each sale. The general mood arising out of the poem is sadness, but what is that sadness directed toward? Toward the poor villagers who have to depend on the sale of dumplings for their livelihood? Toward the villagers who miss the traveling season? Or toward the poet, a lonely traveler? Toward the poet mourning over the passing of summer? Or toward both nature and human life, which must change with time? The word "too" and the verbless last line make the meaning ambiguous. But through that ambiguity the feeling of sadness is universalized, as it were. The sadness is no longer the petty feeling of the villagers grieving over diminished sale. It is "loneliness" shared by the villagers, by the traveling poet, and by the autumn wind. Sadness has been dissolved into that impersonal loneliness.

The concepts of *sabi* and *shiori* explain two of the techniques peculiar to the Haiku: *kireji* or the "cutting-word," and *kigo* or the "season-word." The cutting-word is a word or a part of a word used in a Haiku poem to cut the structure into two parts. It may or may not have its own meaning; its main function is to show that the flow of the meaning is interrupted there. It often follows the subject of the sentence, interrupting the sentence at that juncture and leaving out the predicate verb altogether. The result is of course ambiguity; the reader must supply the verb in his own imagination. In the cicada poem quoted earlier, for instance, a cutting-word follows "Quietness—," in the place of whatever verb there might be. In the Ten Dumplings poem there is a cutting-word after the second line, thereby leaving the last line hanging in the air. All this creates ambiguity, but that ambiguity changes the particular into the universal and transforms a specific personal emotion into a vague, impersonal atmosphere.

Kigo or the season-word is concerned with a rule in the orthodox Haiku tradition which prescribes that every poem must contain a word suggestive of a season of the year. A rule like this would be arbitrary in other verse forms, but in the poetics of the Haiku it does make sense. Each Haiku poem, according to Bashō, must present an atmosphere of nature; it follows, then, that each Haiku must imply a season, for nature is seasonal. Even when the Haiku takes its original material from a personal emotion, it will still show a season since that particular emotion will, by the time it is made into a poem, have been transformed into an impersonal mood of nature. We have already seen an example of this in Bashō's poem on the death of his disciple. Here are two more similar examples, both composed on intensely emotional occasions. Bashō produced the following poem when he revisited his native home, where he wept over a lock of his late mother's hair kept as a memento in a little bag:

If I take it in my hand,
The hair will melt with my burning tears.
The autumn frost—.

He wrote the next Haiku on hearing of the untimely death of another of his disciples:

Move the gravemound!
My tearful cry
Is the wind of autumn.

In both of these two poems an intense emotion is suggested in the first two lines but then in the third line, which contains a season-word, the poet's grief is depersonalized into an object of nature, the autumn frost or the autumn wind. Death is sad, but it is part of nature, just as winter, heralded by autumn, is part of the cycle of the seasons. Grief dissolves into the loneliness of the universe.

The main task for the Haiku poet, then, is to immerse himself into the heart of an object or an incident that he proposes to sing about, and to catch the impersonal mood it shares with the universe. In order to be able to do this, he must have a most delicate, sensitive mind. Bashō has a name for such a special working of mind: slenderness. It is as if the mind were so slender that it could go into any external object and reach its innermost life. The Haiku that Bashō thought showed slenderness is:

The water birds
Must be asleep, too,
On Lake Yogo.

Lake Yogo is a small, quiet lake among the mountains. The poet was staying at a rustic inn near the lake, and as he lay in bed at night he thought of the water birds on the lake. With a slender mind the poet entered into the life of the water birds and found therein the loneliness of a traveler like himself—or, indeed like all men and all changing things in nature.

Another example of a poem that Bashō thought had slenderness is one composed by Bashō himself:

The salted sea bream's
Gums are chilly, too,
At the fish shop.

The sea bream that the poet saw at the fish shop was of course dead. But again with the slenderness of mind he entered into the fish and felt chilly. There is ambiguity as to why he felt chilly. It may be that the fish shop was chilly, or chilly-looking, because it has so few fish on display due to bad fishing weather. Or perhaps the fish's white teeth somehow yielded a chilly impression. The word "too" in the second line creates ambiguity. But the over all impression produced by the poem is unmistakably that of loneliness.

However, no matter what a slender mind the poet may have, it is no easy matter to enter into the innermost life of an external object. It presumes the poet's complete dehumanization, the dissolution of all his emotions. But obviously a man cannot live without his emotions, for he is a biological existence, who must maintain himself, and his species through his physical desires. The poet could dehumanize himself, but only for a brief period of time, perhaps only for a few moments at most. For the poet those moments are precious indeed, since this is the only time when he can get a glimpse of the impersonal essence of the universe, of the innermost life energy shared by all things in nature. Here arises Bashō's concept of inspiration, which he thought was essential to the writings of the Haiku.

Understandably, in Bashō's view poetic inspiration goes through two stages, perceptual and expressive. First, there is the poet's instantaneous perception of the essence of the object; secondly, there must be the poet's spontaneity in recording that perception in the form of a poem. About the first stage Dohō has a passage:

> The Master said: "Learn about a pine tree from a pine tree, and about a bamboo plant from a bamboo plant." What he meant was the poet shall detach the mind from his own self. Nevertheless some people interpret the word "learn" in their own ways and never really "learn." "Learn" means to enter into the object, perceive its delicate life, and feel its feeling, whereupon a poem forms itself. Even a poem that lucidly describes an object could not attain a true poetic sentiment unless it contains the feelings that spontaneously emerged out of the object. In such a poem the object and the poet's self would remain forever separate, for it was composed by the poet's personal self.

Here is a strong plea for objective, impersonal poetry. The poet's task is not to express his emotions, but to detach himself from them and to enter into the object of nature. A pine tree has its own life, so a poet composing a verse on it should first learn what sort of life it is by entering into the pine tree and perceiving its delicate life. The poet will become at one with the pine tree; this is the only way by which he can learn about the inner life of the pine. And, when he identifies himself with the tree, a poem will spontaneously form itself in his mind, without a conscious attempt on his part. Dohō has made a distinction between "growing" and "making" in the process in which a poem is created. "There are two ways in which a verse may be written: "growing" and "making," he says. "When a poet who has always trained his mind along the way of the Haiku applies himself to the object, the color of his mind "grows" into a poem. In the case of a poet who lacks that training, nothing grows into a poem; as a consequence, he has to "make" a poem out of his self." A true Haiku poet can make his mind transparent, as it were, so that an external object dyes it in its color; this color grows into a poem. A mediocre poet cannot do this, so he has to turn to his intellect, learning, conventional poetic technique, and so on; the poem thus made is inevitably artificial. Dohō calls this, "a technician's disease" and cites Bashō's teaching to the same effect. "Let a little child compose the Haiku," said Bashō at one time. "Any beginner's Haiku has something promising," he said at another time.

A poet who has successfully perceived the delicate life of an object must go to the next step: to record that perception adequately. Even if the perception is attained, no good poem will emerge from it if it is distorted or lost in the process of expression. Dohō is referring to this danger when he says: "One of two things might happen to the poet who has entered into the essence of the object: he might nourish that inspiration, or he might destroy it. If he destroys that inspiration, the poem will become spiritless." Then he quotes Bashō's words: "The Haiku must be composed by the force of inspiration." Bashō said the same thing again and again. "If you get a flash of insight into an object," he taught at one time, "record it before it fades away in your mind." "When you are composing a verse," he said at another time, "let there not be a hair's breadth separating your mind from what you write. Quickly say what is in your mind; never hesitate at that moment." Bashō had more colorful similes, too, in stressing the spontaneity of poetic expression. The composing of the Haiku must be done in an instant, he said, "like felling a massive tree, like leaping at a formidable enemy, like cutting a watermelon, or like biting at a pear." All this clearly points to Bashō's idea that the Haiku poet should never lose his inspired moments but write down the instantaneous perception as it is, with no impure thought intervening in the process.

The idea of inspiration explains that extreme brevity of the Haiku form, which consists of only seventeen syllables. The inspired moments never last long; they cannot, as long as they presume the poet's complete submersion in an external object. His momentary perception cannot be described; it defies a logical explanation. The Haiku needs only to present concrete images in the briefest words. The relationship between images does not have to be spelled out, for doing so would mean the imposing of logic upon a fresh, new insight. The omission of the predicate verb and the use of the cutting-word are thus justified, as we have already seen.

It naturally follows that the Haiku need not have logic in its internal structure. This is substantiated by what Bashō and his disciples have written, too. Indeed, they have said little about the methods of structure in the Haiku; but we can guess what their thoughts on the subject must have been, because we have their written comments on the principles of structure in the Renku, or linked verse in the Haiku style. Since the Renku can be said to be the linked Haiku, we can safely assume that what is valid in the Renku can be applied to the Haiku as well.

Bashō and his disciples have conceived a number of structural principles in the Renku, but chief among them seem to be fragrance, reverberation, and reflection. As these terms show, none of them is logical; indeed all are very impressionistic and elusive. Fragrance, as explained by Rogan, is "like the fragrance of a flower drifting." It is as if a faint fragrance flowed out of a stanza and quietly moved to the next stanza in the Renku. Here is an example:

> Enlivened at the top
> Is a pine tree in the shower of summer.
> A Zen monk
> Stark naked
> Enjoys the cool.

There is some vague connection between a pine tree in the summer shower and a naked Zen monk cooling himself. This link is termed as "fragrance." Another example of fragrance is given by Dohō:

> Many different names
> Are all too confusing;
> The spring flowers.
>
> Slapped, a butterfly
> Awakens from its sleep.

The first stanza sings of the beauty of spring flowers; various flowers are all so beautifully blooming that it is confusing to remember them each by a different name. But the expression "confusing" gives one the impression of something unsettled, as if something is fluttering at a corner of a beautiful landscape. The author of the second stanza, Bashō himself, smelled this "fragrance" and therewith created the image of a fluttering butterfly in his stanza.

"Reverberation" is explained by Rogan: "As soon as the first stanza is hit, the second stanza reverberates from it in unison." Kyorai also has a similar explanation and then cites an example:

On the veranda
A silver-glazed cup
Is smashed.

Look! The slender sword
Is about to be drawn.

The first stanza suggests a fierce fight about to start between two warriors at a banquet; one of the warriors, in anger, flings his wine cup at the veranda and smashes it into pieces. The second stanza, continuing that tense atmosphere, creates an equally strained situation where a warrior, ready to fight, is about to unsheathe a long, slender sword. The relationship between the two stanzas is described as "reverberation." Here is another example:

An orphaned crow is yet to find its bed
Somewhere under the moon of tonight.

The spears
Charging at a thief
Have the sound of the deepening night.

The natural order of the universe is disturbed in the couplet with the orphaned crow, and that is echoed in the triplet, which tells of a thief discovered by the guards in the depth of night.

"Reflection" seems to describe the relationship between two successive stanzas in which the atmosphere of the one reflects that of the other. It is sometimes called "movement," too, for the poetic atmosphere moves from one stanza to another. Here is an example:

The brushwood is being cut down
Along a grassy path toward the peak.

Deep amid the pine trees
In the forest on the left
Is a thatch-roofed temple.

Bashō thought that the rough, coarse atmosphere of forest workers cutting down the brushwood, as presented in the couplet, is not reflected in, or does not move smoothly into, the mood of the triplet, which is peaceful and still. So he suggested that the first line of the triplet be changed to "It is hailing—," whose harsh wintry mood would well befit the mood of the couplet.

As seen in those instances, the qualities such as fragrance, reverberation, and reflection are delicate and subtle indeed. It is not easy to distinguish between them, although it has been said that fragrance deals with a quiet, peaceful atmosphere while reverberation occurs when the mood is more forceful and stirring. We saw such an anti-discursive attitude in the structural principles advocated by Yoshimoto; that trend has now been further carried on by Bashō and his disciples. And that is no wonder, since the Haiku, even more than linked verse, has its roots in the poet's pre-logical mentality, in his flash of insight into the nature of things.

Here we might see a few instances in which such impressionistic qualities are used as unifying elements within the individual Haiku:

The chrysanthemum smell—
In the old town of Nara.
Many ancient Buddhas.

Exhausted,
I look for an inn.
The wistaria flowers—.

Quietly, quietly,
Yellow mountain roses fall.
The sound of the rapids—.

Under the crescent moon
Dimly looms the earth
The buckwheat flowers—.

In each of these Haiku two disparate objects are abruptly juxtaposed, with little or no explanation. The scent of chrysanthemums and old Buddhist images, purple wistaria flowers and a tired traveler, yellow mountain roses and the sound of a torrent, the crescent moon and white buckwheat flowers—there is little logical connection between the two objects presented in each Haiku. Yet the juxtaposition of the two objects produces a strangely harmonious mood, a mood that cannot be described except by such impressionistic terms as fragrance or reverberation.

There seems to be one special case, however, in which we can define a structural method of the Haiku with a modern scientific term. This is the case of synesthesia. In some Haiku two objects are juxtaposed in such a way that the merging of different senses may take place. Here are some examples:

Their fragrance
Is whiter than peach blossoms:
The daffodils.

Over the evening sea
The wild ducks' cry
Is faintly white.

It is whiter
Than the rocks of Ishiyama:[6]
The autumn wind.

Onions lie
Washed in white.
How chilly it is!

In these poems a color is used to suggest the quality of a fragrance, a sound, a tactile sensation, or a temperature. Such a method is very effective for presenting an experience in its totality, in contrast with the method of science, which dissolves a whole into its component parts. Synesthesia presumes an attitude that accepts the ultimate interrelatedness of all things and experiences. Bashō's synthesesia, however, seems to differ significantly from its counterpart in French Symbolist poetry. French Symbolists used synesthesia in such a way as to create a shocking effect and the beauty of artifice; their beauty was the perfume of amber, musk, benjamin, and incense—violent, sensual, artificial, sophisticated, often decadent and even abnormal. But the effect of Bashō's synesthesia is like the fragrance of daffodils or the wild ducks' cry over the evening sea—faint, natural, simple, primitive, and never extravagant or shocking. This of course stems from Bashō's basic attitude toward life—*sabi, shiori*, and "return to nature." We might recall that all four instances of synesthesia cited above involved the color white, suggestive of that universal loneliness.

However, the ideas of *sabi, shiori*, and return to primitive nature did not constitute the whole of Bashō's philosophy or his poetics. Here we must turn to the other side of the poetic spirit, which, as we remember, urged one to "return to the world of common men" after attaining a high stage of enlightenment. This emphasis on plain, ordinary life is another essential factor in the Haiku; indeed, that is an important element distinguishing the Haiku from other forms of traditional Japanese poetry. "Chinese poetry, Japanese lyric, linked verse, and the Haiku are all poetry," observed Dohō. "But the Haiku draws upon all things of life for its material, including even those which are left out in the other three." In traditional Japanese poetry, for instance, a warbler frequently sings in the blossoms. But when the Haiku creates a scene with a warbler, it need not be such an elegant picture. Dohō cites an example from Bashō's work:

The warbler—
It pooped on a rice cake
At the veranda.

The difference between traditional linked verse and the Haiku is also made clear by Bashō when he says: "A willow tree in the spring rain is wholly of the linked verse world. A crow digging up a mud-snail belongs entirely to the Haiku." The world of the Haiku includes all things in existence, elegant or not elegant; it contains warblers, blossoms, and the moon, but it does not exclude a muddy crow, a bird's droppings, or a horse's dung. These are also part of nature.

Likewise, the Haiku takes in all things of human life. The Haiku poet, while detaching himself from worldly desires, lives among them. He does not flee from the world of ordinary men; he is in the middle of it, understanding and sharing the feelings of ordinary men; he has only to be a bystander, who calmly and smilingly observes them. Bashō has a poem suggesting that the poetic spirit does not exclude the feelings of common men:

When masked beggars
Come round, my poetic spirit
Is also at the year's end.

According to a custom of the day, beggars masked themselves with red cloth when they went out begging toward the end of the year, so people who saw them were once again reminded that the year's end was approaching. In this Haiku Bashō is saying that he, with his poetic spirit, shared that year-end feeling, too, Dohō proposes to contrast this poem by Bashō with the following Haiku by someone else:

My storehouse burnt down,
I can now enjoy
An unobstructed view of the moon.

The poem, trying to transcend an ordinary man's feelings under such circumstances, is ludicrously pretentious. Bashō's poem, in contrast, is far from vulgar while dealing with common men's feelings.

Bashō repeatedly emphasized the importance of understanding the feelings of plain men in ordinary life. "One need not be a Haiku poet," he said to Shikō. "But if there is a person who does not harmonize with ordinary life and who does not understand ordinary sentiments, he should be called the most unpoetic person." "One need not be a Haiku poet," he told Dohō, too. "But a person cannot be considered a wholesome personality unless he harmonizes with ordinary life and understands ordinary sentiments." The implication is that the Haiku helps one adapt to ordinary life and to understand ordinary sentiments. If one attains this kind of personality, one really need not compose poetry; the poetic spirit is what counts, and not the actual poem written on paper.

The Haiku poet, therefore, takes an attitude somewhat like that of a recluse, but nevertheless lives among ordinary men and enjoys a plain way of living. Bashō, carrying this attitude further, came up with the notion of lightness in the last years of his life. In the year of his death, for instance, when one of his pupils asked him what the future style of the Haiku would be, Bashō answered: "In five or six years the present style will change completely, and will become much lighter." In the same year he wrote a letter to Dohō and another disciple of his, in which he said: "I was greatly pleased to see lightness prevailing in your verse in general." As for the nature of lightness, Bashō had a number of metaphors, "Simply observe," he once said, "what children do."

"The style I have in mind," he said at another time, "is a light one both in form and in structure, like the impression of looking at a shallow sand-bed river." On another occasion someone asked Bashō what the latest style of the Haiku was. Bashō answered: "Eat vegetable soup rather than duck stew." The man who asked was puzzled and wondered how plain vegetable soup could be compared with delicious duck stew. Bashō only smiled and did not reply. Kyorai, who had been listening, told the man: "Indeed, I can see why you are not tired of duck stew; you have never eaten it, so you crave for it day and night." Lightness, then, is a beauty of things plain and ordinary, as against colorful, gorgeous beauty. It is the beauty of naïveté rather than of sophistication; of simplicity rather than the ornate; of the shallow rather than of the deep. It goes without saying that this beauty of the shallow does not imply a total lack of depth, however: only those who have tasted duck stew can appreciate the true delicacy of vegetable soup. A person can see the beauty of lightness in the world of common men only after attaining a high stage of enlightenment.

It is unfortunate that there are few examples left today of the poems said to contain the quality of lightness. Only in one instance do we have a poem which Bashō thought had lightness:

> Under the trees
> Soup, fish salad and all
> In cherry blossoms,

This is a blossom-viewing poem, but instead of those elegant courtiers and graceful ladies, or of that hazy moon in the evening dusk, here is a down-to-earth object, food—and a plain sort of food, too. The poem depicts the scene of a family picnic, where cherry blossoms are falling on all things that are there, including the picnic dishes. The peaceful, happy mood of the family will be broken some time, as suggested by the falling blossoms, but nevertheless the picnickers are thoroughly enjoying that momentary happiness in a plain way. The implication points toward lightness.

In another instance we have a Haiku poem that Bashō thought was lacking in lightness. The poem was written by Etsujin,[7] a friend of Bashō's, and the incident was recorded by Kyorai:

> Spring under His Majesty's reign—
> The color of a mosquito net
> Is light green throughout the ages.

> The late Master once said to me: "A poem cannot be a true Haiku unless it settles down. Etsujin's poetry did seem to settle down, but then it began to show heaviness. In this poem of his, the words "The color of a mosquito net / Is light green throughout the ages" are good enough. Before those words he should have placed a phrase like "The moonshine—" or "The dawning day—" for the first line, thereby making the poem a Haiku on a mosquito net. But he used the unchanging color of mosquito net to suggest the eternal spring of His Majesty's reign, and thereby made the poem a Haiku celebrating the New Year. As a consequence, the poem has become heavy in meaning and does not look neat. Your poetry, too, has settled down where it should, and in that respect you need not worry. But do not stay fixed there."

A poem should be light, but it should not be flippant, frivolous, or trite. It ought to give the impression of having "settled down"; all its parts should be neatly balanced and firmly founded. But that does not mean the poem is weighty and dignified. Etsujin's Haiku is weighty and dignified; it sounds almost like a national anthem. Bashō therefore proposed to change the whole tone of the poem by replacing its first line, which is especially grandiose. The Haiku would then become a poem about a mosquito net, a subject familiar enough. It may not exactly be light, but it would be far lighter.

We have one more instance where Bashō rejected a verse for its lack of lightness. This time it was linked Haiku, and Bashō thought the stanzas were too "sweet"—that is, too heavily loaded with emotion. The stanzas read:

> Without sense or discretion
> He falls deeply in love.
>
> The rustic setting
> Begins to show its charm
> In the vicinity of Fushimi.

The stanzas deal with love, not courtly love, but the love of a common man, probably a young, peddling merchant. So the material is something that could have produced lightness and the writer of the triplet (Bashō) tried to use it that way and created a rustic setting (Fushimi was located in the outskirts of Kyoto, bordering on the countryside). But the result was not lightness but sweetness; emotions of young love were not sublimated enough. This would become clearer if we contrast it with the two stanzas dealing with a similar kind of love included in *A Sack of Charcoal* ("Sumidawara"), a collection of linked Haiku containing Bashō's works in his last years:

> Without telling
> Even his next-door neighbor,
> He brought his bride home.
>
> In the shade of the screen,
> A tray for the cake dish.

The theme is again the sort of love found among the people of modest means. The couple, being poor, had no elaborate wedding ceremony: the bridegroom, in fact, did not mention his wedding to his next-door neighbor, but quietly brought his bride home. Yet, without a gorgeous wedding, the occasion was a happy one to the couple just the same; they celebrated it between themselves with a small cake at the bridegroom's home. The stanzas simply describe facts as they are; the couplet, in particular, merely depicts an impersonal scene. Yet the stanzas are not lacking in deeply felt love; it is merely that that love is here looked at by a smiling bystander. Such would be a manifestation of lightness.

If the idea of lightness were pursued further there would emerge the element of humor, for lightness is the quality that detaches a man from worldly concerns while he is immersed in the mire, and that is precisely what makes humor possible. Life is constant suffering for those who have not attained enlightenment; it is something to flee from for those who long for the life of a recluse. But those who have returned to the earthly world after attaining a high stage of enlightenment can look at life with a smile, for they are part of that life and are not so. Knowing what life ultimately is, they can take suffering with a detached light-hearted attitude—with lightness. Bashō was one of those men, as is clearly shown in the following instance. Here Bashō is describing himself in a journal:

> My straw hat had been worn out in the rains I met on the long journey; my paper robe had been wrinkled in the storms I suffered at various places. Though I was familiar with all the sorrows of traveling, I felt sad this time. Then it occurred to me that a certain comic poet had also traveled in this area some time before, and that led me to compose a poem:

In the wintry gust
I wander, like Chikusai[8]
The comic poet.

The passage well describes the tired, emaciated Bashō, on a rugged journey. The situation was a desperate one indeed; even Bashō says it was sad. But then he detached himself from the sadness and composed a poem with lightheartedness. The Haiku, with its allusion to a whimsical mountebank in popular fiction, has done away with sadness; there is even a suggestion of the poet's smiling at himself.

We shall take one more example of lightness verging on humor. This time it is part of the Renku, the second stanza of which was written by Bashō:

Stealthily,
He braids a straw sandal
In the moonlight.

There she rushes out to shake the fleas
Off her pajamas in the early autumn night.

The first stanza depicts a farmhouse scene where a peasant, unable to support his family with daytime work alone, is making straw sandals late at night. He is working in the moonlight outdoors to save lamp oil, but he has to be cautious not to disturb his neighbors. Bashō's couplet that follows, however, neither mourns over the sad peasant life nor protests against the existing social order; staring at the cold fact of life, he just smiles it away. In his stanza he introduces a new character, probably the peasant's wife, who comes out of the house with sleepy eyes to shake off the fleas in the open. The lines are permeated with lightness, which somewhat brightens the otherwise somber picture.

We may conclude, then, that Bashō's poetic spirit functioned not only as a poetic doctrine but also as a moral, or even religious, discipline for him. *Sabi* and *shiori* are poetic principles advocating impersonality in composition, but they also attempt to show that man could overcome life's sorrow by dissolving it into universal loneliness. Fragrance, reverberation, and reflection are poetic principles referring to the impressionistic ways in which different parts of a poem are related, but they also suggest the interrelatedness of all things in the universe, the common destiny of all things in the world. Plainness and lightness are also poetic principles advocating the Haiku's all-inclusiveness in theme and material, but going beyond they also teach how to live in this grief-laden world with a smile. Bashō was painfully aware of the sorrows of life and once even contemplated entering the priesthood. But he never became a priest, no doubt because he believed in the saving power of poetry, in the sublimating effect of the poetic spirit. "At one time I craved for a high office and a substantial estate; at another time I thought of living within the walls of a monastery," he writes, looking back on his past career. "But I kept wandering aimlessly like a cloud while singing of flowers and birds, until that became even the source of my livelihood. With no other talent to resort to, now I can only cling to this thin string of the Haiku." Under the pose of modesty characteristic of Bashō, we can detect his single-minded devotion to the Haiku as the source of not only material, but spiritual, livelihood.

Unfortunately, the Haiku could not be a religion after all. Bashō seems to have come to that painful realization toward the end of his life. In a short prose piece believed to be written two years before his death, he speaks of his determination to stop writing poetry and says: "No sooner have I decided to give up poetry and closed my mouth than a poetic sentiment solicits my heart and something flickers in my mind. Such is the weird power of the poetic spirit." Lying in his deathbed, Bashō still thought of poetry. He fully knew that it was no occasion for verse-writing, but, as he told Shikō, he wandered through morning clouds and evening mist while asleep, and was startled at the sound of a mountain stream and the cry of wild birds when awake. "All this," he then said, "is a sinful attachment." He further continued, "I simply wish I could forget the Haiku of my lifetime." His last poem was:

> On a journey, ill—
> My dreams roam
> Over a wild moor.

The poem seems to fully substantiate Shikō's record. In the face of death, *sabi*, *shiori*, and lightness were to lead Bashō to a peaceful, serene state of mind. Yet actually they did not; they could not; as long as they remained poetic principles, and as long as Bashō remained a poet. Those principles of depersonalization could give the poet a moment of solace, but only for that brief, inspired period of time; the next moment he had to emerge out of that impersonal self and resume his role as a poet. A poet must necessarily be an active, vigorous personality, for his task is an act of creation; but Bashō tried to set up his poetics and religion at the extreme of passivity. Bashō's mistake lay precisely in this; he sought to attain the passivity of religion by means of poetry, despite the fact that poetry by its very nature demanded a degree of positivism on the part of the poet. This degree of positivism, no matter how slight it might be in the case of the Haiku, inevitably formed an obstacle in the path of religion—a sinful attachment, as Buddhism calls it. Bashō again suffered the fate of all artists who tried the same; we have already seen the instances of Zeami and Rikyū before him.

Notes

1. Mukai Kyorai (1651–1704) was a leading poet among Bashō's disciples and was close to him throughout his later years. Kyorai's writings on the Haiku, published as *Kyorai's Writings* ("Kyorai Shō") in 1775, show his good understanding of Bashō's poetics. Part of this book has been translated by Donald Keene and is included in his *Anthropology of Japanese Literature.*

Hattori Dohō (1657–1730) was born and lived in Ueno, so he had the advantage of seeing Bashō whenever the master visited his native town. A less original poet than Kyorai, Dohō was perhaps even more faithful in recording Bashō's teachings. In this respect, his *Three Books on the Art of the Haiku* ("Sanzōshi"), published in 1776, is invaluable.

2. Kagami Shikō (1665–1731) was probably the most systematic theorizer of poetry in the Bashō school. His ideas on the Haiku, however, became increasingly dogmatic after Bashō's death.

Morikawa Kyoroku (1656–1715) was especially close to Bashō in the latter's last years. *Dialogues on the Art of the Haiku* ("Haikai Mondō," 1698) is an interesting book documenting a lively controversy between him and Kyorai on various aspects of Haiku writing.

Zushi Rogan (d. 1693) was a promising student of Bashō's but died before the age of forty. In 1693 he welcomed his traveling teacher to his home at a town in northeast Japan, and what he heard from Bashō during those seven days resulted in *The Record of the Seven Days* ("Kikigaki Nanukagusa"), the earliest known document of Bashō's poetics.

3. Priest Saigyō (1118–90) was one of the finest lyric poets after Tsurayuki's time. As indicated by the title of his book of poetry, *The Collection of Poems at a Mountain Hut* ("Sanka Shū"), he loved the life of a recluse and spent most of his life wandering all over Japan.

Iio Sōgi (1421–1502) was one of the most influential writers of linked verse following Yoshimoto's time. He was the central figure in composing the celebrated *Minase Sangin Hyakuin.* He also liked to travel.

Sesshū (1420–1506) was a Zen monk, and an expert in brush painting. He studied in China for a while and mastered the art of landscape painting, and after returning to Japan he created a style of his own. The orthodox school of black ink painting in Japan can be said to have started with him.

4. Sado is an island on the Sea of Japan, some fifty miles off the mainland coast. Some eminent people, including Zeami, led a sorrowful life here after being banished from the Capital.

5. The Mogami River is one of the largest rivers in northeastern Japan. Flowing through the mountains, it has many falls and rapids along its way. June is the rainy season in the area.

6. Ishiyama, literally meaning "a stone mountain," is a site of a large Buddhist temple in Omi Province. The place is famous for its bleached rocks.

7. Ochi Etsujin (1656–?) was especially close to Bashō in the 1680s; in 1688, for instance, he was Bashō's sole companion in the famous journey that resulted in *The Journal of a Travel to Sarashina.* After Bashō's death he was engaged in a series of lively controversies with Shikō over principles of the Haiku.

8. Chikusai is the hero of a popular fiction called *The Tale of Chikusai* ("Chikusai Monogatari," 1635 or 1636) attributed to Karasumaru Mitsuhiro. A physician by profession, he writes a number of comic verses on the incidents he meets during his travel to Edo.

Chapter 8

Zeami on the Art of the Nō Drama: Imitation, *Yūgen*, and Sublimity

MAKOTO UEDA

The Nō play is one of the oldest forms of drama in Japan. From its origins in early religious festivals, to its fullest expression in the fourteenth century by the genius of Zeami Motokiyo, it was primarily an entertainment for the court of the Shoguns, and was not generally available to the common public. The plays, by Western standards, are very short, often no longer than a single act of a Western play. There are usually only four or five actors (always male) who appear in the plays, and the use of masks, beautiful costumes, and musical accompaniment make the Nō a spectacle to behold. The acting is very stylized, and the sign of a truly great Nō actor is his ability to perform the play in much the same way it has been performed for centuries. In the following essay, Ueda discusses many of the aesthetic principles which govern Nō and help to make this complex and fascinating theater more accessible to Western audiences. For additional discussion of the aesthetic principles of the Nō theater, see de Bary's "The Vocabulary of Japanese Aesthetics II."

The aesthetics of Japanese theater reached a peak in its history with the writings of Zeami Motokiyo (1363–1443), a great actor, writer, and theorizer of the Nō drama. For one thing, the Nō was a highly refined, sophisticated art form, accepting no immature theory for itself. It had absorbed many heterogeneous elements from the outside, such as Chinese operatic drama and

Japanese folk dance, Shinto rituals and Buddhist ceremonies, and popular mimetic shows and aristocratic court music, eventually integrating them all into a single, harmoniously unified art. This composite nature of the Nō placed a heavy burden on its performer, for he had to be a competent actor, singer, and dancer at the same time. Inborn gift, intensive training, and above all a never-failing passion for self-improvement were required of anyone intending to learn this art. "A man's life has an end," Zeami has said in a typical remark, "but there is no end to the pursuit of the Nō." Zeami's some twenty essays, written at various times during his long theatrical career, discuss a wide variety of topics concerning the Nō drama, but they are all permeated with his passionate concern for the perfection of his art. That is why, despite all their abstruse vocabulary and idioms, they have a powerful appeal to those who know little about the technical details of the medieval Japanese stage.

The most basic principle in Zeami's art theory seems to lie in the idea of imitation. "Objects to imitate are too many to enumerate here," Zeami teaches to beginning actors, "but you should study them thoroughly, because imitation is the essence of our art." Then he adds, "In principle, the aim is to imitate all objects, whatever they may be." An actor cast in a woman's role (as the Nō permitted no actress to perform on its stage) should carefully study the way in which women speak and behave in daily life. An actor who is to impersonate a high-ranking court lady has a more difficult task, because such a lady is seldom seen out of her palace. In a case like this, the actor should seek accurate information from experts on this subject. "In wearing a coat, in putting on a skirt,—in all such and similar cases," says Zeami, "do not decide by yourself. Ask the people who know." If the actor finds a noble courtier in his audience and has a chance to talk with him after the performance, this is a good opportunity to have his imitation scrutinized. "Ask him," Zeami advises, "what he thought of your performance."

Zeami goes on to explain what would happen if an actor did not follow the principle of imitation. The case in question occurs most frequently when the actor is too intent on producing some specific emotional impact upon the spectators. He might be over-anxious to create an impression of elegant beauty, for instance, which was very popular at the time. The result, as Zeami points out, is often a complete theatrical failure, for the actor has neglected the principle of imitation. The actor too anxious to produce an elegant effect often acts out his role elegantly, even in cases where the role requires him to be vigorous and forceful. In such a case, the actual effect produced will not be elegant; it will be weak instead. His performance is weak because his imitation involves a degree of falsehood. "In all acts of imitation," Zeami warns, "if there is a false element, the performance will become rough or weak." Thus, often an actor trying to create elegant beauty produces a weak effect instead; intending to bring out forcefulness from his performance, he ends up with roughness. "An actor makes such a mistake," Zeami explains, "because he thinks that a quality like elegance or forcefulness exists independently of the object. Actually, it lies within the object itself." The beauty of elegance or forcefulness automatically emerges when the actor faithfully imitates an elegant or forceful object. If he successfully imitates a court lady, a beautiful woman, a handsome man, or various kinds of flowers, his performance will naturally become elegant, because the quality of elegance is inherent in those persons and objects. Likewise, a performance will be forceful when the actor faithfully imitates a warrior, a rustic, a demon, a deity, a pine tree, or a cedar tree, all of which have the quality of forcefulness.

Ideally, then, to imitate an object would mean that the actor becomes identical with that thing, that he dissolves himself into nothing so that the qualities inherent in the object would be naturally manifested. Zeami's way of saying this is that the actor "grows into the object." "In performing an act of imitation, of whatever object it may be," he says, "the actor should first learn how to grow into the object." "If he genuinely grows into the object," he says elsewhere, too, "his performance will be neither rough nor weak." The actor's self, in other words, should be completely absorbed by the object of his imitation. If this is successfully done, the actor will have no awareness that he is imitating an object outside of himself, for he is at one with it. The term "imitation" will no longer apply here in its ordinary sense. Zeami calls this "a realm of nonimitation." "In the art of imitation," he says, "there is a realm called 'nonimitation.' When the actor pursues the art to its ultimate and truly grows into the object, he will not be aware of his act of imitation." Identification is the ultimate form of imitation.

But how could an actor identify himself with something which he is not? By knowing the true intent of that thing, Zeami would answer. He explains this in a passage where he teaches how to act a frenzied person's role:

> To impersonate a mentally deranged person is the most interesting of all roles. Since there are so many kinds of mental derangement, an actor competent in this role would be an expert in all other roles as well. That is why this role should be thoroughly studied. In general, a person possessed by various spirits—by, for instance, a deity, a Buddha, a wraith, or a departed soul—could be easily imitated if one knows what it is that has possessed the person. More

> difficult is to imitate a man who has become frenzied from having lost his parent, child, or spouse. Even a fairly good actor does not make a distinction between different kinds of frenzy but acts then all in the same manner; as a consequence the spectators are not moved. In portraying a man who is deranged because of an obsession, the actor should make the obsession the "true intent," and the derangement the "flower." An actor who performs the role with this in mind will never fail to create a glowing climax in his performance.

The "true intent," then, is that which makes the person what he is. In acting out the role of a man possessed by a deity, for instance, the actor should imitate such actions as characteristic not of any possessed person but of that specific deity, for the deity is what lies in the innermost heart of the man and what controls every one of his actions. Likewise, in imitating a person who has become frenzied the actor should first of all learn the cause of his frenzy, that specific obsession which has driven the man out of his mind. The "true intent" is the inmost nature of the man or the thing. The actor, by learning that inmost nature, can grow into that person or object.

Zeami has emphasized the importance of this throughout his essays on the art of the Nō. As he writes in one of his earliest essays, an actor performing the role of a Buddhist monk should fully express deep devotion to religion because that is what is essential to a monk. As Zeami says in one of his later essays, an actor impersonating a woman should make her heart his and then throw away all his masculine strength; he must feel as if he were born a woman. "One who mimics a woman," Zeami says, "is not a woman." Zeami cites a contemporary proverb to describe such an incomplete act of imitation: "It looks similar, but does not look right." It is an imitation of the outward only; it has failed to catch the true intent.

Imitation, in this special sense, is the most basic principle of Nō acting. But there are some cases in which that principle must be somewhat modified. One typical instance of this is when the actor is cast in the role of a demon. Zeami writes: "By its very nature, imitating a demon involves great difficulty, for the more faithfully the actor imitates the demon, the less entertaining his performance will be. The 'true intent' of the demon lies in its horrifying quality. But horror differs from entertainment as black differs from white. Therefore, if there is an actor who entertains the audience by performing a demon's role, he should be considered a truly accomplished artist." Another such special case is when the actor portrays a man of low social status. Zeami remarks: "The actor can imitate in detail the poetic figure of a woodcutter, a grass mower, a charcoal burner, or a saltwater drawer, but not the people of meaner occupations than those. These unsightly appearances should not be shown to gentleman and ladies of the nobility. They would be too lowly to be of delight to the noble audience. You should fully understand this. Imitation should be carried out to a greater or lesser extent, depending upon what it is that you are imitating." In imitating an object, the actor must take into consideration what effect his imitation will produce on the spectators. If the imitation is such that it would horrify or offend the spectators, that performance would be said to be theatrically unsuccessful, no matter how faithfully the principle of imitation may have been followed. The actor, therefore, must know the proper degree to which each object should be imitated. What determines the degree is the nature of the affective response that the performance creates. It is beauty, or what Zeami calls the flower.

The type of beauty that was most welcomed in the Nō can be easily imagined. It was *yūgen*, that elegant, delicate, graceful beauty which was the ideal of linked verse and of medieval Japanese culture at large. Zeami has an apt image to suggest the beauty: "a swan with a flower in its bill." The Nō actor should imitate his object in proportion to the degree to which it has the *yūgen* quality. Flowers and birds, the breeze and the moon, noble courtiers and graceful ladies, for instance, have plenty of *yūgen* in them; the actor, therefore, may imitate these to the fullest extent on the stage. But people of lower status and occupations have less of that beauty; accordingly the actor should take less from what they are in actual life; he should get less from the outside and create more from the inside, from what Zeami calls the spirit. One might assume that this spirit is roughly equivalent to the same term as used by Yoshimoto in linked verse; it is a spirit in pursuit of elegant beauty. The Nō actor can imitate a graceful court lady without reservation, for she has that spirit in herself. But he will have to supply it from himself when he imitates a peasant, for instance, who has little of it. Therefore, when an expert actor is on the stage the beauty of *yūgen* is always there; this is so no matter how many different roles he may perform. Zeami has an apt simile: "This would be like looking at court ladies of high and low ranks, men and women, monks and rustics, even beggars and outcasts, all adorned with a spray of blossoms." Then comes Zeami's explanation: "This spray of blossoms is the beauty of form. What creates a good form is the spirit." When an actor who has this spirit performs a demon's role, even the horrifying demon comes to assume some strange beauty; Zeami describes it as "blossoms on a crag." Even a withered old man can be made beautiful by an actor who has this spirit; Zeami describes the beauty as "blossoms on a dead tree." Kannami, Zeami's father and a celebrated Nō actor, had this spirit: his performance in his old age is compared to an aged tree that has very few branches and leaves but still retains its most beautiful blossoms.

Yūgen, then is the beauty not merely of appearance but of the spirit; it is inner beauty manifesting itself outwards. The emphasis on inner beauty, as against the beauty of the outward appearance, is inevitable so long as the imitation in the Nō is of the inward spirit, of the true intent. It is the beauty of the innermost nature of things, the beauty of hidden truth. If the term *yūgen* is etymologically analyzed, it will be found that *yū* means deep, dim, or difficult to see, and that *gen*, originally describing the dark, profound, tranquil color of the universe, refers to the Taoist concept of truth. Zeami's idea of *yūgen* seems to combine its conventional meaning of elegant beauty with its original meaning of profound, mysterious truth of the universe. Zeami perceived mysterious beauty in cosmic truth; beauty was the color of truth, so to speak.

If *yūgen* contains cosmic truth underneath, it must necessarily have pessimistic implications, for the truth of the universe always points toward the sad destiny of man. When man is set against the great cosmic power, the vision is always a sad, melancholy one; it is all the more so when conceived in medieval Japanese terms. Thus *yūgen*, in its broader sense, has the implication of universal sadness. Zeami has examples to explain this. After pointing out that elegant court ladies in classical times, such as Lady Aoi, Lady Yūgao, and Lady Ukifune of *The Tale of Genji*, make excellent heroines in the Nō drama, he goes on to say: "There are even better materials which produce the jewel among jewels in this respect. These rare examples are seen in such cases as Lady Aoi haunted by Lady Rokujō's spirit, Lady Yūgao taken away by a ghost, or Lady Ukifune possessed by a supernatural being, all of which provide the seed for superb *yūgen* flowers." Noble court ladies are gracefully beautiful in themselves, but they would be even more lovely when they suffer under some strange power beyond their control, under some mysterious force hidden in the universe. Aoi, Yūgao, and Ukifune have to suffer (and die in the first two instances) from causes for which they are not responsible. That is the sad fate of mankind. Even the most beautiful and accomplished person cannot escape from the sufferings common to all men. *Yūgen* is the beauty of seeing such an ideal person go through an intense suffering as a result of being human. Thus one definition of *yūgen*, attributed to Zeami, reads: "elegance, calm, profundity, mixed with the feeling of mutability."

Of the two principal elements of *yūgen*, elegant beauty and sadness of human life, Zeami emphasized the first in his early essays but steadily shifted the emphasis to the second as he grew older. The difference in emphasis is most clearly seen when he classifies Nō singings in terms of their emotive effects. Of the five categories he sets up, elegant singing comes second. Its beauty is described as that of "looking at both a morning and an evening scene of blossoms and the moon in one view." In another metaphor, it is compared to a cherry tree. In a third comparison, it is likened to the effect of this poem:

> Shall I ever see again
> Such a beautiful blossom hunting
> On the field of Katano,[1]
> Where white flakes fall
> Like the snow at spring dawn?

One is reminded of the image of "a swan with a flower in its bill." Cherry blossoms, beautiful in pure white, are dimly seen in the serene darkness of the spring dawn. They are elegantly, exquisitely beautiful. Moreover, those lovely petals are falling as quietly as snow—and as if to symbolize the mutability of life.

Next comes a type called love singing. It is as gentle and beautiful as elegant singing, but it has an added element—pathos. The pathos is that of longing for someone dear missing. The following poem has been cited by Zeami as producing a comparable effect:

> Tinted leaves begin to fall
> From one side of the forest
> As it rains in the evening
> And drenches a deer
> Lonesomely calling for its mate.

Now the season has changed from spring to autumn, and nature from cherry blossoms to maple leaves. With approaching winter in the background, a deer is lonesomely calling for its missing mate in the cold rain. The image certainly suggests a degree of pathos.

Sadness increases even more in the next type of singing, called sorrowful singing. The season is now winter, and all trees are bare. "Flowery spring and tinted autumn are both over," writes Zeami. "Nipped by frost and buried in snow, trees in winter stand with bare branches, as if mournfully recalling the men and things that have passed away." The poem which exemplifies the mood is:

Even on a mountain
Devoid of feelings, there grow
The Trees of Sorrow.[2]
How much more so
In the heart of a deserted lover!

What has been expressed only indirectly in elegant and love singings now becomes more intense, so much so that it turns into a direct outcry of sorrow. The nature of sorrow, however, remains unchanged; it is the sadness over the impermanence of things in this world. The year must sooner or later come to cold winter, and love must eventually end in grief.

Thus we see elegant beauty gradually yielding its place to sadness of life as we move from the second to the third and then to the fourth type of Nō singing as categorized by Zeami. Sadness, indeed, is the dominating mood in the fourth type. Zeami, however, did not stop here: he had the fifth and final type called "sublime" singing, and he rated it above all others. "Sublime singing is the result of consummate artistry," Zeami observes. "This rank can be attained only after the singer learns the ultimate of all other singings, transcends both the good and evil of music, and arrives at the kind of singing that is like others and yet is not." Zeami's metaphor for sublime singing is a cedar tree, and the following poem is cited for illustration:

With the years that have passed by
It has grown austere and holy
On Mount Kagu:[3]
The cedar tree, upright like a spear,
Already has a layer of moss at the root

Impermanence, which imprisons all men and things in this world, has now been transcended. The cedar, being an evergreen tree, symbolizes permanence in nature. Being a holy tree in Shintoism, it also stands for a man who has attained divine immortality. Sadness is no longer there, because death has been overcome. There is neither the graceful beauty of elegant singing nor the cold beauty of sorrowful singing; the beauty here is that of austerity, deep, tranquil, and awesome. And that is the effect produced by sublime singing.

The meaning of Zeami's sublimity will be further clarified when it is seen in the context of an elaborate scheme he devised in order to define and evaluate the emotional impact of various Nō performances. Zeami has classified all theatrical effects into nine categories and given each a name and a rank.

These are, from the lower to the higher, (1) Roughness and Aberrance, (2) Strength and Roughness, (3) Strength and Delicacy, (4) Shallowness and Loveliness, (5) Broadness and Minuteness, (6) a Right Flower, (7) a Calm Flower, (8) a Profound Flower, and (9) a Mysterious Flower. The element of *yūgen* is latent in all styles except the first three. The quality of sublimity lies only in the final three styles.

The Style of Roughness and Aberrance is the lowest of all styles. As the name shows, this style has no delicacy and it has deviated from the orthodox manners of Nō performance. Zeami compares the style to a flying squirrel. In the Confucian tradition, a flying squirrel is an animal with five talents—climbing, swimming, digging, flying, and running—but they are all commonplace talents. Likewise, when a Nō actor of mediocre talents performs a play, he will produce a crude, uninspiring effect even though he follows the technical details of the theater. The performance will be rough and unrefined, far below the desired standard.

The Style of Strength and Roughness is a little better, because it is at any rate forceful. Zeami quotes an old saying to describe it: "A three-day-old tiger cub already has a temper fiery enough to devour an ox." Again the Nō performance of this category has no grace or refinement, but it has a vital force that moves the audience.

The Style of Strength and Delicacy supersedes the two previous styles, obviously because of its added element of delicacy. Zeami's way of suggesting the effect of this style is: "As the metal hammer moves, the precious sword emits a cold gleam." The element of strength is symbolized in the heavy metal hammer held in the muscular hand of a swordsmith. But that strength is used, not to devour an ox, but to create a delicate work of art, a precious sword. The sword, in fact, is emitting a serene gleam from its blade. A Nō performance belonging to this category will have a similar emotive effect.

The Style of Roughness and Aberrance, the Style of Strength and Roughness, and the Style of Strength and Delicacy are the lowest three, because they lack the quality of *yūgen.* A beginning student in the Nō, therefore, should avoid those styles; he should begin with the fourth style, Shallowness and Loveliness, and work upward from there. After attaining the ninth and highest style, he can then come down and perform in the lowest three styles. Those three styles can be made interesting only when played by a most competent performer, an actor who fully knows what *yūgen* is.

So the beginner's style, Shallowness and Loveliness, has a bit of *yūgen*—Loveliness implies *yūgen,* although it is yet of a shallow kind. To explain the style Zeami cites the very opening line of the *Lao Tzu:* "The Way of ways is not an ordinary way." As it seems, Zeami is giving a warning to his beginning students, as Lao Tzu is doing the same to his. There are various ways in the art of the Nō, but they all begin with and return to the Way, *yūgen*, just as in Taoism all ways derive from and lead to the Way, Tao. "Advance along the ways, and learn what the Way is like," Zeami advises. "Loveliness could manifest itself even at an early stage of apprenticeship." A Nō performance in this style may show the actor's artistic immaturity as yet, but it will nevertheless have a bit of loveliness if the actor has begun to understand what *yūgen* is.

The performer's art widens and deepens in the next higher rank, the Style of Broadness and Minuteness. As the name shows, the actor now has both depth and versatility. Zeami tries to illustrate it through a Zen saying: "The heart of mountains, clouds, seas, and the moon are all told." The student has mastered the art of imitation and knows the true intent of all things in the universe; accordingly, when he performs a role on the stage, he can tell through his performance all about the heart of the object he is impersonating. Of course *yūgen* is there: mountains, clouds, seas, and the moon are elegant objects, and even when he portrays something not elegant in itself, he will make it look so out of his artistry.

The highest of the middle three ranks is called the Style of a Right Flower. The term "flower," which indicates an impressive theatrical effect, appears here for the first time. The actor has attained the flower because he has been making progress along the right road. Zeami illustrates the Right Flower by a colorful line: "The spring haze brightens in the setting sun. All mountains in sight are gleaming in crimson." This is natural beauty at its most colorful. The effect is somewhat like the beauty of myriad cherry blossoms in full bloom on the field of Katano, as described in a poem quoted by Zeami elsewhere. *Yūgen* has now blossomed into a most lovely flower.

In Zeami's view, however, a performance producing such dazzling beauty is not quite the ultimate of the Nō, for there are still three more ranks remaining at the top of the scheme. These would be the ones that fall in the category of the sublime singing, although Zeami nowhere says so in plain terms. Common to the highest three ranks is the quality of quiet, subdued beauty, which is, as we recall, the main characteristic of sublimity.

The Style of a Calm Flower occupies the lowest of the top three ranks. The essence of this style is explained by a citation from Zen: "Snow is piled in a silver bowl." If the Style of a Right Flower is the ultimate of the colorful, this style is the ultimate of colorless beauty, the beauty of pure whiteness as symbolized by snow and the silver bowl. Furthermore, the snow, that wonder of nature, is contained in the silver bowl, that wonder of artistry. Art is a vessel containing the purest beauty of nature; art and nature are harmoniously united in the beauty of whiteness.

One rank higher than the Style of the Calm Flower is the Style of a Profound Flower. To describe this style Zeami again relies on a Zen saying: "Snow has covered thousands of mountains. Why is it that a solitary mountain towers unwhitened among them?" Again the setting is of a natural beauty and of pure whiteness, this time on a large scale. But there is an irrational element in that beautiful picture: a black peak towering among snow-covered mountains. The other world has now begun to invade the world of the ordinary senses. Natural beauty is not enough; there must be the beauty of the supernatural, a strange kind of beauty perceptible to only those supreme artists who are endowed with extraordinary sensitivity. A Nō actor able to perform the Style of a Profound Flower leads his spectators to a state of trance, in which they can appreciate the beauty of the strange and wondrous.

Beauty of the supernatural exists only in part in the Style of a Profound Flower. It thoroughly pervades the Style of a Mysterious Flower, the highest of all nine ranks. Zeami, while conceding that this style is beyond description, attempts to illustrate it by another Zen epigram: "In Silla the sun shines brightly at midnight." The statement is apparently a flat contradiction. But it may not be a contradiction to those who can transcend the limitations of time and space. Silla, part of present Korea, is located to the east of China; the sun shines brightly there when it is still night in China. A person in China would be able to see the bright sun at midnight, if only he could overcome the limitation of space and see the sky of Korea. We see contradictions in the universe only because we are confined within space and time. Once we transcend our limited senses, what we have hitherto seen as contradictions may not be contradictions. A superb Nō actor, through the Style of a Mysterious Flower, makes us visualize such a transcendental world, a world of higher reality lying beyond our ordinary senses. It is a realm of permanence, of immortal souls. As its sight we are struck with the feeling of austerity. Such is the impact of a sublime performance.

According to Zeami's idea, then, the Nō is a symbolic drama. The idea seems to be valid when applied to actual Nō plays remaining today. The protagonist of the Nō is usually some strange being from the other world: a deity, a spirit, the departed soul of a man, and the like. The core of the play consists of an account of life narrated by such a protagonist, a transcendental being who has been to the other world as well as to our world. We cannot directly see him or hear him talk; we can do that only through a medium, the deuteragonist of the play, who, aptly, is a Buddhist monk. The protagonist appears in the monk's dream, and we, together with the monk, come to know what the world of dreams is like. That world, of course, is expressed in terms of the things of this world, for this is the only way we can perceive it. In short, the things that appear in the play are symbols. The artist is a manipulator of symbols.

The view that art is magic thus lies in the center of Zeami's aesthetics. This is not a unique view in itself, but Zeami has expressed it in such a beautifully metaphorical language. The following is one of those passages in which Zeami explains the nature of art and the artist:

> If we explain this by comparing it to the notion of Being and Non-Being in Buddhism, Being corresponds to the appearance and Non-Being to the vessel. It is a Non-Being which engenders Being. This is like a crystal, which is transparent and devoid of color or design, yet produces fire and water out of itself. Why is it that two heterogeneous matters like fire and water emerge from a single transparent object? There is a poem saying:
>
> Smash a cherry tree
> And you will find no flower
> In the splinters.
> It is in the sky of spring
> That cherry blossoms bloom.
>
> The seed of the flower that blossoms out in all works of art lies in the artist's soul. Just as a transparent crystal produces fire and water, or a colorless cherry tree bears blossoms and fruit, a superb artist creates a moving work of art out of a landscape within his soul. It is such a person that can be called a vessel. Works of art are many and various, some singing of the moon and the breeze on the occasion of a festival, others admiring the blossoms and the birds at an outdoor excursion. The universe is a vessel containing all things—flowers and leaves, the snow and the moon, mountains and seas, trees and grass, the animate and the inanimate—according to the season of the year. Make those numerous things the material of your art, let your soul be the vessel of the universe, and set it in the spacious, tranquil ways of the void. You will then be able to attain the ultimate of art, the Mysterious Flower.

Running through the passage is a contrast between two sets of reality, ordinary and higher, as symbolized by a series of different images. Ordinary reality is perceptible through our senses, like cherry blossoms, fire and water; it is appearance, or Being. But ordinary reality is in truth a manifestation of higher reality, the reality whose essence is hidden and remains unnoticed in ordinary human life. In its colorlessness and intangibility, higher reality may be compared to a crystal or a cherry tree without blossoms. The artist, endowed with extra sensitivity, can see a glimpse of it and come to conceive a strange landscape within his soul. When he expresses the landscape by means of art, there emerges a moving work. The work of art is the expression of a microcosm formed inside the artist's soul. In the sense that each artist contains this microcosm within himself, he can be said to be a vessel. It is for this reason that he is creative, that he can create everything out of nothing. Thus the artist can be compared to the universe, which produces thousands of things out of itself. The mysteries of the universe are the mysteries of art, which eventually bloom into the Mysterious Flower.

Having such symbolic nature, the Nō conceived by Zeami, inevitably approaches close to music on one hand and to religion on the other. The Nō must rely on the instantaneous emotive power of music inasmuch as it aims not to analyze social problems but to represent ultimate reality lying beyond the realm of the intellect. Music, the most sensuous among the means of communication, is least controlled by reason and is most appealing to the imagination. Thus the Nō play has no dramatic structure in the Western sense; it has little plot and less characterization. Instead it has ample music; all the actor's lines are recited in rhythmical speech, with the accompaniment of orchestral music. Zeami has declared: "Music is the soul of the Nō." The structure of the Nō is musically conceived: it has *jo, ha,* and *kyū*, like traditional Japanese music. The rhythm of the Nō play is suggestive of the great hidden law of the universe; it is, in fact, the universal rhythm of life. "All things in the universe, good or evil, large or small, animate or inanimate, have each the rhythm of *jo, ha,* and *kyū,*" Zeami says. "It is observed even in such things as a bird's singing or an insect's chirping." "Everything has *jo, ha,* and *kyū,*" he says elsewhere. "The Nō follows that, too." In the Nō a segment of life is presented, not as an accumulation of different parts, but as an integral entity animated with a living rhythm. As the universe gives each object of nature a rhythm of life, so does the artist pour life into his work through the rhythm of nature. It follows that the language of Nō must be rhythmical, too; it must be poetry. Zeami, who has advised his students to sacrifice all other pursuits for the sake of the Nō, makes an exception for poetry. A Nō writer is required to be a good poet, too.

The musical quality of the Nō is well described by Zeami through the metaphor of a flowing stream. Water flows slowly and peacefully on a spacious plain. It rushes on, whirling and bubbling, as it comes to the rapids. A landscape gardener imitates all this in making a garden; he creates a beautiful stream, with falls, rapids, curves, deep pools, sunken rocks, and many other things at proper places along its course. The Nō writer should be such a gardener in composing his work, too. He will put forth the "landscape within his soul" by manipulating the varying rhythm of nature. He will use auditory symbols suggestive of intangible reality.

If the Nō intends to present the mysteries of the cosmos by means of visual and auditory symbols, its relationship to religion is obvious, for religion tries to teach the mysterious truths of pre- and after-life through a symbolic or metaphysical system, too. The Nō is a religious drama; it is a ritual. The implications of the Nō are predominately Buddhist; they point toward a Buddhist scheme of salvation. In many Nō plays the protagonist is a sinner, a sinner not because he has committed a crime against society, but because he has suffered from the limitations of humanity, because he was born a human being. Thus he cannot be saved by human means. In his lifetime, however, he was not even aware of his sin; it is only after death that he discovers what life really is and how sinful it is. The awakening, coupled with the prayer of the deuteragonist (who is a monk), redeems him at the end of the play. The spectators, while they watch the protagonist's spiritual metamorphosis enacted on the stage, come to feel their souls purified and elevated. Such is the purging effect of the Nō.

No doubt Zeami believed in the oneness of art and religion. In one of his last essays he quotes a famous Zen saying: "All laws return to the Law. Where does the Law return to? It returns to all laws." This must have been one of his lifelong mottoes in both art and religion. We have already seen his many quotations from religious texts in describing the ultimate of art, too. Zeami, well disciplined in religious classics in his young days, later entered the priesthood. There is even a record of miracles coming upon him. Did he indeed attain the ultimate of religion, that calm, enlightened state of mind, through art? Sadly, the answer seems to be in the negative. Testifying to it is his mournful confession in the last essays on the Nō, which he wrote when met by the untimely death of Motomasa, his eldest son and a talented actor who had seemed to promise a bright future for the Nō drama after Zeami's time. It reads: "I had bequeathed all the secrets of our art to Motomasa and had been calmly waiting for death's call. Then all of a sudden Motomasa died, ending the line of our art and bringing our theater to a close. My grandsons are yet small, and there is no one else who will inherit our art. When I think of this my aged heart feels so much sinful attachment as to disturb my readiness for death." As Zeami had always thought, art would eventually lead the artist to the calm, to a serenity of mind. Imitation was a way to penetrate the surface and reach for hidden reality. *Yūgen* was a way to resign oneself to the sadness of that hidden reality. Sublimity was a way to accept that reality with calm of mind. Yet Zeami had to discover, near the end of his life, that art was not religion after all. Religion, emphasizing the world beyond, preached the abandonment of all things in this life, including art itself. Art, even the impersonal art of the Nō, had to be of this world as long as it was written by human playwrights, performed by human actors, and appreciated by human spectators. Zeami could not attain Nirvana as long as he remained an artist.

Notes

1. Katano, located near present Osaka, was the Imperial Hunting Ground and was famous for its cherry blossoms, too. As hunting is a winter sport, the comparison of cherry blossoms to snowflakes in the poem is especially fitting.

2. Firewood. It is called a Tree of Sorrow because the Japanese word for firewood, *nageki*, also has the meaning of "sorrow."

3. Mount Kagu is located near Nara. It was considered a holy mountain, as it was believed to have descended from heaven.

Chapter 9

The Social Environment of Tokugawa Kabuki

DONALD H. SHIVELY

Kabuki, a theater form reaching its heights during the Tokugawa period, was primarily a theater of the ordinary people. The actors (all male), like the Nō actors, came from long generations of theater families and learned the conventions of the theater from imitation of their predecessors. In kabuki, the actor is supreme and the scripts for the plays are primarily guidelines for the action which the actors may interpret as they see fit. Emphasis is placed on elaborate costuming and make-up and music and dance (including highly stylized posturing and gestures). The stage sets make use of a long runway extending into the audience, trap doors, and other apparatus designed to make the action of the plays more spectacular. Of special interest in kabuki is the onnagata, *the male performer of female roles. These actors were among the most popular and their dress and hair styles affected the fashions of the day among their audiences. In the following essay, Donald Shively provides an in-depth look at the social milieu of eighteenth-century Tokugawa Japan and the social circumstances which gave rise to the kabuki theater. By focusing his attention on the theater buildings, the relationships between actors and audience, the connections between the kabuki and prostitute quarters, and the lives and art of the kabuki actors, he provides important insights into this exciting and popular form of entertainment.*

Tokugawa Kabuki and Kabuki Today

The audience of "classical kabuki" in Tokyo today witnesses a production which closely approximates its eighteenth-century prototype. If the new play is indeed a classical piece, the text was written during the latter half of the Tokugawa period and hence in subject matter and language remains an artifact of that time. The actors, all descendants of professional theater families, seem to have preserved in mime, dance, and elocution, the conventions of their predecessors. Instrumental and singing styles, handed down from father to son by rote imitation, are probably faithful transmissions of the Tokugawa art. Costumes and props follow those depicted in early woodblock prints. Many of the staging techniques also date from premodern times. In short, today's viewer sees on the kabuki stage a world familiar to his Tokugawa forebears.[1]

Although he may enjoy the performance and empathize with the dilemmas enacted on the stage, the modern Japanese brings with him attitudes and experiences substantially different from those of a Tokugawa observer. A more modern logic and a changed ethical orientation separate him from the action on the stage. A considerable part of the kabuki repertoire consists of history plays which, while they concern events of a much earlier era, depict a moral system and feudal psychology ideally characteristic of the Tokugawa samurai class. The domestic tragedies deal with shopkeepers, artisans, prostitutes, farmers, and the tragic-mundane problems of their lives. Specific events in the city—a murder, a double suicide, an arson case, a swindle—were quickly given sensational treatment on the stage. Other plays treat the more fabulous social outrages—the vendetta of the forty-seven *rōnin* or scandals in the mansions of the feudal lords. As it was forbidden to write about the affairs of the ruling families, these plays were cast in an earlier historical period as camouflage.[2] Public curiosity and the daring of the playwright afforded them particular titillation. There are also plays which reflect the aspirations and fantasies of the drifters in society—masterless samurai, gangsters, gamblers, and above all, chivalrous commoners who defy their samurai superiors. The audacity of playwright and actor would be misinterpreted if it were considered an expression of protest against the social and political system. It was, rather, good box office to electrify an audience with bold passages and parodies which spoke to the experience of the commoner.

Both the history and domestic dramas assume inevitable capitulation to the ethical code which governed society. Characters entangle themselves in nets of loyalties and obligations which come into conflict with unexpected personal desires or sympathetic impulses. The code tolerates no generosity of interpretation. The hero transgresses, fully resigned to pay with his life. The fairness of the code remains unquestioned.

The conscientious, perhaps compulsive reenactment of these dilemmas suggests the importance of the plays as emotional outlets for an audience well disposed to weep over tragedies so suggestive of the conflicts in their daily lives. Kabuki taxes every feeling. It shifts from scenes of love or maternal solicitude to violent murders and graphic harakiri. This rather basic function of theater as response to a rigid social system with a relentless ethical code is little perceived by a modern audience. A substantial difference in the content of his moral difficulties isolates a present-day viewer from some of the deeper reactions of a Tokugawa audience to the plays.

The ambience of the theater and its social environment have also undergone fundamental changes. The theater itself has been transformed. Today's Western-style building offers upholstered seating and all the amenities of a lavish opera house. The Tokugawa audience, which might have numbered slightly over a thousand, was less than half the size of a modern audience. Yet it was squeezed together on the floor of a hall only a fraction the size of a new theater. The stage was far smaller than those we know in kabuki today and, normally deprived of the use of even torches for lighting, the old theaters were quite dark.

Yet there was an intimacy between actor and audience, due not merely to physical proximity but to the familiarity of the audience with the actor and the freer interaction between them. Attending the theater was part of the world of sensual entertainment provided in the cities for the pleasure of the commoners. The origins of kabuki were deeply tied to both male and female prostitution, and although the government repeatedly attempted to forge clear separation between the two professions by banning women from the stage and concentrating houses of prostitution in designated quarters detached from the theaters and actors' residences, the distinction of function was not always clearly drawn. Female dancers continued to perform kabuki dances and skits at private parties and many of the actors served as social and sexual companions.

In principle, at least, the theatrical and prostitution quarters became parallel facilities for amusement—the two wheels of the vehicle of pleasure. They were tolerated in the conviction that vulgar diversions for the lower classes, unprepared by education or lineage for more refined recreation, were necessary evils. It was further argued that while the three great cities—Edo, Osaka, and Kyoto—were under Tokugawa control, they would lose their commanding positions in population and hence in commerce without the presence of lively amusement areas.[3] The two professions, therefore, received some official recognition insofar as they were licensed and relegated to separate quarters removed from the rest of society and treated as analogous groups.

Prostitutes and actors, like others who took money from performing, were classified by the officials as pariahs. The operators of houses of prostitution in Edo were placed under the jurisdiction of the head of the eta, Danzaemon, and denied certain privileges given to other residents of the city. They were known by the derogatory name *kuruwa mono.* Kabuki managers and actors, who were treated in much the same way, were called *kawara kojiki* (riverbed beggars) or *koya mono* or *shibai mono,* equally derisive terms.[4] When they did go out of the quarter, they were required to wear woven hats made of sedge grass to hide their faces, the same type of hat worn by outcastes and criminals under arrest.

The common people, while regarding these members of the demimonde as somewhat disreputable, found them endlessly fascinating. They were admired for their beauty and their splendid clothes, their social poise and savoir faire. They were the purveyors of entertainment and pleasure for the nonaristocratic residents of the city, and provided the social stage on which the more prosperous could enjoy their wealth and make reputations as men of importance within their levels of society.

Both quarters were intended for the entertainment of commoners. Yet the excitement of the kabuki theater and the glamor of the pleasure houses were irresistible to the numerous samurai who visited these quarters exercising only a moderate degree of discretion in concealing their faces with large hats or scarves. Since involvement in any altercation would be embarrassing, they could ill afford to insist upon the prerogatives of their class. Muro Kyuso (1658–1734), the Confucian scholar, lamented: "There are even feudal lords and district governors who like to enjoy themselves secretly in houses of prostitution, and there are warriors and great men who vie in learning the customs of the theater."[5]

Prostitutes of the highest grades were reputedly accomplished entertainers, skilled in music or dance and surpassing in coquetry. The leading players of male roles had prodigious reputations as lovers. Some of the beautiful young actors were sought after as sexual partners, and women's roles were played by male actors (*onnagata*) who also had an erotic fascination for both men and women. In a society in which there was an easy acceptance of homosexual relations, the presence of actors on the stage who deliciously exploited sexual nuance occasioned far more excitement than it does today.

Confucian advisors to the government, who expected drama to edify the viewer, were distressed by the pernicious influence of kabuki. One of these scholars, Dazai Shundai (1680–1747) remarked: "Because our kabuki plays of today put on licentious and unrestrained matters which obtain among the people in present-day society in order to cater to vulgar sentiment, they all set examples of licentiousness. There is nothing worse than this in breaking down public morals."[6]

Thus the kabuki performance in Tokugawa times was charged with a far more erotic atmosphere than it is today. The social environment in which the actors lived and the social role they performed off the stage conditioned both their private lives and their style of acting as well as the content of the plays. These were important factors in the shaping of early kabuki and must be taken into account to understand classical kabuki. With the profound changes that have transformed modern Japanese society, and the quite different private lives now led by actors, the sensual elements in the performance have paled and only faintly touch the present-day audience. With the "reform" of kabuki in the last decades of the nineteenth century, by which is meant primarily the ending of public prostitution by actors and the raising of their social status to the level of other artists, the special relationship between kabuki and the pleasure quarters finally ended. Kabuki was removed from the social environment in which it had developed, and it became "classical" theater.

The extent of this change can be appreciated if we recreate the proper social atmosphere of Tokugawa kabuki, describing the physical arrangement of the theater and its surroundings and the sexuality of the actors in the eyes of the Tokugawa audience. Of particular interest is the situation in the early eighteenth century when kabuki first flourished. By that time the style of acting of the various type roles, the structure of the plays, and most of the conventions and traditions of the theater had been established, although they were to be considerably refined and elaborated during the following century or more. To understand the social milieu of the theater and the many interconnections between the kabuki and the prostitutes' quarters (a theme which will be developed later), a review of the early history of these quarters is instructive.

The Beginnings of Kabuki and Licensed Prostitution

The conventional account of the origins of kabuki opens with the appearance in Kyoto of Okuni in 1603 or perhaps earlier. An itinerant dancer who claimed association with Izumo Shrine, she was said to have performed suggestive dances and skits in the dry riverbed of the Kamo River by Gojō Bridge, then the eastern edge of the city proper, which was given over to amusements and sideshows. Shrine dancers from earlier times had engaged in prostitution, and those who traveled around to solicit funds, frequently renegades who performed for their own profit, were called *aruki miko* (walking priestesses) or *uta bikuni* (singing nuns). Okuni's dances were probably standard contemporary skits dressed up with novel dramatic elements and a farcical or erotic twist. Her particular contribution to the development of kabuki may have been no more significant than that of similar entertainers, but it is at least certain that performances by small troupes of female dancers were popular in the first two decades of the seventeenth century. One of these troupes performed in 1608 at Sumpu (the present Shizuoka), where Tokugawa Shogun, Ieyasu, had retired. A brawl erupted, whereupon Ieyasu banned such groups from the town, setting aside a place next to the prostitutes' quarters outside the town at Abekawa.[7]

Within a few years of Okuni's appearance in Kyoto, there were imitations of her performance by troupes of prostitutes. In 1612 Sadoshima Yosanji set up a stage on the riverbed at Shijō, and brothel proprietors in that vicinity followed suit in order to solicit patrons. These shows were known as *yūjo kabuki* (prostitutes' kabuki). Many of the skits demonstrated techniques used by prostitutes to approach prospective clients or mimed the style of gallants accosting a favorite. They were, in fact, a kind of burlesque with risque lines and suggestive dance movements. Occasionally male performers assumed female roles, producing a great deal of sexually confused pantomime. A contemporary Confucian scholar Hayashi Razan (1583–1657) remarks: "The men wear women's clothing; the women wear men's clothing, cut their hair and wear a man's topknot, have swords at their sides, and carry purses. They sing base songs and dance vulgar dances; their lewd voices are clamorous, like the buzzing of flies and the crying of cicadas. The men and women sing and dance together. This is the kabuki of today."[8]

Screens and handscrolls of the time depict the girls swinging their hips and throwing their arms about with an abandon not to be seen in later dancing. Descriptions of performances leave no doubt that they were prostitutes as well. The diary kept by Richard Cocks from 1615 to 1622, while he was head of the English trading post at Hirado, refers to them as "*caboques* or Japan players (or whores)." He mentions being entertained by a Japanese merchant who "provided *caboques,* or women plears, who danced and songe; and when we returned home, he sent eavery one one of them."[9]

Early "theaters" copied the rudimentary structures found in amusement areas around the edge of Kyoto which were used for occasional performances of subscription *nō (kanjin nō)*, staged to raise money from the general public for temple construction or repair. Only the small square stage was covered with a roof. Spectators paid admission to enter an enclosure formed by a high fence of bamboo palings covered with straw mats. There they stood or sat on mats on three sides of the stage.

Fights sometimes occurred among the more hotblooded samurai or footsoldiers in the audience. Many were *rōnin*, samurai who lost employment during the purges of daimyo in the first decades of the Tokugawa period. They drifted to the cities in search of new masters, employment, or excitement, and were often a disorderly element in the streets. Because brawls were touched off by rivalries over the performers, female players were banned from the kabuki stage in 1629. This ban was repeatedly issued, and after a few years actresses ceased to appear in the theaters of the principal cities. Their place was taken by young male actors.[10]

The exile of women from the stage was, of course, the basic step in the separation of the professions of prostitute and actor. It served the government's objective of creating greater social order and stability by recognizing the various trades and affording them a degree of security and protection from competition by new operators.

The practice of licensing prostitutes began in the Muromachi period. At the end of the sixteenth century, Hideyoshi took the first steps to isolate their houses from good society by establishing a quarter in Kyoto at Madenokōji Nijō. It was moved in 1603 to Rokujō (Misujimachi) south of the political and commercial areas. Yet prostitutes continued to scatter through all parts of the city. In 1641 an extremely large quarter called the Shimabara, replete with luxurious establishments, was founded in the fields of the southwest corner of the city. In the shogun's capital, brothels sprang up in various parts of the city in the early years of the Tokugawa rule, but in 1617 they were brought together to form the Yoshiwara, just east of Nihonbashi. Bathhouse girls and other prostitutes in competition with the Yoshiwara were rounded up repeatedly during the next few decades and deposited in the licensed quarters. After the Meireki fire of 1657 which destroyed two-thirds of Edo including the Yoshiwara, the houses were moved outside the city to the open fields beyond Asakusa Temple, some four miles from Nihonbashi. Two hundred houses were licensed there as the new Yoshiwara. In Osaka, Shimmachi was established in 1629, and in other cities and castle towns sections for prostitutes were also set aside.

The prosperous condition of the cities in the seventeenth century supported the creation of opulent houses of assignation in the licensed quarters. These *ageya*, or more properly, *chaya* (teahouses), were tasteful parlors for drinking and dining where dancing girls, reciters, jesters, and other entertainers could be summoned. Prostitutes lived in separate houses called *okiya* to which they were indentured. Several ranks of prostitutes populated each quarter. A guidebook to the Yoshiwara of 1642 mentions 75 girls of *tayū* rank, 31 *kōshi*, and 881 *hashijorō*.[11] By the next century the quarter distinguished among its 4,000 inmates at least six ranks representing a wide range of fees. A girl of the highest rank, indulged like an aristocrat, might refuse a client who did not interest her. Perhaps she would require considerable wooing—several visits and various gifts—before she would bestow her favors.

In addition to the official quarter there were other centers of prostitution, some of which came to be tacitly recognized but were not accorded the same status and privileges. Because of the great distance to the Yoshiwara from Edo and its theaters, unlicensed houses kept appearing in more convenient locations within the city. In 1673, 512 illegal prostitutes were seized in 74 houses near the theater quarter and sent out to the Yoshiwara. A decade later another 300 were rounded up at various unlicensed parlors. Such sweeps on a much larger scale were conducted during the Kansei and Tempō reforms of the late Tokugawa period.[12] Since it proved too difficult to confine all prostitution to one quarter of the city, the authorities in later years permitted prostitution at Shinagawa, Fukagawa, Nakasu, and Ryōgoku, and in Kyoto at Gion, Nijō, Shichijō, and Kitano. There was also a considerable amount of less formal prostitution in public places of entertainment and relaxation. At many bathouses, restaurants, and inns, female attendants liberally sold their fruits. The great variety and gradation among professional sexual practitioners is suggested by the over four hundred terms used to designate prostitutes. There were other female entertainers: dancers (*odoriko*) who entertained at private parties, and geisha who made their appearance in the 1750s. Prostitution was commonly practiced by entertainers of all kinds, both male and female—dancers, actors, jōruri reciters, musicians—as well as by young itinerants calling themselves nuns or monks, and youths who were peddlers of toilet articles and incense. Frequent prohibitions were issued against private prostitution, but the main concern of the authorities seems to have been the prevention of exploitation of girls and boys by unscrupulous panderers. The young kabuki actors as public entertainers, like the actresses before them, could be engaged as sexual partners.

Even before the ban against actresses, at least as early as 1612, there were troupes made up entirely of boys or young men who performed *wakashu kabuki* (youths' kabuki). Homosexual practices had become extremely prevalent during the military campaigns of the fifteenth and sixteenth centuries and were also common in Buddhist monasteries. During the seventeenth century some of the shogun and feudal lords exercised their preference for beautiful youths.[13] Homosexuality was, moreover widely practised among commoners, following the example of their betters. The playlets performed in youths' kabuki were of two types: those in which homosexual love was acted out, emphasizing the loveliness of these boys (*shudō goto*), and those which demonstrated techniques to accost prostitutes (*keisei goto*). The latter was, as mentioned earlier, a popular convention in women's kabuki. City officials attempted to curb the erotic effect of the young female impersonators as rivalries over these youths led to altercations between admirers. Homosexual prostitution was banned in 1648, but to little effect. Finally, in 1652, the authorities seized upon an incident to close the theaters in Edo and other cities and youths' kabuki, or at least kabuki by that name, came to an end.[14]

Following repeated entreaties by theater owners, an agreement evolved which permitted kabuki performances to be staged again, henceforth known as *yarō kabuki* (fellows' kabuki). One basic change required female impersonators to dress their hair in the masculine fashion, shaving the forelock. Further, youths over fourteen were no longer permitted to use girls' clothes or hairstyles.[15] Since men in the Tokugawa period had a shaven pate, a coiffured forelock was erogenous. The young actors were inspected periodically to make certain that they were closely shaved. They hid their bald spot with kerchiefs, although this too was prohibited, and later with patches of dark purple silk to give the impression of glistening dark hair. By the end of the century it became common practice to wear a wig on the stage. While this indicates an enduring concern over appearance, there was a gradual tendency to assign female roles to older performers who relied more on acting resources than on physical attraction, and the art of the *onnagata* (female impersonator) developed. Government repression, ironically, had inspired the transformation of these popular performances from burlesque into a more serious art form.

The beneficial effects of the reforms of 1652 were realized only gradually. For some years the most characteristic scenes continued to be the prostitute-accosting routines, known as Shimabara *kyōgen.* In fact, kabuki was frequently called "Shimabara" until these plays were banned in 1664.

The reforms of 1652 were intended to separate homosexual prostitution from kabuki and to relegate the kabuki theaters and actors' residences to one or two quarters of the cities. In the first respect the reform was only partially successful. It did remove from the stage those youths who were more prostitute than actor. These continued their service in separate sections of the city. Yet in the "reformed" *yarō kabuki*, young actors, especially those apprenticed to the role of *onnagata*, continued to be sought after. *Yarō*, a somewhat derogatory term for "fellow," carries the connotation of homosexuality. An account in an Edo guidebook suggests that even in this form of kabuki there was at first excessive interest on the part of the audience in these beautiful boys:

> When these youths, their hair beautifully done up, with light make-up, and wearing splendid padded robes, moved slowly along the runway, singing songs in delicate voices, the spectators in front bounced up and down on their buttocks, those in back reared up, while those in the boxes opened their mouths up to their ears and drooled; unable to contain themselves, they shouted: "Look, look! Their figures are like incarnations of deities, they are heavenly stallions!" And from the sides others called: "Oh, that smile! It overflows with sweetness. Good! good! and the like, and there was shouting and commotion.[16]

The display of youths on the stage differed little from the line-up of prostitutes within the lattice fronts of the Shimabara houses.

Only four years after the reform, an incident in Kyoto again closed the kabuki theaters in that city for a time. The *onnagata* Hashimoto Kinsaku was drinking in a box with a samurai admirer when the latter, in a fit of jealousy, drew his sword, inspiring Kinsaku to leap into the pit to save himself.[17]

The Development of Theater Buildings

The earliest kabuki performances, as noted, were staged in rudimentary enclosures which could be hastily constructed if subscription *nō* stages were not readily available in the amusement quarters at the edge of cities. From about 1617 Kyoto began issuing licenses to operate theaters. As was true of houses of prostitution, the theaters were increasingly restricted to certain quarters of the city. In Kyoto they were clustered in the area of Shijō, just east of the river, and although as many as seven licenses were issued by 1669, it is not clear how many were in operation at one time.[18] This concentration parallels the establishment of the large prostitution quarters at Shimabara, several miles to the southwest, in 1641. The Shijō theater area and riverbank was a large amusement center in which kabuki was one of many dozens of diversions. There were smaller playhouses, puppet theaters, and a number of wayside entertainers who recited tales from military epics, the *Taiheiki* and *Heike monogatari.* There were fortune-tellers, dentists, sumō wrestlers, jugglers, and tightrope walkers. There were sideshows exhibiting such freaks as the female giant and the armless woman archer. There were exotic animals—tigers, bears, porcupines, eagles and peacocks, performing monkeys and dancing dogs. Teahouses, restaurants, and refreshment stands lined the streets. Paintings of the period show these establishments crowded together, thronged with people of every description.[19]

Edo performances of women's kabuki and youths' kabuki took place as early as 1617 in the Yoshiwara and the nearby amusement area of Nakabashi. The first theater to be licensed was the Saruwaka-za in Nakabashi in 1624, later renamed Nakamura-za, which continued to operate at a succession of locations until 1893. It serves as a particularly remarkable example of the exercise of an hereditary license to operate a theater. This and later kabuki theaters were ordered to move from time to time and finally, after the Meireki fire of 1657 forced the Yoshiwara far outside the city, were restricted to Sakai-chō and Kobiki-chō and shortly limited to four in number. The Tokugawa government continued to follow a policy of treating the prostitution and theater quarters as parallel concerns. When the theater quarters burned in 1841, nearly two centuries later, they were ordered to move to Saruwaka-chō in Asakusa, close by the Yoshiwara. In Osaka too, where the issuing of regular licenses to theaters followed the Edo precedent, they were restricted from the 1660s to Dōtombori and Horie.

With the issuing of licenses permitting the construction of permanent theaters, the buildings became gradually more substantial. The mat fence was replaced by solid board walls, and a row of boxes (*sajiki*) was built along the two sides of the parquet (*doma*) for spectators who required more comfort and privacy. Later boxes were added at the rear of the parquet. City officials, seeking to keep kabuki a simple form of entertainment, forbade the construction of roofs over the parquet. But resourceful theater owners devised a method of stretching mats across the parquet to serve as makeshift shelters which provided shade from the sun and protection against light showers. Over a period of two centuries the theater buildings became gradually more elaborate and comfortable as the authorities made concessions, alternating between a resigned attitude and a stricter policy of sumptuary regulation.

Set back slightly from the street so as not to obstruct traffic, the theater facade was dominated by a tower on which ornamental spears were mounted to indicate possession of an official license. This spear (or drum) tower was draped with a cloth bunting featuring the large design of the theater's crest. The Nakamura-za first used the wheeling crane (*maizuru*) design. The Ichimura-za chose a rounded crane within an octagon.[20] Most theaters placed large billboards on the tower, the center board announcing in bold characters the name of the proprietor, those on either side the names of leading actors. Lower billboards, typically four in number if the offering was a four-act play, gave the titles of each act. From the 1720s a tableau from each act was painted above the title.

Before these signs stood low platforms where barkers waved their fans to attract the attention of passersby and entice them into the theater. In addition to the cruder techniques of whistling and calling to onlookers, they would attempt to draw a crowd by staging impersonations of the leading actors, imitating their voices as they recited tantalizing lines from the play, and parodying their characteristic poses and gestures. Contemporary paintings record the remarkably exuberant commitment of these *kido geisha* (entrance performers) to their task.[21]

The early theaters had only one entrance, located in the center of the building under the drum tower. It was a small opening with a high threshold which the customer had to step over while ducking under a low overhead. Aptly called the mouse-entrance (*nezumi kido*), it was a holdover from the enclosures used for subscription *nō* and was presumably designed to make it difficult for anyone to slip in quickly without paying. As the theaters grew larger in the eighteenth century, an entrance was provided on each side of the drum tower for admission to the parquet. The stoop entrance was abandoned and a short curtain (*noren*) hung across the top of the doorway, as is customary in Japanese shops. Tickets were purchased outside and other fees paid within for the rental of a reed mat (*hanjō*) and a length of smoldering cord to light one's pipe. On each side of the front of the building an entrance was added for guests going to boxes in order to avoid jostling by the plebs. Inside, stairs led to the upper level of boxes.

The price of tickets ranged widely between the cheapest and the best seats. In 1714, boxes in Edo theaters commanded 1200 *mon*, single spaces 200 *mon*. Parquet tickets averaged 64 *mon*. When space was available, single-act tickets were sold for 12 *mon*. Rental of a mat was 6 *mon* additional.[22]

These prices increased rather steadily through much of the Tokugawa period, probably following the general inflationary trend, but exacerbated at certain times by the escalating salaries of the star actors. Attending a major theater was not cheap. The cost of a box seat in 1828 was 1 *ryō* 2 *bu*, the equivalent of 3 bales (*hyō*) of rice or a servant's salary for three or four months. When a performance was popular, the price of tickets rose abruptly.[23]

While the Nakamura-za in Edo provides a detailed illustration of the physical design of a theater, it should be noted that no two were identical. Theaters were, moreover, periodically rebuilt, for fires frequently ravaged Edo. In the 1690s the outer dimensions of the Nakamura-za were 71.5 feet by 97.5 feet, or 6,971 square feet.[24] At its largest in 1809, it measured 80 feet by 138.5 feet, or 11,080 square feet.[25] The structure remained a fraction the size of the present Kabuki-za in Tokyo which has 39,000 square feet of space on the ground floor, seating 1,078 people, approximately the same number as the Tokugawa structure. But the modern building has five floors with 120,000 square feet of floor space and accommodates an additional 1,522 people on the mezzanine and balconies.[26] The Nakamura-za of 1720 had a row of boxes along the two sides and across the back. Although only one tier was allowed at that time, by 1724 a second tier of boxes had been added. It was repeatedly forbidden to hang bamboo blinds across the front of the boxes and to install screens or other partitions which would provide privacy for the occupants. However, a number of paintings from this period show such items in use, partially concealing from the gaze of the populace ladies-in-waiting of the shogun's or daimyo's households, members of the Buddhist clergy, and rich merchants.[27]

The parquet (*doma*) of the Nakamura-za, 52 feet wide and 82.4 feet deep in 1720, had a capacity of 800 persons. Later, the front half with its better seats was divided into partitions (*masu*) not quite five feet square which narrowly accommodated seven or eight people.[28] Rear parquet space was unreserved. The last back seats, called the *ōmukō* (greatly beyond) were so far from the stage that they were also known as the "deaf gallery." Thus including boxes and the cheapest parquet seats the theater held about 1,200.[29] Operating policy was to crowd in as many as possible. According to a book of 1703: "The people came in pushing and jostling, and eight persons sat knee over knee on a mat. It is very pleasant to see them pressed together like human *sushi*."[30]

By the early eighteenth century, wooden roofs occasionally sheltered part of the pit, although not officially sanctioned until 1724. Thereafter tile roofs were recommended to decrease the danger of fire from flying embers.

Even after the theaters added roofs, artificial lighting remained proscribed because of the danger to the wooden structure from the open flame of oil lamps and candles. Performances, expected to end about 5 P.M., depended on natural light from windows with translucent paper-covered *shōji* installed on both sides of the theater behind or above the upper row of boxes.[31]

Dressing rooms, located directly behind the stage, were built in two stories by the 1670s. Before the end of the century the Morita-za in Edo added a third level.[32] This section of the building was built high to take as little ground space as necessary from the stage and parquet. A passageway leading to the dressing room section was constructed behind the boxes. Though intended for use by actors to gain access to the end of the runway (*hanamichi*), it was soon traveled by actors summoned to boxes or patrons visiting dressing rooms.[33] The usual arrangement called for baths and quarters for musicians, writers, and *wakashu* on the first floor, *onnagata* on the second, and players of men's roles on the third. A large rehearsal area also occupied the third level. Leading players had individual dressing rooms, although partitions had not received official sanction.[34]

The early kabuki stage basically recreated the square *nō* stage with pillars in the four corners supporting a thatched roof. The main platform had two narrow appendages, one to the right used by the chorus in the *nō*, the other at the rear for the musicians. Off the left of the stage a "bridge" (*hashigakari*) for entrances and exits extended back at an oblique angle with a railing on each side and a long roof. These features of the *nō* stage were gradually modified in the kabuki theater, although it is surprising how long they persisted. The stage itself was only nineteen feet square at the outset. Rather than alter its design, more space was gained by greatly widening the bridge and eliminating its handrails. It then emerged as a secondary performing area, a rectangle set back slightly from the main stage. A platform was appended to the front of the stage (*tsuke-butai*) which jutted into the audience. Though these changes were not completed until the first decades of the eighteenth century, some stages had already become quite large. That of the Nakamura-za measured 32.5 feet by 37.7 feet in 1724. Not until 1796, however, was the roof over the main stage eliminated.[35]

One of the most distinctive inventions of the kabuki theater is the *hanamichi*, a five-foot-wide runway which extends from the left side of the stage to the rear of the audience. It is used for more dramatic entrances and exits and as an occasional pivot of activity. Its origins are unclear. The more obvious assumption, that it began as a second *hashigakari* directed through the audience, appears to be incorrect. Perhaps as early as the 1650s a small platform was attached to the stage slightly left of center where members of the audience placed gifts (*hana*) of money or goods for their favorite actors. These were called *hana* because the gift was attached to a flower (*hana*) branch. Such a platform appears in a drawing of the Nakamura-za in 1687.[36] By 1724, at least, the *hanamichi* was a runway 52 feet long, set at an oblique angle, probably ending toward the rear end of the row of boxes on the left side of the hall. Although the word *hanamichi* may originally have meant "a path for gifts," by the 1720s and perhaps several decades earlier, it was used primarily as an extension of the stage. Woodblock prints of the next decade show actors standing or seated upon it. Occasionally a small platform called the *nanori-dai* was added about the midway point where an actor could stand almost dead center of the parquet to announce the name and pedigree (*nanori*) of the character he was portraying. After 1780 another narrower runway was sometimes erected on the right side of the hall. Perhaps as a result, the main *hanamichi* was set at right angles to the stage, parallel to its narrower companion.[37]

Most of the physical features of the theater discussed on the preceding pages are illustrated in a woodblock print by Okumura Masanobu (1686–1764) of the Ichimura-za in Edo in 1744. The *nō* stage with its roof and front pillars, the appended *hashigakari* stage right and *tsuke-butai* stage front and the *hanamichi* are clearly evident. There is a raised walk (*ayumi*) across the hall for easier access by customers and vendors to the front part of the pit. A tea and a food vendor pass through the audience. The stage curtain is drawn to stage right. Boxes of the first tier were known as quail boxes (*uzura sajiki*) because their wooden bars made them resemble crates for keeping quail. The second tier of boxes retained eaves from the days, a few decades earlier, when there was no roof over the pit. Sliding doors of translucent paper let in daylight above the boxes.[38]

In such a theater the play moved easily into the audience. The tiers of boxes at the front of the hall were alongside the stage. Later in the eighteenth century a low balcony intruded behind the left corner of the stage (stage right). Known as the *rakandai* (arhat dais), its tightly lined-up spectators hovered over the stage like the five hundred arhats of a Buddhist painting. A seventeen syllable satirical poem (*senryū*) observes: "The five hundred went home, having seen the actors' backs." A second balcony inevitably grew above this. It was called *tsūten* (passing through to heaven) or Yoshino (a mountain district noted for cherry blossoms), as its perspective barely penetrated the artificial cherry blossoms suspended from the ceiling of the hall. A woodblock print of the last decades of the Tokugawa period shows the plebs, crammed in these galleries at the edge of the stage, watching gleefully, mouths agape, as the actors perform, almost within reach.[39] When the play was a great success, the management, not impervious to the potential boon, seated customers on the stage itself. This practice is recorded by the satirical poems: "A big hit—the action is performed in a six-foot square," and "Spectators and actors are lined up together—a big hit."[40] With an audience thus gathered on three sides of the performers and cheap balcony seating available over one corner of the stage, no concept of a platform-framing proscenium arch emerged.

Rapport between Actor and Audience

The intimacy of the theater and the consequent physical closeness between actor and audience was conducive to easy communication. Regulars were familiar with the lineage and careers of the actors whose private lives were examined in critical booklets (*yakusha hyōbanki*) printed for theatergoers. When a new or visiting actor was first presented on stage, or a rising performer given a new name as a mark of promotion, a formal announcement took place between acts. The entire company, seated by rank on the stage, participated in this ceremony called *kōjō*. On such occasions the manager and leading actors would thank the audience for past favors, and with heads bowed to the floor ask for continued patronage. At other times actors addressed the audience in a more informal manner. In the midst of a scene a player might step out of role to welcome another actor back to the city or introduce his protégé or a new colleague and ask the audience's favor. The new names given to less important actors were sometimes announced in the course of the dialogue as informal *kōjō* within the play (*kyōgen no nakaba no kōjō*), and these were especially relished by alert members of the audience.[41] Occasionally an actor would humorously refer to himself or to another performer by a personal name as if to draw attention to the fact that their play was make-believe. Kabuki was never intent upon sustaining the illusion of reality, and the audience considered such asides less an interruption than a familiar confidence.

Another variety of communication was the *homekotoba* (words of praise) which originated in the mid-seventeenth century as the *onnagata* offered a few lines of praise to the male lead as he made his entrance.[42] A variation on this practice was for a member of the audience to interrupt the action of the play by rising to make a declaration of his admiration for an actor, either from his place in the parquet or from the *hanamichi*. This type of *homekotoba* probably began in Edo. Kyoto people, more reticent, first committed their laudatory sentiments to writing and sent them to the dressing room. But by the first decade of the eighteenth century, they too surrendered to speechmaking.[43] This was sometimes annoying to the actors, especially if it stranded them in an awkward moment: an actor playing a ghost, caught in the middle of his haunting scene by an overly long speech, could not fade away.[44]

A less disruptive form of audience reaction involved spontaneous shouts from enthusiastic viewers (*kakegoe*) to applaud an especially skillful pose or vocal coloration in the delivery of a dramatic line. A fan might merely call out the actor's name or his house name (*yagō*). A better compliment is to call out the actor's father's name, indicating the attainment of skill equal to his predecessor. (Such calls are frequently heard in kabuki theaters today, but they usually come from a paid claque or employee of the theater to provide a taste of the atmosphere of the old days.) Often the calls were much more subtle allusions to be savored only by aficionados. Words of criticism or insult were heard too, such as "*daikon*" (radish). The front rows sometimes showed their displeasure by throwing their mats onto the stage (*hanjō o ireru*).[45] Not infrequently, when a critic's remarks angered one of an actor's more rabid admirers, a fight would break out. Woodblock prints of the theater interior show plebs in the front part of the parquet striking each other with fists and with wooden clogs. The theater assigned two of its employees during each scene as "stage guards" (*butaiban*) to quiet such disturbances. The informality of the theater was also expressed in humorous comments from the audience. During a drinking scene an inebriated viewer might call out: "If you don't have enough, I've got more here."

Audience support also found expression in clubs of enthusiasts known as *teuchi renjū* (handclapping groups). Several dozen club members, dressed in identical clothes, would sit together like a cheering section, clapping hands or wooden clappers as they sang rhythmic songs to stir support for their favorites. Sometimes the actors would join in, clapping hands in unison with the group. The handclapping groups originated in Kyoto and Osaka, and then spread to Edo, where clubs were usually composed of men of some standing in the business community. The most active were associations of dealers in fish, vegetables, and rice, and the association of Yoshiwara proprietors. These vied with each other in presenting novel stunts and songs. The Yoshiwara group prided itself on having the honor, when the play *Sukeroku* was performed, of supplying the umbrella and purple headband which play such a distinctive part in the hero's performance.[46] The tradesman groups also supplied gifts of stage curtains and festoons for the boxes of the theater, and sometimes contributed subsidies for the production.

A more artistic kind of rapport was the appreciation of the audience for the skill of both the playwright and the actor. Because kabuki became increasingly a repertory theater in which the story lines of most of the cycles of plays were already known to the audience, and the actors performed largely according to type-roles (*kata*), innovations in the plot and variations in the style of acting were refinements which gave excitement to the performance. As Donald Keene has observed: "Virtuoso actors require virtuoso audiences to appreciate their skill, and in this sense the Kabuki audience forms part of the performance. Unless an actor can be sure that a slight change in *kata* will be noticed and appreciated, there is no temptation to study and vary the parts."[47]

Kaomise: Opening the Season

It became customary for a kabuki theater to offer six programs during the year, each new offering beginning about the first of the odd-numbered month. The season opened in the eleventh month. Since this was the occasion for introducing actors under contract to the theater for the year, it was called *kaomise* (showing the faces). This practice began in Kyoto in the 1650s and 1660s. From the twentieth day of the tenth month the theater began to bustle with activity. The facades of the theater were decorated with bamboo palings and signboards announcing the cast and titles of the play and its scenes. Hawkers went through the streets distributing playbills (*banzuke*) carrying this announcement.[48] Actors dressed in formal clothes and, preceded by runners with lanterns calling "*hyōban, hyōban,*" made the rounds of the patrons' homes to inform them of the *kaomise* program. Gifts received by the troupe—bales of rice, barrels of sake, bundles of charcoal, and trays of seabream and pheasant—were piled in front of the theater. The surrounding streets and teahouses were decorated with lanterns. These also hung inside the theater across the beams and above the boxes.

Actors coming from other cities to join a Kyoto troupe as visiting performers made a formal arrival by palanquin and were borne directly onto the stage where they were greeted by their Kyoto colleagues with the exchange of wine cups. The actors took turns reciting, singing, and playing their samisen. The scholar Motoori Norinaga records such a scene in his diary: "I did not go to see this," he hurries to mention, "but I heard it from other people."[49] Spectators, fearing to miss the opening of the performance during *kaomise,* started from home through the cold morning long before dawn in order to arrive for the 5 A.M. curtain. They stopped at a theater teahouse for a bowl of oyster potage, changed from wooden clogs to slippers, and entered the theater.

An actor's memoir of 1830 describes the special part played by handclapping groups during the *kaomise* in Kyoto. When the first drum was sounded at 2 A.M., the actors were in readiness. Partitions directly before the stage were occupied during each of the first ten days of *kaomise* by one of the handclapping groups dressed in colorful matching costumes and caps. They came down the runway of the theater by twos and threes, and when they were settled in their places, word was sent to the dressing rooms. The curtain was drawn open and the son of the head of the theater, ushered across the stage by the stage manager, took his place at stage left. He was followed by the *onnagata,* the child actors, and the players of male roles, led by the most popular actor and the head of the troupe. The stage manager spread a red carpet at the front of the stage and, seating himself there, offered greetings. The group responded by standing and beating out various rhythms with their clappers. Next the head of the troupe stepped onto the carpet, danced a *Sanbasō,* a short auspicious number, and offered formal greetings. The leading *onnagata* performed a longer dance, followed by welcomes from the other actors. Before each actor spoke, a member of the group read a list of gifts presented in his honor: the number of bales of rice and packhorse loads of sake. The ceremony closed with greetings from the head of the troupe, then the curtain was drawn. After the first ten days of the performance, this ritual was replaced by a one- or two-act filler.[50]

Kaomise at the Osaka theaters had two unique features. The first was the ceremonial arrival by boat of the visiting actors. This was a publicity stunt, enthusiastically backed by the brothel proprietors and others of the entertainment world. A dozen or more boats, colorfully decorated and carrying musicians, carried the guest actors along the river from the Kunosuke Bridge to the theater at Dōtombori where they were welcomed to the stage by the local actors. Further, the Osaka *kaomise* came to be performed at night. This was because competition for seats during the *kaomise* was so keen that the audience crowded the theater by ten o'clock the night preceding the performance. The custom began, therefore, of starting the proceeding at midnight, the hall filled with a great number of lanterns and the stage illuminated by several dozen wooden candlesticks. Because of the danger of fire, the *kaomise* was cut to only ten days.[51]

Going to the Theater

Since normally theater performances were supposed to conclude before dark, they began early in the morning, usually at 6 A.M. or slightly later, with the second sounding of the drum in the theater tower. The first drum sounded hours before, although from time to time the authorities forbade this early disruption of sleep. Since performances could not be given on rainy days in the early years before the theaters had proper roofs, the drum served the neighborhood as a weather forecast. Those who wished to arrive in time for the opening curtain left their homes well before dawn during the winter months. The second drum was the signal for the beginning of the ceremonious *Sanbasō* which preceded the play. From the theater entrance the call rang out "*Sanbasō, Sanbasō,*" but there was only a scattering of spectators in the theater when the performance began. Many were visitors up from the country or servants of city people who were sent early to hold good seats in the parquet.

It was an exciting experience to go to the theater, especially for the womenfolk who had little occasion to appear in their best clothes or to eat and drink in public. Because they would have to start out early in the morning, they began preparations the day before—getting their hair dressed and going to the bathhouse. These preparations were similar, it was said, to those made by men anticipating a visit to the Yoshiwara.

One of the pleasures of going to the theater for women was to be seen in stylish kimono by their favorite actors. While there are a number of paintings showing well-dressed ladies seated in theater boxes, one handscroll has an unusual detail of young ladies drinking and dallying with actors behind the protection of a folding screen in a box.[52]

The theaters were surrounded by small establishments known as theater teahouses (*shibai jaya*), which provided a number of services to theatergoers. The first, which appeared in Edo as early as 1624, served tea and food and reserved tickets for the better seats. Not until the end of the century did they take on the broader social function of the Kyoto houses. In that city the banks of the Kamo River from Sanjō to Matsubara were lined with restaurants and teahouses during the summer months. Among these were some which catered especially to theater patrons, providing food and refreshment between the acts and after the performance. Here too actors could be called to drink with the guests, but it was prohibited to send for prostitutes.[53]

Before long there were various classes of theater teahouses: large (*ō-jaya*), medium (*naka-jaya*), small (*ko-jaya*), front (*mae-jaya*), and finally "water" (*mizu-jaya*) whose function was limited to serving food and drink in the theater. Their proprietors, many of whom were connected with the theater world, some actors and managers themselves, provided part of the financial backing for new performances. Box seats in the theater were consigned to the teahouses for sale to their patrons; large teahouses released most of them and turned the remainder over to smaller establishments. By the late Tokugawa period, when much of the parquet was also reserved, the large teahouses (then also called *omote-jaya*, front teahouses) of Saruwaka-chō assigned both tiers of boxes, and the small teahouses (also known as *ura-jaya*, rear teahouses) had half the parquet but were often favored by enthusiasts because of their better access to the actors' dressing rooms. Attendants from the teahouses prepared the boxes before the arrival of the guests. They arranged ashtrays, mats, and cushions, and hung red carpets over the railings of the boxes. They greeted guests in the street, escorted them to the teahouse to leave wraps, canes, swords, and other articles. Slippers were provided to use instead of footgear and, during the summer, some patrons changed to informal summer dress (*yukata*). After they were offered refreshment, the customers were led to their boxes, in some cases by a direct passageway from the teahouse to the theater.[54]

The attendants in Edo were young men, but in Kyoto and Osaka they were girls (*ochako*). The cheerful solicitations of these maids are described in a guide to the theater district of Kyoto:

> The morning drums of the theaters reverberate to Otowa Hill. The maids with their red aprons bright as the morning sun come out into the street and, with welcoming glances, call out: "Come, buy your tickets. I will pick out a good place or a box for you. I'll take care of your coat, hat, and your cane. I'll bring you tea later on. The performance has already begun. One thousand-kan Mandayū prospers year after year, the Kameya theater has Kumenojō, and in the puppet theater it is the felicitous Kaganojō. Come buy your tickets." So they egg people on like boiling pots—*rin rin shan*.[55]

The girls first brought their customers tea and sweets and illustrated booklets containing a synopsis of the play. As there were no restaurants in the theater, they served appetizers and sake, then lunch, and later an afternoon meal of *sushi*. After the performance dinner was available at the teahouse. An important part of theater-going was eating and drinking. The guests could also go to the teahouses to relax during the long intermissions and to use the toilets, facilities usually lacking in the theater building itself, at least in Edo. The women might make several trips to the teahouse during the day to tidy their coiffure and freshen their make-up. Some changed to a new garment. The practice of wives and daughters of prosperous merchants of changing their kimono at the teahouse during the course of the day is noted in satirical poems: "Wishing to be noticed by the actors, they change clothes frequently," and another, "The Komachi in the box changes seven times."[56] (Ono no Komachi was a famous beauty, poetess and lover of the ninth century.)

The audience in the parquet could also order food and drink. As the parquet was often crowded, it required a great deal of squeezing and maneuvering for the vendors (*dekata*) to deliver food. Vendors brought tea or sake, and a limited choice of food: cakes (*kashi*), a simple lunch (*bentō*) and *sushi*. The acronym *kabesu* was made from these three words to designate a patron who would not leave his box for better fare lest he miss an exciting development on stage.[57]

The Osaka theater teahouses, numbering 47 by 1700, served patrons of any of the theaters of the district. In this way they were like the Kyoto establishments. In Edo, however, a teahouse was affiliated with a single theater and served its patrons exclusively. By 1714 there were at least 58 teahouses surrounding the kabuki and puppet theaters.[58] Their number increased steadily and, after the move to Saruwaka-chō in 1842, totaled 142, classified into four grades. Here at last the Tokugawa bureaucrat's ideal theater quarter layout was realized. Each of the three large kabuki theaters, arranged in a row, was situated in the middle of a separate block and surrounded by its designated teahouses.[59] The quarter itself was enclosed by a high wooden fence with four gates which were closed at night, rather effectively sealing the quarter from the rest of society.

We are provided with a considerable amount of pictorial information about the Nakamura-za in Edo, its dressing room and an adjoining theater teahouse in the excellent pair of painted screens dating from the end of the seventeenth century and attributed to Hishikawa Moronobu (d. 1694), now in the collection of the National Museum in Tokyo.[60] The first two right panels of the left screen show a dressing room, and the third panel shows a gate in the fence leading directly to an elegant teahouse. The remaining three panels display young actors, mostly female impersonators, entertaining guests in the teahouse. In one room a young actor dances, surrounded by musicians and guests. Leaning against the post in the corner, a patron and an actor hold hands and gaze at each other. On the veranda a group gathers around a *go* board, while nearby a guest peeks around the sliding door and makes eyes at a passing youth. Here too an actor plays the samisen to accompany the *shakuhachi* (vertical flute) of a guest. On a Chinese carpet in the garden, one visitor, relaxing with an enormous cup of wine after dancing, waves to an intoxicated companion being steadied on his stool by two young actors. Other couples walk about the garden. To the extreme left, a mounted samurai disguised by a woven reed hat arrives at the gate. Female impersonators and attendants from the house welcome him.

Moronobu and his contemporaries depict the houses of assignation in the courtesan quarter in precisely the same manner. While youths have replaced prostitutes in these scenes of a theater teahouse, the posture and arrangement of figures is common to both worlds. A number of paintings, all attributed to Moronobu, illustrate the similarity in treatment of scenes from the teahouses of the two quarters.[61]

The more opulent teahouses were also first-class restaurants, and they were patronized by wealthy merchants who sought not merely their own amusement; there they entertained the majordomos (*rusui*) of the Edo mansions of feudal lords and other samurai of better rank who served as intermediaries for contracts and purchase orders. They were invited to the theater and teahouses to be plied with food, drink, young actors, and bribes.

Special patrons of the large teahouses in Edo were the ladies-in-waiting from the shōgun's castle and the lords' mansions and, in Kyoto, the Imperial Palace. It was customary for them to receive vacations during the third month to visit their parents, but many headed straight for the theater. Plays were often scheduled during that month on themes drawn from classical literature appropriate to this clientele. Although, in theory, it was not proper for ladies of the samurai class to go to the theater, attendance was not only condoned but encouraged by their lords who wished them to improve their skill in kabuki dances. They came elegantly dressed and added a great deal of color and beauty to the theater during the month.[62]

The Ejima-Ikushima Affair

The fascination which samurai ladies felt for kabuki actors led to a delicious scandal in 1714. Ikushima Shingorō, the most talked about actor in Edo, was a handsome specialist of love scenes, which he played wonderfully, according to a critical booklet of his day, "causing the ladies in the audience to be pleased." Another book states that he enacted love scenes "realistically and provocatively," and that all the women of Edo were mad for him.[63] One whom he well satisfied was Ejima (1681–1741), a high-ranking lady official in the service of the shōgun's mother.

There are differing accounts of the particular incident which brought their affair to light. While the story appears to have been somewhat embroidered and the details are unreliable, the basic facts are verified. Ejima was instructed to make a pilgrimage on the twelfth day of the first month on behalf of Gekkōin, the mother of Shōgun Ietsugu, to the Tokugawa family mausolea at Zōjōji in the Shiba district of Edo. According to usual procedure, Ejima and her entourage were expected to pause for refreshments at the abbot's residence after the ceremony. Instead she left the temple directly and, with eleven attendants, went to the Yamamura-za to see the play. They called actors to their box and drank sake with them. Among the actors was Ejima's lover, Ikushima. News of the theater party leaked out and investigation resulted in full exposure, not only of the party, but of the love affair which had continued for nine years. All those implicated in the affair and the party were given punishments ranging from banishment to death. The lady officials were placed in the custody of different lords, and Ikushima was banished to Miyake Island.[64]

The following is a more colorful account of the incident which should be read less for its factual reliability than for its description of what a rousing theater party could become.

> The scene on this day was a hubbub which cannot be described. In the boxes carpets were spread, and the theater owner, Nagadayū, Ikushima Shingorō, and Nakamura Seigorō, wearing *hakama* and *haori*, were invited to be drinking partners. The party was so noisy that the sounds of the play could not be heard. . . . At this time occupying a lower box was a retainer of Matsudaira Satsuma-no-kami, a person called Taniguchi Shimpei, who was watching the play with his wife. In the upper box, Ejima, quite intoxicated and not knowing what she was doing, spilled her sake, and it poured on Shimpei's head. He sent a messenger to the upper box. A *kachi-metsuke*, Okamoto Gorōemon, made apologies, but this did not satisfy Shimpei. Gorōemon apologized over and over, and finally Shimpei accepted his apologies, and although it was only about midday, he and his wife left the theater. . . . Thereupon Gorōemon several times urged Lady Ejima to leave, but she would not consent, and instead became very angry. At 2 P.M. a passageway was installed

> from the second-floor box by which they went to Yamamura Chōdayū's house, and the capers of the many maids from the castle were beyond words. . . . For the entertainment of Ejima, many actors, young actors, and youths were summoned as drinking partners. . . . At 4 o'clock they left Chōdayū's rooms and went to a teahouse called Yamaya on the street behind. On the second floor the maids and actors kept coming and going and there was a great hubbub. . . . They finally left Kobiki-chō and returned by the Hirakawa-guchi Gate (of the castle) at 8 o'clock.[65]

The most serious consequence of this affair for the history of kabuki was the fate of Yamamura-za. Founded in 1642 and the most popular among the Edo theaters for more than a decade, it was closed, the building demolished, and the assets of the theater and its owner sold at auction.[66] For the remaining one hundred and fifty years of the Tokugawa period there were three, instead of four, large theaters in Edo. All theaters were closed for three months and permitted to reopen only under stringent conditions. The twenty-four leading actors of Edo were required to submit written statements that they would not violate any of the orders of the government. The regulations imposed on the managers were set forth in a document on the ninth day of the third month:

1. The boxes of the theaters have been made two and three tiers in recent years. As formerly, not more than one tier will be permitted.
2. It is prohibited to construct private passages from the boxes or to construct parlors for merry-making backstage, in the theater manager's residence, or in teahouses and such places. Nothing at all should be done by the actors other than performing plays on the stage, even if they are called to the boxes or teahouses or the like. Of course pleasure-making patrons must not be invited to the actors' own houses.
3. In the boxes it is not permitted to hang bamboo blinds, curtains, or screens, and to enclose them in any other way is prohibited. They must be made so that they can be seen through.
4. In recent years the roofs of theaters have been made so that even on rainy days plays can be performed. In this matter also roofs must be lightly constructed as was done formerly.
5. The costumes of actors in recent years have been sumptuous;

this is prohibited. Hereafter, silk, pongee, and cotton will be used.

6. It is strictly prohibited that plays continue into the evening and torches be set up. They should be planned so that they will end by 5 P.M.
7. Teahouses in the vicinity of the theaters should be simply constructed, and parlorlike accommodations are entirely prohibited. Concerning those which are in existence at present, petitions should be submitted to the city magistrate's office and, upon inspection, a decision will be given.

The above must be observed without fail. If there are violations, the principals, of course, and even the representative of that quarter and the five-man group will be considered offenders.[67]

After the order was issued, enforcement was strict for a time as officials were sent by the city magistrates to make periodic inspections, not only of the theater buildings, but of the fifty-six teahouses. It was not very long, however, before the teahouses were again well appointed, and actors resumed making calls on their patrons. Moreover, within a decade, after complaints from theater owners that rainy days were bankrupting them, roofs were permitted as well as a second tier of boxes.[68] After the incident the dressing room section was limited to one story, but by 1720 it was again up to three stories. As a gesture of deference toward regulations, the second floor was called a mezzanine (*chū nikai*), and the third floor the second (*hon nikai*).[69]

The details of the incident and the regulations which it provoked provide considerable insight into the social environment of kabuki. We see that the quarter was equipped with generous facilities for guests of either sex to drink and flirt with actors and other entertainers. They might rendezvous in dressing rooms, in boxes, in the greater privacy of the teahouse parlors, or in the homes of the actors themselves. The personnel of the theater, from the manager to apprentice boy-actors, were in the business of social entertaining which could range, according to the preference of the customer, from genteel conversation and private performances of music, dance, storytelling, impersonations, and skits, to risque banter and lovemaking. Although Tokugawa society was regulated by a class system of finely graduated hierarchical distinctions, in the pleasure quarters even high officials interacted intimately with theater people who, though beautiful, accomplished, and expensively dressed, were outcastes.

The Life and Art of Actors

The life of the actor—his background, training, and professional and social relationships—was fascinating to the wider audience of theatergoers. The main focus of kabuki was less the play than the actor who attracted attention not only because of his dramatic talent but because of his lineage, his physical assets, and his private life. Boyish beauty, unusual acting ability, elaborate reputations for a luxurious lifestyle, and romantic entanglements titillated a public vulnerable to the glamor of the theater world.

Actors were instructed to live in the quarter or in its close vicinity. In Kyoto their homes were found especially in Gion-machi, Miyagawa-chō, and Kawara-machi north of Shijō. The great Genroku actors Sakata Tōjūrō and Mizuki Tatsunosuke lived at the latter address, a few blocks west of the theaters. Minor performers sometimes lived in their dressing rooms under rather wretched conditions, while the established actors and managers usually had fine residences.[70] According to the colorful version of the Ejima story, the home of the manager of the Yamamura-za must have been a large and comfortable building to permit the entourage from the castle to hold one phase of its party there, drinking with "many actors, young actors, and youths."

The most popular actors lived in luxury, commanding high salaries and receiving lavish gifts from admirers and patrons. Some of the more prosperous, particularly in Kyoto and Osaka, became theater owners. Others owned or had a part interest in teahouses. Some kept a considerable number of beautiful youths in their homes whom they trained as actors. Customers of the teahouses could arrange for these boys to entertain and drink with them and serve as sexual partners. Daimyo and men of wealth summoned them to their mansions to entertain and to spend the night. Called *iroko* (sex youths) or *butaiko* (stage youths), they ranged in age from thirteen to about seventeen. Estimates claim that 80 or 90 percent of the *onnagata* during the first half of the Tokugawa period started as *iroko*. Segawa Kikunojō (1693?–1749) was a catamite in Dōtombori before becoming a famous actor. Onoe Kikugorō, Yamashita Kinsaku, Onoe Shōroku, Ichikawa Monnosuke III, Nakamura Rikō II, Sawamura Kitō, and Nakamura Kikuyo are among the many others who emerged from this background.[71]

Most of the youths were given no spoken lines, but merely lined up as extras on the stage with powdered faces and beautiful clothes or were brought on in dance numbers.[72] Those who showed some ability in acting began with children's parts. The less talented were kept in their teacher's home to work as prostitutes, while continuing to be called actors to avoid difficulties with the authorities.[73] During the 1670s and 1680s young catamites were extremely popular and, despite official disapproval, became increasingly numerous.[74] Laws of 1689, 1694, and 1695 forbad actors or catamites to answer summons and specified that troupe managers alone could keep youths exclusively for dramatic training.[75] These were limited to twenty young actors and ten apprentices.[76] Nevertheless, there must have been some kind of understanding on this matter, as a law of 1709 required those on the stage to shave their forelocks while sparing the youths innocent of dramatic appearances. In 1723, "several tens of persons" were punished because of violations and the *iroko* held by troupe managers were freed, that is, contracts indenturing them were cancelled, and they were sent home to their parents.[77]

In time the number of such youths in Edo became so large that it was inconvenient to keep them all in the theater teahouses or other houses in that quarter. Therefore they were placed in establishments in Yoshi-chō. These houses were called *kagema-jaya* (catamite teahouses), and although it appears that in many instances the youths were indentured to the master of the teahouse, the fiction was maintained that they were employees of the theater or troupe manager. Their names appeared on the playbills (*banzuke*) of the three theaters, and in the twelfth month, at the time of the investigation and registration of the populace, a special fee of 100 silver *hiki* was paid to the officials to overlook the irregularity. This fee was paid by the masters of the catamite teahouses.[78] When the youths were called to the stage to appear as extras or members of the chorus, their masters were pleased to have them perform without pay and to supply costumes because of the excellent publicity.[79] As their forelocks were unshaven, the front hair was concealed by a purple crepe cap, slightly larger than the patch worn by the *onnagata* over his shaven pate.[80]

Edo theater practice dictated that these youths be summoned only by customers in the lower level boxes on the west side. Further nicety of convention delicately prevented female geisha from attending the same parlor in a teahouse.[81] The youths who appeared on the stage held a higher status than the ordinary catamites, which was reflected in their different costume and precedence in seating. Their patrons were frequently women, sometimes ladies of the shogun's castle or daimyo mansions, who were referred to by the argot "golden sliding doors" (*kin-busuma*). It was policy, however, that youths decline invitations from Buddhist nuns.[82]

Catamite teahouses which were not directly connected with the theaters also appeared in Edo. The first was probably the Yushima Tenjin houses of the 1740s.[83] They were, however, part of the same social world. The actor Ichikawa Gennosuke became enamoured of a youth from one of these houses, bought him for fifty *ryō*, and later, when he became twenty-one, arranged (with some difficulty) to put him on the stage as an *onnagata*.[84] In the 1760s there were ten quarters in Edo which had catamite teahouses, only three of which had direct connections with the theater quarters.[85] Most were in front of shrines, suggesting the patronage of Shinto and Buddhist priests.

The situation in Kyoto appears to have been much the same. One of the first critical booklets on actors, *Yarō mushi* (Fellow [or Actor] Bugs) (1660), describes the kabuki youths who were sought after by Buddhist monks:

> In these times in the capital there is a great number of what are called "fellow bugs" who eat away the bamboo and wood of the five Zen monasteries and ten abbeys, the books of the learned priests, and even the purses of fathers and grandfathers. . . . "Fellow bugs" are about the size of a human being fifteen or sixteen years old; they are equipped with arms, legs, mouth, nose, ears, and eyes, wear a black cap on the head, fly around Gion, Maruyama, and Ryōzen, and have eyes on people's purses. When I asked someone: "Are those not the young kabuki actors of Shijō riverside?" he clapped his hands, laughed and said: "You are right." These young kabuki actors have multiplied in number especially in the past year and this year. The handsome among the children of lowly outcastes and beggars are selected; their faces never without powder, and dressed in clothes of silk gauze and damask, they are put on the stage to dance and sing, and the old and the young, men and women, become weak-kneed and call out: "Gosaku! Good! Good! I'll die!" Not only do they call to them, but seduced by their alluring eyes, they go with them after the performance to Higashiyama; borne away in woven litters and palanquins, they proceed in high spirits, calling "Here, here! A palanquin, a palanquin." Ah! What grateful affection! Bilked of a large amount of gold and silver for one night's troth, the droll priests of the temples, their bodies wasting away day by day, desire only to engage the fellows. Having no money, they sell the treasure of paintings and tea ceremony utensils that have been handed down generation after generation in the temples, and if these do not suffice, they cut bamboo and timber grove trees, and with that money, engage fellows.[86]

Saikaku devotes the second half of his *Great Mirror of Homosexuality* (*Nanshoku ōkagami*, 1687), to the kabuki youths of Kyoto and Osaka. He states that there were thirty-one of these youths in Kyoto at the time.[87] Catamite teahouses also became numerous; a book of 1766 lists 85 in Miyagawa-chō in Kyoto and 47 in Dōtombori in Osaka.[88]

Apart from the kabuki youths who at best were apprentices or bit players, there were some young actors of ability and beauty known as *wakashu-gata*, usually fourteen to seventeen years of age.[89] They played the roles of boys or handsome young men, gentle and somewhat effeminate. Their slightly plump faces and bodies were said to have a neutral quality intermediate between male and female, and they were likened to statues of Buddhist deities of the style sculpted by Annami Kaikei in the early Kamakura period. Some also played girls' parts, and most turned to *onnagata* roles when they became older. The best of the *wakashu-gata* were given star billing along with the leading players of men's roles (*tachiyaku*) and the mature *onnagata*. This is evidence that despite the abolition of youth kabuki in 1652 and its replacement by *yarō kabuki*, the audiences continued to admire beautiful young actors. This is further attested by the first extant playbill of 1675 which listed them after the *tachiyaku*, but before the *onnagata*.[90]

Most of the *onnagata* had, of course, been kabuki youths. Yet as they grew older, they relied increasingly on a more subtle skill in playing women's roles. They could not merely mimic for, aging and wrinkled, their lantern chins and heavy noses more pronounced, their voices more gravelly, they could hardly be mistaken in appearance for women. A more abstract method of interpretation was required. Thus they singled out the most essential traits of a woman's gestures and speech and gave to these a special emphasis in much the same way that puppets exaggerate human gestures to appear alive. The stylized manner of the *onnagata*, together with the interplay between the *onnagata* and *tachiyaku*, became the essence of kabuki acting to the extent that attempts by women in modern times to play the female roles have not been satisfactory. A number of factors contribute to this situation. The beauty of *onnagata* acting lies in its formalized grace. Women in these roles appear too natural, too realistic. Furthermore, since male roles are played in a strong, sometimes exaggerated manner, women lack the physical strength to project an equal stage presence. And again, women do not exude the peculiar eroticism with its homosexual overtones which has become an inherent characteristic of kabuki. Actresses become plausible only when they play their parts, not by miming women, but by imitating *onnagata*.

The lack of realism in the acting style of the *onnagata* was not a deficiency in the eyes of a Tokugawa audience. One of the more popular styles of male acting, *aragoto* (rough business), which was characterized by the exaggerated movement and bombastic language appropriate to the superhuman prowess of warrior heroes, was equally unnatural. In the earliest kabuki, not only did women play men and men women, but plots were steeped in the fantastic. In later plays as well, action is often illogical and fantastic elements frequently intrude. The art of the theater makes such action plausible, not real. Realistic representation is not an objective in other forms of traditional Japanese drama. This is well illustrated by the puppet theater, a major art which rivalled kabuki in popularity during some decades of the Tokugawa period. As part of the kabuki repertoire was drawn from the puppet theater, the movements of the puppets actually influenced the human acting styles. Earlier dramatic forms, *bugaku, nō,* and *kōwakamai,* are even less concerned with realism of conception and detail.

The actors of women's roles portrayed in an idealized manner chastity, virtue, patience, and tact—embodying the ideals of Tokugawa women prepared to sacrifice their lives for their children or husband or parents, or give themselves solely to enhance the honor of the family. They were also models of etiquette in their bows, their deferential movements, their modesty. They were retiring in the presence of men, often keeping to the back of the stage (upstage), which also served the purpose of making them appear smaller in stature than those playing men's parts. *Onnagata* did not step out in front of an actor in a male role, but sat slightly behind him. They sat on a lower level on the stage more commonly than on a raised set, and never on the stools which were used on occasion by men of high rank. In short, they played women's place in society to an extreme degree.

Some players of women's roles, even after they reached *onnagata* status and were no longer indentured, continued to have homosexual relationships. If they were prominent actors, they would of course be selective. Inasmuch as they were trained and experienced homosexual partners and since their stage roles as *onnagata* depended on assumed femininity, it was their practice to lead rather feminine lives, to live their art. The many stories concerning the practices of *onnagata* in the Tokugawa period include accounts that they dressed like women when off the stage. The younger *onnagata* wore long-sleeved kimono (*furisode*) and flowery patterns appropriate to young girls. They dressed their hair in a unique style resembling a woman's coiffure. Some are said to have entered the women's side of public bathhouses, and "no one thought this strange."[91] They developed the motor habits of women in hand gestures, walking, and sitting, and it has been said that some squatted to urinate. They used women's language—vocabulary, verb endings, honorifics—not to mention female pitch and intonation. The famous early *onnagata*, Yoshizawa Ayame (1673–1729) said that an *onnagata* should continue to experience the feelings of an *onnagata* even in the dressing room, eating only the kind of food appropriate to women, and modestly turning away from the leading man when eating.[92]

The extent to which *onnagata* lived their art is illustrated by an anecdote about the Edo *onnagata* Segawa Kikunojō. A man from Osaka went to call on him at his home, but when he arrived Kikunojō was in the kitchen talking to the fishmonger. The visitor, mistaking Kikunojō for his wife, asked to meet the actor.[93]

The appeal of *onnagata* was not merely to the men of the audience. They were admired by the ladies for the elegance of their gestures and the gentleness of their dispositions—since they played women in an idealized manner. Occasionally they became involved in love affairs with ladies of higher status. In 1706 the *onnagata* Ikushima Daikichi (1671–1706) hid himself in a clothing chest and was smuggled into the Edo mansion of the Tokugawa daimyo of Kii.[94]

The leading players of male roles were also admired for their sexuality and were more openly idolized than the *onnagata*. Sakata Tōjūrō (1647–1709) specialized in playing the part of the great lover and big spender in the prostitute quarters. He was called the "original master of love scenes" and "the first in the line of the engagers of prostitutes." His skill in these scenes, we are told, was due to a great deal of practice off the stage, although, in fact, this may well not have been true in his case. When he died, the women of the entire city of Kyoto wept "crimson tears."[95]

His contemporary, the Osaka actor Arashi San'emon (1635–1690), held a similar title: "pioneer of lovemaking in the West." His biographical sketch in a critical booklet states: "There is not a prostitute with whom he is not intimate."[96] Reputations as free-spending lovers of courtesans were important publicity for actors. Ikushima Shingorō was much admired by the ladies for the way he played love scenes. A description in a critical booklet written many years before his affair with Ejima, seems to foreshadow the danger ahead: "He quickly came to be gossiped about for his amours. It is due to the large-heartedness with which he was born that the cord he uses to tie up his hair becomes undone. The god of Izumo sends a shower which causes him to enjoy love scenes on the stage, pleasing the ladies of the audience."[97]

Actors set fashion in some sectors of society. The new patterns used in their robes, their hair ornaments, their styles of speech were aped even by wives and daughters of prominent merchants. The many examples of popular styles copied from actors include the Kichiya knot, inspired by the manner in which Uemura Kichiya tied his sash, the Mizuki hat, adapted from Mizuki Tatsunosuke, and Rokō brown, a color sported by Segawa Kikunojō (Rokō II).[98]

Some actors opened shops which sold products carrying their endorsement. Shops specializing in cosmetics were the most common, but there were also shops selling fans and clothing material. One of the best known, dating from the 1680s, was established by the actor Uemura Kichiya at the end of the Takasegawa Bridge on Shijō to sell cosmetics.[99] The actor in his shop is occasionally the subject of a woodblock print. Sanogawa Ichimatsu is shown in his establishment where incense and toothpowder were sold, wearing a robe of checkered pattern which he made popular (Ichimatsu-*zome*). In another print, an actor, perhaps Matsumoto Kōshirō IV is seated in his shop which offered a special wafer, writing a poem on a fan for a young woman.[100] The *yagō* or "shop names," which are still associated with the names of famous actors, probably had their origins in the actors' shops, for example, Takashimaya for Ichikawa Sadanji and his disciples.

The craze for actors was extreme among the Edo fans, a reflection of the ebullience and rashness of the Edokko temperament. Their first great actor, Ichikawa Danjūrō, a hero to the plebs in the pit, was referred to as "The Flower of Edo."[101] Excitement shot up to a high pitch when a great star made his entrance on the *hanamichi*, paused, and slowly turned his face toward the audience: "One glance, a thousand *ryō*—Kikunojō on the *hanamichi*."[102] The obsession with actors in Edo is distastefully borne out by a tale of Ichikawa Yaozō II, a great favorite in the role of Sukeroku, chivalrous commoner. At the conclusion of the play he makes his escape by concealing himself in a water barrel. After the performance the water was bottled and sold to his female admirers, some of whom drank it.[103]

From the last decade of the seventeenth century, when the first actors with prodigious reputations began to appear, the salaries paid the leading players rose to large sums. It is not known for certain how much was actually received as figures were sometimes inflated to enhance the fame of the actor. Ichikawa Danjūrō is said to have received 500 *ryō* a year in 1694, but his own record indicates payment of 320 *ryō*. Yet this was a time when ordinary actors might expect about 25 or 30 *ryō*. The highest figure reported for Sakata Tōjūrō, 800 *ryō* is certainly an exaggeration; a critical booklet of 1701 quotes his salary at 500 *ryō* and that of Ikushima Shingorō at 259 *ryō*.[104] In any case, this was the beginning of very substantial payments. A few decades later various actors are listed at 1,000 *ryō*, but in fact some received little more than half the publicized figure.[105] The three Edo managers were hard pressed to restrain demands for higher and higher salaries. In order to check the ruinous competition among themselves, they agreed in 1794 not to pay more than 500 *ryō*. This agreement was soon broken, but the government ordered them to observe this ceiling in 1827 and again in 1842. Actors were expected to provide their own costumes, but when the wage ceiling came into effect, they demanded a supplement for costumes.[106]

The leading actors did live luxuriously with large homes, expensive delicacies, and gorgeous clothing. Attended by many apprentices and disciples, they adopted the style of a wealthy merchant or minor daimyo. Sakata Tōjūrō was renowned for extravagance. He would not wear clothes once they had been washed, would use candles alone rather than the more economical oil lamps, and had his sake heated over a fire of aloes wood, or so we are told. When he went to Osaka to perform, he had drinking water brought in barrels from Kyoto. His rice was checked grain by grain before cooking to insure that there were no pebbles which might damage his teeth. When a member of his household suggested that he refrain from such extravagance, he laughed: "The reason I am receiving a salary now of close to 1,000 *ryō* is because I am not frugal. As I am well known and am called a celebrated man of the theater in the three great cities, I must be large spirited and nothing should be heard or seen concerning me that could be considered small."[107] The publicity value of such stories is undoubted.

Despite the prohibition, some leading actors had residences in the suburbs of Edo: Danjūrō II in Meguro, Danjūrō IV in Kiba, Danjūrō V in Ushijima, and Nakamura Nakazo in Ukechi. The Edo *onnagata*, Segawa Kikunojō II, had three homes, three mistresses, and supported fifty-three people. Over thirty persons lived in Nakamura Utaemon III's residence in Dōtombori, Osaka. He had three additional houses, inflating his living expenses to 3,000 *ryō* a year. During the Tempō Reform of 1842, however, the government strictly enforced laws for the control of actors, confining them to the new quarter at Saruwaka-chō, and investigating those who mixed with commoners. Sawamura Sōjūrō V and Onoe Baikō IV were manacled for appearing without sedge hats, and Nakamura Utaemon II was jailed for going to a bout of *sumō* wrestling. Danjūrō VII (1791–1859) was punished for his opulent style. His residence at Kiba and its expensive furnishings were confiscated, he himself was banished from Edo.[108]

Some actors, men of education and character, were occasionally entertained by daimyo, or at least, by retired daimyo. Danjūrō II tells in his diary of an invitation to the residence of the retired lord of Matsuura where he drank so much that he was forced to stay the night. Nakamura Nakazō frequently went to the Mōri residence for tea with the retired lord, and was presented with an inkstone from Chōshū. The retired lord of Izumo, a Matsudaira and a patron of Segawa Kikunojō II, went to the theater for Kikunojō's final rehearsal and returned for the opening performance.[109]

An account of the 1840s laments the improper behavior of actors of its day who sat in the teahouses with their high-born patrons and behaved as intimates. It contrasts their conduct with earlier times when Onoe Baikō I and Sōjūrō were performing. Retired daimyo came incognito to the theater to watch them and invited them to a teahouse. The actors came dressed in formal clothes, took their seats in a humble position at a distance from the lords, and when they had received cups of sake, they took leave.[110]

The Depiction of Actor and Prostitute in Ukiyoe

Second only to the principal actors in notoriety and public curiosity were the leading courtesans of the pleasure quarter. The fame of the leaders of both professions was spread by woodblock prints and critical booklets. Indeed, the prints and booklets developed in competence, sophistication, and circulation largely in the effort to cope ever more imaginatively with subjects so voraciously consumed by the public. There are numerous parallels in the manner in which actors and courtesans were treated in these two types of publication.

The art of ukiyo paintings and prints dealt largely with prostitutes and actors from its beginning throughout a century and a half of development. Even in the nineteenth century when landscape and bird and flower themes became common, portraits of prostitutes and actors continued to dominate ukiyoe. The popularity of these prints and books has given Japan a larger illustrated record of actors and prostitutes than is found in any contemporary culture.

Hishikawa Moronobu who, more than any other artist, shaped the early development of ukiyo painting and prints, divided his work largely between these two worlds. This is neatly demonstrated by two handscrolls made up of a series of scenes from both Edo kabuki and the Yoshiwara.[111]

In 1690 Torii Kiyomoto did the first poster for the Ichimura-za, thus originating a professional kabuki style, perfected by his son, which remained popular for several decades. From the middle of the eighteenth century, prints which displayed actors posed in their roles were regularly issued with changes of the Edo programs. Many of the actor prints depict a single, strong figure in a dramatic moment of the play. The dramatic climax is not necessarily at the end, for the kabuki play is more a series of striking climactic images as the actor holds a pose to show an intense emotion, rolling his head, crossing one eye, grimacing, flinging out his arms and legs. The most dramatic of these conventional postures, *mie,* are the discrete high points recorded in prints. These are the moments the audience applauds by shouts of praise.

While the word "dance" suggests in the West a fluid, continuous movement, Japanese kabuki dance leads from one dramatic posture to another, and these moments are also recorded in prints. In fact the kabuki scene contains a series of tableaux in which the arrangement and spacing of figures on the stage—the patterns formed by the lines and colors—observe the same principles of composition as an ukiyo print or painting.

This commitment to the depiction of highly conventionalized, tableaulike scenes instead of more natural or unstudied postures is sustained in the courtesan prints. The leading beauty accompanied by an attendant en route to a rendezvous is endlessly repeated. Triptychs of characteristic beauties of the three great cities become familiar exercises. And portraits of courtesans before their shops often occur. All sense of motion is eroded as the static figure is caught in a standardized gesture.

The presentation of a single, bold, voluptuous figure against a plain ground is perfected in the courtesan paintings and prints of the Kaigetsudō during the early eighteenth century. Again there is a close parallel to the artistic treatment of the actor who is most frequently featured alone, poised commandingly before the viewer with little peripheral distraction. The three leading actors of a play frequently appear in a triptych, but as each actor occupies an individual panel, the figures are essentially independent prints as in the case of the courtesan triptychs.

Actors are usually identified in the prints, the majority of them by 1700, although prostitutes remain largely anonymous until after the middle of the eighteenth century. Yet both subjects are represented in a style which gives little attention to individual personality. Most ukiyoe lack the concern for facial detail of true portraits. Costume is recorded more painstakingly than the face, as though both types of print were more fashion plate than portrait. The public preoccupation with clothing and ornament is documented by the loving concentration devoted to fabric and design in these prints.

Women of the pleasure quarter are depicted in much the same unreal style which governs their portrayal by *onnagata* on the stage: as idealized girls of the Yoshiwara, they represent the romance, the fidelity, and half-real, half-fantasy world epitomized in the anonymous portraits by Okumura Masanobu. The courtesans of the domestic plays are simply fictionalized figures from the real pleasure quarter and, indeed, are occasionally biographical versions of a real life (though deceased) figure. The idealization and lack of unflattering comment that characterize the playwright's interpretation of his heroine is paralleled by the treatment of the courtesan prints and is reflected again in the actor print of the courtesan role. The role itself, the representation of the actor in the role, and the basic courtesan study are alike in their fascination not so much with the details of the Yoshiwara but with its appeal to the imagination. That the actor-courtesan so often appears in a conventionalized pose without background, boldly detached from the content of the play, seems to divorce the print from the world of kabuki and return it directly to the Yoshiwara.

The portrayal of actors in stage roles, which significantly dominates more personal, offstage studies, suggest that they too were expressive vehicles for the imagination of artist and audience much like the prostitutes. The basic repertoire of courtesan poses and the studied manner of depiction reduces the idiosyncratic importance of the individual and inflates her value as a symbol of a lifestyle. So too the depersonalization of actor and absorption in the beauty of theatrical pose preserves his identification with a glamorous world, wide enough to accommodate the most flamboyant imagination.

The kabuki prints commonly carry the name of the actor and his role. In the Torii school, identification often depends upon depiction of the actor's crest on his costume. Occasional inclusion of a crest may also offer a clue to identity in the more typically anonymous courtesan prints. Yet the actors are known, not by personal names, but by hereditary stage names which invoke the reputation of a great forbear. Among the courtesans it was also common practice to repeat noted professional names, not to establish any legitimate affiliation, but to borrow the reputation for skill or beauty of a romantic predecessor. This use of traditional names by both actors and prostitutes adds an additional factor of impersonality and anonymity to the prints. As it is the idealized Hanaōgi who is important, so it is the idealized Ichikawa Danjūrō as Benkei who is important. No matter what generation of Hanaōgi or Danjūrō-Benkei the artist portrays, an imaginative ideal replaces reality.

This emphasis on the symbolic importance of the actor and the courtesan prints is not to deny the personality feature altogether. The print did, to some extent, serve the personality cults of actors so ardently sustained by fan clubs. Prints of courtesans were also made in expectation of satisfying an audience which, by dint of the mechanics of her art, was necessarily more limited than that of the actor. However, for the wider audience of both actor and prostitute prints, the idealized treatment of the subject in colorful and stylish costume provided easier entry to the fantasy world of the pleasure quarter.

The faces in the earlier prints are so lacking in individual traits that actors could rarely be identified if their name or crest were not provided. The courtesans' features are feminine and graceful, but they are impassive, and there is no hint of temperament and little sensuality. During the latter half of the eighteenth century, both the actor and courtesan prints undergo a change, more or less simultaneously, due in part to improved techniques in multicolor printing. Close-up facial treatment is given preference by some artists over full-length studies and more personal characteristics are stressed. In some instances an actor might be recognized by face alone in the work of different artists. In the large heads (*ōkubi*), beginning in the 1770s, and shortly in the large faces (*ōgao*) of Bunchō, Shunshō, and Shukō, which lead to the faces of Sharaku, the change lies more heavily on the side of caricature than portraiture. Nonetheless, it signifies a transition from fascination with the symbolic to fascination with the idiosyncratic. A parallel development takes place in the increased attention to individual personality in the depiction of women, but possibly because this subject lends itself less to caricature than the grimacing of actors, the way was opened for the more interesting psychological studies of Utamaro. Unlike the impassive faces of the earlier courtesan prints, sensual beauty now emerges in a variety of physiognomical studies of vanity, fickleness, passion, and so forth. This change toward portraiture was accompanied by the identification of the individual beauty, frequently her name and house, and sometimes the address, written in a cartouche in a corner of the composition.

The intimate connection between the two worlds in the public mind is best illustrated by prints which posed actor with prostitute, geisha, or *kamuro*.[112] The consummate works on this theme are those erotic prints, delicately called "spring pictures" (*shunga*), which show in breathtaking detail a popular actor and a prostitute in the act of love. Considered neither libelous nor invasive of privacy, they simply depicted leaders of the two professions performing as the public expected.

Critical Booklets on Actors and Prostitutes

Critical booklets (*hyōbanki*), quoted earlier, also publicized the leading actors and courtesans. The conception and the design format of these books were very similar for both groups. They developed from the *kanazōshi* tradition of guidebooks to cities and famous places which appeared during the early decades of the seventeenth century. The first booklet on prostitutes (*yūjo hyōbanki*) was probably the *Tōgenshū*, a 1655 guide to the Shimabara quarter and its inmates, followed directly by guides to the quarters in Osaka and Edo. The *Naniwa monogatari* on the Shimmachi quarter of Osaka rated twelve girls of *tayū* rank and thirty of *tenjin* rank. In the next years the first of the guides to actors (*yarō hyōbanki*) appeared, the *Yakusha no uwasa* in 1656 and the *Yarō mushi* in 1660. The latter describes forty-one boys of the theater. These illustrated books extol the physical attractiveness of the young actor-prostitutes but overlook their ability on the stage. The *Muki tokoro* of 1662 shows an advance by making some reference to acting, but not until the end of the century is the main concern of the booklets turned to dramatic talent.

From this time, when not only the youths but the more serious actors are listed, the booklets are known as *yakusha hyōbanki*. In the 1690s the *onnagata* were listed first, followed by youths, and finally by the varieties of masculine roles: *tachiyaku*, villain, and comic character. However, beginning with the *Yakusha kuchi jamisen*, published in 1699, the books increasingly listed the three masculine roles first.[113] This work, like many to follow, devotes one volume to each of the three cities. The usual format is first to give the actor a rating, list the roles he has played, followed by stories about him, and a critique of his skills. Occasionally information on salaries was included. The books came to be published in the first month, focused on the *kaomise* performance of the preceding eleventh month. A second book was published to deal with the program of the first month, and sometimes one was issued concerning the seventh-month performance.

The system of rating performers was modeled on the prostitute booklets. The earliest extant booklet to rate actors, dating from 1687, employed only three ranks, but by 1702 six were in use, from "superior-superior-excellent" (*jōjōkichi*) down to "medium (*chū*). The *Yakusha nichō jamisen* of that year listed 302 actors in the three cities, placing 26 in the highest category and 135 in the lowest.[114] Variations on this scheme were used for some years, but in time the schedule of ratings was devalued by overuse of the higher grades. By the middle of the eighteenth century one book used eleven grades, with "superior-superior-excellent," originally the highest rank, now third from the bottom.[115]

There is also great concern in the professions themselves for a system of hierarchical rank. This is quite clear among the prostitutes of the official quarters. Although the names varied from city to city and changed over time, there was never any doubt about the order. In Shimabara and Shimmachi during the Genroku period, for example, four ranks were recognized.[116] There were also semiofficial quarters and unlicensed brothels, such as bathhouses, which used different names and their own ranking systems. In the case of actors, an order of precedence was acknowledged between the different roles. But further, within each role category, there were levels ranging from master-actor to bit players and apprentices. These are set forth with care in playbills (*banzuke*) which appeared from the 1660s on, initially as handbills for distribution, and later also for posting at crossroads and in bathouses and barbershops.

Playbills recorded a rank list for the year for all actors in a troupe. Others listed the actors of all three cities—Edo, Kyoto, and Osaka. The rating system used for prostitutes was copied in *banzuke* as it was in booklets on actors. In format, however, the playbills came to resemble increasingly the *banzuke* of *sumō* wrestlers.

Interrelation of the Kabuki and Prostitute Quarters

The close relationship between the two social centers of the Tokugawa city also becomes apparent in the fluid exchange of fashion, language, and other cultural innovations which characterized these groups. The current mode and the latest slang of the prostitutes' quarters were introduced in plays and passed on to a wider public. Styles in weaving and dyeing, in color and pattern of dress, in cosmetics, hairstyles, combs and bodkins, constantly passed between them.

The music, the popular songs, the styles of recitation, were shared. The standard instrument of both quarters was the samisen, introduced into Japan in the latter part of the sixteenth century. The samisen of the kabuki and pleasure quarter was higher pitched than that of the puppet theater and had a plaintive, sensuous quality scandalous to Confucian scholars who considered it the most harmful of "licentious music." The numerous schools of recitation used in the kabuki theater were drawn from a variety of sources, but most were shared with the prostitutes' quarters. Some were developed as teahouse music and transported to kabuki, such as Katō-bushi and Shinnai,[117] but by and large, the recitation of teahouse entertainment was adapted from styles found in kabuki. The two worlds were also linked by styles of dance.

Female dancers from the courtesan establishments adopted stage movements and kabuki performers promptly assimilated new material developed in the brothel.

The interconnection between the two worlds appears most fully in those acts of kabuki plays set in houses of assignation. The glamorous but mysterious life of a fine establishment is revealed for an audience thus able to taste vicariously what only a rich man can devour. The personnel of the pleasure quarter, proprietor, madame, courtesan, attendant, maid, and jester, could be amply purveyed. The manner of speaking of these inhabitants of the quarter—the jargon of their trade, the unique honorific verb endings, the peculiar intonation—all attracted great interest. The cultural accomplishments of the *tayū*, focus of so many improbable claims, could be proven on the stage as the courtesan answered the challenge of a guest to perform virtuoso pieces on the koto or samisen and compose a poem in a skillful hand. The presentation of a customer's first meeting with a courtesan, its protocol and characteristic banter, is indeed an ultimate refinement of the prostitute-accosting skits popular in primitive kabuki.

These immensely popular scenes in the licensed houses began as insertions in historical plays. Hence the astonishing anachronism of Minamoto or Taira warriors encountering virtuous wives and beautiful mistresses of both kin and foe in up-to-date brothels. Plays were soon written, however, which centered on the life of the quarter. A piece dating from 1698 is an exuberant tour de force, for it includes scenes in the pleasure districts of each of the three cities.[118] These were early steps toward the full-blown domestic play which dealt entirely with the common people of the day. Among the first were those concerning the double suicides (*shinjū*) of thwarted lovers, the girl usually a prostitute, the man a young clerk or shopkeeper who could not afford to buy her out. The sensational and romantic treatment of these suicides by playwrights such as Chikamatsu seems to have tempted frustrated lovers to rash death covenants, anticipating the publication, if not immortalization, of their passion. To check the popularity of this practice, plays about love suicides were banned in 1722. But the prohibition was effective for only a short time. Each theater tried to scoop the others by getting on the boards first a play concerning a recent suicide or scandal. With the domestic play, theater and society finally met. Real life tragedies were enshrined in a make-believe world.

The best and most challenging role in kabuki is that of the courtesan. The role combines beauty of person and character with attraction as a sexual object. Inasmuch as the prostitute was sold into bondage to relieve her father of debt, her submission to the contract is an act of filial devotion. The courtesan is characteristically portrayed as a person of noble feelings, of dignity and pride. She is courageous and faithful in the midst of feudal intrigue, ready to die rather than betray a samurai lover. This is the *tayū* of the history play. In the domestic play the girl is not of this expensive rank which is meant for the high-born or wealthy but a lower-ranking prostitute, approachable by the commoner, a more girlish and vulnerable lover. But she too is willing to forsake love and sacrifice freedom rather than allow her paramour to fail a family obligation. Her role is a subtle one as her true feelings are rarely revealed before the denouement. This complicated psychology, the tension between honor and passion, considerably enriches the dramatic possibilities open to the *onnagata.*

The life of the quarter revealed in kabuki was glamorized by idealizing the prostitute and romantically depicting the brothel. This was yet another dimension of the sexual fantasy of theatergoing. The content of the plays and the presence of actors with scandalous reputations provided a far more sensual atmosphere than one would suspect from the perspective of kabuki today.

If kabuki was unexpectedly erotic, the brothel could be described as a theater of love, where country girls masqueraded as sophisticated beauties and lowly merchants assumed the airs of men of affairs. Here merchants, to whom the ruling class allowed little dignity, could act out a fantasy of influence and power and be accorded gracious admiration. Here the daughters of impoverished peasants were transformed, their dark skins painted white and rustic dialect replaced by the elaborate polite language of Kyoto. Trained in at least one artistic accomplishment, dressed in sumptuous robes, they were tutored in every technique of the love goddess. A courtesan of *tayū* rank was addressed by her maids in language of formal deference accorded a daimyō's wife by her ladies-in-waiting. The latter-day *tayū* (the *oiran* of the Yoshiwara) was overdressed, overpainted, overloaded by a coiffure bristling with dozens of bodkins. Her entrance into the parlor was staged. She might keep a suitor waiting, his anticipation whetted by the preliminary byplay and solicitous visits of maids and madame while, surrounded by two *kamuro,* one or two maids, and lantern and parasol bearer, she began her deliberate parade from her residence to the house where her guest waited. At last the sliding doors of the parlor were flung open, revealing the *tayū* poised at the threshold with her attendants like an *ukiyo* print. At first she was cool and reserved, fencing verbally with her admirer, now flattering him, now putting him down, besting him in repartee.

The parlor had its subtle rules of sophisticated speech and deportment. There was a dread of blundering in this exchange, of revealing too deeply one's feelings. It was bad form to fall in love. Some common prostitutes and their lovers fell into hopeless infatuations which ended in double suicides; they misunderstood the game. The art, as in kabuki, was to make fiction seem plausible.

Deception was the business of the theater as well. Social outcastes masqueraded as heroes of the past—brave warriors, loyal ministers, even military overlords, analogous to the Tokugawa shogun himself. The chivalrous gallants who defied those of higher status to right injustices were the embodied fantasies of the underprivileged. But the most cherished charade, and that which best portrays the social environment of the theatrical world, was the tender, threatened union of the courtesan and her lover.

Conclusion

The interconnections between kabuki and the pleasure quarter illustrate how specifically the theater was a product of the social environment of Tokugawa cities. The physical presence of attractive youths acting out the roles of glamorous courtesans had more immediacy for an audience which was curious about or knew firsthand the sensual world of prostitute and catamite which was to be found in the cities. But the excitement of kabuki was not limited to such gross features. Kabuki was a stage on which to display many of the accomplishments of the new urban society. These were not limited to the immediate ingredients of drama, such as the elaboration of more subtle plots and variety in acting styles. Kabuki called for new musical forms, recitative styles, composition of songs, and especially choreography. It inspired innovation in fabric and costume design, hairstyles and personal ornamentation. Whatever was new and striking found its way quickly to the stage.

With kabuki as the most exciting form of entertainment, it is not surprising that fashions seen on the stage were copied and that the speech and mannerisms of the popular actors were emulated. Kabuki also provided subjects for painters and printmakers and inspired a new boldness in composition. The traditions and tales on which kabuki drew for its material were returned into the stream of literature to make stories with intricate plots and more dramatic structure. This continuous interchange between the theater and its social environment wove kabuki into the fabric of urban culture.

Notes

1. While this might be unusual in some other cultures, it is not remarkable in Japan, for the Japanese, more than any other modernized people, have managed to preserve a large variety of traditional skills. *Nō* drama is much more faithful than kabuki in carrying on traditions from earlier times, and even the puppet theater, whose development is interwoven with that of kabuki, follows Tokugawa conventions more closely.

2. See D.H. Shively, "Chikamatsu's Satire on the Dog Shogun," *Harvard Journal of Asiatic Studies (HJAS)* 18 (1955): 159–80.

3. The "necessary evil" thesis is discussed in my article, "Bakfu *versus* Kabuki," *HJAS* 18 (1955): 326–56; reprinted in John W. Hall and Marius B. Jansen, eds., *Studies in the Institutional History of Early Modern Japan* (Princeton, N.J.: Princeton University Press, 1968), pp. 231–61.

4. At the time of the Tempō Reform of 1842, actors were counted by the numerary adjunct or counter, *hiki*, used for animals. Gunji Masakatsu, *Kabuki to Yoshiwara* (Tokyo: Asaji Shobō, 1956), p. 68. After the Edo theaters brought a successful suit to free themselves from Danzaemon's jurisdiction (1708), actors were generally considered to be in an intermediate position between commoners and outcaste groups such as *eta* and *hinin*. Gunji Masakatsu, *Kabuki: yōshiki to denshō* (Tokyo: Nara Shobō, 1954), pp. 155–59.

5. *Sundai zatsuwa* (1750), in *Nihon zuihitsu zenshū* (Tokyo: Kokumin Tosho Kabushiki Kaisha, 1929), III:230.

6. *Keizairoku* (1729), in *Nihon keizai sōsho* (Tokyo: Nihon Keizai Sōsho Kankōkai, 1914), VI:55.

7. Ihara Seiseien (Toshirō), "Kabuki no fūzoku," in *Nihon fūzokushi kōza* (Tokyo: Yūzankaku, 1929), no. 18 (IX):44.

8. *Razan sensei bunshū*, quoted in *Dainihon shiryō*, ser. 12 (Tokyo: Tokyo Teikoku Daigaku, 1901), I:260–61.

9. Edward M. Thompson, ed., *Dairy of Richard Cocks*, 2 vols. (London: Hakluyt Society, 1933), I:156, 177, 180, 193, 211, and II:27. Cocks also refers to them as *cabokes, cabukis, coboke, cabukes,* and also as "dansing beares." In an entry at Osaka, he says: "Our host brought us *cabuques*, 3, one the cheefe, with their musick, and staid all night." His notation two days later makes it clear that the "cheefe" was a woman, who evidently stayed two nights.

10. On the history of early kabuki, see Benito Ortolani, *Das Kabukitheater: Kulturgeschichte der Anfänge*, Momumenta Nipponica Monographs no. 19 (Tokyo: Sophia University Press, 1964); Shively, "Bakufu *versus* Kabuki."

11. Gunji, *Kabuki to Yoshiwara,* pp. 186–87, quoting the *Azuma monogatari.*

12. In 1790, 1,200 private prostitutes were seized in Kyoto and were put in the Shimabara quarter. In 1842, 533 girls were again moved in Kyoto, while in Edo, 4,181 were rounded up and placed in the Yoshiwara. Gunji, *Kabuki to Yoshiwara,* pp.188, 197–99.

13. D. H. Shively. "Tokugawa Tsunayoshi, the Genroku Shogun," in A. M. Craig and D. H. Shively, eds., *Personality in Japanese History* (Berkeley and Los Angeles: University of California Press, 1970), pp. 85–126, esp. 97–99.

14. According to the official Tokugawa chronicle, the *Tokugawa jikki,* the shōgun bannermen (*hatamoto*) were addicted to the kabuki youths. In Osaka this year (1652) at the mansion of the *daimyō* Hoshina Masasada, co-commander of the guard of Osaka Castle, there was a drinking party with kabuki youths and a fight broke out. *Kokushi taikei* (Tokyo: Kokushi Taikei Kankōkai, 1932), XLI:53b; Ihara Toshirō, *Kabuki nempyō* (Tokyo: Iwanami Shoten, 1956), I:64–66; Ihara Toshirō, *Nihon engeki shi* (1902; reprint, Tokyo: Waseda Daigaku Shuppanbu, 1924), pp. 92–93.

15. *Kabuki nempyō,* I:66.

16. *Edo meishoki* (1662), by Asai Ryōi (d. 1691), in *Zoku zoku gunsho ruijū* (Tokyo: Kokusho Kankokai, 1906), VIII:757–58.

17. *Kabuki nempyō,* I:70. See C. J. Dunn and Bunz Torigoe, trans. and eds., *The Actors' Analects (Yakusha Rongo)* (Tokyo: Tokyo University Press, 1969), pp. 44, 177.

18. Dōmoto Kansei (Yatarō), *Kamigata engeki shi* (Tokyo: Shun'yodō, 1934), p. 41; Takano Tatsuyuki, *Nihon engeki shi* (Tokyo: Tōkyō-dō, 1948), II: 265–69. Dōmoto believes that seven theaters were licensed as early as 1624, but Takano's opinion that this did not happen until 1669–70 seems more probable.

19. There are many illustrations of the scene at the Shijō riverbank, including performances of *onna kabuki, wakashu kabuki,* and a variety of sideshows in screen paintings of the second quarter of the seventeenth century, as in Kondō Ichitarō, *Japanese Genre Painting: The Lively Art of Renaissance Japan,* trans. R. A. Miller (Tokyo: Charles Tuttle Co., 1961), plates 4, 66–71, pp. 22 and 24; also Kikuchi Sadao et al., eds., *Kinsei fūzoku zukan* (Tokyo: Mainichi Shimbunsha, 1974), II:109; and Kyoto Kokuritsu, Hakubutsukan, comp., *Rakuchū rakugai zu* (Tokyo: Kadokawa Shoten, 1966), unnumbered plates at back.

20. The use of the crane became taboo in 1690 because the word for crane (*tsuru*), was used by the shōgun Tsunayoshi in his daughter's name,

Tsuruhime. Thereafter the Nakamura-za used a gingko leaf design and the Ichimura-za changed its crest to an orange-tree design. Suda Atsuo, *Nihon gekijō shi no kenkyū* (Tokyo: Sagami Shobō, 1957), p. 330.

21. The six-fold screen (Tokyo National Museum) of the Nakamura-za with its new gingko-leaf crest and stage, attributed to Hishikawa Moronobu (d. 1694), appears in Kondō, *Japanese Genre Painting*, plate 76 (identified inexplicably as the Morita-za): Gunji Masakatsu, ed., *Temae miso* (Tokyo: Seiabō, 1969), plate 416; and Suwa Haruo, *Kabuki kaika* (Tokyo: Kadokawa Shoten, 1970), plate 58. See note 60.

22. Takano, *Nihon engeki shi*, II:242–43.

23. Gunji, *Kabuki to Yoshiwara*, pp. 62–63; Gunji, *Temae miso*, pp. 51–52. Only the large theaters of the three cities are discussed in this chapter, but there were also small, low-priced theaters known as *miyachi shibai* located on temple grounds, which were permitted to give performances for one hundred days during the year. Gunji, *Kabuki to Yoshiwara*, pp. 38–40.

24. Suda, *Nihon gekijō shi no kenkyū*, p. 328.

25. Zushi Yoshihiko, *Nihon no gekijō kaiko* (Tokyo: Sagami Shobō 1946), p. 61. The largest Kyoto theaters seem to have been somewhat larger, at least in 1689 when one measured 106 by 196 feet, over 20,000 square feet. Suda, *Nihon gekijō shi no kenkyū*, p. 330.

26. Yoshida Teruji, ed., *Kabuki-za* (Tokyo: Kabuki-za Shuppanbu, 1951), p. 324.

27. Zushi, *Nihon no gekijō kaiko*, p. 60; Suda, *Nihon gekijō shi no kenkyū*, pp. 331–33; Takano, *Nihon engeki shi*, II:341. Three-tiered boxes are mentioned in 1701, but this perhaps means two tiers raised above the floor, allowing space underneath. Suda, *Nihon gekijō shi no kenkyū*, p. 331.

28. From 1772, wooden partitions replaced ropes to divide the *masu*, and later the size of the *masu* was reduced until finally there was space for only four people. Suda, *Nihon gekijō shi no kenkyū*, 339.

29. Takano, *Nihon engeki shi*, II:343; Iizuka Tornoichirō, *Kabuki gairon* (Tokyo: Habubunkan, 1928), p. 469; Gunji, *Temae miso*, p. 50.

30. "*(Kyō-Ōsaka) Yakusha hyōban iro jamisen*," in *Kabuki hyōbanki shūsei* (Tokyo: Iwanami Shoten, 1973), III:327a; Takano, *Nihon engeki shi*, II:343.

31. Suda, *Nihon gekijō shi no kenkyū*, p. 333.

32. Ibid., p. 327.

33. Ibid., pp. 327, 329.

34. Ibid., pp. 335, 345.

35. Ibid., p. 337. The present kabuki-za stage is 77 feet by 95 feet.

36. Ibid., p. 329. There is some evidence that it was used as part of the

stage by 1668. Iizuka, *Kabuki gairon*, p. 421; Takano, *Nihon engeki shi*, II:361–63.

37. Suda, *Nihon gekijō shi no kenkyū*, pp. 337–41.

38. The pillar at stage left bears the name of the play, *nanakusa wakayagi Soga*, followed by the name of the theater, Ichimura-za. The other pillar gives the name of the scene, "Yaoya Oshichi kyōdai biraki." On the beam joining the pillars we see that the Ichimura-za has reclaimed its crane crest. On stage beside her shop counter stands the vegetable dealer (*yaoya*) Oshichi, played by Segawa Kikujirō in this performance of the first month of 1744. Kichizō, played by Onoe Kikugonō, approaches on the *hanamichi*. A stage attendant waves his fan to quiet the audience. This print is an example of the Western-style perspective picture (*ukie*, "floating picture") which came into vogue about 1736. Yoshida Teruji, *Kabuki-e no kenkyū* (Tokyo: Ryokuen Shobō, 1936, 1963), pp. 98–100. The print is in the collection of the Atami Bijutsukan.

39. Detail of a print of a theater interior by Utagawa Toyokuni III (1786–1864), in the collection of the Waseda Daigaku Engeki Hakubutsukan (The Tsubouchi Memorial Theater Museum, Waseda University). The entire print is reproduced in Gunji, *Temae miso*, plate 448.

40. Gunji, *Kabuki to Yoshiwara*, pp. 59–60.

41. Toita, pp. 66, 69.

42. Iizuka, *Kabuki gairon*, p. 484.

43. Dōmoto, *Kamigata engeki shi*, p. 166. Beginning in the last decade of the seventeenth century, *homekotoba* were printed up for wider distribution. For example see Shuzui Kenji and Akiba Yoshimi, *Kabuki zusetsu* (Tokyo: Man'yōkaku, 1931), plates 69 and 72.

44. Iizuka, *Kabuki gairon*, p. 484.

45. Gunji, *Kabuki to Yoshiwara*, p. 61.

46. Iizuka, *Kabuki gairon*, pp. 481–82; Gunji, *Temae miso*, p. 50. A woodblock print of about 1790 by Katsukawa Shun'ei (1768–1819) shows Nakamura Kumetarō II seated on the stage, bowing to the audience, receiving applause, as he takes leave to go from Edo to Osaka. In the foreground we see draped over the heads of three men in the audience identical scarves bearing Kumetarō's crest. These are doubtless members of his booster club. Illustrated in Harold P. Stein, *Master Prints of Japan: Ukiyo-e Manga* (New York: Harry N. Abrams, 1969), p. 173.

47. Toita, p. 65.

48. The earliest copies extant date from 1675; see Shuzui, *Kabuki zusetsu*, plates 29–30.

49. Entry dated 1756; Dōmoto, *Kamigata engeki shi*, p. 246.

50. Gunji, *Temae miso*, the autobiography of Nakamura Nakazō III (1809–1886), Gunji Masakatsu, ed. (Tokyo: Seiabō, 1969) pp. 135b–136a; Dōmoto, *Kamigata engeki shi*, pp. 248–49.

51. Dōmoto, *Kamigata engeki shi*, pp. 249–52; Takano, *Nihon engeki shi*, II:415.

52. On theater-going, see Gunji, *Kabuki to Yoshiwara*, pp. 49–53. The handscroll known as "Hokurō oyobi engeki zukan" (Picture scroll of the Northern Brothels (Yoshiwara) and Theaters), attributed to Hishikawa Moronobu, is in the Tokyo National Museum. It was not originally a single scroll, but it is made up of segments dated and signed by Moronobu, seven of the segments bearing dates ranging from 1672 to 1689. Plate 4 is the left edge of a section, bearing the date 1687, which shows the action on a stage, identified by Suwa, *Kabuki kaika*, pp. 118–19, as the Nakamura-za. The stage, omitting the box, is illustrated in Suwa, *Kabuki kaika*, plate 51, and Gunji, *Temae miso*, plate 408. The handscroll is reproduced in full in *Kinsei fūzoku zukan*, vol. III.

53. Dōmoto, *Kamigata engeki shi*, pp. 169–74. In Osaka, however, prostitutes were allowed to go to the theater teahouses. Sometimes dancing girls appeared in teahouses in Edo and Kyoto, which suggests that enforcement was not always complete.

54. Suda, *Nihon gekijō shi no kenkyū*, p. 336.

55. Takano, *Nihon engeki shi*, II:364, quoting Uji Kaganojō's *Shijō-gawara suzumi hakkei.*

56. Gunji, *Kabuki to Yoshiwara*, p. 52.

57. Ibid., pp. 53–54; Zushi, *Nihon no gekijō kaiko*, pp. 61–62; Gunji, *Temae miso*, p. 50.

58. Suda, *Nihon gekijō shi no kenkyū*, p. 265.

59. Ibid., p. 305. For a sketch map of the quarter, see plate 62 in Suda, *Nihon gekijō shi no kenkyū.*

60. The right screen, depicting the Nakamura-za entrance (plate 1) and interior, is referred to in note 21. The left screen is reproduced in full in Kondō, *Japanese Genre Painting*, plate 77; and the two right and two left panels only in Suda, *Nihon gekijō shi no kenkyū*, plates 59–60. The pair of screens in the Tokyo National Museum is designated an Important Cultural Property.

61. Plate 7 is a detail of Moronobu's "Edo fūzoku zukan" (Picture scroll of Edo customs) in the Atami Bijutsukan. In plate 8, kabuki youths look down from the second-story lattice window of a theater teahouse at two samurai dueling in the street. This detail, like the scene in plate 9 of the latticed front

of a brothel, is from the "Hokurō oyobi engeki zukan" (Tokyo National Museum) described in note 52.

62. Gunji, *Kabuki to Yoshiwara*, pp.54–55. For an illustration of elegant ladies seated in a box, see Kondō, *Japanese Genre Painting*, plate 76; and Gunji, *Temae miso*, plate 416. The women of *daimyō* households were taught kabuki dances by a master (*kyōgen-shi*) who came to instruct in the lords' mansions.

63. *Yarō nigiri kobushi* (1696) in *Kabuki hyōbanki shūsei*, II:65a; and *Yakusha-za no furumai* (1713), *Kabuki hyōbanki shūsei* (1974), V:187b; Takano, *Nihon engeki shi*, II:337. Ikushima appears in a print with two other actors in 1712, reproduced in James A. Michener, *Japanese Prints: From the Early Masters to the Modern*, with notes by Richard Lane (Rutland and Tokyo: Charles E. Tuttle Co., 1959), no. 22.

64. Takano, *Nihon engeki shi*, II:338–39. According to some accounts, Ikushima died in exile in 1733, but others say that he returned to Edo and lived until 1743.

65. In *Chiyoda-jō ōoku*, by Nagashima Imashirō and Ōta Yoshio (1892: reprint, Tokyo: Hara Shobō, 1971), II:86–94, in *Meiji hyakunen-shi sōsho*, no. 168, quoting an unnamed source.

66. Suda, *Nihon gekijō shi no kenkyū*, p. 262.

67. Takayanagi Shinzō and Ishii Ryōsuke, eds., *Ofuregaki Kampō shūsei* (Tokyo: Iwanami Shoten, 1934), no. 2734 and also 2733.

68. Takano, *Nihon engeki shi*, II:340–41: Ihara, *Nihon engeki shi*, I:454–55.

69. Suda, *Nihon gekijō shi no kenkyū*, p. 333.

70. Dōmoto, *Kamigata engeki shi*, p. 262.

71. Ihara, "Kabuki no fūzoku," p. 16; Sekine Shisei, *Tōto gekijō enkaku shi* (Tokyo: Chinsho Kankōkai, 1916), I:73a.

72. Sekine, *Tōto gekijō enkaku shi*, I:72b.

73. Ibid., I:73a.

74. Ibid., I:72a, cites the *Chinjidan* (1692) which claims that catamites surpassed female prostitutes (in popularity or in numbers?), and that there were over five hundred male prostitutes of various types in Edo.

75. Ibid., 63b, 72a; Ishii Ryōsuke, ed., *Tokugawa kinreikō* (Tokyo: S bunsha, 1959–1961), V, no. 3396.

76. Sekine, *Tōto gekijō enkaku shi*, I:57a, 64a.

77. Ibid., I:72a.

78. Ibid., I:73c.

79. Ihara, "Kabuki no fūzoku," p. 16; Sekine, *Tōto gekijō enkaku shi*, I:72b.

80. Ibid., I:72b.

81. Ibid., I:73a. The institution of female geisha did not begin until the 1750s. It was possible for youths and geisha to attend the same box in the little theaters (*miyachi shibai*), ibid., I:73a.

82. Ibid., I:73ab.

83. Ibid., I:72b.

84. Ibid., I:72b.

85. Ibid., I:73b, citing the *Nanshoku shina sadame* (1764).

86. *Kabuki hyōbanki shūsei* (1972), II:27; Takano, *Nihon engeki shi*, II:57–58.

87. Dōmoto, *Kamigata engeki shi*, p. 264.

88. Ibid., p. 264.

89. For a portrait of a *wakashu-gata* of the Genroku period, see Shuzui, *Kabuki zusetsu*, plate 105.

90. Ibid., plates 29–30. Although most *wakashu-gata* were in their teens, this was not always the case by the eighteenth century. Sanogawa Ichimatsu (1722–1762) was a popular *wakashu* at sixteen, and although he did not change to *onnagata* roles until he was thirty-two, he played *wakashu* parts occasionally until he was forty.

91. Ihara, "Kabuki no fūzoku," p. 17.

92. In *Ayame gusa*, cited in *The Actors' Analects*, pp. 61–62.

93. Ihara, "Kabuki no fūzoku," p.17.

94. The affair came to light, Daikichi was imprisoned, and the theater, the Nakamura-za, was closed for a time. Takano, *Nihon engeki shi*, II:331.

95. Ibid., II:433, 440, 460. An anecdote which casts doubt on Tōjūrō's experience as a lover is cited in *The Actors' Analects*, p. 130. He is also quoted as having said that he did not go to teahouses in the prostitutes' quarters, in Iizuka, *Kabuki gairon*, p. 254.

96. Takano, *Nihon engeki shi*, II:396, quoting the *Naniwa tachigiki mukashi banashi* (1686).

97. *Yarō nigiri kobushi* (1696), see note 63.

98. Ihara, "Kabuki no fūzoku," p. 53.

99. Dōmoto, *Kamigata engeki shi*, p. 262.

100. Helen C. Gunsaulus, *The Clarence Buckingham Collection of Japanese Prints: The Primitives* (Chicago: The Art Institute of Chicago, 1955), pp. 207 and 269. I follow Stern, *Master Prints of Japan*, p. 111, in identifying the latter as Koshirō IV, rather than as Sanogawa Ichimatsu, as Gunsaulus does. Stern also suggests the Gunsaulus' "young woman" may be the actor Osagawa Tsuneyo II.

101. Gunji, *Kabuki to Yoshiwara*, p. 65.

102. Ibid., p. 66.

103. Ibid., p. 68.

104. Takano, *Nihon engeki shi*, II:457; Ihara, "Kabuki no fūzoku," pp. 53–54.

105. In 1741 Danjūrō II demanded 2,000 *ryō* to go from Edo to the Sadoshima-za in Osaka.

106. Ihara, "Kabuki no fūzoku," pp. 55–61.

107. Ibid., pp. 51–52.

108. Ibid., pp. 49–52.

109. Ibid., pp. 47–48. It is significant that in each instance the lord was retired, past the age of responsibility, and he could therefore indulge himself without being reprimanded by the Bakufu.

110. Iizuka, *Kabuki gairon*, p. 255.

111. The two handscrolls in the Atami Bijutsukan and the Tokyo National Museum, referred to in notes 52 and 61. I am indebted to Mary Elizabeth Berry for contributions to the interpretation developed in the balance of this section.

112. An example is the first plate in Gunji, *Kabuki to Yoshiwara*: Kikukawa Eisan's portrait of Iwai Hanshirō V (1776–1847) with a Yoshiwara *oiran*. Among other examples are: Kiyonaga's print of Matsumoto Kōshirō IV with a geisha, Michener, *Japanese Prints*, plate 157; Onoe Shōroku with a *tayu* and *kamuro, Ukiyoe zenshi* (1955), vol. 5, figs. 53, 54; Sanogawa Ichimatsu with two *kamuro* looking at a guidebook, probably to the Yoshiwara, Gunsaulus, *Buckingham Collection*, p. 222. On the importance of prostitutes as subject in the development of ukiyoe, see Richard Lane, *Masters of the Japanese Print* (New York: Doubleday and Co., 1962).

113. *Kabuki hyōbanki shūsei*, II:173–289; Takano, *Nihon engeki shi*, II:304.

114. *Yarō tachiyaku butai ōkagami* (1687) is found in *Kabuki hyōbanki shūsei* I:229–68; *Yakusha nichō jamisen* in *Kabuki yakusha shūsei*, III:175–292.

115. *Sangatsu gei gashira*, cited by Iizuka, *Kabuki gairon*, p. 238.

116. *Keisei iro jamisen* (1702), cited in Gunji, p. 135.

117. Iizuka, *Kabuki gairon*, pp. 628, 637.

118. *Keisei Edo zakura*, a Sakata Tōjūrō play, probably written by Chikamatsu Monzaemon, appears in Takano Tatsuyuki, ed., *Chikamatsu kabuki kyōgen shū* (Tokyo: Rikugōkan, 1927), pp. 305–57.

Chapter 10

The *Wabi* Aesthetic through the Ages

HAGA KŌSHIRŌ

One of the most important aesthetic principles in Japanese culture is wabi, *and in this essay Kōshirō focuses on its historical development by first defining the term and then discussing its primary sources. Through Kōshirō's references to the works of Kenkō and Zeami, his discussions of* yūgen *and* sabi, *and his definition of the role of* wabi *in the tea ceremony the reader is constantly reminded of the interconnectedness of all the aesthetic principles discussed in this volume and the immense influence they have had on the shaping of Japanese literature, art, philosophy, and religion.*

Chanoyu seeks to embody a particular kind of beauty: *wabi.* Together with the concept of *yūgen* (mystery and depth) as an ideal of the *nō* drama and the notion of *sabi* (lonely beauty) in *haiku* poetics, *wabi* is one of the most characteristic expressions of Japanese aesthetic principles. This essay attempts to clarify the nature of *wabi* and the beauty it represents by looking at its historical development and the factors contributing to its refinement.

The Three Aspects of *Wabi*

Because *wabi* as an aesthetic brings together many diverse elements, it is difficult to encompass in a simple definition. It can, however, be likened to a three-sided pyramid. Let us briefly look at each of those three sides in turn.

Simple, Unpretentious Beauty

Wabi is a noun derived from the verb *wabiru. Wabiru* and its homophones can have several meanings. The meaning of *wabi* in its aesthetic sense is perhaps best defined by the author of the *Zen-cha Roku,* who wrote: "*Wabi* means lacking things, having things run entirely contrary to our desires, being frustrated in our wishes."[1] This is an extension of the meaning of *wabiru* as being disappointed by failing in some enterprise or living a miserable and poverty-stricken life. The original sense of *wabi,* then, embraces disappointment, frustration, and poverty. The author of the *Zen-cha Roku,* in the section on *wabi,* continues:

> Always bear in mind that *wabi* involves not regarding incapacities as incapacitating, not feeling that lacking something is deprivation, not thinking that what is not provided is deficiency. To regard incapacity as incapacitating, to feel that lack is deprivation, or to believe that not being provided for is poverty is not *wabi* but rather the spirit of a pauper.[2]

From this we can understand that instead of resenting disappointment or hating poverty and trying desperately to escape from it, *wabi* means to transform material insufficiency so that one discovers in it a world of spiritual freedom unbounded by material things. It means not being trapped by worldly values but finding a transcendental serenity apart from the world. This is the way of life of the true exponent of *wabi* and the best expression of *wabi* in action. Consequently, although the beauty of *wabi* is not simply a beauty of mere poverty, unpretentiousness, or simplicity, there are times when, at least superficially, it may seem to be such.

This seemingly unpretentious aspect of *wabi* is evident in the Taian tea room in Myōkian Temple in Yamazaki, in the rustic style of the Urasenke tea room known as Yūin, and in such tea bowls made by Rauku Chōjirō as Hinsō (Impoverished Monk). It is apparent, too, in Takeno Jōō's preference for commonplace objects to use as tea utensils—a bamboo kettlehook, a plain bucket-shaped water container (*mizusashi*), a bentwood washbasin-shaped bowl for used water (*kensui*), and a bamboo lid rest; or in the Southern Barbarian (Namban) style rope screen (*nawasudare*) or a taro-shaped *mizusashi.* This simple, unpretentious—at first glance even impoverished—sense of beauty is certainly one of the more obvious features of the *wabi* aesthetic.

The artlessness of *wabi* beauty, however, should not be confused with an empty simplicity, and its unpretentiousness or external roughness should not be mistaken for mere poverty or coarseness. In this connection it is worth recalling the injunction by Murata Shukō in the *Yamanoue Sōji Ki*: "A prize horse looks best hitched to a thatched hut."[3] Or as it says in the first of the "Ten Resolutions of the *Chanoyu* Practitioner" (*Chanoyu-sha kakugo jittei*): "Truly, a rough and ready, relaxed manner is superior, an overly regimented manner inferior" and "Carrying things out in a relaxed, easy manner demonstrates good taste (*suki*)."[4]

From these injunctions we learn that *wabi* is a kind of beauty which stores a nobility, richness of spirit, and purity within what may appear to be a rough exterior. In offering an unpretentious appearance to the world, *wabi* does not display the attention that has been paid to the smallest details of things nor the cost and effort that have been lavished on what cannot be seen. It is a beauty of great depth which finds its expression in simple and unpretentious terms. *Wabi* is thus an aesthetic of unequal composition in which the most important component lies within that which is being overtly expressed; the internal element is superior to the external. In *wabi* a higher dimension of transcendent beauty is created by the dialectical sublation of an inner richness and complexity into the simple and the unpretentious. It is a beauty, in a word, that detests excess of expression and loves reticence, that hates arrogance and respects the poverty that is humility.

Imperfect, Irregular Beauty

Another side of the pyramid of *wabi* beauty—and one that is closely related to the unpretentious aspect we have just discussed—is that of imperfection or irregularity. In *Zenpō Zatsudan*, Komparu Zenpō quotes Murata Shukō as saying: "The moon is not pleasing unless partly obscured by a cloud."[5] For Shukō, such a moon is preferable to a full moon shining brightly in a clear night sky. This example gives us an insight into Shukō's doctrine that the incomplete is clearly more beautiful than the perfect.

There is another well-known example of this attitude in the *Oboegaki* (Memoranda) section of the *Nampōroku*: "Utensils used in the small tea room need not be entirely perfect. There are people who dislike even slightly damaged objects. This, however, is merely indicative of thinking that has not attained true understanding."[6] Cracks and tears, if properly mended, are not necessarily disliked in *chanoyu.* Indeed, the bamboo flower vase known by the name of the temple Onjōji, made by Sen no Rikyū, is prized precisely because it is cracked. The tea bowl Seppō (Snowy Peak), made by Hon'ami Kōetsu, is particularly admired because it has been repaired. The fact that the old Iga pottery water jar known as Yabure-bukuro (Burst Bag) sagged and split during the firing made it all the more interesting. Other examples include chipped and warped braziers. Thus we arrive at one of the major characteristics of the *wabi* aesthetic: It finds a deeper beauty in the blemished than in the unblemished.

From early times much has been made in *chanoyu* of the word *suki,* meaning taste or refinement but with a hint of eccentricity thrown in. It is found in such combinations as *wabi-suki* (*wabi*-taste), *sukisha* (man of taste), *sukiya* (tea room), and *suki dōgu* (fine utensils). The author of *Zen-cha Roku* praises *suki* as "the very essence of *chanoyu*" and devotes a whole chapter to its elucidation. There the original meaning of *suki* is given as "a form in which the parts are eccentric and do not match."[7] It is further explained as lacking essential parity, being asymmetrical, unbalanced. The true man of taste, *sukisha,* it asserts, is "one who does not march in step with the world, who does not bend to worldly concerns, who does not cherish conformity; an eccentric who takes pleasure when things do not go as he might expect them to."[8] The structure of the tea room is also used to illustrate *suki*:

> Pine pillars, bamboo joists, left as they are,
> curved and straight, square and round,
> up and down, left and right, new and old
> light and heavy, long and short, broad and narrow,
> repaired where chipped, patched where torn.
> Everything at odds, nothing matching.[9]

This irregular beauty of *suki,* too, is an aspect of the beauty of *wabi.*

In early tea gatherings, when the influence of the *shoin* style of tea was still strong, the most commonly used utensils were perfectly symmetrical black glazed *tenmoku* tea bowls and bronze and celadon flower vases. With time, however, as the trend toward *wabi* gathered strength, a preference for warped and irregular forms developed. This tendency is evident in the clog-shaped (*kutsugata*) tea bowls prized by Furuta Oribe or in such Iga, Shigaraki, and Bizen flower vases as the Iga "Crouching Vase" and the bamboo flower vases Fujinami by Kobori Enshu and Natame by Kanamori Sōwa. From this time on, the tendency to find a higher order of beauty in the imperfect grew stronger with the mounting interest in *wabicha.* The beauty of *wabi,* then, is imperfect and irregular. But here too, as in the case of the simple, unpretentious beauty discussed above, it is an irregular beauty which subsumes within itself the beauty of perfect regularity.

Austere, Stark Beauty

A third aspect of the *wabi* aesthetic is a tranquil, austere beauty, the cool stark beauty, of original non-being, *muichibutsu.* In a letter from Murata Shukō to his discipline Furuichi Harima, the priest Chōin, we find the following comment: "Nowadays there are plenty of mere beginners who, mouthing expressions like 'cold' or 'withered,' acquire pottery from Bizen or Shigaraki and put on unpardonable airs. It is really too absurd for words."[10] At the most obvious level this is a warning against the folly of immature beginners who, assuming the airs of connoisseurs, use *wabi*-like Bizen and Shigaraki wares which they are not competent to handle, and, claiming that they are expressing a cold and withered beauty, merely mimic high accomplishments in the art of tea. At the same time, at a deeper level, Shukō reveals that he believes this cold, withered beauty, this austere beauty of age and experience, which can only be attained through a master's accomplishment, to be the epitome of beauty. From this we can glimpse the kind of beauty Shukō perceived as his ideal in *chanoyu.*

This aspect of the beauty of *chanoyu* resurfaces in Tsuji Gensai's frequently cited discussion in *Yamanoue Sōji Ki.* There he refers to Takeno Jōō admiring the expression "withered and cold" by the linked verse (*renga*) master Shinkei and arguing that "the fruit of *chanoyu* too must be like that."[11] From this we can understand Jōō's ideal of *wabi.* Toward the end of *Nampōroku,* Jōō points out that anybody who wants to know the true taste of *wabi* should savor this verse by Fujiwara no Teika:

Miwataseba	Looking about
Hanas mo momiji mo	Neither flowers
Nakarikeri	Nor scarlet leaves,
Ura no tomaya no	A bayside reed hovel
Aki no yūgure.	In the autumn dusk.[12]

The notion of *wabi* that Jōō derives from this poem is that of a tranquil, austere beauty which transcends the vivid beauty of spring light or the striking beauty of autumn leaves. His ideal is closer to that of an inkwash monochrome, the lonely beauty of "a bayside reed hovel in the autumn dusk," a faded beauty of emptiness.

Turning now to Sen no Rikyū, what was his ideal of *wabi*? Perhaps the best way of grasping what Rikyū meant by *wabi* is through a poem continuing in the spirit of the "looking for" poem cited by Jōō above. When Rikyū said "one poem is outstanding," he was referring to the following verse by Fujiwara no Ietaka:

Hana o nomi	To those who wait
Matsuran hito ni	Only for flowers
Yamazato no	Show them a spring
Yukima no kusa mo	Of grass amid the snow
Haru o misebaya	In a mountain village.[13]

Through this poem Rikyū hints at his ideal of *wabi* and its artistic boundaries. To those who think that only a vivid beauty is true beauty, the poet clearly wanted to present the vision of a "spring of grass amid the snow." But what kind of beauty is this "spring of grass amid the snow?"

We can imagine a mountain village in the depths of winter when the seven wild grasses of autumn have withered and the brilliant scarlet leaves have scattered. It is a lonely, cold, and desolate world, a world that is even more deeply steeped in the emptiness of non-being than that of "a bayside reed hovel in the autumn dusk." At first glance this may seem like a cold, withered world at the very extremity of *yin.* It is not, of course, simply a world of death. As proof, we have these lines: "When spring comes it turns to brightness and amid the snow fresh grass sprouts, here two there three blades at a time."[14] This is truly "the merest tinge of *yang* at the extremity of *yin.*" Ietaka expressed this notion as a "spring of grass amid the snow." And Rikyū found in it the perfect image of *wabi.* Thus Rikyū's *wabi,* viewed externally, is impoverished, cold, and withered. At the same time, internally, it has a beauty which brims with vitality. While it may appear to be the faded beauty of the passive recluse, or the remnant beauty of old age, it has within it the beauty of non-being, latent with unlimited energy and change.

Analyzing *wabi* as the ideal of *chanoyu* from the point of view of aesthetics, many other aspects can be raised. The late Hisamatsu Shin'ichi defined the following seven characteristics of *wabi* beauty: irregularity, simplicity, austerity, naturalness, mystery (*yūgen*), ethereality, and tranquility.[15] For the development of my theme, however, it is sufficient to stress that *wabi* has the three characteristics discussed above—the sides of my three-sided pyramid—mutually blended to create a single aesthetic sensibility.

Sources of the *Wabi* Aesthetic

As we have seen in the preceding sections, the *wabi* ideal of beauty sets simple and unpretentious expression above the complex and striking. It abhors excess; it admires restraint. It sees a higher dimension of beauty in the imperfect than in the flawless. While it was certainly Shukō, Jōō, and especially Rikyū who self-consciously defined *wabi* as the aesthetic ideal of *chanoyu*, it was by no means invented by them. *Wabi* was already maturing as part of the aesthetic consciousness of the Japanese long before the appearance of tea masters or the elaboration of *chanoyu*.

The aesthetic consciousness comprising the three aspects of *wabi* was gradually elaborated in the form of literary theories dealing with *waka* and *renga* and treatises on the performing arts centered on the *nō* during the four centuries between the early twelfth and the late fifteenth. In this sense, the *wabi* of *chanoyu* can be described as the culminating distillation of an aesthetic consciousness of the Japanese people that had been cultivated from the late ancient period through medieval times. The *wabi* of *chanoyu* draws upon an ancestry of *yūgen*, the dark and mysterious, which medieval *waka*, *renga*, and *nō* took as their ideal. Moreover, it was through *chanoyu* that *wabi* was realized in practice as an art for everyday life. In the next section, focusing on *yūgen* as an ideal of beauty, I shall trace the transformation of the Japanese aesthetic consciousness from antiquity through medieval times in order to illustrate how the three-sided beauty of *wabi* took shape.

Shunzei and Chōmei: Admiration for the Yojō *and* Yūgen *Styles*

Although the forerunner of literary criticism in Japan was the *Bunkyō Hifuron* by Kūkai, it was really the preface to the *Kokinshū*, with its opening statement that "Japanese poetry, having the human heart as its seed, produces the myriad leaves of speech,"[16] that had the greatest impact on subsequent theories of poetry and the performing arts. In suggesting that *waka* is that which flows of itself from the poet's heart through contact with the beauties of nature or the events of human life, the preface touched the very essence of literature and the arts. In the *Kokinshū* view of poetry, the heart (*kokoro*), which acts as the womb from which *waka* are born, and the leaves of words (*kotoba*), the external expression of the emotions, are equally as important as the two wheels of a cart. In this early stage of literary theory, the ideal of *waka* was that of a perfectly balanced combination of emotion and expression: heart = words.

Ki no Tsurayuki and the other contributors to the *Kokinshū* took as their ideal the fullest expression in words of the inner heart. They called this heart = words expression "the correspondence of heart and words, the complementarity of fruit and flower." It was from this perspective, for instance, that Tsurayuki evaluated the poetic styles of the Six Poetic Geniuses. He commented on the poetry of the monk Henjō (Yoshimne no Munesada) in the following terms: "While it has the semblance of poetry, it lacks inner sincerity."[17] He criticized the poetry of Fun'ya no Yasuhide as "deft in the use of words, but its style does not match its substance. It is like fine robes worn by a common tradesman."[18] In both cases Tsurayuki's criticism suggests that, while the expression was more or less acceptable, inner reality was wanting. In his view, the works of both poets were composed on the basis of heart yielding to lyric and fruit yielding to flower (heart > words, fruit > flower) and thus fell short of the *waka* ideal: an equal balance of emotion and expression.

In contrast, Tsurayuki criticized the poetry of Ariwara no Narihira as "overflowing with heart, inadequate in words. It is like a faded flower drained of color but with the scent still lingering."[19] His criticism suggests that because Narihira's poetry is structured in terms of heart > words, fruit > flower, the heart does not find full expression in words. This unexpressed emotion, like the lingering scent of a faded flower, drifts about the words as an emotional aftertaste (*yojō*) that refuses to leave. Again, if one regards the ideal *waka* as a perfect balance of heart = words the poem is less than superlative. Thus, in the early tenth century, the lingering aftertaste type of expression with "heart in excess, words deficient" was far from the *waka* ideal. In this context there is one more quotation meriting our attention. It is Ki no Tsurayuki's comment on a poem by the priest Kisen: "The words are understated, the opening is taut, but it lacks certainty. It is like trying to view an autumn moon obscured by dawn clouds."[20] From this it is clear that the mysterious and veiled expression later prized as *yūgen* in poetry was not esteemed in Tsurayuki's day.

With the passage of time, however, some poets clearly felt that it was too much to expect them to fully express their hearts within the limited scope of the thirty-one syllables of the *waka* form. This led to the advocacy of what can be called the "lingering emotion" (*yojō*) form of *waka*, particularly by the poet and critic Fujiwara no Kintō. While stressing "mutual realization of heart and form" in which "heart is profound and form pure," Kintō tended to attach more importance to the inner heart than to its expressions: "If mutual realization of heart and form proves difficult, one should give priority to the heart."[21] In the *Waka Kuhon*, which evaluated *waka* in nine grades, poems of the upper-middle rank were those in which "heart and words move in step to create interest." Poems of the mid-upper rank were "graceful with an excess of heart," while those of the upper-upper rank were "exquisite of expression, yet with a surplus of heart."[22] Thus we can see that the *yojō* style of *waka* with "heart in excess, words restrained," which was not particularly appreciated in Ki no Tsurayuki's day, came into vogue in the age of the Fujiwara regents.

In the late eleventh and early twelfth centuries, the period referred to as *insei*, or rule by abdicated emperors, the poets Fujiwara no Mototoshi and his disciple Fujiwara no Shunzei (Toshinari) began to use the term *yūgen* in judging verse-matching contests (*utaawase*). In his comments in the afterward to the *Jichin Oshō Jikaawase*, Shunzei clearly linked the *yojō* style with *yūgen* as superior poetry. For him superior poems were those that "over and above the diction (*kotoba*) and general configuration (*sugata*) of the verse" are suffused with a lingering subtlety of thought and vagueness of emotion "like a trail of mist around spring flowers, or the cry of a deer before an autumn moon, or the scent of spring wind by a plum blossom hedge, or the patter of soft rain on autumn maple leaves among the crags."[23]

However, it was Kamo no Chōmei, the author of *Hōjōki*, who greatly increased the respect for *yojō-yūgen* initiated by Shunzei. In the section entitled "*Kindai katai no koto*" (Recent Verse Styles) in his critical work on poetry *Mumyōshō*, Chōmei points out that verse forms change over time. The dominant characteristic of his day, he says, was the prevailing high regard for *yūgen*. He defines *yūgen* as "lingering emotion not apparent in the diction, a mood not visible in the configuration of the verse," which drifts faintly about the expression. Among the examples of *yūgen* he offers are the following:

> It is like an autumn evening under a colorless expanse of silent sky. Somehow, as if for some reason that we should be able to recall, tears well uncontrollably.

or:

> It is rather like the resentment of a beautiful woman, which she does not display in words but endures silently. . . . Instead of exhausting her vocabulary in recriminations and making a show of wringing tears from her sleeves, she grieves within her heart, tasting the depths of sorrow.

Or again:

> When looking at autumn mountains through mist, the view may be indistinct yet have great depth. Although few autumn leaves may be visible through the mist, it is alluring. The limitless vista created in imagination far surpasses anything one can see more clearly.[24]

Moreover, in the *Eigyokushū* Chōmei states: "Expressing the whole of one's heart in words, rather like describing the moon without clouds or praising flowers for being beautiful, is not at all difficult."[25] Thus Chōmei suggests that the heart = words form of poetic expression is a lesser aesthetic. It is the *yojō-yūgen* style that is the essence of *waka.* Moreover, he says, "poetry which takes its form from *yūgen*" is "an uncertainty of heart and words like looking upon a mirage of shimmering heat waves in an azure sky. . . . Being, they are not. Not being, they are."[26] This is precisely the poetic style of the priest Kisen which was earlier criticized by Ki no Tsurayuki.

Thus by the time of Kamo no Chōmei at the end of the twelfth century, the *yojō* style of Ariwara no Narihira and the cloudy, indistinct style of Kisen, which had been looked down upon in the age of the *Kokinshū* in the tenth century, had come to be labeled *yūgen* and regarded as the most admirable of *waka* styles. The aesthetic consciousness of *wabi,* then, suppresses the outward display of expression while storing within itself a rich depth of emotion. In this it realizes a profound and simple inner beauty in which *wabi* is differentially structured "inner outer" beauty.

The *yojō-yūgen* style that was regarded as the epitome of *waka* from the time of Shunzei to Chōmei has a connection in its heart > word structure with the *wabi* of *chanoyu,* which it preceded. In this way, at least one of the sources of *wabi* can be detected in the poetic theories extolling this *yojō-yūgen* form and in the intellectual currents of the age surrounding them. It is perhaps worth noting that Fujiwara no Teika, Shunzei's son, who was the leader of the poetry world in the early Kamakura period and a man later regarded as a "sage of poetry," favored the word *ushin* (literally, to possess heart) and set the *ushin* form above *yūgen.* Although there was a slight nuance of difference, his *ushin* was virtually the same as *yūgen.* The reverence for *yūgen* aesthetics became the mainstream in subsequent poetry circles. It was especially strongly advocated by the Reizei family in the middle and late fourteenth century. Because of this, the *wabi* aesthetic was further deepened from the Kamakura through the Northern and Southern Courts period.

Yoshida Kenkō: The Discovery of Imperfect, Irregular Beauty

We have already seen that the *wabi* aesthetic prizes the imperfect over the flawless and classically elegant as one expression of a higher dimension of beauty. It would be incorrect to suggest, however, that such as aesthetic ideal only came into being with *chanoyu.* This ideal of imperfect beauty had already been described by Yoshida Kenkō in his *Tsurezuregusa.*

There is a natural human desire to admire the perfection of cherry blossoms at their peak and the full moon shining in a clear night sky. Like other peoples, the Japanese have from ancient times regarded such images as the highest expressions of beauty. In section 137 of the *Tsurezuregusa,* however, we find the following famous lines:

> Are we to look at cherry blossoms only in full bloom, the moon only when it is cloudless? To long for the moon while looking on the rain, to lower the blinds and be unaware of the passing of spring—these are even more deeply moving. Branches about to blossom or gardens strewn with faded flowers are worthier of our admiration . . . .
>
> The moon that appears close to dawn after we have long waited for it moves us more profoundly than the full moon shining cloudless over a thousand leagues. And how incomparably lovely is the moon, almost greenish in its light when seen through the tops of the cedars deep in the mountains, or when it hides for a moment behind clustering clouds during a sudden shower![27]

Kenkō sets aside the perfect beauty of the flower in full bloom to claim that there is a still higher dimension of beauty in the partly opened flower or in the lingering blossom. And while he allows that the beauty of an unclouded moon is attractive, he insists that a moon obscured by rain or veiled by clouds or a waning moon sinking behind the trees is a still deeper expression of beauty.

In the same section Kenkō argues:

> In all things, it is the beginnings and ends that are interesting. Does the love between men and women refer only to those moments when they are in each others' arms? The man who grieves over a love affair broken off before it was fulfilled, who bewails empty vows, who spends long autumn nights alone, who lets his

> thoughts wander to distant skies, who yearns for the past in a dilapidated house—such a man truly knows what love means.[28]

Here Kenkō suggests that it is only by tasting fully the pangs (*aware*) of an unrequited love or a broken love affair that one come to understand true love. Later in the same passage he criticizes the attitude of spectators at the Kamo festival for being interested only in the highlights of the procession. For him, the early morning prelude to the festival and the lingering loneliness afterward, when the crowds have gone, enhance and validate the beauty of the occasion:

> By the time it is growing dark you wonder where the rows of carriages and the dense crowds of spectators have disappeared to. Before you know it, hardly a soul is left, and the congestion of returning carriages is over. Then they start removing the blinds and matting from the stands, and the place, even as you watch, begins to look desolate. You realize with a pang of grief that life is like this. If you have seen the avenues of the city you have seen the festival.[29]

That Kenkō's discovery of beauty in imperfect things and quiet moments is not mere whimsy or paradox but rather an aesthetic consciousness shared with other cultured persons of his day can readily be seen from section eighty-two of *Tsurezuregusa.* At the opening of this section he writes:

> Somebody once remarked that thin silk was not satisfactory as a scroll wrapping because it was so easily torn. Ton'a replied, "It is only after the silk wrapper has frayed at top and bottom, and the mother of pearl has fallen from the roller that a scroll looks beautiful." This opinion demonstrated the excellent taste of the man. People often say that a set of books looks ugly if all volumes are not in the same format, but I was impressed to hear the Abbot Kōyū say, "It is typical of the unintelligent man to insist on assembling complete sets of everything. Imperfect sets are better."[30]

Clearly Kenkō approved of the attitudes of the priests Ton'a and Kōyū that the old and faded, the mismatched and incomplete, can be more beautiful than the unblemished, the uniform, or the complete. One notes with interest that Kenkō, Ton'a, and Kōyū—three men of culture who lived in the Kamakura to early Northern and Southern Courts periods—should all agree in praising the imperfect and irregular or the worn and aged as a higher dimension of beauty. To claim that things are most beautiful not when they are "perfect and round" but when they are irregular and mismatched is an expression of *suki* in its original meaning, and here we can detect one of the currents of the *wabi* of *chanoyu*.

Zeami and Zenchiku: Toward a Beauty of Reticence and Non-Being

Chanoyu was refined from the late fifteenth century as one part of what has been called the culture of the Eastern Hills (Higashiyama) because of its association with the eighth Ashikaga shogun, Yoshimasa, who built his retreat, the Silver Pavilion, in the eastern hills of Kyoto. The more fully articulated *chanoyu* of this period was based on the practices of tea drinking by Zen monks, courtiers, members of the warrior elite, and merchants that had been spreading from the Kamakura period. The cultural life of this era was rich and diverse. Since other important elements of Higashiyama culture were linked verse and *nō*, it would not be surprising to find that the *wabi* aesthetic which came to play such a central role in *chanoyu* also owed something to their influence. In the case of *nō*, one way to gauge its influence on *chanoyu* is to look at the dramatic theories formulated by Zeami Motokiyo.

Kan'ami Kiyotsugu and his son Zeami were actors in the Yamato *sarugaku* tradition, which originally prized mime (*monomane*) or representational performance. But they established a new dramatic style by assimilating the singing and dancing styles of Ōmi *sarugaku* and *dengaku* (field music). This new artistic style attracted the notice of the third Ashikaga shogun, Yoshimitsu. Yoshimitsu's backing opened the way to success and to patronage by the Bakufu and by daimyos. Under this elite patronage, Kan'ami and Zeami refined their dramatic performances to establish the elegant dance-drama that we still enjoy as *nō*.

Zeami had been trained in mime, the traditional dramatic style of his *sarugaku* lineage. But in treatises written to transmit his teachings secretly to his followers he emphasized *yūgen* as the highest expression of beauty attainable in *nō*. In *Kakyō*, for instance, he wrote: "*Yūgen* is regarded as the highest level of attainment in various artistic traditions. In our art, in particular, the mood of *yūgen* is the most important feature of style. . . . However we may vary the elements of mimicry, we must not depart from *yūgen*,"[31] Zeami's *yūgen* cuts off the search for verisimilitude pursued through mime at a certain limit and, by converting expression into poetry and dance, injects a mood of lingering emotion, *yojō*. In this way Zeami took the edge off realistic expression, made it more rhythmical, and created a romantic world of *yūgen-yojō* beauty suffused with subtle emotion and delicate feeling. Although there is no space here to discuss Zeami's view on the beauty of *yūgen* in detail, I can at least present some of his conclusions.

In *"Mondo jōjō,"* the third section of his *Fūshi Kaden*, Zeami writes: "Irrespective of the role he is playing, the principal actor (*shite*) should be vivid (*hanayaka*). This constitutes *yūgen.*"[32] In the section "On Entering the Boundaries of *Yūgen*" (*Yūgen no sakai ni iru no koto*) in *Kakyō*, he gives the following examples of *yūgen*: "the fine bearing of a nobleman or woman" and "the elegant manner of speech of a nobleman or religious dignitary." He also says that "a simple softening of form is the essence of *yūgen.*"[33]

In his *Nō Sakusho*, Zeami mentions fitting subjects for the characterization of *yūgen*: Ariwara no Narihira, Ōtomo no Kuronushi, and Hikaru Genji among men and Ise no Osuke, Ono no Komachi, Giō, Gijō, Shizuka Gozen, and Hyakuman among women.[34] All of these personages—both historical and fictional—convey a beauty tinged with lingering emotion, an aristocratic, feminine beauty derived from the emotional aesthetic tastes of Heian court literature, a vivid, gentle, elegant beauty. This *yūgen* style of beauty was, for Zeami, the fundamental expression of *nō*. But there was an even higher form of beauty to be achieved only by master actors at the very peak of performance. Zeami called this extreme beauty the "flower" (*ka*). As is obvious from the titles of such secret treatises as *Fūshi Kaden* and *Kakyō*, he loved the character for flower. In the *Mondō jōjō* section of *Fūshi Kaden* he goes so far as to say that "the flower is the life of *nō*." In the same section, however, he observes: "There is a beauty that must be spoken of as even higher than flower."[35] That is the beauty of *shiore*, literally the "withered." *Shiore* is the higher level of beauty, known only to those who attain the limits of flower.

From this it is clear that even when writing *Fūshi Kaden*, while he was still under the influence of his father, Kan'ami, Zeami set a higher value on the imperfect, negative, emaciated beauty of *shiore*, the negation of "flower," than he did on the perfect, affirmative beauty of "flower" itself. Moreover, this aesthetic deepened in later years as his experience and ideas matured. This development is clear from the "*Hihan no koto*" (On Criticism) section of *Kakyō*, where he distinguishes three levels of artistic accomplishment in *nō*: There are three faculties through which *nō* is expressed—sight, hearing, and heart."[38] Fundamental, but at the lowest level, is what we might describe as "*nō* emerging through sight." Zeami writes: "From the first the theater is colorful. The dancing and chanting are animated, the spectators high and low exclaim their praises, the atmosphere is brilliant."[37] He is describing a *nō* that is visually appealing, easily understood, vivid and ostentatious. Thus it is a form of *nō* that is readily appreciated by the general public: "Not only connoisseurs, but even those who know little of *nō*, all in the same spirit, think it interesting."[38]

The second stage is that of "*nō* emerging from hearing." It is a *nō* in which "from the beginning there is a seriousness, music and mood harmonize, and the effect is graceful and interesting." Rather than being seen with the eyes, this *nō* is gracefully absorbed by hearing and the other senses. For this reason, "it may not appeal strongly to rural enthusiasts,"[39] but actually it is a very sophisticated level of *nō*.

The final stage of "*nō*" emerging from the heart" is a *nō* which appeals not to hearing or the other senses but succeeds by stirring the heart. Zeami describes this *nō* as "like the performance of a peerless *sarugaku* which after countless times has shed all variation, mimicry, or forced movement." It is like a master who has transcended the extremes of the vivid and, from an artistic domain beyond this, has reduced the movements of dance and mimicry to the minimum. It is a *nō* which does not have to rely on twists of plot, a "wordless *nō*," a *nō* which in the midst of desolation (*sabi*) has something of awe in it." It is an austere drama—a "*nō* of no-mind (*mushin*)." Consequently, it is the very aesthetic pinnacle of the art of *nō*: "unknown even to true connoisseurs and even more beyond the comprehension of rural admirers."[40]

We note here that Zeami set an auditory beauty—that is, "a penetrating, gentle beauty"—above a visually appealing, "vivid" beauty. But on an even higher plane, at the very pinnacle of his aesthetic, he set a simple, "wordless" beauty, an "austere cold beauty" that appeals to the heart. It is clear, then, that the aesthetic consciousness later known as *wabi* was being gradually forged by Zeami in the middle Muromachi period.

Zeami's son-in-law Komparu Zenchiku, who was active in the Higashiyama epoch at the time of the shogun Yoshimasa, pushed this aesthetic even further. The principal works for understanding Zenchiku's theories of *nō* are his *Shidō Yōshō* and *Rokuin Ichiro no Ki*. In the former he categorizes the varieties of music used in *nō* in the following terms: "Although there are many types of qualities of music in the performance of *sarugaku*, you should know the eight fundamental sounds."[41] Having divided musical styles into eight types, he places the sound of *yūgen* at the middle range, fourth rank. In the eighth rank of "unsurpassed perfection" he puts the music of "leisurely ease" (*kankyoku*), which he says is "supremely elegant, tranquil and graceful." Zenchiku, in a telling analogy, compares the beauty of *kankyoku* to that of aged cherry trees which, after enduring years of rain, dew, wind, and snow, put forth only a few scattered blossoms: "It is like seeing fine rain on the sparse blossoms of the few mossy branches of the framed ancient trees of Yoshino, Ōhara, and Koshio. The mood is tranquil, graceful, and haunting."[42] This austere and serene beauty is the negative counterpart of sumptuous and vivid beauty. It is a simple and reticent form of expression which subsumes within itself the colorful and flamboyant.

Rokurin Ichiro no Ki expounds a Zen-infused view of the performing arts in which "the way of the *sarugaku* performer lies in the secret of detachment from self and object."[43] Zenchiku's assertion that the arts of *nō* are intrinsically detached from self and object is identical with the Zen ideal of "seeing one's original face before one's parents were born." From this view of performance he divides the art of *nō* into six stages, or rings: the ring of longevity, the ring of verticality, the ring of dwelling, the ring of images, the ring of fragmentation, and the ring of emptiness. The six stages are depicted by circles, starting from the ring of longevity, which is described as "a state of nondifferentiation and emptiness, a mysterious expression of movement and stillness."[44] The stages gradually unfold through more colorful expression. When the process reaches its zenith, it transcends set forms and, passing through the ring of fragmentation, once again "becomes unrestrained and returns to the original ring of longevity."[45]

This final stage, the ring of emptiness, is depicted with the same circle as the ring of longevity. How did Zenchiku perceive of his highest level of performance—the beauty of the ring of emptiness? As we can understand from his explanation of the ring of emptiness as "empty and traceless, hushed and wordless, shedding and shedding until nothing is left to shed, emptying until nothing remains to empty,"[46] the ring of emptiness involves an utter simplicity in which expression is restrained to the very minimum. However, as the structure of *Rokurin Ichiro no Ki* hints in such expressions as "realizing enlightenment is the same as being unenlightened,[47] the artistic ideal of the ring of emptiness, although it is expressed through the same ring as the original ring of longevity, is a simple artless beauty which subsumes within itself the colorful, skillful beauty that precedes it.

Explaining the artistic concept of the ring of emptiness, Zenchiku uses the expression "the performance is thoroughly withered, a few blossoms clinging to an aged tree."[48] Clearly the beauty of the empty ring has much in common with that of *kankyoku.* But Zenchiku also explains that "all things withered are faintly rejuvenated, each sound, each step returning to where it first sprouted."[49] The imagery he conjures up here is of silent winter fields, empty of cherry blossoms, autumn leaves, and all emotional quality. While superficially this may seem to be a withered world of death, within the barren fields the life force is inherent, ready to burst forth in the coming spring. The aesthetic of the ring of emptiness advocated by Zenchiku is a stark and withered beauty like that of winter fields. It is a kind of beauty in which one can sense, despite its coldness and reticence, a pulse of life. It is not off the mark to liken this aesthetic ideal to the beauty of *wabi* alluded to by Takeno Jōō in his reference to the poem "Looking about" or by Rikyū in his reference to "a spring of grass amid the snow."

Shinkei: Aspiration to Stark, Cold Beauty

As we have seen, the roots of the *wabi* aesthetic can be detected in the vogue for *yojō-yūgen* among poets of the early Kamakura period. In the Muromachi period, as *renga* outstripped *waka* in popularity, it too contributed to a deepening of the aesthetic consciousness of *wabi*. We can explore this development through a representative poet of the early Muromachi period, the Zen monk Seigen Shōtetsu of the Tōfukuji lineage of the Rinzai school.

Shōtetsu, who studied *waka* with the warrior-poet Imagawa Ryōshun of the Reizei school, admired the two poetic treatises *Gubishō* and *Sangoki*, which were prepared by the Reizei school and spuriously attributed to Fujiwara no Teika, and on that basis adopted *yojō-yūgen* as a poetic ideal. In his *Shōtetsu Monogatari*, Shōtetsu has the following to say about *yūgen*: "What is called *yūgen* is something in the heart that cannot be expressed in words. The moon lightly veiled in clouds or the reddening autumn hills shrouded in mist are viewed as forms of *yūgen*. But when asked where exactly is the *yūgen* in these things, we find it hard to say."[50]

That Shōtetsu thought of *yūgen* as a form of expression in which lingering emotion, *yojō*, clings subtly to feelings that end before being fully expressed we can understand from this comment: "If racing clouds and swirling snow can be called the *yūgen* style, then clouds trailing faintly in the sky or snowflakes drifting gently on the wind are surely in this style."[51] At the same time, Shōtetsu expressed the quality of the beauty of *yojō* in such analogies as "the feeling that four or five noblewomen in silken robes might be singing of flowers bursting into full bloom at the southern palace"[52] or "thinking so raptly of a beautiful court lady that one is speechless."[53] It is clear that for Shōtetsu the *yūgen* ideal of beauty was an elegant, flamboyant, and femininely voluptuous beauty. As such, it was close to the earlier Zeami model of the *yūgen* aesthetic.

Shōtetsu's student, the *renga* poet Jūjūin Shinkei, a contemporary of Komparu Zenchiku, forged a very different conception of the *yūgen* aesthetic. In *Sasamegoto,* his representative critique of *renga,* Shinkei writes:

> While many paths serve the same cause, this path especially takes as its end emotions, appearances, and lingering feelings *(yojō)*. *Yūgen* and pathos (*aware*) are to be found in what is left unspoken and unformed in thought. With poetry, too, its unclear form speaks only of appearances. This is the utmost expression of poetic form.[54]

This comment should be sufficient to show that Shinkei, like his teacher Shōtetsu, prized the *yūgen* style—that is, an expressive style overflowing with *yojō*. The quality of *yojō* that Shinkei admired was very different from Shōtetsu's, however. Reading the *Shinkei Sōzu Teikin* (Bishop Shinkei's Instructions), we find the following passage:

> One should set one's heart only on the indistinct. The most interesting verses are like those in which we find a spray of single-leaf white plum blossoming in the depths of a bamboo grove or glimpse the moon through clouds. On the other hand, red double plum blossoms in wild profusion or a full moon like that of the fifteenth night of the eighth month are not agreeable.[55]

As if imitating the voice of Yoshida Kenkō in the *Tsurezuregusa,* Shinkei's heart was drawn more to an imperfect, implied beauty than to perfect, rounded beauty whether it be the radiant loveliness of the shining harvest moon or the red double plum blossoms in full bloom. We can understand from this that he did not appreciate gorgeous self-display but rather loved an understated, modest, and simple beauty. But even more noteworthy are his statements in *Sasamegoto*: "The heart requires few words. Excellence is to be found in verses that are cold and spare." The poetic form of the ancients was "like lapis lazuli piled on crystal," their poems being "cold and pure."[56] In the same work he remarks:

> Somebody asked one of the ancient poet immortals (Fujiwara no Mototoshi): "How do you compose poetry?" He replied: "Pampas grass in the withered fields, the moon at dawn." By this he meant putting the heart into what is not stated and recognizing that which is cold and desolate. The verses of those who have entered this realm of understanding display such qualities.[57]

In *Oi no Kurigoto* Shinkei appreciates most highly the beauty that is "elevated, aloof, cold, and frozen" by arguing that "of all who penetrate the very depths of their art, those whose forms are aged and worn, *sabi*, are most respected."[58] The words he used to express the highest beauty of *renga* are words that connote a negative beauty, a beauty of age, like "cold" (*hieru*), "emaciated" (*yaseru*), "frigid" (*samushi*), "withered" (*kareru*), "dried out" (*karabiru*), "spent" (*karekajikeru*), and "aged and worn" (*fukesabiru*). In his *Hitorigoto*, written when, having fled the capital in the Ōnin War, Shinkei was wandering in the eastern provinces of Musashi and Sagami, there is a description of water in its various seasonal manifestations. He finds in the scenery of ice and withered landscape a fathomless beauty:

> Nothing is more beautiful than ice. The thin crust of morning ice on the stubbled rice fields, icicles hanging from eaves of aged cypress bark, the feeling of withered trees and grasses locked in hoar frost. Are these sights without interest and beauty?[59]

Thus we can appreciate that Shinkei's notion of the ideal *renga* and the highest expression of beauty was the same as that of Komparu Zenchiku. It was a beauty in utter contrast to the emotional, vivid beauty of spring cherry blossoms or autumn maple leaves. It was, instead, a tense, stern beauty of barren fields, a winter-withered beauty in which the pulse of the life force is just discernible beneath the awesome desolation of outward appearances, a beauty of starkness and tranquility.

We should note, too, that Murata Shukō might have been quoting Shinkei when he said that "the moon is not pleasing unless partly obscured by a cloud"[60] and that Takeno Jōō, admiring Shinkei's expression "*renga* should be withered and cold," commented that "the fruit of *chanoyu* too must be like that."[61] Why this admiration for Shinkei? Because he celebrated a type of beauty very much like that of the *wabi* of *chanoyu*.

Other Influences Shaping the *Wabi* Aesthetic

Up to this point we have considered *wabi* exclusively as a Japanese aesthetic development that emerged from the arts of *waka*, *renga*, and *nō* during the four centuries of the medieval age from the late Heian period through Muromachi and was gradually refined on the basis of the ideas and reflections of masters in those arts. At the same time, as with other aspects of the thought and culture of the Japanese people, imported ideas may have played a role in shaping *wabi* and the aesthetic concepts leading to it. Although it is difficult to pinpoint sources of direct influence, the Chinese made several contributions to the general intellectual environment within which *wabi* developed.

Confucius, Lao Tzu, and Hsün Tzu

From ancient times Confucianism guided the education of nobles and officials in Japan as in China. The *Analects* (*Lun-yü*), in particular, was regarded as indispensable reading. Confucian values penetrated deeply into the lives of the Japanese people of all social levels as a morality regulating everyday life and imperceptibly came to shape the way people viewed their world and thought about things. Although there were slight modulations in different periods, this current remained fairly steady throughout the medieval period.

In the opening book of the *Analects*, entitled "On Learning," Confucius states:

> It is rare, indeed, for a man with cunning words and an ingratiating face to be benevolent (*jen*).[62]

And later we find reference to its obverse:

> Unbending strength, resoluteness, simplicity and reticence are close to benevolence.[63]

Taken together these statements stress that people who embellish words and show off through their appearance or attitude are wanting in benevolence and sincerity. In contrast, people who are simple and unpretentious in manner and reticent in speech are likely to be sincere and imbued with *jen*. Clearly this view of human nature rejects flamboyance in favor of understatement and reticence. Again, there is this statement:

> With the rites, it is better to err on the side of frugality than on the side of extravagance.[64]

This is to say that on such occasions as coming-of-age, marriage, and funeral rites or the presentation of gifts it is better to be restrained than ostentatious. This is because the essence of such rites lies not in their externals but in the heart.

Furthermore, Tseng Tzu, praising Yen Yüan, the youngest and favorite disciple of Confucius, made these observations:

> To have yet appear to want.
> To be full yet appear empty.[65]

Tseng Tzu is saying that while Yen Yüan had great learning and knowledge he did not make a display of it to others but rather acted as if he were ignorant. While building true ability and force of character he acted modestly as though he were powerless. He was truly a man of great depth.

A similar anecdote describing Lao Tzu can be found in the "Tales of Lao Tzu and Chuang Tzu" in the *Historical Records* (*Shih-chi*) of Ssu-ma Ch'ien:

> Just as a good merchant stores things away and may seem empty of stock, so the sage may outwardly seem foolish and empty of attainments.[66]

Whereas the upstart merchant is likely to enlarge the front of his store and display his goods gaudily, the well-established merchant will maintain a restrained appearance and display his wares sparingly. To outward appearances this wealthy merchant's store may seem sparsely stocked or even empty. But when a customer requests something, an unlimited quantity of precious things are brought from the back. Lao Tzu was exactly like this good merchant. At first glance he might be taken for an empty fool. Yet he was the kind of fathomless sage who offers more wisdom the more he is pressed. The message here is that what should be prized is a poverty of appearance behind which lies a wealth of inner meaning. Moreover, in the *Classic of the Way and Its Power (Tao Te Ching)*, we find such expressions as "One who knows does not speak, one who speaks does not know" and "To know, yet to think one does not know is best."[67] They stress the idea that eloquence is disdained and reticence admired. Again, Taoist thought suggests that the very highest, most mysterious states of being seem rather to take the forms of their opposites. Chapter forty-five, for example, states that:

> Great perfection seems chipped,
> Yet use will not wear it out;
> Great fullness seems empty,
> Yet use will not drain it;
> Great straightness seems bent;

> Great skill seems awkward;
> Great eloquence seems tongue-tied.[68]

The *Tao Te Ching* was read by Japanese men of letters from the Nara period. As the following statement from the *Tsurezuregusa* indicates, the *Tao Te Ching* was also read with pleasure among medieval scholars and especially studied by Gozan Zen monks, who led the world of medieval learning and culture:

> The pleasantest of all diversions is to sit alone under the lamp, a book spread out before you, and to make friends with people of a distant past you have never known. The books I would choose are the moving volumes of *Wen-hsüan*, the collected works of Po Chu-i, the sayings of Lao Tzu, and the chapters of *Chuang Tzu*.[69]

Thus we seem to be safe in assuming that these aphorisms and ideas relating to Lao Tzu were known by learned men of the medieval period.

Similar ideas may be found in the writings of Hsün Tzu. In his *Book on the Seat of Admonition* (*Yu-tso p'ien*) there is a description of Confucius' audience at the court of Duke Huan of Lu. Seeing a tipping vessel that the duke had placed to the right of his seat as a warning to himself, Confucius explained the principle to his followers: "When it is filled it topples."[70] This was an admonition against the evils of overindulgence. The tipping vessel was a water jar which sat at an angle when empty, stood upright when half full, and tipped over when filled to the brim.

This rejection of satiety or completeness was already being advocated in Japan by the Heian period. In the latter part of the eighty-second section of the *Tsurezuregusa* we find the following:

> In everything, no matter what it may be, uniformity is undesirable. Leaving something incomplete makes it interesting, and gives one the feeling that there is room for growth. Someone once told me, "Even when building the imperial palace, they always leave one place unfinished." In both Buddhist and Confucian writings of the philosophers of former times, there are also many missing chapters.[71]

This passage is followed in the eighty-third section by a reference to the eulogy offered by Tōin (Fujiwara) Saneyasu to Saionji Kinhira when the latter declined a promotion to chief minister and requested to be allowed to end his career in the subordinate post of minister of the left. Saneyasu learned this from the act:

> Nothing stood in the way of the lay priest Chikurin'in and minister of the left (Saionji Kinhira) rising to be prime minister, but he said, "I doubt that being prime minister will make much difference. I'll stop at minister of the left." He subsequently took Buddhist orders. The Tōin minister of the left (Saneyasu), impressed by the story, himself never entertained any ambitions of becoming prime minister. The old adage has it, "When the dragon has soared to the summit he knows the chagrin of descent." The moon waxes only to wane; things reach their height only presently to decline. In all things, the principle holds true that decline threatens when further expansion is impossible.[72]

It is not hard to guess from this that in Yoshida Kenkō's day the current of Chinese thought which rejected satiety permeated the intellectual world around him. Nor would it be far off the mark to suggest that this thinking nourished an aesthetic that emphasized an unequal, irregular beauty.

The Shih-jen yü-hsieh *and Muromachi Ink Painting*

In Sung dynasty China there were innovative movements in thought and literature. The intellectual world saw the rise within Confucianism of so-called Sung studies, or Neo-Confucianism. At the same time there was a parallel renaissance in letters marked by a surge in literary criticism. In the late Northern Sung dynasty there was a sharp political conflict between a newly emerging reform faction, known as the "new policies" faction, led by Wang An-Shih, and a more conservative establishment, a counterreform faction, including the historian Ssu-ma Kuang and the poet Su Shih (Su Tung-p'o). This conflict was reflected in written debates as a bitter literary feud developed between the two factions. In the course of this rivalry many "discourses on poetry" (*shih-hua*), such as the *Shih-lin shih-hua* and *Ch'eng-chai shih-hua*, were published and transmitted to Japan by the hands of Zen monks.

Noteworthy among these discourses were two works that conveniently classified the main types of poetic discourse under various topical headings: the *Yü-yin ts'ung-hua* edited by Hu Tzu and the *Shih-jen yü-hsieh* edited by

Wei Ch'ing-chih. The latter had been imported and was being read in Japan by the late Kamakura period. We can be sure that the *Shih-jen yü-hsieh* actually was being read because there is a ten-volume edition of it in the Kyoto Library which contains an afterword by the famous Zen monk-scholar Gen'e:

> In this collection the punctuation is difficult. The mind grows dizzy, errors are many. Later scholars can hope to correct them. Inscribed the latter part of the eleventh month of the first year of the Shōchū era (1324) with purified heart by Gen'e.[73]

From this we know that by 1324, the late Kamakura period, the *Shih-jen yü-hsieh* was being read in Japan. Moreover, entries in the *Hanazono Tennō Shinki* for 1325:12:28 and 1332:3:24 reveal that Emperor Hanazono and his mentor in *waka*, Kyōgoku Tamekane, who breathed new vitality into the poetic circles of his age, both read and admired the *Shih-jen yü-hsieh* as the "core" of poetry. They praised it highly for "being perfectly in harmony with the meaning of Japanese verse (*waka*)." Moreover, the Zen monk Kokan Shiren, well known as the author of the *Genkō Shakushō*, and Gidō Shūshin, one of the leading figures in the Gozan literary movement, as well as other Muromachi period Zen monks, read it with great appreciation. It is clear, too, that Nijō Yoshimoto, the commanding literary figure of his age and cultural adviser to Ashikaga Yoshimitsu, read the *Shih-jen yü-hsieh.* He quotes from it and promotes its views in his *Jūmon Saihishō* (Most Secret Extract in Ten Questions).

Thus the *Shih-jen yü-hsieh* was transmitted to Japan at an early period, published there, read by men of letters from the late Kamakura period, and highly praised as the core of poetry. It contains a quotation from the *Hou-shan shih-hua* (Poetic Discourses by Ch'en Shih-tao) at the beginning of volume five, "The Path of Beginning Scholarship," that bears directly on our theme:

> Be awkward rather than skillful. Be plain rather than florid. Be rough-and-ready rather than delicate. Be eccentric rather than conform to the popular norm. Poetry is all like this.[74]

Or again there is a quotation from the *Lü-shih t'ung-meng-hsün* (Master Lu's Instructions to Children):

> For the beginner composing poetry it is better to fail through artlessness than it is to fail through excessive stylishness.[75]

In the general discussion of "Latent Implications" in the tenth volume, an assertion from the *Shan-hu-kou shih-hua* (Coral Hook Poetic Discourse) is introduced:

> This book takes the latent and natural as superior. It takes the fragmentary and modeled as inferior. . . . The plain and disinterested are superior, the prodigious and affected are inferior.[76]

Although the *Shih-jen yü-hsieh* presents literary theories from a variety of standpoints, its underlying thesis is simple: The unskillful is better than the skilled, the plain is better than the ornate, the rough-and-ready is better than the delicate, the eccentric is better than the worldly. It is a view in which the artless and natural are superior to a decorative style abounding with literary flourishes. This is the literary view of the Yüan-yu school (of Su Tung-p'o and his fellows) that "simple aged austerity is to be prized, skillfully wrought elaboration to be despised."

Thus it is not too much to argue that Sung literary theories transmitted via the *Shih-jen yü-hsieh*, especially those of the Yüan-yu school, exerted both direct and indirect influences on medieval Japanese theories of poetry, *waka* and *renga*, and through them contributed to a deepening of the *wabi* aesthetic.

A similar stimulus to the *wabi* aesthetic can also be seen in the case of monochrome ink painting (*suiboku*, literally "water and ink"), which had developed in China and was transmitted during these centuries to Japan where it also flourished. Ink painting had its origins in the T'ang dynasty, when color painting was very advanced, and it flowered in the Sung. It continued to thrive into the Yüan dynasty, where it became the mainstream of academic painting. Its flowering owed much to its close ties with the Zen sect of Buddhism.

From the *Butsunichian Kōmotsu Mokuroku* transmitted in Engakuji Temple we know that already before the end of the Kamakura period a large number of Chinese ink paintings had been imported to Kamakura.[77] Then, in the Northern and Southern Courts period of the middle and late fourteenth century, the appreciation of ink painting spread into elite warrior society, while Zen monks like Kaō, Mokuan, and Gyokuen began to paint them as avocational accomplishments. In the Muromachi period, when painter-priests like Josetsu, Shūbun, and Sesshū and academic painters like Kanō Masanobu appeared, Sung-Yüan style ink painting reached its highest level of achievement in Japan.

Monochrome ink painting is based on the suppression and abbreviation of expression. It is sufficient for it to grasp the essence of its subject directly and to express that essence in simple lines and washes. Ink painting rejects color as superfluous because the colors of things change with time and are thus not essential characteristics. Ink monochrome is not simply black or gray; rather, by negating all color, it includes all. Like the *wabi* of *chanoyu*, it is a simple, impoverished beauty which sublates more vivid beauty. At any rate, ink painting prizes the subjective expression of ideas and images more than the objective representation of the visual. Thus it esteems the simplification of expression and of unstated emotions, *yojō*, and the refinement of spirit that accompanies it. It does not seem farfetched, then, to see the rise of ink painting as a mood of the age and one more factor in the deepening of the *wabi* aesthetic. Considering that in early *chanoyu* the most prized hanging scrolls for the alcove were ink paintings by Mu Ch'i and Yü Chien, this conjecture seems reasonable.

The Zen Spirit

As we have seen, the *wabi* ideal of *chanoyu* originated and matured within the aesthetic consciousness of the medieval Japanese. In this sense it was a very Japanese feeling for beauty. At the same time, Zen, which was introduced from China and had an inseparable connection with the establishment of *chanoyu*, was another powerful force in deepening and refining the *wabi* aesthetic.

The Ōryō teachings of Rinzai Zen were introduced by Eisai in 1187. Fujiwara no Shunzei and Kamo no Chōmei were both still alive in that year, but neither showed any interest in Zen and, consequently, we have to conclude that their admiration for the *yojō-yūgen* ideal of beauty was not inspired by Zen. By the early fourteenth century, the age of Yoshida Kenkō, the Rinzai and Sōtō Zen schools were well established in Japan. This was also the age when great Zen masters like Shūhō Myōchō and Musō Soseki were active. We can recognize certain parallels between the ideas of Kenkō and those of Dōgen, but there is no firm evidence that Kenkō was particularly influenced by Zen. Again we have to conclude that Kenkō's reverence for imperfect, irregular beauty did not derive from Zen.

In contrast, Zeami Motokiyo practiced Sōtō Zen under the spiritual guidance of Chikusō Chigan of the Hoganji Temple in Yamato province and attained some degree of enlightenment. In *Fūshi Kaden* and other works, for example, he uses Zen expressions correctly. Especially in the secretly transmitted text *Kui* (The Nine Levels) he uses Zen sayings like "at midnight in Silla, the sun is bright" or "piling snow in a silver bowl" to hint at the nine levels of accomplishment in the art of *nō*. And the chapter title in *Kakyō*, "On Linking All Things in *Nō* with a Single Mind," is nothing other than the application to *nō* practice of the basic Zen principle "proper mindfulness and uninterrupted practice." Thus it should be clear to what extent Zen thought permeated Zeami's *nō* and *nō* theory.

Komparu Zenchiku studied with Ikkyū. From the detailed entries in the *Ikkyū Osho Nenpu* and other sources there is no doubt of his deep attainment in Zen as a layman. We have already seen that the structure of his *Rokurin Ichiro no Ki* draws on Zen thought. Moreover, the form and aesthetic of the empty ring, which he raised to the highest realm of performing art, was greatly influenced by Zen or at least could be described as a Zen-inspired aesthetic. The poet Seigan Shōtetsu was a Zen monk who served as record keeper for the Kyoto Gozan monastery of Manjuji, and the *renga* master Shinkei, although a monk of the Onjōji lineage of the Tendai school, had a deep understanding of Zen. Thus we can conjecture that Zen was applied indirectly through Zeami, Zenchiku, Shōtetsu, and Shinkei to deepen and refine the *wabi* aesthetic.

Even more important than this, however, Zen had a direct impact in shaping the personalities and aesthetic sensibilities of tea masters in the formative stages of *chanoyu*. For example, Murata Shukō, who is regarded as a founder of *chanoyu*, was a lay student of Zen master Ikkyū. Shukō's successor Murata Sōju was a good friend of Daikyū Sōkyū of Myōshinji Temple. Takeno Jōō's teacher, Jūshiya Sōgo, practiced Zen under the guidance of Kogaku Sōsen of Daitokuji, and Jōō himself studied Zen under Kogaku's dharma heir, Dairin Sōtō. Jōō became an enlightened lay practitioner who "understood that the flavor of tea and the flavor of Zen are the same." Imai Sōkyū and Tsuda Sōgyū also committed themselves to Zen. Sen no Rikyū studied Zen under Shōrei Sōkin of Daitokuji and then Shōrei's dharma heir Kokei Sōchin and was known as a great lay practitioner who "practiced eagerly for thirty years." Furthermore, those who played major roles in the way of tea in the early modern period—men such as Furuta Oribe, Kobori Enshū, Katagiri Sekishū, Kanamori Sōwa, Rikyū's sons Dōan and Shōan, and Shōan's son Genpaku Sōtan, who revived the Sen family tradition of tea—all studied and consorted with Zen monks such as Shun'oku Sōen of Daitokuji.

The following words by Rikyū are found at the beginning of *Nampōroku*, the most sacred text of *chanoyu*:

> *Chanoyu* of the small tea room is first of all a Buddhist spiritual practice for attaining the way. To be concerned about the quality of the dwelling in which you serve tea or the flavor of the food served with it is to emphasize the mundane. It is sufficient if the dwelling one uses does not leak water and the food served suffices to stave off hunger. This is in accordance with the teachings of the Buddha and is the essence of *chanoyu*. First, we fetch water and gather firewood. Then we boil the water and prepare tea. After offering some to the Buddha, we serve our guests. Finally we serve ourselves.[78]

As we can guess from this instruction, Zen had permeated *chanoyu*. It was the backbone for the way of tea. But exactly how did Zen contribute to the deepening of the *wabi* aesthetic and the enhancement of *wabi* beauty?

Zen enlightenment is literally beyond words. Even using a billion words its truth cannot possibly be transmitted to, or from, another. There is no recourse other than to "know hot and cold for oneself." For this reason Zen rejects reliance on written texts or concepts and denies their logical explanation and expression. Nevertheless, having said this, Zen recognizes that without some kind of expression there would be no way of transmitting one's enlightenment to another person and no way to discuss and deepen Zen. Therefore, the primary means of transmitting thought in Zen is indicating things directly with the things themselves or, by some simple gesture, having the inquirer recognize for himself from his own experience: "Yes, that's it exactly!" Although this is a very effective method, alone it would be impossible to transmit anything to persons not present on the occasion or to later generations. What is delightedly used, then, is metaphorical allusion or hints of scenes from nature or actual things—as in response to the question: "What then is this admantine Dharma Body?" The answer: "Mountain flowers blooming resemble brocade, the valley streams tumble like indigo." Moreover, Zen is a determinedly self-power (*jiriki*) school of Buddhism. A basic principle of Zen teaching is that if one corner is revealed, you should be able to discover the other three corners for yourself. For this reason Zen leans toward metaphorical, allusive, or symbolic expression and prizes restraint and reticence. Thus one can conjecture that the tea masters' esteem for simple expression as one aspect of *wabi* was—besides being in the tradition of *yojō-yūgen* in medieval literature and the performing arts—also due to the influence of Zen.

Reading the *Shōbō Genzō Zuimonki* (Records Heard from the Treasury of the True Dharma Eye), which was taken down from Dōgen's evening talks by his disciple Ejō, one finds that Dōgen repeatedly warned his disciples that "those intent upon learning the way must first learn poverty." In book three of this work we find the following passage:

> Those who are called excellent followers of the Buddha wear sack-cloth and always beg for their food. The Zen school is called "the good school" and Zen monks are different from those of other schools. In the beginning, when Zen was emerging and Zen monks lived in temples of the older schools or in Ritsu (Vinaya) school temples, they scorned worldly things and lived in destitution. With regard to the life-style of the Zen school you should first of all know this.[79]

Thus, for Dōgen, poverty itself is the primary religious characteristic of the Zen life-style.

In book four Dōgen gives the example of the Rinzai patriarch Yangch'i Fang-hui (Yogi Hōe) who forbade repairs to his monastery and lived among dilapidated buildings, stating that "*satori* is not determined by the quality of one's residence. It is determined only by the quantity of effort put into *zazen*."[80] Dōgen follows this observation with a remark by the monk Lung-ya Chu-tun (Ryuge Kyoton): "In learning the Way of Zen one should first study poverty. Only after studying poverty and being poor will one become familiar with the Way."[81] He further emphasizes that "from the time of the Buddha until today among true practitioners of the Way, one does not hear of or see any who are wealthy."[82] In book five Dōgen cites the example of Tao-ju (Dōnyo), a senior monk of Mount T'ien-tung monastery: "In Great Sung the good monks who are known to the people are all poor."[83]

At first reading, these comments might be taken as a glorification of poverty. But of course they are not simply an idealization of penury. They stress, rather, that the true Zen seeker does not trouble himself about clothing or food, nor is he distracted by thoughts of fame and profit in the secular world. That is to say, he is not concerned that he is poor in a material sense, but devotes himself single-mindedly to Buddhist practice, destroying illusion and breaking through into enlightenment. The important thing is to be a good Zen man, no matter how wretched and unsightly one may outwardly appear.

In the Zen classic *Verses Testifying to the Way* by Yung-chia Hsüan-chüeh (Yōka Genkaku), one finds the following lines:

> I am a destitute follower of Buddha.
> Although I may be called poor,

> this is merely a material poverty.
> I am not poor in the Way.
> Because I am poor I dress in rags.
> But in finding the Way
> I bear a priceless jewel in my heart.[84]

These lines express the great confidence of a man of Zen. The poverty of which Dōgen spoke is exactly this. Prizing poverty in this sense was not confined to Genkaku or Dōgen, of course. It was the most Zen-like life-style from antiquity. Extolling the appearance of the Zen man as "poor of body but not poor in the Way" is based on the Zen saying that "tattered robes are filled with a pure breeze," which means "although clad in rags the heart is pure."

Here we naturally recall the words of Shukō explaining the taste of *wabi* tea as "a prize horse hitched to a thatched hut,"[85] or the first injunction of *Jittai no Koto* (On the Ten Forms) that "one should place one's trust in someone who is coarse on the outside but strict and proper within."[86] As we have seen, *wabi* is a beauty that may seem superficially impoverished and unrefined. Internally, however, it stores a depth of richness and purity. Clearly this is the same structure as the ideal of the Zen seeker: "poor of body but not poor in the Way," whose "tattered robes are filled with a pure breeze." This is just one example of Zen's influence on the *wabi* aesthetic or, conversely, of how the *wabi* of *chanoyu* derived nourishment from Zen.

I wish to make one final point. The man of Zen, as we have seen, feels bitterness and shame at poverty in his spiritual practice (the Way) but does not feel the slightest concern for material poverty. Believing that "the distasteful, this too is tasteful," he lives beyond the range of external conditions. There is certainly no harm in being wealthy, perfectly satisfied, and having things go as one pleases. One does not go out of one's way to despise or avoid such things. On the other hand, there is no need to despise the poor, the imperfect, or what does not go as one wishes, inasmuch as these things can be seen as possessing the flavor of human life. That is, they too are "tasteful," living in the spirit of the *waka*:

Harete yoshi	Fine against a brilliant sky
Kumoritemo yoshi	Fine when wrapped in clouds
Fuji no yama	Fuji Mountain.
Moto no sugata wa	The original form
Kawarazarkeri.	Does not change.[87]

This is the way of life of the man of Zen. Not clinging to riches, perfection of things, or having everything as one wishes but rather finding a higher value in poverty, the irregular, and that which goes against one's wishes, recognizing that "the distasteful, this too is tasteful": This is the Zen-like way of the Zen seeker.

As noted, Jōō suggested the beauty of *wabi* and the *wabi* aesthetic by citing Fujiwara no Teika's poem "Looking about/Neither flowers/Nor scarlet leaves/A bayside reed hovel/In the autumn dusk,"[88] and Rikyū indicated them with Fujiwara no Ietaka's poem "To those who wait/Only for flowers,/Show them a spring/Of grass amid the snow/In a mountain village."[89] In contrast to those who seek beauty only in the splendor of spring's cherry blossoms and autumn's maple leaves or in the abundant, the perfect, and the rounded, Jōō and Rikyū looked for true taste and deep beauty in the ostensibly distasteful, such as "a bayside reed hovel in the autumn dusk," in "a spring of grass amid the snow in a mountain village," and in the destitute and undesirable. In finding that these things too are "tasteful," they learned from the Zen seeker's way of living and view of life and taught what it is to be a *wabi*-suffused man of tea.

Notes

1. Jakuan Sotaku, *Zen-cha Roku*, in Sen Sōshitsu, ed., *Chadō Koten Zenshū*, vol. 10 (Kyoto: Tankōsha, 1961), pp. 296–97.

2. Ibid., p. 297.

3. Yamanoue Sōji, *Yamanoue Sōji Ki*, in Sen Sōshitsu, ed., *Chadō Koten Zenshū*, vol. 6 (Kyoto: Tankōsha, 1958), p. 101.

4. Ibid., pp. 90, 104.

5. Kitakawa Tadahiko, ed., *Zenpō Zatsudan*, in Hayashiya Tatsusaburō, ed., *Kodai Chūsei Geijutsu Ron* (Tokyo: Iwanami Shoten, 1983), p. 480.

6. Nambō Sōkei, *Nampōroku*, in Sen Sōshitsu, ed., *Chadō Koten Zenshū*, vol. 4 (Kyoto: Tankōsha, 1956), p. 10.

7. Jakuan Sōtaku, *Zen-cha Roku*, in Sen Sōshitsu, ed., *Chadō Koten Zenshū*, vol. 10, p. 301.

8. Ibid.

9. Ibid.

10. In Hayashiya Tatsusaburō, ed., *Kodai Chūsei Geijutsu Ron*, p. 448.

11. Yamanoue Sōji, *Yamanoue Sōji Ki*, in Sen Sōshitsu, ed., *Chadō Koten Zenshū*, vol. 6, p. 97.

12. Nambō Sōkei, *Nampōroku*, in Sen Sōshitsu, ed., *Chadō Koten Zenshū*, vol. 4, p. 16.

13. Ibid.

14. Ibid., p. 17.

15. Hisamatsu Shin'ichi, "Chadō Bunka no Seikaku," in *Chadō no Tetsugaku* (Tokyo: Risōsha, 1973), pp. 59–69.

16. See the translation of the Japanese preface in Laurel Rodd and Mary Henkenius, *Kokinshū: A Collection of Ancient and Modern Poems* (Princeton: Princeton University Press, 1984), pp. 35–47.

17. Ibid., p. 43.

18. Ibid., p. 44.

19. Ibid.

20. Ibid., p. 45

21. Fujiwara no Kintō, *Shinsen Zuinō*, in Ōta Tōshirō, ed., Zoku Gunsho Ruijū (Tokyo: Zoku Gunsho Ruijū Kansei Kai, 1911), vol. 456, p. 663.

22. Fujiwara no Kinōto, *Waka Kuhon*, in Hisamatsu Shin'ichi and Nishio Minoru, eds., *Karonshū, Nogakuronshū* (Tokyo: Iwanami Shoten, 1961), p. 2.

23. Jichin, *Jichin Oshō Jikaawase*, in Hanawa Hokiichi, ed., *Gunsho Ruijū* (Tokyo: Zoku Gunsho Ruijū Kansei Kai, 1930), vol. 218, p. 380.

24. Kamo no Chōmei, *Mumyōshō*, in Hisamatsu Shin'ichi and Nishio Minoru, eds., *Karonshū, Nōgakuronshū*, p. 224.

25. *Eigyokushū*, in Sasaki Nobutsuna, ed., *Nihon Kagaku Taikei*, vol. 13 (Tokyo: Kazama Shobō, 1973), p. 312.

26. Ibid., p. 323.

27. Donald Keene, trans., *Essays in Idleness: The Tsurezuregusa of Kenkō* (New York: Columbia University Press, 1967), pp. 115, 118.

28. Ibid.

29. Ibid., pp. 119–20.

30. Ibid., p. 70.

31. See the translation of this passage in J. Thomas Rimer and Yamazaki Masakazu, trans., *On the Art of the Nō Drama* (Princeton: Princeton University Press, 1984), pp. 92, 94.

32. Ibid., p. 28.

33. Ibid., pp. 93, 95.

34. Ibid., pp. 148–49.

35. Ibid., p. 28.

36. Ibid., p. 99.

37. Ibid.

38. Ibid.

39. Ibid., p. 100.
40. Ibid., p. 101.
41. Komparu Zenchiku, *Shidō Yōshō*, in Omote Akira and Itō Masayoshi, eds., *Komparu Koden Sho Shūsei* (Tokyo: Wanya Shoten, 1969), p. 266.
42. Ibid., p. 271.
43. Komparu Zenchiku, *Rokurin Ichiro no Ki*, in Omote Akira and Itō Masayoshi, eds., *Komparu Koden Sho Shūsei*, p. 197.
44. Ibid., p. 198.
45. Ibid., p. 203.
46. Ibid.
47. Ibid., p. 218.
48. Ibid., p. 219.
49. Ibid., p. 218.
50. Seigen Shōtetsu, *Shōtetsu Monogatari*, in Hisamatsu Shin'ichi and Nishio Minoru, eds., *Karonshū, Nōgakuronshū*, p. 224.
51. Ibid., p. 232.
52. Ibid.
53. Ibid., p. 233.
54. Jūjūin Shinkei, *Sasamegoto*, in Kidō Saizō and Imoto Nōichi, eds., *Rengaronshū Haironshū* (Tokyo: Iwanami Shoten, 1961), p. 178.
55. Jūjūin Shinkei, *Shinkei Sōzu Teikin*, in Ōta Tōshirō, ed., *Zoku Gunsho Ruijū*, vol 497, p. 1126.
56. Jūjūin Shinkei, *Sasamegoto*, p. 129.
57. Ibid., p. 175.
58. Jūjūin Shinkei, *Oi no Kurigoto*, in Hanawa Hokiichi, ed., *Gunsho Ruijū* (Tokyo Zoku Gunsho Ruijū Kansei Kai, 1960), vol. 17, p. 72.
59. Jūjūin Shinkei, *Hitorigoto*, in Ōta Tōshirō, ed., *Zoku Gunsho Ruijū*, p. 1028.
60. Kitakawa Tadahiko, *Zenpō Zatsudan.*
61. Yamanoue Sōji, *Yamanoue Sōji Ki.*
62. D.C. Lau, trans., *Confucius: The Analects* (London: Penguin, 1979), p. 59.
63. Ibid., p. 123.
64. Ibid., p. 67.
65. Ibid., p. 93.
66. Ssu-ma Ch'ien, *Shih-chi* (Peking: Chung-hua Shu-chü, 1959), vol. 7, p. 2140.
67. D.C. Lau, trans., *Lau Tzu: Tao Te Ching* (London: Penguin, 1963), pp. 117, 133.

68. Ibid., p. 106.

69. Keene, *Essays in Idleness,* p. 12.

70. Harvard-Yenching Institute Sinological Index Series, Supplement no. 22, *A Concordance to Hsün Tzu* (Taipei: Chinese Materials and Research Aids Service Center, 1966), p. 102.

71. Keene, *Essays in Idleness,* pp. 70–71.

72. Ibid., p. 71.

73. Haga Kōshirō, *Chūsei Zenrin no Gakumon oyobi Bungaku ni kan suru Kenkyū* (Tokyo: Nihon Gakujutsu Shinkokai, 1956), p. 318.

74. Wei Ch'ing-chih, *Shih-jen yü-hsieh,* vol. 1 (Shanghai: Shanghai Ku-chi Ch'u-pan-she, 1978), p. 113.

75. Ibid.

76. Ibid., p. 209.

77. *Butsunichian Kōmotsu Mokuroku* was written in 1363. Material was added to it during the succeeding sixty-five years.

78. Nambō Sōkei, *Nampōroku,* in Sen Sōshitsu, ed., *Chadō Koten Zenshū,* vol. 4, p. 3.

79. Ejō, comp., *Shōbō Genzō Zuimonki,* in *Nihon Koten Bungaku Taikei,* vol. 81 (Tokyo: Iwanami Shoten, 1965), p. 387.

80. Ibid., p. 408.

81. Ibid.

82. Ibid.

83. Ibid., p. 413.

84. *Taishō Shinshū Daizōkyō,* vol. 51, p. 460b.

85. Yamanoue Sōji, *Yamanoue Sōji Ki,* in Sen Sōshitsu, ed., *Chadō Koten Zenshū,* vol. 6 (Kyoto: Tankōsha, 1958), p. 101.

86. Yamanoue Sōji, *Yamanoue Sōji Ki,* in Sen Sōshitsu, ed., *Chadō Koten Zenshū,* vol. 6, p. 90.

87. This *waka* is by Yamaoka Tesshū and is inscribed on a painting he did of Mount Fuji.

88. Nambō Sōkei, *Nampōroku,* in Sen Sōshitsu, ed., *Chadō Koten Zenshū,* vol. 4, p. 16.

89. Ibid.

Chapter 11

Bushidō: Mode or Ethic?

ROGER T. AMES

Bushidō, *"the way of the warrior," a term known, but often misunderstood, in the West, is defined and explained in this descriptive essay by Roger Ames, who uses the life and death (by* seppuku*) of Yukio Mishima as the context for his discussion of the importance of* seppuku *in* bushidō. *In his desire to understand and explain Mishima's suicide, Ames provides us with insight into* bushidō as *"mode" rather than "ethic".*

On November 25, 1970, Yukio Mishima, undoubtedly the most widely read Japanese author ever, killed himself in the traditionally Japanese way, by committing *harakiri* (腹切り). The location—the Ichigaya Headquarters of the Army National Defense Forces in Tokyo. It has been a personal exigency to understand the mentality behind Mishima's death that has led me into the larger task of exploring the relationship between his suicide and the traditional social ethic. In so doing, Mishima's life and death will be drawn on as a practical example to test certain of our conclusions. This will, I hope, serve us in putting some flesh onto our abstractions, and hopefully serve him in providing some insights into a death that I believe has been sorely misunderstood.

The sheer profusion of "explanations" that followed upon Mishima's death show how much misunderstanding there has been. Theories have been advanced to explain it as the final, desperate act of a political extremist, the dramatic exit of an author of exhausted resources, the "Chinese revenge" of a homosexual lover embroiled in an unmanageable passion, the administration of euthanasia for an invalid suffering from a terminal illness, and quite simply, an inexplicable deed performed by a man bereft of his sanity. The only common denominator among these various explanations is that the suicide was an act of desperation, and this is probably wrong. In assessing his motivations and providing a starting point in analyzing the traditional social ethic, let us look into a very brief synopsis of the events on Mishima's last day.

At about 11:00 a.m. Mishima presented himself along with four members of his Tatenokai ("Shield Society") at the Ichigaya Headquarters of the National Defense Forces to keep a prearranged appointment with General Matsuda, the commanding officer. His uniformed appearance at the headquarters was not unusual—the National Defense Forces had often assisted the Tatenokai with training facilities and their off-the-record encouragement. After the general had received his guests in his second floor office, he commented on the fact that Mishima was carrying a long, samurai sword, and asked to examine it. This set off a pre-rehearsed series of events among Mishima and his four cohorts. The general was seized, bound and gagged; the doors were barricaded; a list of demands were made known to those in command. If the demands were not met, the group threatened to execute the general.

In compliance with Mishima's demands, the entire contingent of approximately one thousand soldiers was assembled in front of a large balcony leading off of the general's office. Mishima then appeared on the balcony and, shouting over the din of circling helicopters, sirens and the persistent jeers of a less than sympathetic crowd, he mustered his best attempt to give them a moving speech. He cut his address, or perhaps more properly, his inaudible harangue, from a projected thirty minutes to barely seven, and ended with the traditional "*Tenno Heika Banzai* (天皇階下萬歳) (Long live his Imperial Majesty)." Thereupon Mishima withdrew and committed *seppuku* (切腹) in traditional form. His *kaishaku-nin* (介錯人) (second) gave him the coup de grace, and then followed him in death. Significantly, Mishima was successful in inflicting a death wound upon himself—there is no mystery surrounding the formal satisfaction of his *seppuku.* His *kaishaku-nin,* by contrast, barely scratched himself before calling upon his second.

When Donald Keene, Mishima's long-time friend and translator, heard of the death, he contended that "the manifest motive for Mishima's death—his charging into the military headquarters—was trivial."[1] Keene rejected the thesis that Mishima had hoped to fuse some kind of right-wing coup d'état. In fact, few have taken Mishima's role as the inflamed right-wing zealot seriously—his strained politics are regarded as a device rather than a sincere conviction.[2] The only people who seem to have taken the "revival of Japanese militarism" thesis to heart were the Chinese who reported the incident as "new iron-clad evidence," and suggested complicity on the part of the Japanese government.[3] And even here, there would seem to be more polemic than insight.

If his political stance was "a device rather than conviction," Mishima must have killed himself for a cause that he probably did not believe in, a cause he knew his death would contribute little to. In fact, he ostensibly killed himself for an emperor about whom he had his own serious misgivings, an emperor who could only have been embarrassed by the circumstances surrounding the *seppuku*. Where in this death then is his espoused patriotism? What was the true meaning of his suicide?

The answer to these questions lies in *bushidō* (武士道)—variously translated as "the way of the warrior," "the way of the samurai," and even as broadly as "the traditional Japanese social ethic." In this essay, I would like to offer a basis for understanding *bushidō*, and in the process, to hopefully dispel some less than adequate assumptions surrounding it. Second, most people who have an interest in Japan are aware of the valuable contributions to our understanding of Japanese thought made by the philosopher, Nakamura Hajime; the psychologist, Doi Takeo; and the sociologist, Nakane Chie. The works of these three scholars characterize the Japanese as reflecting an "absolute devotion to a closed social nexus,"[4] a characterization which tends to minimize if not preclude the possibility of individuated human freedom and personal fulfillment. I hope to clarify, refine, and perhaps qualify this position. And third, I hope that this interpretation of *bushidō* will shed some light on the motivations behind Mishima's death, and show him to be an earnest if anachronistic proponent of a rich but fading tradition.

What is *bushidō?* Historically, there has been some debate over the meaning if not the very existence of this philosophy. B. Hall Chamberlain, an early cultural historian, claimed:

> *Bushidō,* as an institution or code of rules, has never existed. The accounts given of it have been fabricated out of whole cloth, chiefly of foreign consumption. . . . The very word appears in no dictionary, native or foreign, before the year 1900. . . . *Bushidō* was unknown until a decade or so ago.[5]

This position was reinforced by John Buchan in his *Japan:*

> *Bushidō*—"The Precepts of Knighthood"—is a modern product, so very modern that the present writer cannot now recollect ever having heard the word mentioned during a residence of over thirty

> years in Japan, in constant association the whole time with the military and official classes. It is not mentioned in any dictionary, in any of the works of Satow, Aston, Brinkley or Chamberlain, nor in any of the Transactions of the Asiatic Society of Japan, published prior to 1900.[6]

Nitobe Inazo who played a pivotal role in interpreting Japan to the world in this century offered a strong, contrasting opinion in his book *Bushidō*:

> "as applied to fundamental ethical notions . . . *Bushidō*, the maker and product of Old Japan, is still the guiding principle of the transition and will prove the formative force of the new era.[7]

He saw *bushidō* not only as the "commanding moral force of his country" but as the "totality of the moral instincts of the Japanese race."

Chamberlain and Buchan claimed that *bushidō* was an out-and-out ruse while Nitobe sees it as the primary ethical force that has shaped Japan. To clarify this dilemma, we must move from secondary materials to the *bushidō* literature itself. Although *bushidō* cannot be traced to any one source or particular individual, it is not an exaggeration to say that *Hagakure* (葉隱), an early eighteenth-century document which was compiled from the conversations of a Nabeshima samurai named Yamamoto Tsunetomo, articulated many of the central concepts of *bushidō* and evaluated many of its proponents. It is an interpretation of the *bushidō* way of life that has been taken by some, Mishima included, as a veritable bible of this philosophy.

The basic difficulty in understanding *bushidō* may be due to a confusion between it and the prevailing moral or social ethic that it has traditionally served. If we take "social ethic" to mean a standard or set of standards whereby the social man can guide and evaluate his conduct, there is a serious question as to whether *bushidō* can be construed as a social ethic at all, This is made clear in *Hagakure* I-140[8] where the text insists upon a distinction between the two:

> It is not good to divide your concentration. Seeking only *bushidō*, one should not pursue anything else. Hearing Confucianism or Buddhism and taking it for *bushidō* on the basis that the final character is the same will not lead to the realization of *bushidō*. If one bears this in mind, then even if he studies various schools of thought, he will assuredly realize *bushidō*.

If *bushidō* in essence is not a social ethic, what is it and how can we define it? Returning to *Hagakure* I-2 and I-114, we find an explicit and unequivocal definition:

> I have discovered that *bushidō* is to die. (I-2) *Bushidō* is a mania for death. . . . In *bushidō*, there is only this mania. (I-114)

Bushidō is not a willingness to die, not a once-off decision to die, but is rather a *resolution to die.*[9] A more difficult and perhaps intellectually insoluble question is the meaning of this *resolution to die.* Again *Hagakure* I-2 provides some explanation:

> When the choice arises between life and death, one immediately settles on death. This is all it means. Once this is understood, one need only rush in. To call a death short of the objective "death in vain" is the counterfeit *bushidō* of the Kyoto-Osaka area. When a choice arises between life and death, it is simply not possible to know that one is going to reach his objective. Now people generally like to live, and most will find some pretext for doing what they like. If then one fails to reach his objective and yet goes on living, he is guilty of cowardice. This is the difficulty. If one dies without reaching his objective, it is death in vain, but there is no dishonor. And this is the most important thing is *bushidō.*

The resolution to die and the strength and intensity of this commitment is constantly reinforced through meditation, making it the focal point of the *bushidō* existence. It is the center of the *bushi* mentality from the moment of decision until the moment of consummation. It is a resolve which must be total and immediate, and which can only be achieved through daily contemplation on and affirmation of this single principle.

In short "death" becomes the essential meaning of life. *Hagakure* describes the gradual process of steeling this resolution to die in the following terms:

> When someone examines himself every morning and every evening and dwells constantly on death and resides permanently in a living corpse, he will find freedom in *bushidō*, will live his life without fault, and will be able to fulfill his duties. (I-2)
>
> Indeed, there is nothing beyond the resolve of the "very now." Life is but the accumulation of one resolve after another. When

> someone grasps this, there is nothing beyond it that can cause him consternation or that he must seek. Giving pre-eminence to this resolve, he simply lives out his life. . . . Giving pre-eminence to this resolve without wavering from it is the result of long, continuous effort, but once having achieved this level of mind, even without conscious reinforcement, there will be no departure from it. (II-17)

As I have suggested, *bushidō* being centered in this resolution to die, is not in any strict sense an ethical system at all. In essence, it does not represent any particular code of conduct or normative standards. On the contrary, it is free of any implicit commitment to any given set of beliefs or values. Of course, historically the proponent of *bushidō*, the samurai, did align himself with a prevailing morality, or more likely, was born into circumstances where the decision of moral alignment was predetermined. That is to say, through the historical association of the *bushi* with the strict social ethical system of Tokugawa Japan, the resolution to die and the prevailing morality which this resolution supported have become mistakenly identified as one and the same.

However much the distinction between the Tokugawa social ethic and *bushidō* has blurred, the resolution to die that lies at the heart of the *bushidō* matrix has provided the framework for the people of other ages as well. The resolution to die of *bushidō* can therefore be seen as a constant while the cause it serves is a historical variable. While *bushidō* was an important support of particular *daimyo* (大名) during the Tokugawa period, in the post-Meiji era it has supported a variety of causes and moralities, from extreme political factions to the militarism of imperial Japan, from the *kamikaze* (神風) pilots to the exploits of the Red Army. The "resolution" of *bushidō* is ultimately mobile and neutral. It can be attached to any cause or purpose, no matter how trivial or contrary that might be to prevailing morality. The morality, the cause, the purpose determines the action—*bushidō* simply describes the manner in which that action is carried out.

Before correlating *bushidō* and human freedom, let us first identify the avenues open to the *bushidō* proponent in consummating his death resolve. The most obvious path is to die defending the integrity of his cause, to give his life for the protection or support of his morality, whatever that moral reference might be. In the case of the samurai, this would be "death on the battlefield." An alternative to death on the battlefield would be *seppuku* or ritual suicide. Where disembowelment to an objective observer might seem an inconvenient if not blatantly untidy method of departing this earth, certain cultural assumptions and predispositions in Japan support it. In the Western traditions, the brain is considered the seat of the intellect and the heart the seat of the emotions, while the Chinese combine these two functions as the heart-and-mind *shin* (心). The Japanese, on the other hand, identify the *hara* (腹) or "lower abdomen" as the center of a human being's essential nature—the English mind and heart rolled into one—as is revealed in the following Japanese idioms:

1. *Hara o kimeru* (腹を決める), literally "to make up one's *hara*" means "to make up one's mind."
2. *Hara o watte hanasu* (腹を割って話す), literally "to open the *hara* and talk" means "to have a heart-to-heart talk."
3. *Hito no hara o yomu* (人の腹を読む), literally "to read another's *hara*" means "to read someone else's mind."

Consequently, the emotive force of cutting out one's lower abdomen would perhaps be comparable to a Western person cutting out his heart.

In addition to the central role the *hara* plays in Japanese psychology and epistemology, stomach wounds are excruciating. *Seppuku* is, consequently, a fair test of a person's mental fortitude. In fact, in most cases where *seppuku* was a mitigation of capital punishment, the *kaishaku-nin* or "second" would decapitate the individual even as he reached for the knife. As Jack Seward in *Harakiri* points out, this deviation in form eventually lead to *sensu-bara* (扇子腹) and *mizu-bara* (水腹) where the individual would be presented with a fan or cup of water rather than an actual knife.[10]

Seppuku, the so-called "flower of *bushidō*," although consistent in action, has many faces and corresponding functions. Traditionally, the most common "category" of *seppuku* has been *chūgi-bara* (忠義腹), or suicide for the sake of loyalty to one's lord. This could be either *junshi* (殉死), self-immolation to follow one's lord in death, or *kanshi* (諫死), suicide as a protest against a given measure or as a remonstration with one's lord on his course of conduct. Beyond this there are also cases of *sokotsu-shi* (粗忽死), expiatory *seppuku* as a contrition or atonement for one's imprudent or rash behavior, and *munenbara* (無念腹) or *funshi* (憤死) which expresses indignation or resentment at the way one has been treated by one's superiors. And in the eyes of the *bushidō* proponent, *seppuku* in any of these forms as a reflection of the strength of one's resolve was no less honorable than "death on the battlefield."

The principle that underlies *bushidō* is in essence the resolve to die honorably. If the aim is death, the next question that arises is how the *bushi* deals with determinism—the sense that actions are beyond his own control. What is the effect of this resolve on human action and human freedom? And finally, where does life enter into a philosophy that seems on the surface at least to be totally pessimistic?

The first and perhaps most obvious function of the *bushi's* death resolve concerns the fear of dying, a fear that seems to feed on and grow in proportion to an individual's unwillingness to face his inevitable end. The proponent of *bushidō*, in his initial decision and his meditative reinforcement of that decision, tempers his resolve to an unequivocal and uncontingent point. It is fair, I think, to describe this state of mind as a perfect willingness to die.

Yet, death must be put into its cultural framework. *Bushidō* arose in an environment dominated by an admixture of Confucian moral precepts and Buddhist philosophy, and owes some of its most fundamental characteristics to both traditions. Given the currency of Zen ideas and their influence on *bushidō*, the proponent of *bushidō* would probably not see death as "self-destruction," "self-annihilation," or "self-abnegation"—the Hobbesian "leap into a black hole." Rather, he would be inclined to view it in a way more consistent with *mujō* (無常)—"impermanence"—expressed in the popular metaphor of the fleeting cherry blossoms with petals that fall at the height of their beauty when they are fully what they are. It is their temporality that enhances the intensity and poignancy of the experience. There is a soft determinism implicit in this attitude, but it is a determinism qualified by cultivation, refinement, and the attainment of self-fulfillment.

A second function of the *bushi* death resolve is a complete and total separation of morality and self-interest. A central issue in Confucian moral philosophy dating back to Confucius himself is the need to disengage morality—the most appropriate thing to do *yi* (義) in a particular situation—from the contamination of self-interest *li* (利). What the Confucian thinkers were seeking was a devotion to maximizing community interests such that personal interests would enter the picture only as one consideration among many. Confucius and his later adherents did *not* suggest that a tension *necessarily* exists between what one ought to do and one's own interest. What they did advocate, however, was that in a situation where a conflict did arise between the two, the good man would opt for what he saw as right rather than what he saw as personally advantageous. In the words of Confucius himself:

> If a man considers what is right at the sight of profit, is ready to lay down his life in the face of danger, and does not forget his ordinary commitments for the sake of an old promise, he may be said to be a complete man.[11]

Self-interest then is the most formidable, most persistent, and most insidious threat to any community-based morality.

The concern of the Confucian theorist is the purification of moral action. Mencius reiterates this sentiment:

> I want life and I also want rightness. But if I cannot have them both, I will opt for rightness over life.[12]

The function of *bushi's* death resolve is to establish a clear distinction between morality and self-interest, and to absolve him of any concern for the latter. The resolution is a purgative, a catharsis, which purifies the decision to act by removing any tension which may exist between what one believes to be right and the decision to act on it accordingly. As observed above, the resolution to die is independent of the morality to which it offers service. In not only rejecting any attachment to the ego-self, but further in committing himself to die, the *bushi* becomes the uninhibited agent of his morality, whatever morality that might be. The freedom implicit in such a philosophy is the mobility to assign his "purity of action" to any cause or purpose that he might decide is worthy of his support. Such freedom has been the mark of the post-Meiji era.

A third function of the *bushidō* death resolve is spontaneity in action and freedom from the conscious reflection and calculation that usually attends decision. In the death resolve, the dilemma of decision has been expunged and circumstances alone determine the time and place of death. The degree to which the *bushi* evidences this spontaneity, immediacy, and impulsiveness of action has long been taken as an indication of the strength of his resolve to die, and as such has served as a normative measure or standard of *bushi* conduct.[13] By contrast, the calculating mind is despised because it hedges on total commitment and avoids bold action.

> *Hagakure* I-112 attacks backsliders explicitly and in no uncertain terms: A calculating person is a coward. This is because calculation is the weighing of gain and loss, and as such, the person can never extricate himself from this gain-and-loss mentality. If he takes death to be "loss" and life to be "gain," because he dislikes death, he will end up a coward.

The rejection of rational decision-making and careful deliberation in favor of spontaneous action, of course, is consistent with the basic Zen emphasis on action and experience.

A corollary to this "spontaneity of action" is the fact that, since the final moment is always imminent, the man of *bushidō* is forced to live in the immediate "now." This *satipatthana*-like "mindfulness" or attention to present action releases him from common human stress and anxiety about future developments, the bulk of which never materialize. In *Hagakure* I-61, this "mindfulness" is an essential element of human cultivation:

> Let's try to answer the question: "What is the cultivation that a man must undertake to attain his highest objectives?" It is to live focusing a tranquil mind on the very now. . . . Then, in carrying out all of one's various activities, there is this one established thing in mind. Toward the lord it becomes loyalty, toward one's parents it becomes filial piety, toward *bushidō* it becomes courage and toward everything else it is a foundation. This principle, however, is difficult to discover, but even more difficult than discovering it is to maintain it consistently. There is nothing more important than living in the very now.

A forth function of *bushidō* is self-assertion. The proponent of *bushidō* has been typically characterized as "blindly obedient" to his lord where such obedience would be nothing less than a total surrender of free-will. Such stereotypes must be qualified. While the *bushi* indubitably makes a solemn commitment to the values and order represented by his overlord, little in the popular literature about Japan is ever said about the obligations obtaining in the other direction. The *bushi's* dedication to the interests of the lord is balanced by a pledge on the part of the lord to guarantee the affairs of his retainers. The absolutely sincere and selfless services of the ideal *bushi*, therefore, cannot simply be construed as "blind obedience." Rather, consistent with the Confucian ideal of the filial son remonstrating with an erring father and a loyal minister risking his life to expostulate with his ruler, *bushi* had both the right and the inescapable duty to dissuade the lord against any given course of action ill-advised or detrimental to the lord's interests.[14]

Nitobe describes the *bushi* who neglects this obligation and who simply follows the dictates of the lord in very unflattering terms:

> Such a one was despised as *nei-shin* (佞臣), a cringeling, who makes court by unscrupulous fawning, or as a *chō-shin* (寵臣), a favourite who steals his master's affections by means of servile compliance. . . .

> When a subject differed from his master, the loyal path for him to pursue was to use every available means to persuade him of his error.[15]

When all else has failed and the lord remains obdurate, the *bushi* can offer him a final protest to demonstrate the degree of his commitment and the extent of his sincerity. He can commit *kanshi seppuku*, suicide as remonstrance. While this suicide is certainly self-immolation, paradoxically, it is also self-fulfilling in that it consummates one's resolve and it is self-assertive in that it advances one's personal point of view with the optimum degree of emotive force. Consequently, suggesting that *bushidō* simply means "blind obedience" is a distortion that ignores the obligation of the *bushi* to speak his own mind and act according to his own conscience.

By single-mindedly resolving to die, all life activities, human interests, attachments and entanglements are placed in perspective. They must, by definition, be secondary to this resolve. In this setting aside of human attachments, we can at once detect a strong sympathy with the Zen notion of repudiating attachments as a necessary step toward the elimination of the subject/object dichotomy. As in Zen, the *bushidō* meditation that seeks freedom from personal desires and attachments implies a dogged discipline, self-control, determination, and total mastery over one's own natural inclinations. And again as in Zen practice, the absolute commitment of *bushidō* must engender a certain tranquility and serenity of mind.

The question arises: if the proponent of *bushidō*, relative to his resolution to die, eliminates all attachments and entanglements, what is the significance of the "loyalty" and "devotion" so often associated with this philosophy? To once again put this in Zen terms, this problem is similar to the characterization of the monk as one "attached to" or "devoted to" his practice. The judgment is made from the outside by the spectator, not from the perspective of the monk himself who has no attachments. Similarly to someone outside of the world of the *bushi*, he seems to be "loyal" and "devoted" because he acts without hesitation in the interests of his lord. Yet the *bushi* himself allows no such attachments; loyalty and devotion are simply givens. This is what *Hagakure* I-114 means by the following:

> Great deeds cannot be effected by sober means. One must become mad and work at them with a mania for death. In *bushidō* if one stops to ponder the situation, he has already lost. Loyalty and filial

> piety do not enter into it. In *bushidō* there is only this mania for death. Within its scope, loyalty and filial piety are implied as a matter of course.

As the man *bushidō* makes himself the selfless agent of his morality, the spontaneity and energy of his action are no more interrupted by attachment to his lord than the precision of an arrow is hampered by the attachment to the bow. It is at this level that we can perhaps begin to understand how a man like Mishima can offer his life for a "trivial" cause which seems entirely unworthy of his action.

In addition to the *bushi* death resolve forcing a person to accept the imminence of death and to live constantly in the "very now," it also releases him from any blame or censure for the *outcome* of his action. He is totally absolved of guilt and/or responsibility for the consequences of his mission. It is the quality of his commitment that is important, not the ultimate success or failure of his specific actions. *Hagakure* I-55 clarifies this point:

> Victory and defeat are determined by circumstances. Conduct that does not incur dishonor is a different matter. It needs only the determination to die. Even when one is going to be defeated, he must strike back at once. Intelligence and strategy do not enter into it. A person who can be called a "tough customer" gives no thought to victory or defeat, but, totally indifferent to all other considerations, rushes forward to his death. In doing so, he awakens himself to his true self.

The quality of *bushi's* action is evaluated not according to success or failure, but rather on the basis of the strength or weakness of his single resolve.

He is not judged on *why* he dies, but rather on *how* he died. That the strength of his resolve supersedes all considerations of ability, intelligence, and physical prowess is underscored in *Hagakure* I-13[16]:

> Even a man who has no versatility and is not particularly good at anything, if he has the determination to devote himself earnestly to his lord, is a retainer who can be depended upon. Service based only upon intelligence and skills is service of a lowly calibre.

Yet it would be just as fallacious to generalize and say the proponent of *bushidō* has no concern with the ultimate efficacy of his actions. Strength of determination is related to success. The *bushi*, who objectively speaking, is only mediocre, can amplify his ability immeasurably through the strength of his determination:

> There is nothing that is impossible. Where one manifests a determination of purpose he can penetrate the cosmos. There is nothing that cannot be accomplished. Hence, it is not that one "can't," but that he is faint-hearted and lacking in resolve. Indeed, without prowess even entering into it, one can shake the world through sheer singleness of purpose.

The difficulty inherent in stopping someone who has no qualms about exchanging his own life for the success of his action needs no elaboration.

Efficacy aside however, it is *how* the *bushi* consummates his resolve that stands as the single measure of his conduct. Since the performance is so crucial, consistent with Zen aesthetic sensibilities, the importance of formal refinement becomes a significant element in the way the man of *bushidō* frames his life. On the battlefield as in the highly formalized *seppuku*, any equivocation or faint-heartedness, any reluctance or violation of form would seriously detract from the quality of one's actions, or even more irreparably, from the quality of one's death.

A final function of the death resolve is the freedom of total and uninhibited comradery among *bushi* who have committed themselves to the same cause or purpose. The strength and the intensity of this comradery can only be known by those who come together in a single and all-encompassing purpose. Since self-interest has no part in this kind of relationship, the individual is not judged on the basis of ability or intelligence, but rather, given his absolute commitment, is accepted on his own terms and on the basis of his own merits.

The dominance of the death resolve further serves to defuse conventional sources of disharmony by relegating them to the margins in interpersonal relationships. Again, these relationships must be seen in terms of the quality and sincerity of action rather than in terms of love or attachment. There is a frequent association between *bushidō* and homosexual love *shudō* (衆道). While *Hagakure* does allow that a homosexual relationship may develop within the parameters of *bushidō*, this particular relationship has no special claim. Like all relationships, it is peripheral relative to the death resolve (I-182):

> Ryōtetsu asked, "Is your understanding of homosexual love to put yourself into it heart and soul?"

> Edayoshi replied, "I see it as loving but not loving." . . . Years later someone asked Edayoshi what he had meant by this answer. At that time, Edayoshi explained, "To give up one's life is the essence of the lover's way. Where this is not the case, there is dishonor. Now, if one gives up his life for his lover's sake, he has no life to give for his lord. Hence, I understood it to be a matter of loving but not loving."

Returning to Mishima as our practical example, to what extent, greater or lesser, is his death congruent with this interpretation of *bushidō*? First, the importance and persistence of the death-theme and, especially, the notion of suicide in the corpus of his work spanning almost three decades would certainly indicate at least a preoccupation with death—a constant meditation on death and suicide. In Mishima more than in most proponents of *bushidō*, we can identify a clear line between his espoused political convictions, that is, his "cause," and his death resolve. We must make a strong distinction here between the revival of prewar militarism which he used as a device, and his commitment to *bushidō*, the spirit of Japan to which he was sincerely devoted.

In his impassioned speech to the National Defense Forces and in the act of *seppuku* itself there was no equivocation. While we cannot say that he had overcome his fear of death, his self-control was such that he was at least able to contain his fear. His *kanshi*—his death of remonstration—was unquestionably self-assertive, forcing his death before the Japanese people as a protest against their spiritual degeneration and degradation. In spite of his role as a family man and a doting son, these conventional attachments collapsed in his death resolve. Although it is widely believed that Mishima and his *kaishakunin* were homosexual lovers, this hypothesis is irrelevant to his final act. The most prominent and identifiable elements of his death are consistent with our interpretation of *bushidō*, and there can be little doubt that Mishima saw himself as a proponent of this philosophy. However, *bushidō* seeks self-fulfillment in acting as the unselfish agent of one's morality, and only at that point Mishima may perhaps have fallen short of the mark. He seems to have been more concerned with death as his own vehicle to self-fulfillment than as a means to furthering his stated cause.

In summary, the "resolution to die" has been a key for unlocking the *bushidō* mentality, and on the basis of this we have been able to identify *bushidō* as something distinct from and independent of the morality or cause with which it is aligned. *Bushidō* describes the action rather than precipitates it, explains *how* the action be carried out rather than *why* that particular course of action has been chosen, qualifies the action rather than determines it. This is, of course, consistent with the *dō* (道 "way") of *bushidō*: the modality of a *bushi's* action rather than the reason for it. In exploring the application of *bushidō's* death resolve, the nature and the extent of its influence on the actions of the person of *bushidō* can be clarified. *Bushidō* is not the core of the samurai ethic and feudal subservience; it is the consciousness behind the post-Meiji *ronin*, the imperial soldier, the *kamikaze*, the Red Army activist and perhaps even Mishima.

To the uninitiated, *bushidō* might appear to be negative and even nihilistic. There is support, however, to suggest that it is a discipline requiring persistent cultivation and effort, and that the dividends for this discipline do include a very real degree of personal freedom and fulfillment. Where the proponent might lack free-will in the sense of choice among alternative possibilities of action, he does have the freedom of self-determination in accordance with his own dispositions, motives and ideals. His freedom is not the freedom of choice based on a calculating and deliberating rational mind, but rather, like his Zen counterpart, freedom from the very calculating and deliberating mind that would constrain and delimit his action.

Notes

1. *New York Times*, 26 November, 1970.

2. John Nathan in his excellent biography, *Mishima* (Boston: Little, Brown, 1974): 163–64, suggests and illustrates this lack of conviction in right extremist politics by taking an excerpt from one of Mishima's characters in *Kyoko's House*. That character, commenting on his own rightist politics, states quite baldly:

> I wouldn't say I believe it exactly. It's just that phrases like that give me a *fine feeling*. I feel as if my body can melt into each phrase as I say it. Probably because phrases like this are closer than anything to *death*. . . . I see this ideology outside of myself, and I use it as a tool to obtain an indescribable rapture, to feel that my own death and the death of others is always close to me. The feeling is my qualification as an effective member of the group, as effective as you can be.

3. See the *Peking Review* following Mishima's death in November-December, 1970. J. Araki, "The Mishima Incident," in *University of Hartford*

Studies in Literature 10, nos. 1–3 (1978) contains an insightful discussion.

4. See Nakamura Hajime, *Ways of Thinking of Eastern Peoples* (Honolulu: East-West Center Press, 1964), p. 430ff.; Nakane Chie, *Japanese Society* (Middlesex: Penguin, rev. ed. 1973), pp. 20, 61; Doi Takeo, *The Anatomy of Dependence* (Tokyo: Kodansha, 1973), p. 40ff.

5. See *Things Japanese* (London, 1972), p. 564, cited from K. Singer, *Mirror, Sword and Jewel* (New York, 1973), p. 155.

6. See *Japan*, ed. John Buchan (London: Hodder and Stoughton, 1923), pp. 235–36.

7. See *Bushidō: The Soul of Japan* (New York: Knickerbocker, 1905), pp. 172–73. See Nitobe's essay in W. Stead, *Japan by the Japanese* (London: 1904), pp. 266, 279. Nitobe's analysis inspired other writers such as A. Stead, *Great Japan* (London: John Lane, 1905) to develop chapters in their own works such as his "*Bushidō*: The Japanese Ethical Code."

8. All citations from *Hagakure* refer to the Watsuji Tetsuro and Furukawa Tetsuchi edition (Tokyo: Iwanami Shoten, 1941).

9. D.T. Suzuki in his *Zen and Japanese Culture* (Princeton: Princeton University Press, 1959), p. 61ff. also identifies the obsession with death as a central notion in the samurai tradition, and supports it with references to several different *bushidō* texts.

10. See Jack Seward, *Hara-kiri, Japanese Ritual Suicide* (Rutland, Vt.: C.E. Tuttle Co., 1968) for a fuller discussion of the various expressions of *seppuku* and the details of the ritual.

11. See *Confucian Analects* 14/12.

12. See *Mencius* 6A10.

13. See *Hagakure* 1–55, 114, 190. The contrast drawn in favor of the impulsive Nagasaki incident at the expense of the deliberating 47 *ronin* is a good example of the value placed on spontaneity.

14. See *Hagakure* 1–43, 107, 137, 158, 192.

15. Nitobe Inazo, *Bushidō*, pp.92–93.

16. See also *Hagakure* I-114.

Chapter 12

Culture in the Present Age

H. PAUL VARLEY

In this last chapter of his book, Japanese Culture, *H. Paul Varley discusses the literary work of Dazai Osamu, Tanizaki Junichirō, Kawabata Yasunari, Mishima Yukio, Abe Kōbō, Ōe Kenzaburō, and several other lesser-known writers in the context of post–World War II Japanese literary movements. In addition to an upsurge in literary production in the postwar years, film also became "one of the most important media for the transmission of Japanese culture to the West" during this period. The work of Mizoguchi Kenji, Kurosawa Akira, Ozu Yasujirō, three of the most famous directors, is discussed in some detail by Varley. Finally, short discussions of* shingeki *(modern theater), architecture, and the rise of the new religions* (shinkō shūkyō), *complete the picture of culture in postwar Japan.*

After more than three and a half years of fighting, during which its early victories in the Pacific and Southeast Asia were inexorably reversed, Japan finally acceded to the ultimatum of the Allied powers from Potsdam in July 1945, and in August surrendered unconditionally. The last agonies of the war produced, on one side, the horror of suicidal air attacks by *kamikaze* pilots—who were exhorted to recreate the glorious defense of the homeland by "divine winds" directed against the Mongol invaders of the thirteenth century—and, on the other side, the unspeakable holocaust of atomic destruction in the American bombings of Hiroshima and Nagasaki.

In an unprecedented radio broadcast on August 15 (August 14 in the United States), the emperor informed his subjects that "the war situation has developed not necessarily to Japan's advantage, while the general trends of the world have all turned against her interest." In fact, Japan's war-making capacity had been reduced to a pitiful remnant, many of its cities lay in charred ruins, and thousands of its citizens faced starvation. There remained no practical alternative to surrender or, in the words of the emperor, no alternative but "to endure the unendurable and suffer what is insufferable."[1]

Although the emperor's forebodings proved excessively dire, one cannot minimize the suffering the Japanese were forced to endure in the first few years following defeat, despite the vigorous efforts of the Occupation regime—monopolized by the United States through General Douglas MacArthur as Supreme Commander of the Allied Powers (SCAP)—to reestablish order. People were not only hungry and homeless, they were also spiritually exhausted; jobs were scarce and in some sectors nonexistent; inflation raged and black markets sprang up everywhere.

By contrast, GIs strolling the streets of Tokyo and elsewhere and patronizing military post exchanges seemed to be blessed with undreamed of material prosperity. The Japanese could observe this prosperity not only among GIs in Japan but also through American movies. For once movies became widely available again, some 38 percent of the theatres throughout the country were devoted exclusively to the showing of films from America in which capacity crowds saw, day after day, "the refrigerators, cars, modern houses, highways and all the other accoutrements of the 'Good Life.'"[2]

As in other war-torn countries, luxury commodities such as cigarettes, chocolate, chewing gum, and nylon stockings were coveted in Japan in gross disproportion to their intrinsic values. Prostitution and other forms of fraternization between GIs and Japanese girls became commonplace and highly conspicuous. It was also a time when Americans arrogantly believed that their civilization, if not they themselves, had been proved superior in the modern world. To the Japanese, ever sensitive to matters of face, the swaggering of some GIs must have seemed almost intolerably humiliating.

Yet the Occupation was a considerable success, at least if judged by the extraordinary cooperation between occupiers and occupied and by the new, extremely favorable national attitude the Japanese came to hold toward Americans and the United States. This attitude can be observed, for example, in postwar popularity polls in which for years the Japanese identified the United States as their favorite foreign country or the country they most admired.

The stated goals of the Occupation were to "demilitarize and democratize" Japan. In the name of the former goal the country was stripped of the overseas empire it had painstakingly acquired during the preceding half-century; its army and navy were demobilized and its remaining war machinery dismantled; war criminals—including former Prime Minister (and General) Tōjō Hideki—were brought to trial; and militarily tainted people were extensively purged from government, business, and other sectors of society. In keeping with MacArthur's utopian vision of making Japan the Switzerland of the Far East, a provision was even incorporated into the SCAP-imposed Constitution of 1947 that declared, "the Japanese people forever renounce war as a sovereign right of the nation. . . . The right of belligerency of the state will not be recognized."[3]

Meanwhile, the democratization phase of Occupation policy was implemented in a series of sweeping political, social, and economic reforms. Of these the most radical (and, in retrospect, probably the most lastingly successful) was the land reform, whereby tenantry was virtually eliminated through the expropriation of most absentee land-holdings. Other reforms were directed toward decentralization of the national police force and the education system, elimination of morals training in public schools based on the prewar *kokutai* ideology, encouragement of labor unions, and dispersal of the economic combines through a process of *zaibatsu*-busting.

The new Constitution, written by SCAP Headquarters and presented to the Japanese government in 1946, was premised on the emperor's renunciation of his putative divinity (after the decision not to prosecute him as a war criminal) and on the converse assertion that the people of Japan were now sovereign. Henceforth the emperor was to be a symbol of state, and the state itself was to be representative of the people through a system of responsible party government. A thoroughly Anglo-American type of government, the Constitution dramatically reversed what SCAP regarded as the most illiberal and oppressive features of the Meiji Constitution. Probably most conspicuous and most in keeping with the democratizing zeal of the Occupation authorities was the inclusion in the new Constitution's provisions of an American-style Bill of Rights.

Even before promulgation of the new Constitution and its Bill of Rights, SCAP had abolished the wartime Japanese Propaganda Ministry and Board of Censors (although the Occupation authorities did their own censoring) and released all political prisoners. Some of these prisoners were Marxists who had been in jail since the late 1920s, when prewar Communism was brutally suppressed. One concomitant to the release of such prisoners and the guarantee of basic political freedoms was reestablishment of the Japan Communist Party, which soon acquired about 10 percent of the voting electorate. Japanese intellectuals rushed with eagerness to the previously forbidden fruit of Marxist ideology, and during the first decade of the postwar period, when there was a marked abandonment of the more simplistic doctrines of historical determinism in the West, Japanese scholars and other intellectuals vociferously proclaimed that history had already progressed and would eventually turn out exactly as Marx (and perhaps also Lenin) had said it would.

Even some of the more vocal critics of the United States and its postwar policies agree that the early, New Deal phase of the American occupation of Japan was an exceptionally progressive undertaking. But rapidly changing world conditions in the late 1940s—the advent of the Cold War and the fall of China to the Communists—exerted pressures that brought policy shifts on the part of SCAP to the point where the second half of the Occupation (from about 1948 until 1952) has been labeled a time of undisguised reaction or a reverse course. Clearly the revised aim of SCAP during these years was to transform Japan from an occupied enemy country into a revitalized bastion of the Free World in its struggle to contain the spread of Communism in Asia.

One aspect of the reverse course of the Occupation was a general relaxation of the *zaibatsu*-busting program in the hope of stimulating the Japanese economy, which had remained largely dormant after its devastation during the war. Although they are alleged no longer to have the potential for regaining their prewar stranglehold on national affairs, such combines as Mitsui and Mitsubishi certainly have in the intervening years once again become pervasive entities in Japanese business and commerce. But undoubtedly the single most important boost to the economy was American military spending in Japan during the Korean War (1950–53). Partly because of this spending and the freedom attained through national independence when the Occupation was ended in 1952 (in accordance with the San Francisco Peace Treaty of 1951), Japan was launched upon one of the most vigorous and sustained periods of economic growth of any country in modern history. With its gross national product expanding by about 10 percent annually from the mid-1950s, Japan became, by the late 1960s, the third largest economic power in the world.

Despite the devastation of war and the chaos of defeat (or perhaps because of them), the postwar period brought an immediate, unprecedented expansion in literary output. Released from the severe restrictions of wartime controls, writers rushed to complete manuscripts and get them into print. Newspapers and magazines, traditionally among the most important media for the publication of literature in modern Japan, fought fiercely to acquire the most promising manuscripts and thereby to expand their circulations. Established writers such as Nagai Kafu, who had remained silent during the war in protest against the militarists, received fees for their stories that seemed astronomical.

The alacrity with which some Japanese perceived the potentialities for a postwar publishing boom in all kinds of printed matter can be illustrated by the example of the head of Seibundō Company who, after listening at a provincial railway station to the emperor's August 15 broadcast announcing the surrender and after purportedly shedding tears with others gathered at the station, got the idea on the train back to Tokyo that night of publishing a new Japanese-English dictionary. Completed and issued a month to the day after the emperor's speech, the dictionary, helped by a flood of advance orders, surpassed the three million mark in sales within a brief period of time. Such was the demand for reading material of every kind that printers and publishers sought frantically to obtain paper—then very scarce—wherever it could be found, and before long there appeared a flourishing black-market trade in this commodity, most of which seems to have come from surplus Japanese army and navy supplies.

One especially strong demand that arose in reaction to the nationalistic exclusivism and xenophobia of the militarist years was for new translations of Western literature, both classical and contemporary. Before the war, Western literature in Japan had been represented chiefly by French, English, German, and Russian writings, but owing to the United States's dominant role in the war and Occupation, American literature was for the first time also comprehensively explored by the Japanese. Major writers such as William Faulkner and Ernest Hemingway drew the most serious and sustained attention, while current American best-sellers about the war, such as John Hersey's *Hiroshima* and Norman Mailer's *The Naked and the Dead*, enjoyed great popularity. In addition to American literature, the writings of Jean-Paul Sartre, Albert Camus, and their philosophic precursor Sören Kierkegaard attracted considerable readership among Japanese intellectuals who, spiritually adrift, discerned a new truth in the doctrines of Existentialism.

In assessing the native postwar literature, Japanese critics commonly discuss it in terms of an explosion in mass communications. Referring to a process much more dynamic than the prewar exposure to mass culture, they speak of reaching out to a truly mass audience and of a heightened sensitivity to the need to deal with mass social problems. Among the organizations calling for the expansion of literary horizons in a spirit of postwar liberation and renovation was the Shin-Nihon Bungakkai (Society for a New Japanese Literature). Attracting some of its membership from the suppressed prewar movement of proletarian writers, the society pronounced democracy to be the highest literary ideal, implying thereby a rejection of most prewar movements in literature, including naturalism, Neoperceptionism, and even the so-called social realism of the earlier proletarian writers.

Among the most dramatic of the authors to emerge to prominence in the Occupation period were those loosely referred to as *burai-ha* or "dissolutes." Profoundly influenced by the doubts, uncertainties, and sense of crisis that had permeated their formative years as writers before and during the war, the *burai-ha,* whose most famous representative was Dazai Osamu (1909–48), viewed the world as a place of existential chaos, distorted values, and universal hypocrisy and tried to find humanity in it even as they drowned their anxieties in lives of debauchery and dissoluteness. Claiming a debt to Camus and Sartre, the *burai-ha* writers rose meteorically for a brief period in postwar letters and left a legacy of romantic self-destructiveness that continues to hold a powerful attraction for the Japanese.

Dazai Osamu was born in 1909 into a wealthy landowning family in northern Japan and began what proved to be an exceptionally prolific writing career in the early 1930s. A chronically unstable person, Dazai had already attempted suicide four times before the postwar period, including one effort with a bar maid in which she died and he survived. His fifth attempt, in 1948, a suicide pact by drowning with his mistress at the time, was successful and brought his life to a pathetic end at the age of thirty-nine.

Like the other *burai-ha* writers, Dazai loudly disparaged the narrow egoism, especially of the prewar naturalist school, that constituted the main theme of the persistent Japanese I-novel tradition. Yet Dazai himself relied overwhelmingly on his own life experience for subject material in his writing—many of his stories are diary-like, autobiographical accounts—and may even be regarded as the last great I-novelist.[4] The difference, as Dazai would contend, was that, whereas the I-novelists of the naturalist school were unremittingly self-centered, the aberrant behavior he portrayed with examples of his own life represented an anguished *cri de coeur* against the falsity and deceit of others (if not of mankind as a whole). At times—for example, in the following passage from *No Longer Human (Ningen Shikkaku,* 1948), the story of a man who despairs of living "the life of a human being" and who eventually descends into the abyss of drug addiction—Dazai's attitude is misanthropic:

> Society. I felt as though even I were beginning at last to acquire some vague notion of what it meant. It is the struggle between one individual and another, a then-and-there struggle, in which the immediate triumph is everything. *Human beings never submit to*

> *human beings.* Even slaves practice their mean retaliations. Human beings cannot conceive of any means of survival except in terms of a single then-and-there context. They speak of duty to one's country and suchlike things, but the object of their efforts is invariably the individual, and, even once the individual's needs have been met, again the individual comes in. The incomprehensibility of society is the incomprehensibility of the individual. The ocean is not society; it is individuals. This was how I managed to gain a modicum of freedom from my terror at the illusion of the ocean called the world. I learned to behave rather aggressively, without the endless anxious worrying I knew before, responding as it were to the needs of the moment.[5]

Dazai's most celebrated novel is *The Setting Sun (Shayō,* 1947), an account of an aristocratic family, much reduced in circumstances, in the immediate postwar period. A widowed mother and her divorced daughter appear to be all that is left of the family, but before long a Dazai-like son, thought lost in the South Pacific, returns home. Addicted to drugs, the son promptly renews the life of dissolution and self-destruction he had charted before entering the army and in a short time commits suicide, leaving a final testament—representing the kind of confessional Dazai so much favored—in which he reveals his alternating fear of and disgust toward the world and the personal yearning for love that actually underlay his appalling outward conduct:

> I wanted to become coarse, to be strong—no, brutal. I thought that was the only way I could qualify myself as a "friend of the people." Liquor was not enough. I was perpetually prey to a terrible dizziness. That was why I had no choice but to take to drugs. I had to forget my family. I had to oppose my father's blood. I had to reject my mother's gentleness. I had to be cold to my sister. I thought that otherwise I would not be able to secure an admission ticket for the rooms of the people.[6]

The decline of Japan's old order is a major theme in *The Setting Sun,* and the death of the mother before her son's suicide may be interpreted as symbolizing the fate of that order after defeat in war. But, to millions of fervid readers, what seemed more importantly to have set was the sun of Japan itself, and perhaps no other novel of the period so effectively evokes the sense of spiritual disintegration that engulfed the Japanese at the war's end. Only through the character of the sister, Kazuko (the book's narrator), does Dazai suggest a glimmer of hope for the future. Determined to have a child by a tubercular, drunken artist friend of her brother's, Kazuko proclaims with a ferocity of will totally lacking in Dazai himself:

> I must go on living. And, though it may be childish of me, I can't go on in simple compliance. From now on I must struggle with the world. I thought Mother might well be the last of those who can end their lives beautifully and sadly, struggling with no one, neither hating nor betraying anyone. In the world to come there will be no room for such people. The dying are beautiful, but to live, to survive—those things somehow seem hideous and contaminated with blood. I curled myself on the floor and tried to twist my body into the posture, as I remembered it, of a pregnant snake digging a hole. But there was something to which I could not resign myself. Call it low-minded of me, if you will, I must survive and struggle with the world in order to accomplish my desires. Now that it was clear that Mother would soon die, my romanticism and sentimentality were gradually vanishing, and I felt as though I were turning into a calculating, unprincipled creature.[7]

If the *burai-ha* writers represented an extreme of overreaction to the social devastation of defeat and occupation, some of the more noted authors from the postwar period, at the other extreme, began writing again after the war almost as though nothing had happened. For example, Nagai Kafu, though distinctive for having remained silent while so many other writers spoke out to one degree or another in favor of the war, began immediately to publish the same kind of pleasure-quarter stories he had always favored. To the *apure (après-guerre)* generation of writers, the most infuriating symbol of continuity with the outmoded literary past was Shiga Naoya. Shiga was associated with the patrician White Birch school of writers who made their debut about 1910, and devoted himself as a writer to a minute analysis and reanalysis of his emotional life and psyche and of his relations with his father, his wife, and others close to him. There was no one else who continued to be so thoroughly naturalistic—and thus, according to his critics, so egoistical—in his approach to writing as Shiga, and when he had the temerity to express his distaste for the work of one of the darlings of the new age, Dazai Osamu, the latter insultingly denounced him: "A certain Literary Master feigns distaste for my writings. But what of this Literary Master's own writings? Do they presume to impart —truth—? What do they claim to be?"[8]

Other famous writers who flourished once more in the postwar period were Tanizaki Junichirō and Kawabata Yasunari. Tanizaki had begun to publish *The Makioka Sisters* serially during the war but was forced to stop by the military authorities, and publication was completed after the war. *The Makioka Sisters* is the story of the decline of a once affluent merchant house as revealed in the lives of four sisters after the death of their father, the head of the family. Perhaps Japan's finest modern novel, the book is exceptional because of its considerable length and its plot construction. Most Japanese novels are quite short and structurally loose; many so-called novels are really novellas. This appears to reflect, on the one hand, the native taste for the suggestive instead of the fully delineative—the "art of silence," as one authority[9] has put it—and, on the other hand, the classical tradition whereby the author of prose tended to write episodically and to devote much more care to the transitional elements or passages in a work than to its overall structure. The reader of *The Makioka Sisters* is drawn into a highly complex and detailed narrative of the interwoven lives of the sisters as they seek collectively to find a proper husband for one, to deal with the independent and headstrong ways of another, and above all to grapple with the vicissitudes that have so altered their lives since their father's death. Although Tanizaki informs us only in passing that the time is the advent of the China war in the late 1930s, the reader is absorbed with a powerful sense—intensified by his own knowledge of the coming of World War II—that he is witnessing the decline not only of a single family but of the entire way of life of prewar Japan.

This sense of decline is intense, for example, in the passage where Sachiko, the second sister and central figure in the novel, visits her elder sister as she is about to move out of the main family residence in Osaka. With the dwindling of the Makioka family business, the elder sister's husband—the titular head of the family—had returned to his former position in a bank. The bank has transferred him to Tokyo, and the Osaka house must be sold:

> The house was built in the old Osaka fashion. Inside the high garden walls, one came upon the latticed front of the house. An earthen passage led from the entrance through to the rear. In the rooms, lighted even at noon by but a dim light from the courtyard, hemlock pillars, rubbed to a fine polish, gave off a soft glow. Sachiko did not know how old the house was—possibly a generation or

> two. At first it must have been used as a villa to which elderly Makiokas might retire, or in which junior branches of the family might live. Not long before his death, Sachiko's father had moved his family there from Semba; it had become the fashion for merchant families to have residences away from their shops. The younger sisters had therefore not lived in the house long. They had often visited relatives there even when they were young, however, and it was there that their father had died. They were deeply attached to the old place. Sachiko sensed that much of her sister's love for Osaka was in fact love for the house, and, for all her amusement at these old-fashioned ways, she felt a twinge of pain herself—she would no longer be able to go back to the old family house. She had often enough joined Yukiko and Taeko in complaining about it—surely there was no darker and more unhygienic house in the world, and they could not understand what made their sister live there, and they felt thoroughly depressed after no more than three days there, and so on—and yet a deep, indefinable sorrow came over Sachiko at the news. To lose the Osaka house would be to lose her very roots.[10]

The main reason why the military authorities objected to *The Makioka Sisters* was because it was given over so completely to a portrayal of the private (i.e., selfish) affairs of a single family at a time of international crisis, when all citizens were expected to devote themselves wholeheartedly to the nation. Nevertheless the book, with its delicate handling of the nuances and shadings of human relations, was based on a venerable native tradition—the tradition of *mono no aware* (a sensitivity to things)—that dated back at least to the literature of the middle Heian period and such masterpieces as *Kokinshū, The Tales of Ise,* and *The Tale of Genji.* Tanizaki, who became more and more absorbed from mid-life on with the Japanese past, translated *The Tale of Genji* into modern Japanese in the late 1930s, during the time when he began writing *The Makioka Sisters.* In many ways, *The Makioka Sisters* is a "tale of Genji" set in the present age.

One of Tanizaki's most extraordinary pieces of writing is the essay entitled *In Praise of Shadows.* Reminiscent of the fourteenth-century *Essays in Idleness* by Yoshida Kenkō, it is a miscellany of comments about the traditional tastes and ways of the Japanese as set against those of the modern West. The essay is full of nostalgia for the passing of these older tastes and ways; and so beautifully has Tanizaki pleaded for them that *In Praise of Shadows* has powerfully inspired contemporary architects and others not simply to preserve the past but to use it as a source for art in the present. The meaning of the essay's title is made clear in this passage on the special qualities of the traditional Japanese house:

> A Japanese room might be likened to an inkwash painting, the paper-paneled shoji being the expanse where the ink is thinnest, and the alcove where it is darkest. Whenever I see the alcove of a tastefully built Japanese room, I marvel at our comprehension of the secrets of shadows, our sensitive use of shadow and light. For the beauty of the alcove is not the work of some clever device. An empty space is marked off with plain wood and plain walls, so that the light drawn into it forms dim shadows within emptiness. There is nothing more. And yet, when we gaze into the darkness that gathers behind the crossbeams, around the flower vase, beneath the shelves, though we know perfectly well it is mere shadow, we are overcome with the feeling that in this corner of the atmosphere there reigns complete and utter silence; that here in the darkness immutable tranquility holds sway. The "mysterious Orient" of which Westerners speak probably refers to the uncanny silence of these dark places. And even we as children would feel an inexpressible chill as we peered into the depths of an alcove to which the sunlight had never penetrated. Where lies the key to this mystery? Ultimately it is the magic of shadows. Were the shadows to be banished from its corners, the alcove would in that instant revert to mere void.
>
> This was the genius of our ancestors, that by cutting off the light from this empty space they imparted to the world of shadows that formed there a quality of mystery and depth superior to that of any wall painting or ornament.[11]

Kawabata Yasunari expressed perhaps more poignantly than anyone the shattering despair felt by so many Japanese at war's end when he wrote: "I have the strong, unavoidable feeling that my life is already at an end. For me there is only the solitary return to the mountains and rivers of the past. From this point on, as one already dead, I intend to write only of the poor beauty of Japan, not a line else."[12] Even though he asserts that the defeat in war has driven him to it, Kawabata was by artistic temperament drawn to write about the "poor beauty of Japan," both the land and its people. In spite of his Neoperceptionist and modernist dabblings in the late 1920s and the 1930s,

Kawabata is probably more Japanese in what is generally understood as the traditional sense than any other modern novelist. Often called a writer of *haiku*-like prose, he uses the spare, aesthetically polished language of poetry to sketch his settings and evoke his moods. One is, for example, always keenly aware in a Kawabata novel, as in the poetry by ancient courtier masters, of nature and the seasons, or more precisely, of the particular nature and seasons of Japan that have shaped the temperament of its people.

Kawabata's postwar work *The Sound of the Mountain (Yama no Oto,* 1949) illustrates the characteristically loose-flowing Japanese novel to which *The Makioka Sisters* stands in such contrast. To Kawabata, the natural world and life within it have their own ways of moving and functioning; the things that happen to us and around us are infinitely varied and ever changing, and any effort to impose too much rationality upon them is bound to fail and is in itself a false or dishonest act on the part of an artist. Such an attitude enabled Kawabata to exhibit a striking "sensitivity to things," and in the larger sense joined him to the aesthetic tradition of *mono no aware* that permeated the classical literature with which he, like Tanizaki, was so intimately familiar. But whereas Tanizaki had, in *The Makioka Sisters,* explored chiefly the intimacies of human relations, Kawabata in his writings also used *mono no aware* to deal with the subtle responses of people to the natural settings within which they lived.

An example of Kawabata's poetic handling of perceptions—like the linking of verses in a *renga* sequence—is the following passage from *The Sound of the Mountain:*

> The moon was bright.
>
> One of his daughter-in-law's dresses was hanging outside, unpleasantly gray. Perhaps she had forgotten to take in her laundry, or perhaps she had left a sweat-soaked garment to take the dew of night.
>
> A screeching of insects came from the garden. There were locusts on the trunk of the cherry tree to the left. He had not known that locusts could make such a rasping sound; but locusts indeed they were.
>
> He wondered if locusts might sometimes be troubled by nightmares.
>
> A locust flew in and lit on the skirt of the mosquito net. It made no sound and he picked it up.

> "A mute." It would not be one of the locusts he had heard at the tree.
>
> Lest it fly back in, attracted by the light, he threw it with all his strength toward the top of the tree. He felt nothing against his hand as he released it.
>
> Gripping the shutter, he looked toward the tree. He could not tell whether the locust had lodged there or flown on. There was a vast depth to the moonlit night, stretching far on either side.
>
> Though August had only begun, autumn insects were already singing. He thought he could detect a dripping of dew from leaf to leaf.[13]

The perceiver in this scene is the main character of the novel, Shingo, a man in his sixties who is engulfed in the unhappiness of himself and those around him—a wife he has long ceased to love, a son who callously ignores his own wife for a mistress, and an embittered daughter just returned home from a disastrous marriage. In the midst of this turmoil of personal relationships, Shingo increasingly senses the specter of his own death. His forgetfulness, at first seemingly attributable to age, leads to a blurring of his awareness between consciousness and dreaming, between things that happened long ago and events as they unfold in the present.

To Kawabata the world is a whole and man and nature are one, and he brilliantly handles Shingo as a perceiver both of human relations and of nature and its phenomena. In mood, *The Sound of the Mountain* is very much part of what appears to be the enduring Japanese tradition of sad beauty that is also connoted by *mono no aware.*

A category of writing that inevitably made its appearance in the postwar period was that of books dealing with the war itself. Virtually without exception they were harshly critical of the war (indeed, all wars) and of Japan's military establishment that conducted it. Perhaps the most terrifyingly stark depiction of the collapse of the once triumphant Japanese Imperial Army is Ōoka Shōhei's *Fires on the Plain (Nobi,* 1952), the story of a soldier who is expelled from his unit in the last days of the campaign in the Philippines because the unit, far from having a capacity to continue fighting, no longer possesses even the means to attend to the barest needs of its members. Wandering through the forests of Leyte with only the vaguest hope of eventually reaching a place from which he can be evacuated, the soldier comes upon a deserted village where he finds the corpses of Japanese soldiers piled at the steps leading to a church and, without pausing to consider his act, murders a defenseless Filipino woman who has returned to the village with her lover in search of salt. Upon leaving the village, the soldier encounters other soldiers similarly separated from their units and hears ominous rumors that famine is so widespread within the Japanese army that some men have even resorted to cannibalism. Later he comes across a dying officer who, in a last stage of delirium, raises his arm and exclaims: "When I'm dead, you may eat this." The climax of the novel is reached when the soldier meets two former companions and partakes with them of "monkey meat." It is not long before the soldier has occasion to learn the true source of his food when he witnesses one of his companions on a "monkey"-hunting excursion:

> There was a bang in the distance.
>
> "He's got one!" shouted Yasuda.
>
> I rushed out and ran through the forest in the direction of the shot. Presently I reached a spot where the trees grew sparsely and from where I could see across the river bed. A human form was flying over its sun-drenched surface! His hair was in disorder and he was barefoot. It was a Japanese soldier in a green uniform. And it was not Nagamatsu!
>
> Again there was the report of a gun. The bullet went wide of its apparent mark and the crouched figure continued running. He ran steadily along the river bed, now and then glancing back over his shoulder. Then, evidently confident that he was out of range, he gradually straightened his back and slowed down to a walking pace. Finally he disappeared into a clump of trees.
>
> Now I had seen one of the "monkeys."[14]

Whereas *Fires on the Plain* describes the degradation of the Japanese soldier in the field,[15] *Zone of Emptiness (Shinku Chitai,* 1952) by Noma Hiroshi reveals a scarcely less extreme form of brutalization and degradation of the military man in camp at home. A young soldier, Kitani, has just returned from the prison stockade, where he has spent two years for the falsely alleged theft of a lieutenant's wallet. Japan's "holy war" has entered its final stage of deterioration and disillusionment, and men of all ranks are now engaged in a bestial struggle to secure rations and to avoid the certain death implicit in overseas assignment. But Kitani is fired only with the determination to avenge himself against those responsible for his conviction and unusually harsh sentence and to see once again the prostitute he loved, but who may also have betrayed him. As the true story of Kitani's case is gradually revealed, we are shown the horror-filled inner workings of a totally corrupt system of military life whose every official act is shrilly justified in terms of military reverence for, and selfless devotion to, emperor and nation. In the confessional words of his chief accuser, the lieutenant, whom Kitani finally tracks down:

> The army is cruel. . . .There's nothing to keep me from saying it now. The army of the interior is rotten to the core, to the very core. When I was overseas, I used to hear it said that the army of the interior had preserved the old traditions of honor and dignity. . . . Unfortunately, when I returned I realized that this was completely untrue, that everything was worse than I could ever have imagined. At first, I did what I could, as an officer, to maintain standards. That's what caused my downfall. I loved the army with all my heart. It was impossible for me to tolerate the people who jeered at it and besmirched it, but then I found myself coming up against powerful obstacles, colonels, majors . . . the regiment. . . . the division. . . . It's all a matter of pleasing your superiors. And not only the officers, but even, if I may say so, their families. . . . I once knew a quartermaster's sergeant who was regarded as the most level-headed noncommissioned officer in the entire corps. . . .Well, his wife was unable to leave the house of the battalion head . . . because her presence was indispensable to her husband's advancement. . . . That kind of thing filled me with shame. . . . The supplies that are delivered go straight to the commanding officer, who uses them for making personal gifts. . . .You know Lieutenant Shimorai, don't you? He had a house built for himself, the one he now lives in. I was unable to put up with such corruption. I tried to do something about it, but I was beaten. It's too big a job for one man . . . I was kicked out. I got sick. I no longer count. Kitani . . . I thought that you had been bought by Lieutenant Nakabori. That was why I let you be brought up before the court-martial. When I realized the truth, it was too late.[16]

In *Zone of Emptiness* Noma, a leftist writer from prewar days and himself a veteran of the army, attempts once and for all to demolish the most sacred sustaining myths of emperor worship and the *kokutai* ideology.

A third book of major importance that deals with the war is Ibuse Masuji's *Black Rain (Kuroi Ame),* an account of the dropping of the atomic bomb on

Hiroshima. Based on actual records of the material destruction and human agony caused by the bomb, *Black Rain* is the story of many people, but especially of Shigematsu and his niece Yasuko. In a narrative consisting largely of diary accounts of Shigematsu and others, we meet the inhabitants of Hiroshima and its environs on the day of the bomb, observe their fate with horror at the moment of the bomb's detonation, and then join the survivors as they wander in bewilderment through the nightmarish labyrinth of a devastated city. The present of the novel is set several years after the war's end, and the tale of the bomb and its aftermath is recounted by Shigematsu essentially in the wish to set the record straight about Yasuko who, because of her exposure to the bomb's radiation, is unable to find a husband. In fact, Yasuko is seriously ill with radiation sickness, and the description of her suffering once the symptoms of the sickness become manifest is heart-rending.

The semidocumentary material contained in this long book could easily have been presented in an exploitative and sensationalistic way; but the author has exercised considerable artistic restraint, and has thereby fashioned *Black Rain* into a devastatingly effective indictment of the evil futility of war. It should not be supposed, however, that *Black Rain* is all darkness and grief. There runs through it the theme, although it is sometimes only dimly perceivable, of hope and the will to survive. This is made symbolically explicit at the end when, as others listen indoors to the emperor's broadcast announcing surrender, Shigematsu wanders aimlessly around outside and, upon gazing into a stream, makes a surprising discovery:

> How had I never realized there was such an attractive stream so near at hand? In the water, I could see a procession of baby eels swimming blithely upstream against the current. It was remarkable to watch them: a myriad of tiny eels, still at the larval stage, none of them more than three or four inches in length.
>
> "On you go, on up the stream!" I said to them encouragingly. "You can smell fresh water, I'll be bound!" Still they came on unendingly, battling their way upstream in countless numbers. They must have swum all the way up from the lower reaches of the river at Hiroshima.[17]

Along with translated novels, film became one of the most important media for the transmission of Japanese culture to the West in the postwar period, which soon developed into a golden age of cinema.[18] The main impetus for this was the excellence in cinematic work already achieved in a remarkably short time by prewar Japanese filmmakers. The film industry was also able to expand its activities rapidly after the surrender because the facilities of the major studios—Shōchiku, Tōhō, and Daiei—had suffered no serious war damage and because SCAP adopted a policy of encouraging the reconstruction and building of movie theatres to provide entertainment for the people. At the same time, despite its generally liberating attitude toward freedom of speech and expression elsewhere, SCAP saw fit to impose a fairly wide-ranging censorship on the themes that could be treated in movies. Among those forbidden were nationalism, revenge, patriotism, the distortion of historical facts, racial or religious discrimination, feudal loyalty, suicide, the oppression of women and degradation of wives, antidemocratic attitudes, and anything that opposed the provisions of the Potsdam Declaration and the directives of SCAP.

In their efforts to live with the censorship—or, when possible, to circumvent it—Japanese producers and directors were forced to resort to stratagems and persuasive arguments. For example, in order to secure permission to make *Utamaro and His Five Women (Utamaro o Meguru Gonin no Onna,* 1946), its director, Mizoguchi Kenji (1898–1956), pointed out to SCAP that the late-Tokugawa-period woodblock artist Utamaro was not only a cultural hero to the common man in Japan, he was even a kind of prototype of a modern democrat! Mizoguchi also hinted that he would like to take up the theme of female emancipation in a subsequent film.[19]

Inundated by American culture, customs, and fads, Japanese filmmakers began experimenting with new practices and techniques of acting that, if not revolutionary, were at least attention-getting. One of the most widely heralded of these practices was the kiss, an act strictly banned from Japanese films before the war and even deleted from foreign imports. To the prewar Japanese the kiss had been "an act reserved solely for the privacy of the bedroom, if not indeed something of an occult art."[20] Even after the kiss became generally accepted, it was often faked by having the actors angle their heads away from the camera and merely touch cheeks. Some actors apparently even sought to avoid pollution while kissing by covering their mouths with gauze and applying an extra layer of makeup to conceal it.

Among the most popular postwar films, both in Japan and abroad, have been those of Kurosawa Akira (1910–), including *Rashōmon* (1950), *Ikiru (To Live,* 1952), and *Seven Samurai (Shichinin no Samurai,* 1954). Kurosawa has been called the most Western of Japanese film directors, and it is true that in content his films, particularly those that are highly action-oriented (such as *Seven Samurai)* or deal with events by means of an Existentialist kind of psychological probing (such as *Rashōmon*), are more readily and universally comprehensible than the films of many other Japanese directors. Yet Kurosawa, a consummate cinematic craftsman by any international standard, is also a master of those techniques—the creation of moods and settings that perfectly blend people and their natural environments, the meticulous attention to the details and textures of life and things—that are the stylistic glories of the Japanese film.

Based on a story by Akutagawa Ryūnosuke, *Rashōmon* recounts an incident set in ancient times involving a lord and his wife who, while journeying through a forest, are confronted and set upon by a bandit. At least two facts in the ensuing series of events are undisputed: the bandit violated the wife, and the husband was killed. Otherwise we are presented with a startling set of contradictory interpretations of what truly happened, as the story is told and retold through the eyes of the wife, the bandit, the dead lord (speaking through a medium), and a woodcutter who chanced to witness the incident. Depending upon which version one believes, the husband was killed in a duel with the bandit to uphold his wife's honor, or he killed himself in mortification over the ravishment of his wife, or he was killed when incited to duel with the bandit by the wife after first seeking to disassociate himself from her behavior.

Seven Samurai, an action film of enormous vitality, tells the story of a group of *rōnin,* or masterless samurai, who are hired by a farming village in the sixteenth century to protect it against marauding bandits. It is one of the finest war films ever made, and as such it shows men in the most extreme circumstances faced with choices that must be irrevocably made—choices that openly, even brutally, call into question the most firmly held values and perceptions, however dimly sensed, relating to the meanings of their lives. Much of the humanism that forms the basis of the story is exemplified in the conduct in life and in death of the last samurai (really a peasant masquerading as a warrior), who is played in a grandly swashbuckling manner by Mifune Toshirō, the quintessential Kurosawa hero. But *Seven Samurai* is much more than simply a war film. It is a visually and aesthetically magnificent work of art presented in a setting that, in the most venerable native tradition, reveals the eternal Japanese sensitivity to the flow of time, especially as experienced in the passage of the seasons, and to the finite quality of man *in* nature and not opposed to it. There could be no more eloquent statement of this sensitivity than the ending of the film when, after the bandits have been repulsed for good, the villagers must turn their attention to spring planting and the surviving samurai are obliged, after briefly paying their respects at the graves of their comrades, to move on. Thus they resume the status of *rōnin*—a status that implies social uncertainty and, once again, an absence of direction or meaning in life.

In *Ikiru* Kurosawa deals, in a contemporary setting, with the crisis of a man who is informed that he is terminally ill with cancer. A petty bureaucrat nearing retirement, the man realizes that for years he has led a joyless and robotlike existence, his private life a void and his public vision restricted to his own worm's-eye view of the functioning of government. He determines to do one socially meaningful, good thing before he dies, and he thereupon embarks upon a campaign to bring about the construction of a small park after the petition for it by a group of neighborhood people has been interminably delayed and misdirected through a maze of bureaucratic offices, including his own. *Ikiru* is an uncompromising critique of officialdom and the world of bureaucratic inertia.

If Kurosawa is to be regarded as the most Western of Japanese film directors, then his polar opposite is Ozu Yasujirō (1903–63), the most Japanese of all directors. A leader in film since the prewar period, Ozu focused his attention almost entirely on the conflict between the traditional and the modern as seen through changing relationships in the Japanese family. The historical antecedents of films on the family (the *shomin-geki*) were the domestic plays *(sewa-mono)* of the puppet and *kabuki* theatres of Tokugawa times and the I-novels of naturalists and other writers in the modern age. The classic dilemma that confronted the individual in the Tokugawa domestic play, it will be recalled, was between the demands of duty *(giri)* and the pull of human emotions (*ninjō*). In the stylized plots of the period—for example, the prototypical story of the passion of a merchant, who is already married and has children, for a prostitute—the dilemma was characteristically resolved by double suicide *(shinjū)*. Social pressures today, of course, are much less severe, and double suicide is no longer common; but the domestic dilemma remains, with *giri* often taken to mean the demands of the traditional Japanese family and *ninjō* the pull of modern ways.

To understand why this should represent a specially Japanese, rather than universal, problem, we must note that there are few analogues to the Japanese family and the enormous importance it continues to hold in Japanese society. It is simply a fact, as outsiders constantly observe, that the Japanese are overwhelmingly group-oriented: they work in groups; they play in groups; they seem happiest in groups. Such extraordinary feeling for collective behavior has its origins in the family, and any rejection of, or failure to conform to, the family raises for the Japanese the most serious questions about his role in society as a whole.

In Ozu's films, such as the powerful and moving *Tokyo Story (Tōkyō Monogatari,* 1953), the clash between the traditional and the modern is commonly portrayed in generational terms—that is, in the conflict between a traditional parent and an independent-minded modern child. But the social implications of such a clash are far greater in the Japanese setting than they would be in the Western. Whereas the Western child would most likely think of his parent merely as too conservative or old-fashioned, the Japanese youth is intensely conscious that the parent represents a traditional and still precisely understood pattern of conduct that continues to call all Japanese, to one degree or another, to account.

Ozu prefers scripts constructed less in narrative than in chronicle form, providing dialogues that are closer to the way people normally speak and scenes that are extremely natural in feeling. He also uses almost exclusively a single camera shot taken from the eye level of a person seated on *tatami.* As Donald Richie observes, "This traditional view is the view in repose, commanding a very limited field of vision but commanding it entirely. It is the attitude for watching, not listening; it is the position from which one sees the Noh, from which one partakes of the tea ceremony."[21]

The message typically conveyed by an Ozu domestic or popular drama is that life (which is suffused with the same kind of sadness derived from the sense of *mono no aware* that we find in the novels of Kawabata) will go on pretty much as it has. Young people will still be drawn to the modern, and their elders will continue to find contentment, if not total solace, in the carefully defined world of tradition. Other directors, however, have by no means shared Ozu's timeless, almost fatalistic view of things. An important example is the work of Naruse Mikio, another established director from the prewar period, whose postwar films include *When a Woman Ascends the Stairs (Onna ga Kaidan o Agaru Toki,* 1960) and *Flowing (Nagareru).* Naruse sees the traditional family-oriented ways as even more binding than Ozu implies and seems to doubt that few Japanese, if any, can fully escape them. In *When a Woman Ascends the Stairs,* the still young and attractive proprietress, or *mama-san,* of a walk-up bar in Tokyo's Ginza section accepts, in violation of her professional code, the advances of a patron and agrees to marry him. In fact, the man is already married, and when the woman meets his wife she realizes that, despite what she had regarded as her own modern and even liberated views, she cannot be responsible for the destruction of a family. In the end she once again ascends the stairs alone to her bar, resigned to resuming the role of a *mama-san* who banters with and flatters her patrons but does not get seriously involved with them.

The contemporary Japanese cinema is of such rich diversity that discussion of the films of a few directors, no matter how important they may be, obviously cannot cover the subject adequately. But, along with Ozu and Kurosawa, the greatest master of film has been Mizoguchi Kenji, director of the incomparably beautiful *Ugetsu (Ugetsu Monogatari,* 1953).[22] Viewed from different perspectives, Mizoguchi can be seen as the most romantically traditional of Japanese directors and also as an artist concerned with modern social issues. His traditional side is essentially aesthetic and is probably most fully revealed in his ability to create and sustain atmosphere, particularly in films of the past or some mythical age long ago, such as *Ugetsu,* the tale of a craftsman in the medieval age of civil wars who journeys to a city to sell his pottery and is drawn into an affair by a lovely patroness. In this atmospherically most perfect of films, much of the sense of wonder derives from our uncertainty about what is real and unreal. The craftsman discovers that his affair with the lovely patroness is part of an enchanted spell under which he has fallen; yet when he seeks to return home to his wife, he finds that she also no longer exists but has been dead for many years.

Mizoguchi's modern side is to be found mainly in his treatment of women, including the themes of the importance of their love to men and the fearful way in which they were victimized in traditional, feudal Japan. The latter theme is starkly drawn in *Sansho the Bailiff (Sanshō Dayū,* 1954) an overpoweringly tragic story of the wife, son, and daughter of a provincial official in ancient times who are kidnapped by outlaws and sold into slavery, the son and daughter to one group and the wife to another. Upon growing to manhood the son escapes, thanks to his sister, who sacrifices her life to delay his pursuers. The son soon becomes an important official himself, but he abandons his position in order to search for his mother. When he finally finds her, she is a blind old woman who has been used over the years as a prostitute and has even had the tendons of her legs cut to prevent her from running away.

Although in *Sansho the Bailiff* Mizoguchi introduced social criticism into a historical setting, he remained—like his compeers Ozu and Kurosawa—strongly sentimental about the old Japan and its traditional ways. Other directors, such as Kobayashi Masaki, have rejected what they regard as this all too easy sentimentalism and have instead focused uncompromising attention on the cruelty and crushing inequities of traditional society. In *Harakiri (Seppuku,* 1962) Kobayashi presented the story of a Tokugawa period *rōnin* who visits a domain to request sustenance and vows that he will disembowel himself if it is refused. Regarding the *rōnin* as a mere nuisance, officials of the domain summarily reject his request and order him to make good his vow by performing *harakiri* in their presence. As he prepares for the grim ceremony, the *rōnin* speaks to the officials about another masterless samurai who had called upon them a short while before with a request identical to his and who had been forced to perform *harakiri* with a bamboo sword, the only weapon he carried. The *rōnin* reveals that the earlier samurai was his son, who had been driven in desperation to come to the domain to obtain food for his starving wife and child. Informing his captors that he has already taken the topknots (the symbols of samurai manhood) of three of their fellow officials who were responsible for his son's death, the *rōnin* seizes his sword and, in classic *chambara* style, kills a number of the enemy before he is finally destroyed.

Along with other filmmakers of the postwar period, Kobayashi has also directed severe criticism against modern Japanese society. His most ambitious undertaking, for example, was the three-part drama of the horrors of Japan's participation in World War II—the setting is Manchuria—entitled *The Human Condition (Ningen no Jōken,* 1958–61). In an interview with the American critic Joan Mellen, Kobayashi said that he regarded *Harakiri* and *The Human Condition* as similar in theme insofar as they both deal with the "tenacious human resilience" of individuals under the authoritarian pressures of society.[23]

Other branches of the performing arts, including the modern theatre *(shingeki)* and *kabuki,* also flourished after the war, though on admittedly much smaller scales and not before overcoming their own particular postwar traumas.

The basis of *shingeki* since its inception has been the theatrical company rather than the independent producer as in American theatre. During the war there was only one active company—the Literary Theatre (*Bungakuza*)—and the number of theatre houses accessible to it was severely reduced by bombing raids. Peace brought a feeling of theatrical revolution within *shingeki* as part of the general hope that accompanied the end of the war.

But the most fundamental difficulties confronting *shingeki* in the postwar period were the same that had always bedeviled it. Foremost was the fact that the very word for theatre—*engeki*—overwhelmingly connoted to the Japanese a presentational rather than representational kind of performing art. Specifically, it meant *kabuki,* and the *shingeki* people had been obliged from the first to try to distinguish theirs as a "new" or "modern" theatre. Even as *shingeki* struggled to establish its own acting and theatrical traditions, it was upstaged by a rapidly rising film industry, which was able to advance just a step behind the cinema in the West to become a truly modern, realistic theatre of representation in its own right. Still another difficulty encountered by *shingeki* in its early stages of development was the deep rift that arose between those who wished to keep it an exclusively literary or theatrical medium and those who aspired to transform it into an ideological *(kannen-teki)* form of theatre. This led, as we have noticed, to the dominance in *shingeki* of proletarian writers in the late 1920s and the 1930s and to its suppression by the military authorities. Once again, in the postwar period, political ideology became a source of contention within *shingeki.*

If *shingeki's* difficulties remained the same after the war, some of its attempted solutions also evoked a familiar feeling. One of the means by which *shingeki* sought to deal with poor attendance figures, for example, was to stage Western plays in translation, including Shakespeare's *A Midsummer Night's Dream, Romeo and Juliet,* and *Hamlet.* Among contemporary works, Tennessee Williams's *A Streetcar Named Desire* and Arthur Miller's *Death of a Salesman* (the latter produced by a left-wing theatrical company) enjoyed successful runs. But foreign plays could in the long run contribute little to the advancement of a native theatre, and the relative prosperity *shingeki* has had since the war is attributable also to the original work of Japanese playwrights. Of particular interest has been the writing of plays for *shingeki* by well-known novelists, most notably Mishima Yukio (1925–70) and Abe Kōbō (1924–).

Mishima, who had strong neoclassical tastes, is perhaps best remembered as a playwright for his use of both the Japanese and Western pasts. Among his writings are modern *nō* plays, several *kabuki* pieces, and works drawn from Western history, such as *Madame de Sade* (1965), which is set at the time of the French Revolution. Abe, on the other hand, has devoted himself to avant-garde, experimental theatre, as we can see in such plays as *Friends* (1967) and *The Man Who Turned into a Stick* (1969). But even though Mishima and Abe may differ in the periods—past and present—they have chosen to explore, they have both significantly advanced Japanese theatre by avoiding the pitfalls of earlier, prewar playwrights, who tried to create modern Japanese plays essentially by incorporating into them elements from the realistic tradition of theatre in the West.[24] The plays of Mishima and Abe are original works, free from the constraints of realism, that have served to inspire other playwrights to press forward in the development of a truly modern Japanese theatre.

Kabuki faced a situation and prospects quite different from those of *shingeki* in the postwar period. In its origins, of course, *kabuki* was a bourgeois theatre that the Tokugawa authorities at first had barely tolerated. Yet by modern times *kabuki* had unchallengeably become the main theatre of Japan. Although its low beginning may never have been entirely forgotten, part of its repertory was also viewed as a repository of traditional morality and the feudalistic values of the premodern samurai class. It was for this reason that the military authorities generally favored it during the war[25] and for the very same reason that SCAP cast such a jaundiced eye upon *kabuki* after the war and strictly forebade the performance of "feudalistic" works, such as *Chūshingura* (Treasury of Loyal Retainers), the perennially popular dramatization of the vendetta carried out by forty-seven *rōnin* in the early eighteenth century. But by about 1947 the SCAP-imposed restrictions on *kabuki* were relaxed, and it promptly began to enjoy a brisk revival. Today, *kabuki* enjoys enormous favor and at least one of its actors, Bandō Tamasaburō, is a popular star of the magnitude of a leading rock-and-roll musician.

One of the arts that perforce drew much attention in the postwar period, owing to the destructiveness of the war itself, was architecture. Many of Japan's largest cities, including Tokyo, had been devastated by Allied high-explosive and incendiary bombing raids, and there was a desperate need for new buildings of all kinds. But because of the relatively low priority given by SCAP to the physical reconstruction of Japanese cities and the gap between any drawing up and implementation of large-scale architectural projects, the postwar building boom in Japan did not begin until the early 1950s. To understand the directions then taken in building, it will be helpful to review briefly the general course of architectural development during the preceding century.

Traditional Japanese architecture was based almost entirely on the use of wood in construction. The advent of Western influences about the time of the Meiji Restoration brought a sweeping technological revolution in architecture through the introduction of an array of new building materials, including cement, steel, and bricks. By the beginning of the twentieth century, as modern capitalist industries began to achieve significant growth in Japan, techniques of reinforced-concrete construction were also widely applied in the erection in Tokyo and other great cities of large plant- and office-type buildings.

The earliest Western-style buildings erected during the Meiji period—in a conglomeration of modes, including Gothic, Renaissance, and Baroque—were actually designed by foreign architects, such as the Englishman Josiah Condor, who arrived in Japan in 1877. Among the buildings done by Condor were the National Museum at Ueno Park and the Rokumeikan (Deer Cry Mansion) which became a symbol of what many regarded as the over-Westernization of Japan in the late nineteenth century. Condor taught at the Tokyo Technical College (which later became the Department of Architecture at Tokyo University) and greatly influenced many of the young Japanese architects who rose to prominence in the late Meiji period. But, as one scholar has put it, the Japanese architects of this age used "only the techniques and external forms of the industrial civilization of the West, without understanding its spiritual background. Consequently it was quite natural that they placed more stress on the engineering side in adopting Occidental customs."[26] In addition, the engineering side of architecture was also stressed because of the importance attached by the Japanese government to structural design for the purpose of protection against earthquakes.

It was not until the second decade of the twentieth century—at the same time as the modernist movement in Western architecture commenced—that Japanese architects began to display a more sophisticated and discerning attitude toward the problems and potentialities of modern building construction. Stimulated by the ideas of Walter Gropius, Le Corbusier, and others from the West, they were given new opportunities through increased building demand resulting from the economic boom that Japan enjoyed when the European powers withdrew from competition for Far Eastern markets during World War I. Among the questions Japanese architects began to grapple with in this period were the relationship between function and decoration (functionalism was then much in vogue in Europe), how materials should be used to accent or enhance their special qualities, and how architecture could best be directed toward humanistic rather than dehumanizing ends.

Probably the most important issue approached by Japanese architects during the period of World War I and its aftermath was how Japan's traditional tastes in building could be combined with the modern architectural values of the West. Among the most obvious of these traditional tastes were: the natural use of materials, such as unpainted wood and rough, earthen-type walls; the handling of space—essentially by means of thin, adjustable partitioning—to create a sense of continuity or flow between one part of the interior of a building and another and even between interior and exterior; and an emphasis on geometrically arranged straight lines in design, deriving mainly from retention of the ancient post-and-beam style of construction. All of these qualities are perfectly represented in that most flawless of traditional Japanese architectural masterpieces, the Tokugawa-period Katsura Detached Palace in Kyoto. Yet the modern Japanese themselves remained almost totally oblivious to Katsura's virtues until prodded into reflecting upon them in the 1930s by an expatriate from Nazi Germany, Bruno Taut.

Shortly after Taut's arrival in Japan in 1933, a Japanese architectural authority noted, "Fifty years ago Europeans came and told us, 'Nikkō is the most valuable,' and we thought so too; now Bruno Taut has come and told us, 'It is Ise and Katsura which are the most valuable,' and again we believe."[27] In a speech in 1936 to the Society for International Cultural Relations (Kokusai Bunka Shinkōkai) in Tokyo, Taut had this to say about the Ise Shrine:

> Everything in Ise is artistic, nothing is artificial. There are no peculiarities: the natural wood is faultless and marvellously polished, and the straw roof is equally perfect in its gorgeous curve, without the upcurve of the ridge or of the eaves. Equally flawless is the joining of the wood with the stone of the foundations, and there is no ornament which is not integral to the architectonic character. The golden globules on the cross-beams under the ridge join the harmony of straw and *hinoki* [cypress] wood, and the white papers and green branches of the Shinto sect are unsurpassably in accord with the whole.[28]

Taut went on to observe that, though the "Japanese pretend that the atmosphere of age exerts a particular fascination on them," it is the eternal newness and freshness of the Ise Shrine that impresses him as being most fundamentally Japanese. Of the Katsura Detached Palace, he said:

> Only at Katsura does there exist that overwhelming freedom of intellect which does not subordinate any element of the structure or the garden to some rigid system. At Nikkō, as in many architectural attractions of the world, the effect is gained by quantity—about in the same way that an army of two hundred thousand is larger than one of twenty thousand. At Katsura, on the contrary, each element remains a free individual, much like a member of a good society in which harmony arises from absence of coercion so that everyone may express himself according to his individual nature. Thus the Katsura Palace is a completely isolated miracle in the civilized world. One must speak of its "eternal beauty," which admonishes us to create in the same spirit much more than is the case with the Parthenon, with the Gothic Cathedral or with the Ise Shrine. That which is peculiar to Japan, the local, is insignificant;

> but the principle is absolutely modern and of complete validity for any contemporary architecture.[29]

For Taut, "Japan's architectural arts could not rise higher than Katsura, nor sink lower than Nikkō."

One of the great events in the history of modern architecture in Japan was the construction of the Imperial Hotel in central Tokyo by Frank Lloyd Wright between 1919 and 1922. Wright, who had visited Japan as early as 1905, was a keen admirer of East Asian art, acquiring Buddhist statuary and an extensive collection of Japanese woodblock prints from the Edo period. Among the most daring innovators in modern architecture, he forcefully advocated an "organic" approach to design and construction, by which he meant that the architect should not only seek to achieve unity and harmony in the functional features of a building but also allow it—whether home, office building, or hotel—to emerge organically within its particular setting and social context. Facing on Hibiya Park, not far from the emperor's palace, the Imperial Hotel was a low, rambling structure made of reinforced concrete with a brick-encrusted and heavily decorated exterior. In the interior, Wright made dramatic use of space, raising and lowering ceiling height. Determined to achieve total unity of structural planning and decoration, he even went so far as to design personally the contents of the guest rooms, including beds, chairs, tables, and wall hangings. To the undying dismay of its many admirers, Wright's original Imperial Hotel, having survived both the 1923 Tokyo earthquake and the bombing raids of World War II, was demolished in the late 1960s to make way for the present multistory New Imperial Hotel. But the old structure remains vivid in historical memory, not only for its intrinsic qualities as an architectural masterpiece but also as a direct statement to the Japanese by one of the most powerfully individualistic Western artists of the early twentieth century.

One of the most interesting aspects of Wright's impact on Japanese architecture after World War I was that in part it was a kind of feeding back of influences Wright had himself received earlier from the Japanese. Westerners had displayed interest in Japanese architecture, especially the traditional house, since at least the 1870s. The American Edward Morse, known for his discovery of prehistoric Jōmon remains at Ōmori in the outskirts of Tokyo, made a detailed study of Japanese domestic architecture about this time, and in 1885 published *Japanese Homes and Their Surroundings,* a text that over the years has gone through many printings. Styles of Japanese architecture were also introduced at fairs and exhibitions in the late nineteenth century, most notably in the display prepared for the World's Columbian Exposition at Chicago in 1892, which commemorated the four hundredth anniversary of the discovery of America. Designed and constructed by the Japanese themselves, the Chicago display was modeled loosely on the Phoenix Hall of the eleventh-century Byōdōin Temple at Uji. The original Phoenix Hall consists of a central hall with galleries extending like wings to the right and left (and terminating in open pavilions) and like a bird's body and tail to the rear. At Chicago the rear gallery was eliminated and the pavilions were enclosed. This created an arrangement of three linked structures of extremely graceful design, situated on raised platform floors and covered with gently sloping and deeply recessed tile roofs. The interior of each structure was designed and decorated to represent a different period of domestic styling in Japanese history: Fujiwara, Ashikaga, and Tokugawa.

The Japanese display at the 1892 World's Columbian Exposition, called the Phoenix Villa, was particularly striking in contrast to the oppressively heavy type of architecture adopted for the general exhibition halls, which were "cast in the pure classic, or neo-classic style, employing the familiar design vocabulary of columns, entablatures, arches, vaults and domes, the group unified by a gigantic architectural order sixty feet in height."[30] Although architects throughout the country visited and were impressed by the Phoenix Villa, it was the Chicago School, including Frank Lloyd Wright, that benefitted most from study of this excellent, near-at-hand model of Japanese structure and design, which was presented to the city of Chicago and preserved until 1946. Wright expressed his enthusiasm for traditional Japanese architecture in the following words:

> I saw the native home in Japan as a supreme study in elimination—not only of dirt but the elimination of the insignificant. So the Japanese house naturally fascinated me and I would spend hours taking it all to pieces and putting it together again. I saw nothing meaningless in the Japanese home and could find very little added in the way of ornament [the equivalent of ornament being achieved] by bringing out and polishing the beauty of the simple materials they used in making the building. . . and strangely enough, I found this ancient Japanese dwelling to be a perfect example of the modern standardizing I had myself been working out. The floor mats, removable for cleaning, are all three feet by six feet. The size and shape of all the houses are both determined by these mats. The

> sliding partitions all occur at the unit lines of the mats [and the] polished wooden posts . . . all stand at the intersection of the mats.[31]

Despite the example of Wright and the promise of more independence and even innovation of approach inherent in the new sentiments of Japanese architects, the 1920s and 1930s witnessed a general continuation of the earlier reliance upon, and imitation of, Western architectural trends.[32] For example, rather than attempt in the best traditional manner—and with the encouragement of Taut—to allow structure to determine design (as in the classical straight-line patterning of buildings, such as Katsura, based on post-and-beam construction), they succumbed to the Western use of massive walls that obliterated all structural features. It is true that, with the approach of the China and Pacific wars, the emergent military leaders of Japan sought to promote the development of a "national style" in modern architecture, but this tended to be an effort more to excise Western elements from Japanese buildings than to encourage the pursuit of new and progressive native lines of development.

Whereas before World War II the Japanese had been influenced chiefly by European architectural styles, after the war the main foreign influence was, probably unavoidably, American. One result of this trend was that, while such countries as England, France, and Germany placed great emphasis on city planning in the rebuilding of their wartorn cities, the Japanese—in the absence of a significant American interest in it—devoted little attention to overall planning once postwar rebuilding had begun in earnest during the early 1950s.[33]

To the general neglect of housing needs, highest priority in the early part of the postwar building boom in Japan was given—especially in the largest cities—to the construction of office space. Also under American influence, the Japanese sought to equip their new office-type and other buildings with the most advanced facilities and amenities, including extensive fluorescent lighting and air conditioning. In addition, both in commercial and industrial construction and in later home building, they tried where possible to use fireproof materials to modify the traditional tinderbox character of cities like Tokyo.

The Japanese had always lived in small wooden homes, usually incapable of accommodating more than one or two families. Hence the construction of multistory concrete apartment buildings in the postwar period constituted a truly revolutionary development in living style for many urban dwellers in

Japan. Although even these more modern apartment homes are exceedingly modest by American standards, the Japanese viewed them as first steps toward achievement of what they perceived as a kind of earthly utopia of informal and leisurely living derived from the model provided by the United States.

As part of the postwar building boom, architects experienced a renewal of both self-confidence and pride as Japanese building styles and aesthetic values began truly to attract international attention. One of the leaders in this postwar renewal was Maekawa Kunio, a former student of Le Corbusier and his Cubist-inspired emphasis on geometric forms in architectural design. Among Maekawa's postwar buildings are the main branch of the Japan Mutual Financing Bank (Nihon Sōgo Ginkō, 1952) in Tokyo and the Tokyo International House (Kokusai Bunka Kaikan, 1955), both of which were awarded the annual prize of the Japan Architectural Academy.[34] But the greatest fame in Japan's postwar world of architecture has gone to Tange Kenzō, who began winning prizes in architectural competitions during the war and later was for a time associated with Maekawa. Tange's triumphs include the Hall Dedicated to Peace (Heiwa-ki Kaikan) at Hiroshima and the main Sports Arena for the 1964 Tokyo Olympics. In the same way that the 1964 Olympics symbolized for many Japanese the true end of the postwar period and Japan's resumption of international status and dignity, the Sports Arena represents an important milestone in the country's modern architectural history. Far from requiring further tutelage and inspiration from the West, the Japanese now stand among the leaders in international architecture, and architecture has become an aspect of Japanese culture that has exerted great influence on the world outside Japan.

It is often said that postwar Japan has evolved a one and a half-party system. This means that for the past four decades or so national power has been held uninterruptedly by the conservative camp of politicians, who in 1955 merged to form the Liberal-Democratic Party, and whose opponents in the left-wing, or progressive, camp (led by the Socialist Party) have during this same period been consistently held to a minority—and thus a permanently out-of-power—status with no more than one third of the seats in the Diet.

As the seemingly permanent rulers of the country, the Liberal-Democratic Party has pursued policies of economic development and intimate alignment with the United States based on a Mutual Security Pact that has made the former conqueror responsible for Japan's national defense. The pact, originally signed in 1950, has been a great boon to Japan in enabling it, unlike other major countries, to limit military spending to a small fraction of its national income. At the same time, the pact has at times aroused intense hostility among some Japanese and has even symbolized the complex love-hate feelings of Japan for the United States, which derive from the special kind of relationship that has evolved between the two countries since the end of the war.

An event that was important in restoring some semblance of equality or at least partnership in relations between the United States and Japan was the rioting in Tokyo in 1960 over renewal of the Mutual Security Pact and the consequent cancellation of President Eisenhower's planned visit to Japan. The leftist-inspired rioting occurred against a confused background of Cold War tensions (including the fear that Japan, with American troops still stationed on its soil, might be the first target of the Soviets in a nuclear war with the United States), resentment against the high-handed tactics of Prime Minister Kishi Nobusuke (1896–) in seeking renewal of the pact, and an ambivalent kind of anti-Americanism. For the left wing in Japan, the United States was the principal threat to international peace. A staunch supporter of the conservatives, who were in power, the United States even advocated amendment of the American-imposed 1947 Constitution to eliminate the antiwar article and enable Japan to enter more actively into military association with it. But among the great majority of the Japanese people the United States was probably viewed in 1960 in various, sometimes conflicting ways: as a former enemy, as a humane and beneficent occupier, as an invaluable trading partner, and as a military colossus within the gates of East Asia.

Although Eisenhower was prevented from visiting Japan and Kishi was forced out of office, the Mutual Security Pact was renewed for another ten years and the left-wing opposition was badly fragmented by internal disputes after the rioting. It is therefore debatable who won the victory in 1960. At least one significant result of the incident was a stirring, for the first time in the postwar period, of Japanese nationalism. After a decade and a half of political passivity caused by feelings of guilt and humiliation over the war, action had been taken—whether or not it was fully supported by all of the Japanese people—on a truly national issue, and the United States as Big Brother had been at least partly rebuffed.

This is not to suggest that 1960 marked the charting of a new course for Japan or the definition of a new national purpose. Japan was on the threshold of its decade of greatest material fulfillment, a decade that propelled its gross national product to third highest in the world. What started as a "leisure boom" attained the level of an almost undreamed of prosperity, measured in terms of washing machines, television sets, motor cars, and overseas travel. At the same time, the Japanese were afflicted by those apparent inevitabilities of progress: urban sprawl, pollution, and the psychological tensions and social malaise of the modern condition.

A major phenomenon in postwar Japan has been the spectacular rise in the so-called new religions *(shinkō shūkyō).* Although loosely categorized as new, many of the most important of these religions were founded before the war, some as early as the mid-nineteenth century. But by far the greatest proliferation of the new religions occurred in the period following World War II. By the end of the Occupation in 1952, for example, their number was estimated at more than seven hundred, a figure that prompted one Western scholar to refer to the immediate postwar years as a time of the "rush hour of the gods."[35]

Despite the diversity of the new religions, they share certain general characteristics. For example, they have tended to spring up during times of intense crisis or social unrest, such as the early Meiji and post-World War II periods; their founders have typically been charismatic figures who have served as vehicles for the revelation of religious truth; they are highly syncretic, often partaking freely of Shinto and Buddhism, as well as Christianity;[36] and they are millenarian in that they characteristically promise the advent of a paradise on earth. Also, the new religions have always appealed chiefly to people lower on the social and economic scales: to those who have in some sense been left behind in the march of modern progress.

What makes the new religions most fascinating within the larger context of Japanese cultural history is the degree to which they reflect fundamental religious values and attitudes that have been held since ancient times. This can be seen perhaps most tellingly in the kinds of charismatic figures who have founded new religions, the most interesting of which are the female shamanistic types. Shamanism derives from northeast Asia and exerted enormous influence on early Japanese religion. It centers on belief in the transmission of a deity's will through a human intermediary, or shaman. This form of divine transmission, known in Japanese as *kami* possession *(kami gakari),* is vividly described in classical works of literature such as *The Tale of Genji* and entails a process whereby, in the face of personal affliction or natural calamity, the deity believed to be responsible is invited to enter the body of a medium, usually a girl or woman. Once the deity possesses her, the medium enters into an ecstatic, sometimes frenzied state and a voice, clearly not her own, speaks forth to indicate what must be done to placate the aroused deity.

An excellent example of a modern shaman of this sort is Nakayama Miki (1798–1887), founder of Tenrikyō, one of the earliest and most successful of the new religions. A woman of peasant origins (as so many of the founders have been), Nakayama underwent much suffering and experienced personal tragedy in her early life: the famines of the late Tokugawa period, an unhappy marriage, illness and death of her children. Then, in 1838, while serving as the medium for ministration to the leg pains of one of her sons, she was seized by a deity who proclaimed through her mouth that he was "the true and the original god who has descended from Heaven to save all mankind."[37] The deity demanded that Nakayama's body thenceforth be made available to him.

In addition to becoming the instrument for transmission of divine revelations by the "true and original god," Nakayama developed extraordinary powers to heal, and thus entered the tradition of faith healing that has been a powerful and recurrent feature of Japanese folk religion throughout history.

Faith healing, as stressed in Tenrikyō and other new religions, is simply one of a number of concrete promises of personal happiness, material fulfillment, and even entry into an earthly paradise that constitute the millenarian aspect of those religions. It is also in this millenarianism that the new religions, otherwise so much within the mainstream of the little tradition of folk religion in Japan, reveal themselves to be products of the modern age. Earlier utopian thinking in Japan about life in this world focused almost invariably on the recapturing or restoration of a golden age, and thus implicitly rejected existing conditions.[38] But the new religions not only do not reject the modern world, they boast that their followers will joyously attain the highest rewards that this world offers. To dramatize this promise, the more affluent of the new religions have constructed lavish national centers—equipped with the most modern luxuries and conveniences—to serve as meccas for visits and pilgrimages of the faithful and to enable them to sample the paradisiacal sweets conjured by their religions. Yet, as Carmen Blacker observes, even in the building of such meccas there is a harking back to the traditional—in this case, an attempt to "impose on the present world a kind of mythical or eschatological geography,"[39] much like, for example, the representation of the Pure Land Buddhist paradise in the Phoenix Hall and garden of the eleventh-century Byōdōin at Uji.

The most important of the new religions—and one of the most startling religious, social, and political phenomena in postwar Japan—is Sōka Gakkai, the Value Creation Society. Founded in the early 1930s for the purpose of religious education, Sōka Gakkai is a modern outgrowth of a branch of Nichiren Buddhism. In contrast to most of the new religions, which are highly syncretic, it shares the exclusivism and intolerance of other religious sects that have always been the hallmarks of Nichiren Buddhism.

Sōka Gakkai achieved only minor success in prewar days and was even disbanded when its leaders were jailed during the war because of their refusal to show reverence to state Shinto. But after the war, under the dynamic if not fanatical leadership of Toda Josei (1900–1958), the society enjoyed a phenomenal expansion. Employing such strong-arm, browbeating methods of proselytizing as *shakubuku* (breaking and subduing) and seeking to recruit not merely individuals but entire families, Sōka Gakkai claimed a membership by the early 1960s of ten million. In addition, through its political arm, Kōmeitō (Clean Government Party), Sōka Gakkai went to the polls and established itself as the third largest force in the upper house of the Japanese Diet.

Sōka Gakkai is in many ways a model for realization of the expectations that have been aroused by the new religions in postwar Japan. Although intellectuals may shun it and some people may denounce it as neofascist, Sōka Gakkai is one of the greatest mass movements in Japanese history. Along with its vast following, it possesses enormous material opulence, observable in its sumptuous center at the foot of Mount Fuji, which drew more than two million people to its opening in 1958. The attractions of Sōka Gakkai are many. For one thing, it offers people the opportunity to belong to a great and flourishing movement, an opportunity that appealed with particular force to the Japanese in the wake of the widespread social disorientation caused by defeat in war. Sōka Gakkai makes extravagant claims for its power to induce healing through faith, and even boasts that it can prevent illness. Not content with the slogan "Join us and you won't become sick," the society has gone so far as to threaten, "If you don't join us, you will be sure to *get* sick."[40]

If the resurgence of the new religions since the war has directed additional attention to the extraordinary group instincts and group orientation of the Japanese, there has also been much consideration given during the same period to the matter of individualism in a Japan liberated from the anti-individualistic fetters of the *kokutai* ideology. This is probably most conspicuous in the writings of such authors as Mishima Yukio, Abe Kōbō, and Ōe Kenzaburo (1935–), who have subjected the individual to the most intense psychological scrutiny, observing his unlimited potentiality for erratic, perverse, and bizarre behavior and his often desperate struggle against the dictates of social conformity.

Mishima, who committed suicide by disembowelment in 1970 at the age of forty-five, was one of the most fascinating individuals—at least to foreigners—in recent Japanese history.[41] A small and sickly youth of upper middle-class stock (his father was a moderately successful bureaucrat), Mishima had a most unwholesome childhood under the fanatically possessive domination of his grandmother, with whom he lived and in whose bed he slept until age twelve. Quite likely this early experience nourished the homosexuality that became so central not only to his later social behavior but also to his artistic vision.

Mishima attended the lustrous Peers School in Tokyo, where he achieved an outstanding academic record and even received an award from the hand of the emperor for graduating at the head of his class in 1944. He showed considerable precocity in writing, and although, at the urging of his father, he attended Tokyo University Law School and began a career in the Finance Ministry in 1947, he soon abandoned this to become a full-time author. In 1949 he vaulted into fame with the publication of an extraordinary, painfully revealing autobiographical novel entitled *Confessions of a Mask (Kamen no Kokuhaku).*

One of Mishima's purposes in writing *Confessions of a Mask* was to debunk the I-novelists, many of whom he believed merely chronicled in excruciating detail the dullness of their lives without ever really probing into the dark inner realms of human psychology. Whether or not the I-novelists as a group were, in fact, guilty of not telling the ultimate truth about themselves or getting to the roots of their existences, Mishima himself certainly revealed enough in *Confessions of a Mask* about his own emotional essence to explain the main course of his life and even his manner of death.

The Mishima we see in *Confessions of a Mask* is a narcissistic young man powerfully attracted from an early age to such things as the sight of a night soil man dressed in close-fitting thigh-pullers, the odor of sweat emanating from soldiers, and the "black thickets" in masculine armpits. But far more importantly, these homosexual cravings were associated with an aesthetic of blood and death.[42] This fact is startlingly impressed upon us in the famous passage from *Confessions of a Mask* wherein Mishima reveals that he had his first ejaculation upon viewing a reproduction of Guido Reni's painting of Saint Sebastian in which the martyr is shown tied to a tree, his nearly nude and expiring body pierced with arrows. The effect on Mishima was immediate and fierce:

> That day, the instant I looked upon the picture, my entire being trembled with some pagan joy. My blood soared up; my loins swelled as though in wrath. The monstrous part of me that was on the point of bursting awaited my use of it with unprecedented ardor, upbraiding me for my ignorance, panting indignantly. My hands, completely unconsciously, began a motion they had never been

> taught. I felt a secret, radiant something rise swift-footed to the attack from inside me. Suddenly it burst forth, bringing with it a blinding intoxication.[43]

The latter part of *Confessions of a Mask* is devoted to Mishima's determined but futile attempt to prove his normality by courting a young lady named Sonoko. Mishima—or, I should say, the novel's protagonist—derives no pleasure from physical contact with Sonoko, and when she falls in love with him, he balks at marriage. Still, they renew their liaison even after she marries another man and continue until the climactic scene of the book when they visit a rather sleazy dance hall and he sees something that strikes him with the force of a "thunderbolt":

> He was a youth of twenty-one or -two, with coarse but regular and swarthy features. He had taken off his shirt and stood there half naked, rewinding a belly-band about his middle. The coarse cotton material was soaked with sweat and had become a light-gray color. He seemed to be intentionally dawdling over his task of winding and was constantly joining in the talk and laughter of his companions. His naked chest showed bulging muscles, fully developed and tensely knit; a deep cleft ran down between the solid muscles of his chest toward his abdomen. The thick, fetter-like sinews of his flesh narrowed down from different directions to the sides of his chest, where they interlocked in tight coils. The hot mass of his smooth torso was being severely and tightly imprisoned by each succeeding turn of the soiled cotton belly-band. His bare, sun-tanned shoulders gleamed as though covered with oil. And black tufts stuck out from the cracks of his armpits, catching the sunlight, curling and glittering with glints of gold.
>
> At this sight, above all at the sight of the peony tattooed on his hard chest, I was beset by sexual desire. My fervent gaze was fixed upon that rough and savage, but incomparably beautiful body. Its owner was laughing there under the sun. When he threw back his head I could see his thick muscular neck. A strange shudder ran through my innermost heart. I could no longer take my eyes off him.
>
> I had forgotten Sonoko's existence. I was thinking of but one thing: Of his going out into the streets of high summer just as he was, half-naked, and getting into a fight with a rival gang. Of a

> sharp dagger cutting through that belly-band, piercing that torso. Of that soiled belly-band beautifully dyed with blood. Of his gory corpse being put on an improvised stretcher, made of a window shutter, and brought back here.[44]

Mishima, at about twenty-three, fantasized a death for the young man in the dance hall that was the one he chose for himself some twenty-two years later. It may well be, as Masao Miyoshi hypothesizes,[45] that Mishima's adult life was dominated by a longing for the death he felt he was denied during the war when he failed the physical examination for induction into the army and when all the American bombs missed him. But it is clear in retrospect that he needed much time to prepare both mentally and physically for what he envisioned as the aesthetically perfect form of self-destruction. In the mid-1950s he took up body-building, and during the radicalism of the 1960s, which accompanied the involvement of the United States in the Vietnam War, he assumed an extreme right-wing political stance based on traditional reverence for the emperor. Mishima transformed himself into a modern-day samurai, a warrior of pure spirit who would think only of one thing: "a sharp dagger. . . piercing [his] torso."

Mishima was a disciplined and prolific writer, producing more than thirty novels and many plays and essays. His output is striking not only for its quantity but also for its thematic diversity. Nevertheless, the Mishima that matters—the Mishima driven by an aesthetic of death as both the ultimate sexual experience and the supreme realization of beauty—is fully adumbrated in *Confessions of a Mask.* In his subsequent writing, Mishima gave probably the most artistic and memorable expression to this aesthetic in *The Temple of the Golden Pavilion (Kinkakuji).* Published serially in 1956, *The Temple of the Golden Pavilion* was inspired by the burning six years earlier of the fourteenth-century Golden Pavilion (or Temple) by an unbalanced Zen acolyte. The acolyte of Mishima's novel, Mizoguchi, is a young man, rendered inarticulate by a stutter, who enters into the service of the Golden Pavilion during World War II. When he had first been shown the Pavilion by his father on a visit to Kyoto, Mizoguchi had been disappointed to discover that it was "merely a small, dark, old, three-storied building." But after he returned home he found that

> the Golden Temple, which had disappointed me so greatly at first sight, began to revivify its beauty within me day after day, until in the end it became a more beautiful Golden Temple than it had

> been before I saw it. I could not say wherein this beauty lay. It seemed that what had been nurtured in my dreams had become real and could now, in turn, serve as an impulse for further dreams.
>
> Now I no longer pursued the illusion of a Golden Temple in nature and in the objects that surrounded me. Gradually the golden Temple came to exist more deeply and more solidly within me.[46]

Mizoguchi fixes on the Golden Pavilion as an ideal of externalized beauty and, at the same time, identifies it with the beauty he feels within himself but cannot bring out because of his speech impediment. All goes reasonably well as long as the war continues, because the danger of the Pavilion's possible destruction by bombing balances Mizoguchi's always threatened interior world of beauty. But, when the war ends, there is an abrupt and terrible change in the relationship between the building and the acolyte:

> From the moment that I set eyes on the temple that day [of surrender], I could feel that "our" relationship had already undergone a change. When it came to such things as the shock of defeat or national grief, the Golden Temple was in its element; at such times it was transcendent, or at least pretended to be transcendent. Until today, the Golden Temple had not been like this. Without doubt the fact that it had in the end escaped being burned down in an air raid and was now out of danger had served to restore its earlier expression, an expression that said: "I have been here since olden times and I shall remain here forever."
>
> The most peculiar thing was that of all the various times when the Golden Temple had shown me its beauty, this time was the most beautiful of all. Never had the temple displayed so hard a beauty—a beauty that transcended my own image, yes, that transcended the entire world of reality, a beauty that bore no relation to any form of evanescence! Never before had its beauty shone like this, rejecting every sort of meaning.
>
> It is no exaggeration to say that, as I gazed at the temple, my legs trembled and my forehead was covered with cold beads of perspiration. On a former occasion when I had returned to the country after seeing the temple, its various parts and its whole structure had resounded with a sort of musical harmony. But what I heard this time was complete silence, complete noiselessness.

> Nothing flowed there, nothing changed. The Golden Temple stood before me, towered before me, like some terrifying pause in a piece of music, like some resonant silence.
>
> "The *bond* between the Golden Temple and myself has been cut," I thought. "Now my vision that the Golden Temple and I were living in the same world has broken down. Now I shall return to my previous condition, but it will be even more hopeless than before. A condition in which I exist on one side and beauty on the other. A condition that will never improve so long as this world endures."[47]

Thus Mizoguchi embarks on the line of thinking that leads to the conclusion that he must destroy the Golden Pavilion in order to live. In this application of Mishima's aesthetic, it is the Golden Pavilion as the embodiment of the highest beauty (in contrast to the beauty that Mizoguchi imagines is within him) that must "die" to realize its finest potential.

Mishima committed suicide with another member of his private army, known as the Shield Society (Tate no Kai), on November 25, 1970, at the headquarters of the Japan Self-Defense Force in Tokyo after exhorting a hastily assembled group of its members to join him in smashing the liberal postwar constitutional structure and restoring, in the name of the emperor, a Japan of "true men and samurai."[48] It is difficult to take seriously the radically right-wing politics Mishima espoused in his last years, especially in view of the fact that for most of his life he had been notably apolitical. It seems far more likely, as suggested earlier, that he conceived these politics as a necessary part of the staging for the glorious and beautiful death he so ardently desired. Also part of the staging was delivery to his publisher on the day he had chosen to die of the final installment of his last novel, the massive tetralogy entitled *The Sea of Fertility*. Set in the twentieth century and based on the theme of reincarnation through several generations of the soul of a young Japanese aristocrat, *The Sea of Fertility* was obviously intended by Mishima to confirm his stature as one of the world's great writers. But to many critics it confirms, instead, the sad fact that Mishima's best writing had been done years earlier. As Marleigh Ryan observes, "In [the tetralogy's] more than 1,400 pages of plots and subplots, births and rebirths, violence and sickness, we have a repetition of virtually every theme Mishima used in his earlier novels. From peepholes to ritual suicide, we have been through it all before, and we remain curiously unmoved."[49]

Mishima's delvings into the wellsprings of human behavior was characteristically Japanese at least insofar as he limited himself generally to the particularities of his own psyche (however abnormal) as the only source of true experience. Abe Kōbō, on the other hand, appears to have transcended this particularism of so many Japanese writers and to deal more universally with the self of modern man. A writer of enormous imaginative power—much influenced by Kafka—who weaves his bizarre tales as parables on the plight of contemporary existence, Abe is preoccupied with the themes of personal freedom, the urge to attain it, and the equally powerful urge to prevent or escape from it. In *The Ruined Map (Moetsukita Chizu,* 1967), for example, his hero is a private detective investigating a man's disappearance, who eventually confuses his own identity with that of the man he is seeking. The cause of this confusion is suggested in the following dialogue the detective has with a possible witness to the disappearance. The witness speaks first:

> "Why does the world take it for granted that there's a right to pursue people? Someone who hasn't committed any crime. I can't understand how you can assume, as if it were a matter of course, that there is some right that lets you seize a man who has gone off of his own free will."
>
> "By the same reasoning the one left behind might insist that there was no right to go away."
>
> "Going off is not a right but a question of will."
>
> "Maybe pursuit is a matter of will too."
>
> "Then, I'm neutral. I don't want to be anyone's friend or enemy."[50]

Abe seems to be telling us that some people will always try to escape from the restraints of society and their humdrum existences and that others will just as surely pursue them and attempt to entrap them again. Pursuer and pursued are likely to be motivated by the same force of will and, in their special relationship, may indeed appear to be very similar, if not identical.

Abe's concern is with freedom not as an intellectual ideal but as an emotional craving. The paradox of his message is that freedom, once achieved, may incite the same desire to escape as did one's previous state of real or imagined captivity. Abe's finest statement of this paradox is *The Woman in the Dunes (Suna no Onna,* 1962). Like *The Ruined Map,* it commences with the disappearance of a man, in this case a nondescript schoolteacher who is an amateur entomologist going on a holiday to the seaside in quest of bugs. The man can be seen both as a pursuer of bugs (who possess freedom) and as one who yearns for freedom in his fascination with sand, the natural habitat of the bugs he pursues. No other substance—except water, to which Abe frequently compares it—so clearly represents both freedom and its potential denial. Forever free itself, as it constantly shifts and flows, sand can also relentlessly pursue and totally engulf.

Missing the last bus home, the man accepts shelter for the night in a nearby village, only to discover the following day that he is a prisoner. He has been placed in a house in a deep sand pit to live with a recently widowed but still young woman. Together they constitute one of a score of enslaved families in pits facing the sea that must constantly dig sand to prevent it from inundating the village. Much of *The Woman in the Dunes* is a narrative of the man's schemes and efforts to escape to freedom, but on another level it is the story of how the man, forced into confinement in the microcosmic world of the sand pit, comes to realize the futility for most people of regarding life—whether in his kind of captivity or in society beyond it—as anything other than a pit, a place where freedom is stifled. Some people may think they have round-trip tickets that enable them to come and go as they please, but they need all the strength and will they possess to avoid losing the return halves of their tickets and being forced onto the one-way track that entraps everyone else:

> *Got a one-way ticket to the blues, woo, woo. . . .*
>
> If you want to sing it, sing it. These days people caught in the clutches of the one-way ticket never sing it like that. The souls of those who have a one-way ticket are so thin that they scream when they step on a pebble. They have had their fill of walking. "The Round-Trip Ticket Blues" is what they want to sing. A one-way ticket is a disjointed life that misses the links between yesterday and today, today and tomorrow. Only the man who obstinately hangs on to a round-trip ticket can hum with real sorrow a song of a one-way ticket. For this very reason he grows desperate lest the return half of his ticket be lost or stolen; he buys stocks, signs up for life insurance, and talks out of different sides of his mouth to his union pals and his superiors. He hums "The One-Way Ticket Blues" with all his might and, choosing a channel at random, turns the television up to full volume in an attempt to drown out the peevish voices of those who have only a one-way ticket and who keep asking for help, voices that come up through the bathtub drain or the toilet hole. It would not be strange at all if "The Round-Trip Ticket Blues" were the song of mankind imprisoned.[51]

After a futile and humiliating attempt to escape from the pit, the man sets about constructing a ground trap in the hope of ensnaring a crow to carry his plea for help to the outside world. The trap project has little chance of succeeding, but it leads the man to an incredible discovery: beneath the sand there is water that could be invaluable to the villagers. With this secret knowledge about the water, the man's attitude toward his situation begins to change, and when shortly thereafter the villagers forget or neglect to remove the rope ladder leading to the bottom of the pit, he does not seize the opportunity to make another attempt to escape. For now he has a "two-way ticket" to life and can afford to weigh his options more carefully:

> There was no particular need to hurry about escaping. On the two-way ticket he held in his hand now, the destination and time of departure were blanks for him to fill in as he wished. In addition, he realized that he was bursting with a desire to talk to someone about the water trap. And if he wanted to talk about it, there wouldn't be better listeners than the villagers. He would end by telling someone—if not today, then tomorrow.
>
> He might as well put off his escape until sometime after that.[52]

The themes of freedom and escape from the fetters of modern society are important also in the work of Ōe Kenzaburō, although Ōe presents the issue more clearly as that of alienation and anomie. In Ōe's typical schema, the individual is caught in a society that makes stifling demands upon him, demands that he cannot meet and that, therefore, render him a failure, at least in his own mind. Compounding the personal alienation and fear that he is going nowhere in life is the more widely shared social malaise of anomie that sees no direction in the life of society as a whole (that is, postwar Japan, the home of economic animals who have poured their souls into the transistor radio).

Such an individual—held in the grip of alienation and anomie—is Bird, the hero of Ōe's *A Personal Matter (Kojinteki na Taiken,* 1964), a novel startlingly similar in conception and plot to John Updike's *Rabbit, Run.* As the story begins, we find Bird at age twenty-seven, married and awaiting the birth of his first child. We learn how he was drunk for four weeks after his marriage two years earlier, how he had to withdraw from graduate school, and how he subsequently turned to his father-in-law to obtain an unpretentious job as teacher in a college-preparatory cram school. Bird dreams of going to Africa and has just bought a set of Michelin road maps of the distant continent.

Wandering the streets while waiting for news of his wife from the hospital, Bird is attacked by a gang of dragon-jacketed hoods and is beaten to the ground:

> It occurred to Bird that the maps must be getting creased between his body and the ground. And his own child was being born: the thought danced with new poignancy to the frontlines of consciousness. A sudden rage took him, and rough despair. Until now, out of terror and bewilderment, Bird had been contriving only to escape. But he had no intention of running now. If I don't fight now, I'll not only lose the chance to go to Africa forever, my baby will be born into the world solely to lead the worst possible life—it was like the voice of inspiration, and Bird believed.[53]

Bird counterattacks and "the joy of battle. . . reawakened in him; it had been years since he had felt it. Bird and the dragon-jackets watched one another without moving, appraising the formidable enemy. Time passed," and the gang withdrew.

Bird, trapped and bewildered by life, sees in the dragon-jacketed gang a well-defined enemy he can attack, daringly and against great odds. But the euphoria he experiences over victory in physical battle is short-lived, and the oppressiveness of life becomes even more terrifyingly real when he learns that his baby has been born a monster with a rare brain hernia protruding from its head. Africa suddenly becomes more unattainable than ever before, and Bird tries to escape from the dilemma of what to do about the baby by fleeing in a totally opposite direction. Purchasing a bottle of whiskey, he seeks sanctuary—in a symbolic kind of return to the womb—in the dark, cluttered apartment of a former girl friend. Later, when the baby fails to die in the hospital as Bird had agonizingly hoped, he and the girl friend take custody of it and deliver it to an illicit doctor for disposal. With the baby gone, they plan to fulfill Bird's dream of going to Africa.

Ōe had to this point written a splendid and poignantly moving story. Inexplicably, he chose to conclude it with a brief, less than convincing epilogue that informs us that Bird came to his senses in time to retrieve the baby and return it to the hospital, where it was operated on and fixed—it did not have a brain hernia after all, merely a benign tumor. Bird's attitude is now mature and stable, and he is planning for the future of the baby.

The story of Bird, a true product of postwar Japan, brings us to the contemporary period and will serve to end this survey of Japanese cultural history. If there is a central theme to the book, it is that the Japanese, within the context of a history of abundant cultural borrowing from China in premodern times and the West in the modern age, have nevertheless retained a hard core of native social, ethical, and cultural values by means of which they have almost invariably molded and adapted foreign borrowings to suit their own tastes and purposes.

But the Japanese have also exported their culture in modern times; and Japan's prominence in the world in the mid-1980s is based not only on its phenomenal achievements in manufacturing, business management, and international trade, but also on its great influence in the arts and fashion. Exhibitions of art and craft, ranging from ancient Buddhist statuary and paintings to the utensils of the tea ceremony and signs used by merchants in the Tokugawa and Meiji periods, have drawn large crowds in the United States and other countries. Touring theatrical groups performing plays from the puppet and *kabuki* theatres are perennially popular abroad. Japanese tastes in architecture, interior decoration, and garden design are known and imitated throughout the world; and Japanese designers have recently ascended to high levels in the field of women's fashion. Clearly, major aspects of Japanese culture have become an important and vital part of the lives of people everywhere.

Notes

1. Theodore McNelly, ed., *Sources in Modern East Asian History and Politics*, (New York: Appleton-Century-Crofts, 1967), pp.169–70.
2. Asahi Shimbun, ed., *Pacific Rivals*, (New York: Weatherhill, 1972), pp. 134–35
3. Hugh Borton, *Japan's Modern Century*, (New York: Ronald Press, 1970), p. 572.
4. Comments on the postwar "end of the I-novel tradition" may be found in Yoshida Seiichi and Ingaki Tatsurō, eds., *Nihon Bungaku no Rekishi* (History of Japanese Literature) (Tokyo: Kadokawa, 1968), 12:410–11.
5. Dazai Osamu, *No Longer Human*, translated by Donald Keene, (New York: New Directions, 1958), pp. 124–25.
6. Dazai Osamu, *The Setting Sun*, translated by Donald Keene, (New York: New Directions, 1956), p. 166.
7. Ibid., pp. 132–33.
8. Yoshida and Inagaki, *Nihon Bungaku no Rekishi*, 12:410.
9. Masao Miyoshi in *Accomplices of Silence: The Modern Japanese Novel* (Berkeley, University of California Press, 1974).

10. Tanizaki, *The Makioka Sisters*, translated by Edward G. Seidensticker, (New York: Knopf, 1957), p. 99.

11. Tanizaki Junichirō, *In Praise of Shadows*, translated by Thomas J. Harper and Edward G. Seidensticker, (New Haven: Leete's Island Books, 1971), pp. 20–21.

12. Quoted in John Nathan, *Mishima: A Biography* (Boston: Little Brown, 1974), p. 83.

13. Kawabata Yasunari, *The Sound of the Mountain*, translated by Edward G. Seidensticker, (New York: Knopf, 1970), p. 12.

14. Ōoka Shōhei, *Fires on the Plain*, translated by Ivan Morris, (New York: Knopf, 1957), p. 216.

15. In a translator's introduction to the Penguin edition of *Fires on the Plain*, Ivan Morris points out that the hero did not commit the "ultimate abomination": he did not kill another person in order to eat his flesh.

16. Noma Hiroshi, *Zone of Emptiness* (New York: World, 1956), p. 286.

17. Ibuse Masuji, *Black Rain*, translated by John Bester, (Tokyo: Kodansha, 1969), pp. 296–97.

18. Richie, *Japanese Cinema* (New York: Doubleday, 1971), p. 58.

19. Joseph L. Anderson and Donald Richie, *The Japanese Film* (New York: Grove Press, 1959), p. 162.

20. Ibid., p. 176.

21. Richie, *Japanese Cinema*, p. 64.

22. Based on Ueda Akinari's *Ugetsu Monogatari*, written in the late eighteenth century. See Ueda Akinari, *Ugetsu Monogatari: Tales of Moonlight and Rain*, translated by Leon Zolbrod, (Vancouver: University of British Columbia Press, 1979).

23. Joan Mellen, *Voices from the Japanese Cinema* (New York: Liveright, 1975), p. 147.

24. Ted T. Takaya, ed. and tr., *Modern Japanese Drama: An Anthology* (New York: Columbia University Press, 1979), p. xxx.

25. Although it too was banned in the later stages of the war as an unnecessary extravagance.

26. Kawazoe Noboru, *Contemporary Japanese Architecture* (Tokyo: Kokusai Koryu Kikin, 1973), p. 19.

27. Quoted in Bruno Taut, *Fundamentals of Japanese Architecture* (Tokyo: Society for International Cultural Relations, 1936), p. 6.

28. Ibid., pp. 15–16.

29. Ibid., pp. 19–20.

30. Clay Lancaster, *The Japanese Influence in America* (New York: Walton Rawls, 1963), pp. 76–77.

31. Quoted from Wright's *An Autobiography* (1942), in Lancaster, *Japanese Influence*, p. 88.

32. Yamamoto Gakuji, *Nihon Kenchiku no Genkyō* (The Present State of Japanese Architecture) (Tokyo: Shokokusha, 1969), pp. 23–24.

33. Kodama Kōta et al., *Nihon Bunka-shi Taikei*, 13:287.

34. Maekawa's 1955 International House has been torn down and replaced by another, larger structure.

35. H. Neill McFarland *The Rush Hour of the Gods* (New York: Harper and Row, 1967).

36. Harry Thomsen, *The New Religions of Japan* (Tokyo: Tuttle, 1963), p. 16.

37. Carmen Blacker, "Millenarian Aspects of the New Religions in Japan," in Shively, *Tradition and Modernization* (Princeton: Princeton University Press, 1971), p. 575.

38. This was true, for example, of the spirit of the Meiji restoration.

39. Blacker, "Millenarian Aspects," p. 587.

40. Thomsen, *The New Religions of Japan*, p. 90.

41. Nathan Glazer, citing a poll by the Japanese newspaper *Asahi*, notes that Mishima is one of the very few Japanese whom even a small percentage of Americans can, at least, identify by name. See Akira Iriye, *Mutual Images* (Cambridge, Mass.: Harvard University Press, 1975), p. 142.

42. This theme is developed in John Nathan's biography of Mishima, *Mishima: A Biography*.

43. Mishima Yukio, *Confessions of a Mask*, translated by Meredith Weatherby, (New York: New Directions, 1958), p. 40.

44. Ibid., pp. 251–52.

45. Miyoshi, *Accomplices of Silence*, p. 157.

46. Mishima Yukio, *The Temple of the Golden Pavilion*, translated by Ivan Morris (New York: Knopf, 1958), p. 29.

47. Ibid., pp. 63–64.

48. Nathan, *Mishima: A Biography*, p. 275.

49. Marleigh Ryan, "The Mishima Tetralogy," *The Journal of Japanese Studies* 1, no. 1 (Autumn 1974): p. 165.

50. Abe Kōbō, *The Ruined Map*, translated by E. Dale Saunders, (New York: Knopf, 1969), p. 162.

51. Abe Kōbō, *The Woman in the Dunes*, translated by E. Dale Saunders, (New York: Knopf, 1964), pp. 161–62.

52. Ibid., p. 239.

53. Ōe Kenzaburō, *A Personal Matter*, translated by John Nathan, (New York: Grove Press, 1969), pp. 15–16.

GLOSSARY

In order to make this glossary most helpful, some of the more commonly used aesthetic terms are defined by several scholars, other terms are presented with shorter definitions. While most of these terms appear in the essays in this collection, there are a few that do not but are provided for the reader's general information.

Aware "According to Norinaga, *aware* consists of two interjections, *a* and *hare* both of which are used when one's heart is greatly moved. *Aware*, which combines these two interjections, is primarily a word describing a deeply moved heart, a heart filled with intense emotion. The emotion could be joy, happiness, wonder, horror, hatred, love, grief, anger, jealousy, or anything else. It may be said, however, that two of the emotions, love and grief, tend to dominate, since they are the most heart-engaging emotions" (quoted in Makoto Ueda. "Shintoism and the Theory of Literature," in his *Literary and Art Theories in Japan*, 1967). (See de Bary, ed., "The Vocabulary of Japanese Aesthetics, I," for further discussion; see also *Mono no aware*.)

Bakufu Name given to warrior government under the leadership of the shōgun. Also sometimes referred to as shōgunate.

Buddhism Religion which made its way from India and China to Japan. The goal of Buddhism is interior enlightenment; through "right thinking" and the denial of "earthly pleasures" the soul will reach Nirvana. Various sects of Buddhism emerged in Japan including Tendai and Shingon in the Heian period, Zen and Tendai in the medieval period. (See Graham Parkes' chapter for influence of Buddhism on "ways of thinking.")

Bugaku	Ritual court dance introduced from China in the eighth century A.D.
Bunraku	Puppet theater popular in the seventeenth century. Usually included chanters, samisen players, and puppeteers who manipulated nearly life-size puppets.
Bushidō	Literally the way (*dō*) of the warrior (*bushi*). A term used during the Edo period to describe the ethical code of the samurai warriors. Found in literature in Miyamoto Musashi's *The Book of Five Rings* (*Gorin no sho*, 1643), and Yamamoto Tsunetomo's *Hagakure* (1716). (See Roger Ames' chapter for discussion of the "mode and ethic" of *bushidō*.)
Chanoyu	The tea ceremony. An important part of Muromachi period culture. Most often associated with the great tea master Sen no Rikyū (1521–91), who established many of the guidelines for the use of instruments and the procedures for serving tea in this highly ritualized ceremony. (See also the chapter by Kōshirō "The *Wabi* Aesthetic through the Ages" for more detailed description of the aesthetic of the tea ceremony.)
Chōka	A long poem (in contrast to the shorter *waka*) which uses alternating phrases of five and seven syllables. The subject matter was often about domestic situations; *chōka* were also often used to praise the emperor or members of the imperial family or to commemorate a trip taken by the emperor. They are often accompanied by short *waka* as companion pieces called *hanka* or "envoys."
Confucianism	Originating in ancient China, it is a set of moral and religious teachings which emphasize duty to one's family and friends and ancestor worship. It came to prominence in Japan during the Tokugawa period. (See Graham Parkes' chapter for influence on "ways of thinking.")
Daimyō	Warrior chieftains next in power to the shōgun. They exerted a powerful cultural influence in the medieval period by developing such activities as the tea ceremony (*chanoyu*), Nō theater, and calligraphy.
En	"Charming." "Its use as a term of praise indicates that not only the melancholy but also the colorful surface of the *Genji*

was appreciated. *En* invokes the visual beauty in which much of the literature of the time was clothed" (de Bary, ed. "The Vocabulary of Japanese Aesthetics, I"). (See this essay for more complete discussion).

Gagaku — Music of the imperial court imported from China in the eighth century A.D. Most often comprised of a large number of players of chimes, bells, drums, flutes, and many other instruments.

Giri — Social obligation or duty. Points out the kind of behavior necessary in relation to those people with whom one has contact, especially those who have done one a favor. This sense of duty was particularly important during the medieval period as the means by which warriors served their lords.

Ha — Part of *jo, ha,* and *kyū,* which is the rhythmical progression of *renga* poetry as well as the musical structure of Nō. "All things in the universe, good or evil, large or small, animate or inanimate, have each the rhythm of *jo, ha,* and *kyū,*" says Zeami. "It is observed even in such things as a bird's singing or an insect's chirping." "Everything has *jo, ha,* and *kyū,*" he says elsewhere. "The Nō follows that, too" (quoted in Makota Ueda, "The Art of the Nō Drama: Imitation, *Yūgen,* and Sublimity"). (See this essay for a more complete discussion.)

Haiku — Popular poetic form which uses 3 lines, 17 syllables arranged in a 5-7-5 pattern. Probably developed by taking the first three lines from *renga* (linked verse) and making an independent form from it. Matsuo Bashō is one of the early and most important proponents of haiku. It is still a very popular poetic form in Japan and has also had widespread popularity in the West. [See Yasuda's "The Japanese Haiku" and Ueda's "Impersonality in Poetry: Bashō on the Art of Haiku" for more complete discussions. See also *kigo, kireji* below].

Harakiri — The more popular term for ritual suicide (see also *seppuku*) by disembowelment. The knife was inserted in the abdomen (*hara*), the spot considered by the Japanese as the place where the soul resides. The abdomen was also considered the center of a person's will and spirit. (See Ames', "*Bushidō*: Mode or Ethic" for further discussion.)

Jo See *Ha* above.

Jōruri Dramatic texts associated with the puppet theater (*bunraku*). [See de Bary's, "The Vocabulary of Japanese Aesthetics, III" for further discussion.]

Kabuki Theater form which became popular during Tokugawa period. It was largely a theater of the ordinary people (unlike Nō, which became the theater for the samurai and aristocracy). In *kabuki* the emphasis is on the actors, so the scripts do not emphasize the literary aspects, although in recent years more attention has been given to the literary merit of the scripts. All parts are played by men and there are beautiful costumes, elaborate make-up, and much music and dance. (See Donald Shively's "The Social Environment of Tokugawa Kabuki" for further discussion.)

Kana Japanese syllabary (a set of written signs or characters of a language representing syllables). *Hiragana* and *katakana* are two kinds of *kana*. (See Notes on Language, Pronunciation, and Names.)

Kendō The Way of the Sword. During the Kamakura period there was a great flourishing of skills in swordsmanship. *Kendō* is a kind of swordsmanship involving the techniques of the two-handed sword used by the samurai.

Kigo "'Season-word.' *Kigo* or the 'season word' is concerned with a rule in the orthodox haiku tradition which prescribes that every poem must contain a word suggestive of a season of the year. Each haiku poem, according to Bashō, must present an atmosphere of nature; it follows then, that each haiku must imply a season, for nature is seasonal" (Ueda, "Impersonality in Poetry: Bashō on the Art of Haiku"). (See this essay for further discussion.)

Kireji "'Cutting-word.' The 'cutting-word' is a word or a part of a word used in a haiku poem to cut the structure into two parts. It may or may not have its own meaning; its main function is to show that the flow of the meaning is interrupted there. It often follows the subject of the sentence, interrupting the sentence at that juncture and leaving out the predicate verb altogether. The result is, of course, ambiguity" (Ueda, "Impersonality in Poetry: Bashō on the Art of Haiku"). (See this essay for further discussion.)

Kōan These are the famous riddles used by the Renzai sect of Buddhism to help in the art of meditation. "What is the sound of one hand clapping?" is one of the more well known examples of a *kōan.*

Kyōgen These short, often humorous pieces are associated with the Nō theater. They occurred between performances of Nō plays, and were much more down-to-earth than the more symbolic and abstract Nō plays.

Kyū See *Ha* above.

Makoto Comes from *ma* (true or genuine) and *koto* (words or conduct). Sincerity of mind or heart which should be at the center of relationships between individuals. "[T]he spontaneity and the natural response to situations and surroundings unique to the Japanese. Sincerity was often seen as a court of last appeals in a literary debate" (Thomas Rimer, *Introduction to Modern Japanese Fiction and its Traditions*).

Miyabi Courtliness, elegance, refinement. "The aesthetic ideal of life during the court tradition and particularly in the early classical period. In poetry, it meant an avoidance of the ugly and a tradition of decorous diction and good taste" (Earl Miner, *Introduction to Court Poetry*). "*Miyabi* was perhaps the most inclusive term for describing the aesthetics of the Heian period. It was applied in particular to the quiet pleasures which, supposedly at least, could only be savored by the aristocrat whose tastes had been educated to them—a spray of plum blossoms, the elusive perfume of a rare wood, the delicate blending of colors in a robe. In lovemaking too, the 'refined' tastes of the court revealed themselves. A man might first be attracted to a woman by catching a glimpse of her sleeve . . . or by seeing a note in her calligraphy, or by hearing her play a lute one night in the dark" (de Bary, ed., "The Vocabulary of Japanese Aesthetics, I"). (See this essay for further discussion.)

Monogatari — Tales written primarily in prose though they may contain poetry. *Kodansha Encyclopedia* delineates several types of *monogatari:* " *Uta Monogatari*, stories about poems or poem tales [such as] *Tales of Ise*; *Gunki Monogatari*, military tales [such as] *Tale of the Heike; Tsukuri Monogatari*, courtly romances or prose fiction [such as] *Tale of the Bamboo Cutter, Tale of Genji.*"

Mono no Aware — *Mono* (things) *no* (possessive particle of) *aware* (pathos, sorrow, grief) thus a deep feeling over things, "The 'ahness' of things." "*Mono no aware* might be said to represent a deep sensitivity to things, an ability to grasp the movements, the possibilities, the limitations of life in the context of a single incident, sometimes of a trifling nature." (Thomas Rimer, *Modern Japanese Fiction and Its Traditions*). "Literally the suffering of things. The term suggests an anguish that takes on beauty as a sensitivity to the finest—the saddest—beauties. Both the condition and the appreciative sensibility are implied" (Earl Miner, *An Introduction to Japanese Court Poetry*). A person who understands *mono no aware* is a more complete human being because he/she is more perceptive and understands true human reality.

Mujō — Impermanence or transience. A major theme in literature which is based on the Buddhist notion that everything that is born must die. *Mujō* "[is] expressed in the popular metaphor of the fleeting cherry blossoms with petals that fall at the height of their beauty when they are fully what they are. It is their temporality that enhances the intensity and poignancy of the experience" (Roger Ames, "*Bushidō*: Mode or Ethic?"). Chōmei's *Hōjōki* (An Account of My Hut) is a good example.

Nikki — A popular literary form was the *nikki* or diary. One of the first of this form was the *Tosa Nikki* (935) written by Ki no Tsurayuki. It was written in third person and in the voice of a woman since this was a form most favored by women. The *nikki* helped to introduce the prose work of women which became so important in the Heian period. (See Thomas Rimer's chapter "Four Polarities in Japanese Literature," for further discussion.)

Ninjō — Human feelings as distinct from *giri* (see above). It refers to more universal human feelings, those which one naturally feels as opposed to those feelings tied to social obligation (*giri*).

Nō (Noh) — A form of classical drama which emerged in the Muromachi period. The development of this theater is attributed in large part to Kan'ami and his son Zeami (Seami) who both wrote and acted in Nō plays and were responsible for the aesthetic treatises which defined this form. The themes of Nō often reflect the Buddhist notion of the sinful attachment to things of the world. The use of masks, highly stylized dance, an almost bare stage with few props are features of this dramatic form and set it apart from the more flamboyant *kabuki* (see above). Also unlike *kabuki*, the scripts of Nō plays are more readable as a literary form. (See Makoto Ueda's "Imitation, *Yūgen*, and Sublimity: Zeami and the Art of the Nō Drama," and de Bary, ed., "The Vocabulary of Japanese Aesthetics, II," for further discussion.)

Okashi — A term used to describe something light or witty in contrast to the more serious *aware*. "It seems originally to have meant something which brought a smile to the face, either of delight or amusement. It was not applied to serious or sad things of life except ironically and thus, as one Japanese critic has pointed out, in its making light of the tragic was just the opposite of the attitude of *aware* which sought to impart to the otherwise meaningless cries of a bird or the fall of a flower a profound and moving meaning" (de Bary, ed., "The Vocabulary of Japanese Aesthetics, I") (See this essay for further discussion.)

Onnagata — The term used to describe the male actors who played female roles in *kabuki* theater. Women were not allowed to perform in *kabuki* after 1629, so men had to learn to play women's parts. They were often extraordinarily popular and were accorded the same status as the male actors. (See Shively's "The Social Environment of Tokugawa Kabuki" for further discussion.)

Renga — Linked verse. *Renga* was a popular verse form which developed from splitting the 31 syllable *waka* into two shorter sections of 17 and 14 syllables. One poet would produce the first half and the second would be added by another poet. Sometimes another short piece would be added by a third poet. The verses were linked by repetition of ideas, seasonal references, and mood. At first the form was developed as a sort of game, but by the fourteenth century it had developed into a serious poetic form.

Rōnin "Masterless samurai or floating men." These were masterless samurai who had lost their commanders and stipends. They became the subject of many literary works most notably *Chūshingura* (Treasure House of Loyal Retainers) which was the story of the famous forty-seven *rōnin.*

Sabi Loneliness. "Tone of sadness and desolation . . . primarily used to describe a mood, but also associated with images of a withered, monochromatic nature," (Earl Miner, *Introduction to Court Poetry*). "One modern rendering of the term that captures something of the feeling meant to be conveyed is 'tranquillity in the context of loneliness.'" (Thomas Rimer, *Introduction to Modern Japanese Fiction and Its Traditions*). Most important in connection with haiku of Bashō. (See Keene's, "Japanese Aesthetics"; Kōshirō's, "The *Wabi* Aesthetic through the Ages"; Ueda's "Impersonality in Poetry: Bashō on the Art of Haiku" for further discussions.)

Samurai Literally "one who serves." Also known as *bushi.* Term given to professional soldiers and eventually to warrior class. They were warriors in service to the daimyō lords. (See also *daimyō, rōnin, bushidō* above).

Seppuku Ritual suicide. This is the more formal term for *harakiri* (see above).

Shinjū Double suicide which often came about as a result of people from the wrong classes falling in love and choosing suicide as a way out. These real life suicides often became the subject matter for plays in the puppet theater and for novels. Chikamatsu's *Love Suicides at Amijima* is a good example.

Shintō Indigenous religion of Japan. Emphasis is on the worship of *kami* or spirits, nature, ancestors, and the emperor. Even though it eventually fused with Buddhism, it still remains a force in Japan today. (See Parkes' "Ways of Japanese Thinking" for further discussion.)

Shiori — "Etymologically, *shiori* stems from a verb *shioru*, which means 'to bend', or 'to be flexible'. Originally, therefore, *shiori* described a poem flexible in meaning, a poem ambiguous enough to allow several different interpretations. But . . . there was another verb, *shioru*, written differently and declined differently but pronounced the same, which meant 'to wither', 'to droop', or 'to wilt'. This meaning seems to have found its way into the other meaning of *shiori*, too. Thus, when the poets of the Bashō school use it, *shiori* appears to refer to a poem containing several levels of meaning and yet altogether yielding the mood of loneliness, an atmosphere created by the image of a withering flower." (Ueda, "Bashō on the Art of the Haiku: Impersonality in Poetry.") (See this essay for further discussion.)

Shite — Principal actor or protagonist in Nō play.

Shōgun — Military rulers who generally controlled Japan between 1192 and 1867. Even though they were appointed by the emperor and were responsible for keeping the peace, they were in virtual control of the country while the emperors were only figureheads. Their regimes were referred to as *bakufu* (see above) or *shōgunate*.

Suiboku — Also *sumi-e*. "Literally 'water and ink' . . . developed in China and was transmitted . . . to Japan where it also flourished. Monochrome ink painting is based on the suppression and abbreviation of expression. Like the *wabi* of *chanoyu*, it is a simple, impoverished beauty which sublates more vivid beauty" (Kōshirō, "The *Wabi* Aesthetic through the Ages"). (See this essay for further discussion.)

Suki — Term related to *chanoyu* (tea ceremony). "[M]uch has been made in *chanoyu* of the word *suki*, meaning taste or refinement but with a hint of eccentricity thrown in. Thus the original meaning of *suki* is given as 'a form in which the parts are eccentric and do not match.' It is further explained as lacking essential parity, being asymmetrical, unbalanced"

(Kōshirō, "The *Wabi* Aesthetic through the Ages"). (See this essay for further discussion.)

Tanka — Short (as opposed to long *chōka*) poem of 31 syllables. (See *waka* below.)

Ukiyo — "[A] term which came to prominence about this time [Genroku era] was *ukiyo,* a word which in another meaning was much older. In Heian literature the word was used to mean 'sorrowful world,' and was a typical Buddhist description of the world of dust and grief. However, about 1680 the same sounds acquired a new meaning, by making a pun between *uki* meaning 'sorrowful' and *uki* meaning 'floating.' The new term, the 'floating world,' was quickly taken up, probably because it gave so vivid a picture of the unstable volatile society which had succeeded the medieval world of sorrow and gloom. *Ukiyo* was used especially of the licensed quarters—the brothels and other places of amusement which were the center of urban society at the time" (de Bary, ed., "The Vocabulary of Japanese Aesthetics, III"). (See this essay for further discussion; see also Shively's, "The Social Environment of Tokugawa Kabuki.")

Ukiyo-e — Literally, "pictures of the floating world." Artists of the Genroku era depicted the activities of the floating world. Woodblock prints were the most characteristic art form, especially the depictions of prostitutes and actors from the *kabuki* theater.

Wabi — Term most often associated with the aesthetics of *chanoyu* (tea ceremony). "*Wabi* is a noun derived from the verb *wabiru. Wabiru* and its homophones can have several meanings. The meaning of *wabi* in its aesthetic sense is perhaps best defined by the author of *Zen-cha Roku* who wrote: '*Wabi* means lacking things, having things run entirely contrary to our desires, being frustrated in our wishes.'" The original sense of *wabi,* then, embraces disappointment, frustration, and poverty. The author of the *Zen-cha Roku* continues:

> Always bear in mind that *wabi* involves not regarding incapacities as incapacitating, not feeling that lacking

> something is deprivation, not thinking that what is not provided is deficiency. To regard incapacity as incapacitating, to feel that lack is deprivation, or to believe that not being provided for is poverty is not *wabi* but rather the spirit of a pauper.

From this we can understand . . . *wabi* means to transform material insufficiency so that one discovers in it a world of spiritual freedom unbounded by material things" (Kōshirō, "The *Wabi* Aesthetic through the Ages"). (See this essay for further discussion.)

Waka — Short poems of five lines, 31 syllables in groups of 5-7-5-7-7. Was most common form of early Japanese poetry. "The preface to the *Kokinshū*, with its opening statement that 'Japanese poetry, having the human heart as its seed, produces the myriad leaves of speech,' . . . in suggesting that *waka* is that which flows of itself from the poet's heart through contact with the beauties of nature or the events of human life, . . . touched the very essence of literature and the arts. In the *Kokinshū* view of poetry, the heart (*kokoro*), which acts as the womb from which *waka* are born, and the leaves of words (*kotoba*), the external expression of emotions, are equally important as the two wheels of a cart. In this early stage of literary theory, the ideal of *waka* was that of a perfectly balanced combination of emotion and expression: heart = words" (Kōshirō, "The *Wabi* Aesthetic through the Ages"). (See this essay for further discussion).

Yūgen — "If the term *yūgen* is etymologically analyzed, it will be found that *yū* means deep, dim, or difficult to see, and that *gen*, originally describing the dark, profound, tranquil color of the universe, refers to the Taoist concept of truth. Zeami's idea of *yūgen* seems to combine its conventional meaning of elegant beauty with its original meaning of profound, mysterious truth of the universe. Zeami perceived mysterious beauty in cosmic truth; beauty was the color of truth, so to speak" (Ueda, "Zeami on the Art of the Nō Drama: Imitation, *Yūgen*, and Sublimity"). (See this essay for further discussion].)

"The term *yūgen* has no exact equivalent in English; literally it means 'obscure and dark,' but, as used by Zeami, it carries the connotation of half-revealed or suggested beauty, at once elusive and meaningful, tinged with wistful sadness" (*The Noh Drama: Ten Plays from the Japanese).*

"*Yūgen* is a term which it is difficult either to define or translate. It primarily means 'mystery,' and however loosely used in criticism generally retains something of the sense of a mysterious power or ability. . . . *Yūgen* is considered to be the mark of supreme attainment in all of the arts and accomplishments. In the art of the Nō in particular the manifestation of *yūgen* is of the first importance." "*Yūgen* may be comprehended by the mind, but it cannot be expressed in words. Its quality may be suggested by the sight of a thin cloud veiling the moon or by autumn mist swathing the scarlet leaves on a mountainside. . . . *Yūgen* is the quality of the highest realm of art, an absolute domain to which all forms point" (de Bary, ed., "The Vocabulary of Japanese Aesthetics, II"). (See this essay for further discussion).

Zuihitsu Literally "following the brush." A tradition of literary works where the author allowed "[his] writing brush to skip from one topic to another in whichever direction it was led by free association" (Keene, "Japanese Aesthetics"). Important works in this tradition include Kenkō's *Tsurezuregusa* (Essays in Idleness) and Chōmei's *Hōjōki* (An Account of My Hut).

ANNOTATED BIBLIOGRAPHY

For the reader who would like additional information on Japanese aesthetics, culture, and literature, the following bibliography should prove useful. The works listed are intended to supplement the essays included in this collection and are aimed at the general, non-specialist reader. The list moves from general to specific, beginning with bibliographies, guides, encyclopedias, to anthologies of literary works, to general background reading, to specific works about fiction, poetry, drama/theater, and film. There are, of course, many more works than have been included here, but these works are likely to be found in most college and university libraries and they provide a general rather than narrow focus. Also included are those works which might be most useful to the teacher preparing to teach Japanese literature.

Since many articles in scholarly journals tend to be of a more specialized nature, or focus more on individual works, they are not generally included in this bibliography. So many works by individual Japanese fiction writers, poets, and playwrights are now available in translation that it is impossible to list them all here. (For a comprehensive listing of works available in translation, see *Modern Japanese Literature in Translation: A Bibliography*, cited below). There are also numerous critical studies of individual writers, as well as biographies and autobiographies which are not included. Many of the titles in this bibliography have their own bibliographies which will be helpful in locating more specific studies.

General Reference, Bibliographies, Encyclopedias

Association for Asian Studies. *Bibliography of Asian Studies.* Ann Arbor, Michigan. This is the annual index for the *Journal of Asian Studies* and covers journal articles, monographs, book reviews. A comprehensive reference tool for material published in this journal.

Colcutt, Martin, et al. *Cultural Atlas of Japan.* New York, Oxford: Facts on File, 1988. This single volume cultural atlas is perhaps one of the most useful tools for the general reader, as well as the scholar in Japanese studies. Divided into three parts: "Origins," "The Historical Period," and "Modern Japan," it is filled with information on geography, history, culture, arts, literature, and economics. There are copious maps, charts, and beautiful color illustrations. A must for college and university libraries; this is the one book I would recommend to anyone interested in Japan.

Kodansha Encyclopedia of Japan. Tokyo: Kodansha, 1983 (9 vols.). This is a must for every college and university library. Many entries are signed articles by both Western and Japanese scholars. The entries are often essay length and cover every topic of importance to the student of aesthetics, culture, and literature. A new, revised, illustrated, two volume edition is also available.

Mamola, Claire. *Japanese Women Writers in English Translation: An Annotated Bibliography.* New York and London: Garland Publishing, 1989. A comprehensive bibliography divided into three sections: Heian Period Writings, Fiction Writings from the Nineteenth Century through 1987, and Non-Fiction Writings from the Nineteenth Century through 1987. The preface also gives a complete list of the sources used by the author in her research. An important work on women writers in Japan.

Pronko, Leonard. *Guide to Japanese Drama.* Boston: G.K. Hall, 1973. An important annotated bibliography with sections on general works, Nō and Kyōgen (criticism and texts), Kabuki and Bunraku (criticism and texts), other traditional forms, and the modern theater. This bibliography also includes a good general introduction to Japanese theater.

Rimer, J. Thomas and Robert E. Morrell. *Guide to Japanese Poetry.* 2nd ed. Boston: G.K. Hall, 1984. An annotated guide for the study of poetry, this bibliography provides information on history, translations, and criticism.

Shulman, Frank Joseph. *Japan.* Oxford: Clio Press, 1989 (vol. 103, World Bibliographic Series). This major bibliography provides coverage for generally accessible information (including reference books and bibliographies) in English about Japan. The comprehensive nature of this work (1,500 titles which are cross-referenced) makes this an invaluable tool.

Staff of the International House of Japan Library, eds. *Modern Japanese Literature in Translation: A Bibliography.* Tokyo: Kodansha, 1979. Includes close to 1,500 authors of fiction, poetry, drama and covers the mid-nineteenth century to the 1970s. Although much has been published since then, this is still a valuable source of work in translation.

The International House of Japan Library. *A Guide to Reference Books for Japanese Studies.* Tokyo: The International House of Japan Library, 1989. The preface to this work states that it is designed for "People without the expertise in either spoken or written Japanese [who are] seeking information on contemporary Japan." It covers English and Japanese language titles, and a variety of disciplines. The lists of general reference works for the arts, literature, and history will be particularly useful.

General Anthologies

Carter, Steven, trans. *Traditional Japanese Poetry: An Anthology.* Stanford: Stanford University Press, 1991. A comprehensive introduction discusses the *chōka, haiku,* and *tanka* as poetic forms. The book is divided into six chronological periods with an introduction for each; there are also biographical introductions to major poets, and marginal notes for each of the poems. These notes and introductions make this a useful text for the beginner.

Hibbett, Howard, ed. *Contemporary Japanese Literature: An Anthology of Fiction, Film, and Other Writing since 1945.* New York: Alfred A. Knopf, 1992. This anthology is perhaps the best collection of postwar Japanese literature. In addition to the fiction, poetry, and plays, of particular interest is the inclusion of two film scripts (Kurosawa's *Ikiru* and Ozu's *Tokyo Story*). Each entry has a short biographical introduction.

Hiroaki Sato and Burton Watson, eds. and trans. *The Country of Eight Islands: An Anthology of Japanese Poetry.* Seattle: University of Washington Press, 1981. A thoughtful and readable introduction by J. Thomas Rimer introduces another comprehensive collection of poetry from the beginning to the modern period. There are no notes to accompany the poems which makes this a little less useful for the reader new to Japanese poetry. It does include a number of works not otherwise available in translation and also has a good bibliography.

Keene, Donald. *An Anthology of Japanese Literature, from the Earliest Era to the Mid-Nineteenth Century* and *Modern Japanese Literature.* New York: Grove

Press, 1956. This two volume set is still the most widely used anthology of Japanese literature. The selections are comprehensive, especially in the first volume, and the two volumes together are a good introduction for students. They have not been revised since their publication in 1956, so the second volume does not contain the most modern writers.

Lippit Noriko and Kyoko Selden, eds. and trans. *Japanese Women Writers: Twentieth-Century Short Fiction.* Armonk, New York: M.E. Sharpe, 1991. A good introduction provides a brief history of the role of women in Japanese literature and discussions of the writers included in the anthology. There are also short, but good biographical essays for each of the writers.

McCullough, Helen, ed. *Classical Japanese Prose: An Anthology.* Stanford: Stanford University Press, 1990. Covering the period from the ninth to seventeenth centuries, this collection of prose works is more comprehensive than Donald Keene's anthology of the same period. The introduction provides an interesting discussion of the role of women as writers during this period, as well as a good, but short, history of the period. Each work has a short introduction which provides information about the work in its entirety and how the excerpt is related to the whole. The excerpts are generally long and give a good sense of the larger work.

Mishima, Yukio. *Five Modern Nō Plays.* Translated and with an introduction by Donald Keene. Rutland, Vermont and Tokyo: Charles Tuttle, 1967. Mishima's adaptation of several classic Nō plays provide insights into the traditional Nō as well as modern theater in Japan. The short introduction by Keene is good and discusses the differences between the original plays and Mishima's adaptations.

Morris, Ivan, ed. *Modern Japanese Stories: An Anthology.* Rutland, Vermont and Tokyo: Charles E. Tuttle, 1962. Although the collection is a little dated, the thirty-page introduction by Ivan Morris makes this collection an important one. The twenty-five full-page woodcuts make this one of the few illustrated collections and provide added interest.

The Noh Drama: Ten Plays from the Japanese. Selected and Translated by the Special Noh Committee. Rutland, Vermont and Tokyo: Charles Tuttle, 1960. This collection has a good general introduction as well as individual introductions for each of the plays. Each play has textual notes and line drawings to illustrate the action of the play. A double-page diagram of the Noh stage is also very helpful.

General Background

de Bary, Wm. Theodore, ed. *Sources of Japanese Tradition.* New York: Columbia University Press, 1958. In addition to the "Vocabulary of Japanese Aesthetics" found in this collection, *Sources* . . . also includes excerpts from works of fiction, poetry, and drama which shaped the Japanese tradition.

Katō Shūichi. *A History of Japanese Literature.* 3 vols. Vol. 1, *The First Thousand Years,* covers the seventh to mid-sixteenth century; vol. 2, *The Years of Isolation,* covers the seventeenth through mid-nineteenth centuries; vol. 3, *The Modern Years,* covers from the Meiji Restoration (1868) to the present. Tokyo: Kodansha International, 1979–83. A very good introduction to the literary and intellectual history of Japan.

Keene, Donald. *Appreciations of Japanese Culture.* (Previously published as *Landscapes and Portraits.*) Tokyo: Kodansha International, 1993. Informative essays on aesthetics, fiction, poetry, drama, and Japanese culture make this a must read for the new student of Japanese literature. His essay "Feminine Sensibility," appears in this collection. The final chapter, "Confessions of a Specialist," is particularly charming.

———. *The Pleasures of Japanese Literature.* The source for the essay "Japanese Aesthetics," in this collection, this gem of a book is important background reading. Keene's discussions of aesthetics, poetry, fiction, and theater are accessible to the general reader.

———. *Dawn to the West: Fiction* (vol. 1) and *Dawn to the West: Poetry, Drama, and Criticism* (vol. 2). New York: Holt, Rinehart and Winston, 1984. This comprehensive two-volume edition looks at Japanese literature since the Meji Restoration. There are general essays which cover literary movements during this period, as well as essays on individual authors. Both volumes provide invaluable reference material for teachers.

———. *Seeds in the Heart: Japanese Literature from the Earliest Times to the Late Sixteenth Century.* New York: Henry Holt and Company, 1993. The last volume (though it covers the earliest period) in Donald Keene's monumental history of Japanese literature. As in earlier works, the essays are insightful and interesting and he has continued to write, as he says, "subjectively and enthusiastically, in the hopes of stimulating others to love Japanese literature as I [do]." The introduction gives a particularly good overview of the "genres" and "special features" (his headings) of Japanese literature.

Miner, Earl, Hiroko Odagiri, Robert Morrell. *The Princeton Companion to Classical Japanese Literature.* Princeton: Princeton University Press, 1985. An excellent companion for readers new to Japanese literature. It includes a brief literary history, sections on major authors, works, and literary terms, and a separate section on theater. There are also several sections which include maps, diagrams, drawings of many things incidental but important to understanding the way of life in classical Japan.

Morris, Ivan. *The World of the Shining Prince: Court Life in Ancient Japan.* Penguin Books, 1964. Using *The Tale of Genji* as a backdrop, Morris presents an in-depth study of the society, politics, and culture of Heian Japan.

Rimer, J. Thomas. *Pilgrimages: Aspects of Japanese Literature and Culture.* Honolulu: University of Hawaii Press, 1988. This series of essays presents an interesting study in comparative literature. Professor Rimer looks at the connections between the Japanese and the French traditions in such various fields as fiction, painting, language, and theater. Because, as Rimer points out, many of the essays were first lectures, the style is very readable and accessible.

———. *A Reader's Guide to Japanese Literature.* New York and Tokyo: Kodansha, International, 1989. This general reference work includes discussions of twenty classical and thirty modern works, each two to three pages in length. These short essays provide a good overview of the work for the beginning reader.

Sansom, George. *Japan: A Short Cultural History.* New York: Appleton-Century Crofts, revised ed. 1943. (Reprinted Stanford University Press, 1978.) Although first published in 1931, this work remains one of the classics of Japanese studies. Taking a chronological approach, Sansom begins with "Origins" and comes up to the end of the Tokugawa period, providing the reader with insights into Japan's "cultural history."

Ueda Makoto. *Literary and Art Theories in Japan.* Cleveland: Press of Western Reserve University, 1967. (Recently published in a reprint edition, Michigan Classics in Japanese Studies 6 [Ann Arbor: Center for Japanese Studies, The University of Michigan, 1991].) This important discussion of literary and art theories contains essays not only on Japanese literature but also on flower arrangement, the tea ceremony, narrative singing, painting, and calligraphy. Each of the essays is very readable and provides valuable insights. (See his essays on Zeami and Bashō in this collection.)

Varley, H. Paul. *Japanese Culture.* 3rd, ed., Honolulu: University of Hawaii Press, 1984. In his preface, Varley states that the book "is intended as a survey, for the general reader, of Japanese culture, including religion, thought, the visual arts, literature, the theatre, the cinema, and those special arts, such as the tea ceremony and landscape gardening, that have been uniquely cherished in Japan." His chapter "Culture in the Present Age," appears in this collection.

Poetry

Blyth, R. H. *A History of Haiku.* 2 vols. Japan: Hokuseido Press. 1968. Vol. 1, from the beginnings to Issa, and vol. 2 from Issa to the present, make up this classic study of haiku poetry. Both volumes give a commentary on the history and development of the haiku form as well as extensive examples, with commentary, of the poetry itself. This volume includes romanized Japanese versions of the poems.

Brower, Robert and Earl Miner. *Japanese Court Poetry.* Stanford: Stanford University Press, 1961. This general introduction is "primarily a critical study, rather than a literary history" and covers "The Nature of Japanese Court Poetry"; "The Ideals, Practices and Development of Japanese Court Poetry"; and "The Tradition of Court Poetry." The section "Japanese Poetry and the Western Reader: The Problem of Limitations" is particularly helpful to the non-specialist.

Henderson, Harold. *An Introduction to Haiku.* New Jersey: Doubleday, 1958. This little gem of a book is an "outgrowth" of his *The Bamboo Room,* and is an uncomplicated introduction to haiku. While some readers object to his use of rhyme in his translations, he provides a rationale for doing so. The book contains a good selection of haiku with the romanized Japanese and Japanese word order included.

Miner, Earl. *An Introduction to Japanese Court Poetry.* Stanford: Stanford University Press, 1968. Several introductory chapters on "Courtly and Human Values" and "Forms and Conventions," followed by four chapters on the work of individual poets, and a final chapter on "Major Themes" make up this "little" but important work on court poetry.

———. *Japanese Linked Poetry.* Princeton: Princeton University Press, 1979. Early chapters provide an overview of the role of linked verse in Japanese poetry. Later chapters which focus on some of the *renga* and haiku sequences are more complex, but provide an in-depth discussion of this major form of Japanese poetry.

Ueda Makoto. *Modern Japanese Poets and the Nature of Literature.* Stanford: Stanford University Press. 1983. This in-depth study of eight contemporary Japanese poets provides insights and useful information about "each poet's concept of poetry." Discussions of specific poems are included. A necessary work to gain an understanding of modern Japanese poetry.

Yasuda, Kenneth. *The Japanese Haiku: Its Essential Nature, History, and Possibilities in English.* Rutland, Vermont and Tokyo: Charles Tuttle, 1960. A classic study of the haiku as part of the Japanese tradition in poetry. His "Approach to Haiku" and "Basic Principles" appear in this collection.

Fiction

Miyoshi Masao. *Accomplices of Silence: The Modern Japanese Novel.* Berkeley: University of California Press, 1974. This work focuses on "four basic aspects of the art of fiction—the narrative situation, character, plot, and language"—in the works of Futabatei, Ōgai, Sōseki, Kawabata, Dazai, and Mishima. A good introduction to some of the most important Japanese writers of prose fiction.

Okada, H. Richard. *Figures of Resistance: Language, Poetry and Narrating in The Tale of Genji and other Mid-Heian Texts.* Durham: Duke University Press, 1991. A recent work which looks at the three important *monogatari* (tales) of *Taketori (The Tale of the Bamboo Cutter), Ise (The Tale of Ise),* and *Genji (The Tale of Genji)* in the context of recent "reader-response" theories. Okada addresses the problems of reading texts from cultures not of "our time or place." A complex text, not, I think, for the beginner in either Western literary theory or Japanese literature.

Pollack, David. *Reading against Culture: Ideology and Narrative in the Japanese Novel.* Ithaca: Cornell University Press, 1992. In his preface, Pollack states: "This book is addressed to the general reader of the novel . . . my hope is that it will prove useful to those interested in the relationship between literature and culture and its reflection in Japanese practice. My major concern . . . has been to bring close readings of particular Japanese novels to bear on Western and Japanese ideas concerning that relationship." The introduction raises the questions of "reading against culture" and following chapters focus on the work of Sōseki, Kawabata, Abe, Mishima, and others. An interesting and different approach to the works of many of the most well-known Japanese writers.

Rimer, J. Thomas. *Modern Japanese Fiction and Its Traditions: An Introduction.* Princeton: Princeton University Press, 1978. A good introduction including discussion of some of the important critical terms in the vocabulary of Japanese criticism. The focus of the book is to "provide an explication of certain important literary structures and themes in the Japanese tradition." Includes chapters on Dazai Osamu, Natsume Sōseki, *The Tale of Genji,* Kawabata Yasunari, as well as discussions of the tale, the diary, the *monogatari,* and the essay.

Ueda Makoto. *Modern Japanese Writers and the Nature of Literature.* Stanford: Stanford University Press, 1976. A thorough analysis of six great modern novelists.

Yamanouchi, Hisaaki. *The Search for Authenticity in Modern Japanese Literature.* New York: Cambridge University Press, 1978. A study of twelve writers (including Shōyō, Shimei, Tōson, Sōseki, Abe, and Mishima) after 1868 to focus on "the ways in which these writers tackled different questions—personal, social, and intellectual—including the confrontation with the West, and the way in which they tried, with or without success, to represent their experiences in an authentic form of literary art." In several chapters, two writers are discussed together to show their similarities and differences. An interesting study of some of Japan's most important fiction writers.

Drama/Theater

Bowers, Faubion. *Japanese Theater.* New York: Hermitage House, 1952. This standard introductory work attempts to cover all aspects of Japanese theater—with special emphasis on the kabuki, including three kabuki plays. A shorter discussion of Nō, Kyōgen, and Bunraku are also included. Some drawings and illustrations are good complements.

Brandon, James, et al. *Studies in Kabuki: Its Acting, Music, and Historical Context.* Honolulu: University of Hawaii Press, 1978. As the title suggests, there are three essays which focus on acting, singing, and historical contexts. Donald Shively's essay, "The Social Environment of Tokugawa Kabuki," is included in this collection.

Dunn, Charles and Bunzo Torigoe. eds., and trans. *Actor's Analects.* New York: Columbia University Press, 1969. This work is a collection of essays by actors and playwrights on the "practice and aesthetics" of acting in the kabuki theater in the late seventeenth/early eighteenth century. It also has a good introduction.

Ernst, Earle. *The Kabuki Theatre.* New York: Oxford University Press, 1956. This classic study of the kabuki theatre includes chapters on the stage, the actors, the plays and characters, and elements of the performance. Good illustrations complement the text.

Kato Shuichi. "The Age of *Nō* and *Kyōgen*," in Kato Suichi, *A History of Japanese Literature,* trans. David Chibbett, vol. 1. Tokyo: Kodansha International, 1979–83. This long essay provides a thorough intellectual history of the period of development of Nō, as well as a discussion of the conventions of Nō and Kyōgen.

Rimer, J. Thomas and Yamazoki Masakazu, trans. *On the Art of the Nō Drama: The Major Treatises of Zeami.* Princeton: Princeton University Press, 1984. A translation of some of Zeami's major treatises. What makes this work particularly useful are the two excellent introductory essays by Rimer and Masakazu, particularly Masakazu's essay on artistic theories which provides useful comparisons between Eastern and Western concerns.

Rolf, Robert and John Gillespie, eds. *Alternative Japanese Drama: Ten Plays.* Honolulu: University of Hawaii Press, 1992. A combination of essays, plays, and illustrations, with good introductions, make this collection dealing with the theater of the 1960s and 70s an important work on contemporary Japanese drama.

Yasuda, Kenneth. *Masterworks of the Nō Theatre.* Bloomington: Indiana University Press, 1989. A short, but very definitive introduction which touches on all aspects of Nō, including *yūgen* and *hana.* Each of the eighteen plays included has an introduction and a romanized Japanese version side by side with the English. The book concludes with a Nō play written by Yasuda in honor of Martin Luther King.

Zeami, Motokiyo. *Kadensho,* trans. Chuichi Sakurai et al. Kyoto: Sumiya-Shinobe Publishing Institute, 1968. The forward to this collection of treatises by Zeami gives a good discussion of *hana* and *yūgen* as aesthetic principles. The beautiful color plates in this edition make it especially interesting.

Cinema

Anderson, Joseph and Donald Richie. *The Japanese Film: Art and Industry.* Princeton: Princeton University Press, 1982. A historical account of film in Japan beginning with background from 1896–1917 and ending in 1959. There are additional chapters on "content," "technique," "directors," "actors," "theatres and audiences," with two new essays by Anderson and Richie about film since the first publication of the book in 1959.

———. "Japanese Cinema," in *Encyclopedia of Japan.* Tokyo: Kodansha International. Like so many of the entries in this encyclopedia, this one is packed with information to give the reader a general background in Japanese film.

Bordwell, David. *Ozu and the Poetics of Cinema.* Princeton: Princeton University Press, 1988. Like Donald Richie, Bordwell has written an in-depth study of Ozu's films and film techniques.

Mellen, Joan. *Voices From the Japanese Cinema.* New York: Liveright, 1975. A series of interviews with fifteen Japanese film artists/directors, including Kurosawa, Ichikawa, Kobayashi, and a very interesting interview with the young director Susumu Hani and his actress wife Sachiko Hidari. Hidari speaks about the role of women in Japan and their portrayal in film.

Richie, Donald. *The Films of Akira Kurosawa.* Berkeley: University of California Press, 1965. An in-depth look at the films of Kurosawa by one of the foremost scholars of Japanese film. For each film Richie includes a synopsis of the plot, discussion of the treatment of the story, information on the production, and comments on music, camera work, and characterization.

———. *Ozu.* Berkeley: University of California Press, 1974. An in-depth study of the films of Ozu.

Films

There are numerous Japanese films available on videotape and laserdisc. Below is a partial list (with thanks to Graham Parkes) of some of the films discussed in the essays in this collection as well as other films which have achieved wide public acclaim. Most of these films are available for rental at video stores or for sale through film and audio-visual catalogues.

Ozu Yasujiro	*Late Spring* (1949)
	Early Summer (1951)
	Tokyo Story (1953)
	Floating Weeds (1959)
Kurosawa Akira	*Rashomon* (1950)
	Ikiru (1952)
	Seven Samurai (1954)
	Throne of Blood (1957) (*Macbeth* story)
	Yojimbo (1961)
	Dodes'kaden (1969)
	Kagemusha (1980)
	Ran (1985) (*King Lear* story)
	Dreams (1990)
Mizoguchi Kenji	*The Life of Oharu* (1952)
	Ugetsu (1953)
	Sansho the Bailiff (1954)
	A Story from Chikamatsu (1954)
Shinoda Masahiro	*Double Suicide* (1969)
Juzo Itami	*Tampopo*
	A Taxing Woman
Masaki Kobayashi	*Kwaidan*

Audio-Visual/Curricula Materials

The National Precollegiate Japan Projects Network has regional centers which provide assistance to teachers in preparing curriculum materials and serve as lending libraries for films, books, and other Japan related materials. The list of regional centers for this network will direct the reader to sources of information for materials which can be used in the classroom. While some of their materials are aimed at the precollegiate level, they may be useful to the teacher and student new to Japanese studies.

National Clearinghouse for U.S.-Japan Studies
Social Studies Development Center
Indiana University
2805 East Tenth Street, Suite 120
Bloomington, Indiana 47408-2698
(812) 855-3838 Fax: (812) 855-0455
Nationwide

"The foundation for all Clearinghouse activities is a computer-searchable database of curriculum materials, journal articles, research reports, and other materials. . . . The Clearinghouse collects, analyzes, abstracts, and creates a database . . . that can assist . . . teachers in developing and implementing curricula. . . . Many of the resources included in Clearinghouse database are cross-referenced in ERIC. However, the Clearinghouse also includes data such as videos, films, some simulations, artifact kits and the like."

The Mid-Atlantic Region Japan-in-the-Schools (MARJiS) Program
Benjamin Building, Room 3113
College of Education
University of Maryland
College Park, Maryland 20742
(301) 405-4773 Fax: (301) 405-4773
MD, VA, DC, WV

Japan Project/Stanford Program on International and Cross-Cultural Education (SPICE)
Littlefield Center, Room 14
300 Lasuen Street
Stanford University
Stanford, CA 94305-5013
(800) 578-1114 Fax: (415) 723-2592
CA, NV, OR, UT, WA

Mid-America Japan-in-the-Schools Program (MAJIS)
202 Bailey Hall
University of Kansas
Lawrence, KS 66045
(913) 864-4435 Fax: (913) 864-3566
IA, KS, NE, MO

New England Program for Teaching About Japan (NEPTAJ)
Five College Center for East Asian Studies
8 College Lane
Smith College
Northampton, MA 01063
(413) 585-3751 Fax: (413) 585-2075
CT, ME, MA, NH, RI, VT

Northeast Regional Program on Japan
East Asian Institute
International Affairs Building
Columbia University
420 West 118th Street
New York, NY 10027
(2120 854-1734 fAX: (212) 749-1487
NJ, NY, PA

Rocky Mountain Region Japan Project (RMRJP)
Social Science Education Consortium
3300 Mitchell Lane, Suite 240
Boulder, CO 80301-2272
(303) 492-8154 Fax: (303) 449-3925
AZ, CO, ID, ND, SD, WY

Midsouth Japan-in-the-Schools Program
Japan Project
University of Tennessee at Chattanooga
615 McCallie Avenue
Chattanooga, TN 37403
(615) 755-4118 Fax: (615) 755-5218
AR, KY, MS, TN

Great Lakes Japan-in-the-Schools Project
Global Education Center
College of Education, Peik Hall #152A
University of Minnesota-Twin Cities
159 Pillsbury Drive SE
Minneapolis, MN 55455
(612) 625-1896 Fax: (612) 626-7496
MI, MN, OH, WI

The Japan Society
333 East 47th Street
New York, New York 10017
(212) 832-1155 Fax: (212) 755-6752

The Japan Society provides a number of services to the teacher interested in Japan. The Film Center has a number of films for purchase as well as some interesting and inexpensive publications on film. Of particular interest is "Japan in Film," a catalog of documentary and theatrical films on Japan available in the U.S. For film publications contact Bob Lazzaro at (212) 715-1216 or Fax (212) 755-6752.

Japan Information and Culture Center of the Embassy of Japan
Lafayette Centre III
1155 21st Street, NW
Washington, DC 20036
(202) 939-6900

Videos (mostly Japanese government-funded documentaries) that the public can borrow. Also a great deal of information on Japan in general and a small library. This is also a good place to visit in Washington as there is a beautiful art gallery attached to the center.

INDEX

Entries to literary works have the English or Japanese title in parentheses followed by the author's name in brackets. Names are give in traditional Japanese order with family name first followed by given name. In cases where authors are referred to several ways, I have included both with a *see* reference.